TABLE OF CONTENTS

CULTS INSIDE OUT

How People Get In and Can Get Out

RICK ALAN ROSS

ISBN: 149731660X
ISBN 13: 9781497316607
Library of Congress Control Number: 2014905061
CreateSpace Independent Publishing Platform
North Charleston, South Carolina

FOR HAO HUIJUN AND HER DAUGHTER, CHEN GUO

I met Falun Gong survivors Hao Huijun and her daughter, Chen Guo, after attending an international cultic studies conference in China. Their painfully acquired insight, wrought by a horrible Falun Gong–inspired self-immolation, which took place at Tiananmen Square during 2001, is both compelling and inspiring. They quite literally bear the scars of their experience and are icons of truthfulness, compassion and forbearance. This book is dedicated to Hao Huijun and Chen Guo and all former cult members who have moved on to find freedom of mind.

FOREWORD

My work has placed me in legal settings, and I have been qualified as an expert in courts of law. I know firsthand what is considered the state of art within this field. I have a PhD in psychology and have worked with current and former cult members as a licensed counselor for over twenty years.

In this book Rick Ross describes situations in which a current cult member could be persuaded that he or she needs a replacement for his or her current or former cult leader. This is one reason why we must proceed with caution and due diligence when educating former and current cult members and their families.

This book is unique among the books written about cults. My hope is that people will carefully read it. The author has firsthand knowledge of the subject and is qualified to explain cults based on his many years of experience.

We don't know how many cults actually exist, but we have witnessed the harm they have done. Critics of the term *cult* generally object to its standardized application, claiming that it denigrates "new religious movements." But since many cults are not religious, this objection seems misplaced. Any meaningful investigation into the nature of cults must forego specific beliefs and instead focus on the practices that make a group or relationship harmful. Whatever the cult, there is almost always sustained deception. This fact raises the issue that there is an absence of informed consent.

Ross's decades of inquiry and work related to cults have provided him with knowledge of their pernicious attributes. This background has provided Ross with the tools and ability necessary to recognize their true nature. Not afraid of controversy, he tries to find that delicate balance between exposing cults and encouraging the freedom of undeterred choice.

Cults employ secretiveness, because most people would otherwise not knowingly affiliate with them. Neither intelligence nor family background precludes being tricked and caught by a cult. People who have been caught weren't necessarily "seeking" or looking for "something." This book doesn't unfairly stigmatize cult victims; instead it thoroughly discusses the real history of cults and how they trap people. Telling the truth about cults based on facts and research, not speculation, is important.

This is not another book about counseling cult members, though some recovery suggestions are appropriately discussed. We don't know whether everyone in a cult has been traumatized. We do know that many have had very difficult and painful experiences. We don't have the data to support the contention that *every* former cult member needs professional counseling. But we *do* know that education about cults has been helpful and is an important facet of recovery, which often alleviates the confusion and suffering of former cult members.

Professional counseling is, by its very nature, a persuasive process. Education focused on critical thinking, the power of persuasion, deception, and indoctrination practices with the support of research is, in my opinion, a better choice to assist former or current cult members.

My concern is that reliance on counseling rather than on education has the potential to create dependence on an authority figure and doesn't necessarily nurture the autonomy and knowledge one needs to make decisions in a rational and systemic fashion. This book is designed to provide its readers with important information that can lead to genuine independence and freedom.

Over the years Rick Ross has established the single-largest website devoted to the topic of cults and their associated practices. This book is a type of capstone to his long-standing work. Ross is effectively in the information and education business. He has labored tenaciously toward providing educational tools for others to help them deal with the ongoing and often misunderstood world of cults.

Some who have encountered the main content of research used in this book in an intervention, counseling, or a legal setting have criticized it. Criticism and dissent are good; they make our theories better. There are no theories that are absolutely proven in science. Some research is better supported than other research. Ross has chosen some of the most familiar models, and they are not without limitations. Good research acknowledges that it needs more ongoing support.

By the end of her life, Dr. Margaret Singer had provided a rich body of work and insight into cult formation. It is impossible for anyone to operate in the realm of cultic studies and not know about Drs. Margaret Singer, Robert Lifton, and Richard Ofshe. However, we must still continue to look for more models of education that can be helpful. This book is a step in the right direction. Instead of merely repeating various theories without attribution, this book is carefully footnoted and offers rare insight into how these theories actually work in real situations with real people.

Contained within the book are illustrations and examples of cultic histories, interventions, and statements about the problems associated with cults. This book will not disappoint, but rather it will provide insight and understanding.

We can all be students, academics, and adventurous seekers of the "truth" and overcome adversity. But as seekers we must recognize that some organizations are harbingers of danger. Finding the truth is a process that is ideally transparent, engaging, and respectful of each person's unique human spirit.

Cathleen A. Mann, PhD

Lakewood, Colorado

October 2013

INTRODUCTION

My work in the field of cultic studies began rather suddenly and ser-endipitously in 1982. People associated with a controversial religious group that targeted Jews for conversion infiltrated the paid profes-sional staff of a Jewish nursing home where my grandmother was a resident. A person associated with the group tried to recruit my grand-mother. When that attempt failed, the encounter quickly escalated into a hateful confrontation. When I arrived to take my grandmother out for lunch that same day, she was still quite upset about the unsettling experience. She was eighty-two years old at the time and nearing the end of her life.

This covert activity aimed at the elderly angered me. My grandmother had the right to expect privacy, not to suffer the intrusion of an un-wanted group bent on somehow exploiting her. In the years since this disturbing encounter, I have learned that destructive cults frequently target and exploit the elderly.

Volunteers often provide meaningful help in nursing homes. There were many volunteers who regularly visited my grandmother's nurs-ing home. Some came specifically in response to requests residents made. But the idea that a group deliberately circumvented the usual process for entry and planted people in the nursing home staff to pur-sue a hidden agenda was deceptive and unethical.

At the time I had no interest in cultic groups. My only purpose was to make sure my grandmother was as comfortable and happy as possible. She had survived enough hardships during her life and had the right to receive respect and live what was left of her life with dignity. I immediately reported the incident to the executive director of the nursing home. We then worked together, and the people who had surreptitiously infiltrated the nursing home staff, were exposed and summarily dismissed.

My work with the director of the nursing home came to the attention of the organized Jewish community in Phoenix, Arizona, where I had grown up and lived at the time. Suddenly I became an activist. I served on various committees locally, nationally, and internationally.

Within those committees we came to a consensus concerning ethical boundaries for proselytizing or recruitment efforts. We agreed that targeting a particular group, such as Jews, was unethical; that minor children shouldn't be approached without prior written parental notification and consent; that privacy must be protected at hospitals and nursing homes; and that any group trying to recruit new members must do so honestly without misrepresentation or deception.

Working with the Jewish Federation of Greater Phoenix, I helped to develop an educational pamphlet, which was widely distributed throughout the local religious community. The publication, which most of the religious leaders in Phoenix endorsed, was titled "What in God's Name Is Going On in Arizona?"

A national committee I served on for the Union for Reform Judaism produced an educational video titled *You Can Go Home Again*, which is a study of cults as seen through the eyes of former cult members and their families.

I once told a rabbi who served with me on committees in the early 1980s that I certainly didn't consider myself an authority on the subject of cults and that personal interest had drawn me to the issue. The rabbi said, "In the land of the blind the one-eyed man is king," citing an old adage attributed to the scholar Erasmus. What he meant to say was that at that time cults were still largely a mystery and often misunderstood.

After the publication of the pamphlet about proselytizing, someone brought to my attention that cults and hate groups were targeting Jewish prisoners in the prisons and jails of Arizona. In response I began a Jewish prisoner program. That program was later incorporated into the services provided by Jewish Family & Children's Service (JFCS), a social service agency in Phoenix. I served as the staff coordinator for that program at JFCS.

In the following years my efforts included opposing hate groups, cult recruitment, and unethical proselytizing within and outside prison walls. My work included teaching a course about destructive cults for the Bureau of Jewish Education of Greater Phoenix. The curriculum was used to inform young people before they entered college. At that time I also began my cult-intervention work, which was then commonly called "cult deprogramming." Typically families would contact me at the social service agency regarding cultic problems, and I would facilitate an intervention. All these efforts were on a voluntary basis and took place either at my office or at a family home with the consent of the cult-involved adult.

By 1986 I felt the strain of simultaneously being pulled in two directions, between my work related to cults and the program for Jewish prisoners. I decided to focus all my attention on cultic studies. My reasoning was that unlike Jewish prisoners, who had done something wrong, cult members had done nothing to warrant the punishment they received.

At this juncture my work expanded beyond the Jewish community and began to take me first across the United States and later around the world as a private consultant, lecturer, and cult-intervention specialist. Most often the requests for help I received came from parents, but there were also calls from spouses and at times from the adult children of cult members. Over the past thirty years, I have done hundreds of cult interventions, working within almost every state in the United States. My work has also taken me across Canada and to China, England, Ireland, Europe, Israel, India, Australia, and Thailand.

At one time I agreed to cooperate with parents to do what has been called "involuntary deprogramming." This involved the physical restraint of an adult cult member under the supervision of his or her family. The use of such restraint guaranteed that the family would have time to adequately address their concerns without cultic interference. Repeated court rulings regarding the involuntary deprogramming of adults have effectively ended this form of cult intervention in the United States. I no longer recommend that any family consider such an approach due to the legal consequences.

In involuntary deprogramming parents often hired people to serve as security guards to ensure that an adult cult-involved child couldn't leave until parents determined that the intervention had concluded. This is unlike a voluntary intervention, which is based on the willing cooperation and consent of the cult-involved individual, who is free to leave at any time.

In fairness I feel obligated to point out that families felt involuntary deprogramming was necessary because cults trained and sometimes urged their members to run away rather than talk to their families in an intervention. Successful interventions require substantial time allotted for discussion and exchange of ideas. Concerned families used restraint to guarantee them that time.

A form of temporary conservatorship was once used in the United States to address the concerns of families about cults and enable them to legally intervene on an involuntary basis to help an adult cult victim.

The courts, however, later eliminated this legal option. Temporary legal authority or conservatorship over an adult cult member was ruled a violation of the US constitutional provision for freedom of religion.

At this point it is important to note that many groups called "cults" are not based on religion. For example, cults can be based on some form of training, therapy, business plan, philosophy, diet, or exercise that forms the outer facade a group uses when the general public sees it.

My limited involuntary deprogramming work with adults ended more than twenty years ago. I do only intervention work on a voluntary basis unless the cult-involved individual is a minor child. Under certain circumstances minor children may be mandated to participate in an intervention under the direct supervision of a custodial parent or authority figure. These are the legal boundaries regarding cult-intervention work today in the United States.

In voluntary interventions adult cult members are free to go at any time. Most cult members willingly stay and agree to participate due to the expressed concerns of family members, friends, and others. Most of my intervention cases have been successful—that is, at the conclusion of the intervention, the cult-involved individual decides to leave the group that has created concern.

Public education about the dangers of destructive cults is the best deterrent. Destructive cults have historically targeted college campuses for recruitment. My lecture work has included universities and colleges in the United States, such as the University of Chicago, Dickinson College, Carnegie Mellon, Baylor, Rutgers, and the University of Pennsylvania in Philadelphia. My experience has taught me that a cult can potentially recruit anyone regardless of his or her education or social background. No one is invulnerable or somehow immune.

Cults have been a focus of interest for the US judicial system. My work has included expert testimony regarding cultic groups in ten states within the United States, including US Federal Court. This legal work has involved both civil and criminal cases, such as the prosecution of homicides and civil actions concerning child custody and personal injuries. I have also worked with local police departments across the United States, the Federal Bureau of Alcohol Tobacco and Firearms and Explosives (BATF), the Federal Bureau of Investigation (FBI), and the Department of Justice.

The media have often been the means of exposing destructive cults that have become a global phenomenon. My media work, both in the United States and internationally, has been extensive. Publications and wire services, such as the *Associated Press, Reuters, New York Times, London Times, China Daily News, South China Post, Washington Post, USA Today, Los Angeles Times, Time Magazine, Newsweek,* and *Forbes,* have often quoted me in press stories.

Over the years my radio work has included more than one hundred interviews across the United States through such US outlets as National Public Radio, CBS, and ABC as well as internationally on the BBC, RAI in Rome, CKO National Network of Canada, and the Australian Broadcast Corporation.

My work through television has included virtually every national network in the United States and most of the major news programs, such as ABC's *Nightline* and *Good Morning America*; NBC's *Dateline, Today Show,* and *Evening News*; CNN; FOX; and MSNBC. The issue of destructive cults isn't limited based on geography, a demographic, a nationality, or one's political ideology; rather it is an issue of human welfare, which transcends such boundaries.

The Internet has revolutionized cult education. Access to information through the World Wide Web is ubiquitous, and virtually anyone anywhere at any time can access historical information about destructive cults. In an effort to use this resource, I launched what became known as the Ross Institute Internet Archives in 1996. Today that website is a database known as the Cult Education Institute (CEI), which is the largest and most comprehensive cult-related online library that is freely accessible to the general public. CEI features a database of information about controversial groups and movements, some of which have been called "cults." The attached public message board at CEI contains more than one hundred thousand individual entries, including the comments of former cult members, current cult members, affected families, and others concerned about cultic groups and related issues. Thousands of individual and unique users visit CEI daily. I personally respond to hundreds of inquiries every month.

The scope of my work has increasingly included international concerns. Many groups called "cults" are global entities, such as Scientology, the Kabbalah Centre, Landmark Education, Falun Gong, and the Reverend Moon's Unification Church. Israel's Ministry of Welfare and Social Services sought my input in 2011 for its report about cults. And I have attended international conferences about cults in China, Thailand, and Canada.

My first visit to China was at a conference in 2009. The paper I presented, which the Chinese Academy of Social Sciences published, was titled "Is Falun Gong a Cult?" In my opinion Falun Gong fits well within the core criteria forming the nucleus for the definition of a destructive cult. Some people seem to think that defining Falun Gong as a destructive cult is somehow politically motivated. But the real issue is, does the group hurt people? After receiving complaints from affected families in the United States and interviewing former members of Falun Gong as well as corresponding with current practitioners through e-mail, I have concluded that Falun Gong *does* hurt people through its practices. And in my opinion Falun Gong fits the profile of a personality-driven and defined group dominated by a charismatic leader—which is the most salient single feature of destructive cults. This book contains two chapters about Falun Gong, which has affected millions of lives in China and has reportedly contributed to the deaths of more than a thousand people.

The most poignant and heartbreaking meeting I have ever attended with any former cult member was my visit with self-immolation survivors and former Falun Gong practitioners Hao Huijun and her daughter, Chen Guo. The two women, once followers of Li Hongzhi, the founder of Falun Gong, participated in a staged protest at Tiananmen Square on the Chinese New Year's Eve on January 23, 2001. At that time a small group consisting of seven Falun Gong practitioners set themselves on fire. A twelve-year-old girl and her mother died. Hao Huijun and her then twenty-year-old daughter, Chen Guo, survived but paid a horrible price for their involvement with Falun Gong. Both women were hospitalized and endured multiple surgeries. Today they live together in welfare housing and are severely scarred and disabled. Hao Huijun told me she regrets encouraging her daughter to embrace the teachings of Li Hongzhi. She lamented, "You can see the disastrous effect this caused my daughter. I really regret that now." This book is dedicated to Hao Huijun and Chen Guo.

My work spans three decades and has included consulting with thousands of families and cult victims. In the 1980s there were dozens of deprogrammers doing cult-intervention work across the United States. But today there are only a handful due to the rigors of the work and also largely as a result of cult harassment. Over the years I have received death threats, I've been stalked, and I've even been a target of cyber warfare. I can easily understand why some cult-intervention specialists have dropped out or burned out, and I can understand the reluctance of new people to pursue what is often an emotionally draining and ethically challenging career.

Considering the shrinking resources and limited alternatives available to families and others concerned about destructive cults, this book is necessary now. My intention is to provide a practical and accessible synthesis of both relevant research and working experience regarding destructive cults. Rather than try to "reinvent the wheel," this book carefully connects and footnotes the most meaningful research and relevant information.

Here are also historical accounts of those affected by some of the most horrible cults in modern history. There are chapters about large, organized groups as well as about small but deadly cults. These historical chapters reflect the diversity and disturbing behavior of destructive cults. It is this history that demonstrates so vividly the cause for concern about cults—that is, because they hurt people. It is this history that forms the basis for why people remain concerned about groups called "cults." It is the harm they have done, which is neither random nor accidental, that reflects their systemic and systematic practices.

Specifically defining a destructive cult has generated considerable debate over the years. Some scholars and academics say any attempt to put forth a definition is pejorative and based on bigotry without any objective basis. A chapter of this book is focused on explaining the nucleus for the definition of a destructive cult. This nucleus definition is based on a specific set of objective criteria, which encompass the most common features and core characteristics found within all groups that have been considered destructive cults. This nucleus definition is based on behavior, not on beliefs.

Also much debated is the subject of cult brainwashing. That is, how do groups called "cults" control people? A chapter in this book focuses on the existing body of research, which explains the process of cultic manipulation and control. The same process we can see in the context of large organizations called "cults" is also used by smaller groups. There is also evidence of similar manipulation in abusive, controlling relationships and in families that behave like cults. Some multilevel marketing companies and large-group-awareness training seminars have also employed a similar blend of coercive persuasion techniques to gain undue influence and control over people's lives.

When I began my intervention work back in the early 1980s, I largely built upon the existing foundation constructed by the first cult deprogrammer Ted Patrick. It was Patrick who first formulated and tested the basic approach of cult intervention during the 1970s. Despite the controversy surrounding Patrick's illegal "kidnap deprogrammings," he was the first deprogrammer. It was Patrick who did the first cult interventions, which he devised as an educational process that included thought-provoking questions and dialogue. I have never met or spoken with Ted Patrick, but I read about his work in *Snapping: America's Epidemic of Sudden Personality Change*, a seminal book about cults first published in 1978.

Patrick sought to unravel the programming of cults; therefore, his process became known as "deprogramming." Cult expert and psychologist Margaret Singer explained this succinctly. "Deprogramming... [is] providing members with the information about the cult and showing how their own decision-making power had been taken away from them." Singer's description continues to form the basis for cult-intervention work today, though information technology since the advent of the Internet has continuously refined and greatly enhanced the process.

In this book I have broken down the cult-intervention process into simple, easy-to-understand blocks that identify the categories of questions and corresponding dialogue that provides their substance. It is my hope that by explaining this process in detail, others can use and further refine its elements. Within this book is a detailed examination of each step of the process necessary to evaluate and respond to a cultic situation that has drawn concern. This includes the initial assessment, ongoing coping strategies, preparation for an intervention, and the intervention itself. Each chapter serves as a potential template and practical guide, taking the reader from the initial point of identifying a possibly harmful cultic situation to the use of relevant research information and practical tools that can effectively address such concerns. There is also a potentially helpful chapter about moving on after a cultic experience.

To provide a better understanding of the practical application of the intervention approach described in this book, there are also chapters that recount actual cult interventions. These case vignettes include an array of groups, which vividly illustrate the fact that groups called "cults" may appear in many forms. They often appear as a religious or spiritual group, but they may also appear in other guises, such as a commercial enterprise, diet or exercise program, therapy, or a political cause or movement. What all destructive cults share in common, regardless of the facade they present to the public, is essentially the same organizational structure, dynamics, and practices that exploit and hurt people.

I have also included a chapter specifically about failed interventions so others might avoid mistakes that may contribute to, or cause, failure. This chapter also very specifically defines my basis for determining success or failure in any of my professional consultations and interventions, which center on concerns about someone's involvement in a cultlike situation of undue influence.

CHAPTER 1

GROWING CULT AWARENESS

There have probably been cult groups following charismatic leaders since the beginning of human history. But relatively few have been historically noted or have garnered the attention of the modern media. The cult phenomenon as a contemporary issue began creeping into the public consciousness during the 1960s and 1970s. For the most part destructive cults chiefly hurt people through some form of exploitation. This might be done by persuading members to relinquish assets or by profiteering through free labor. There is also the personal damage done to cult members both psychologically and emotionally; this damage remains a factor in their recovery from cult involvement in many situations for some time.

Many cult groups seem to gain influence and control over their members through a process of increasing isolation and estrangement from mainstream society. This process has often largely included cutting people off from family and old friends. In the most extreme groups, this may be accomplished by relocating members in so-called intentional communities, frequently called "cult compounds."

Some destructive cults have physically hurt people. This harm has included both children and adults in sexual abuse, harsh corporal punishment, and/or mandated medical neglect. In the most severe situations, cult members have been mutilated, murdered, or asked to take their lives in orchestrated suicides.

No one has determined conclusively through research the number of destructive cults or an exact count of their total combined membership. Michael Langone, Executive Director of the International Cultic Studies Association reports that "during the last 30 years, we and other cult-awareness organizations, have received inquiries about more than 5,000 groups."[1] But whatever their number, destructive cults or extreme "cult-like" groups remain a continuing problem that has not abated, as news reports, criminal arrests, and subsequent prosecutions have demonstrated.

The problems posed by destructive cults have also proliferated around the world. Many of the larger cults have grown to become international concerns. There is no continent or seemingly few countries that could plausibly claim this phenomenon hasn't affected them. And with the increasing portability and ubiquitous nature of Internet access, a cult group can potentially touch virtually anyone anywhere in the world, since many maintain a presence on the World Wide Web. The Internet can also provide relatively easy access to critical information about destructive cults.

Groups historically referred to as "cults," such as Scientology and the Unification Church, may arguably be in decline, but others have risen to prominence. This has included the relatively recent appearances of such groups as Aum Shinrikyo in Japan and Falun Gong of China. Both of these organizations have historically succeeded in spreading far beyond Asia.

In the United States destructive cults are perhaps more plentiful relative to the population than in any other single country. This may be because many groups called "cults" are largely based on religious beliefs, which receive special protections and tax-exempt status in the United States. Some groups called "cults" may have conveniently defined themselves as "religions" to obtain such protections and tax-exempt status.

There is considerable legal protection for any religious group, as provided by the First Amendment of the US Constitution, which specifically states, "Congress shall make no law respecting an establishment of religion, or prohibiting the free exercise thereof; or abridging the freedom of speech."[2] But as some have noted, the First Amendment isn't a "suicide pact." That is, it doesn't provide the basis to do anything in the name of religious freedom, thereby preventing authorities from enforcing the law equally regarding all religious groups.

Dr. John G. Clark, a Harvard psychiatrist known for his study of contemporary cults, observed some years ago, "The new youth cults, though usually self-styled as religious for purposes of First Amendment privileges, are increasingly dangerous to the health of their converts and menacing to their critics."[3] John Clark's criticism of cults certainly made him a target. Scientology reportedly launched a "series of threats, harassment, and false and malicious accusations" against Clark.[4] But in the United States, the First Amendment ideally protects the constitutional rights of groups called "cults" and their critics through its provisions for freedom of expression.

For us to better understand the issue of destructive cults, knowing their history is important. What follows is a historical examination of some of the largest and most destructive groups called "cults," reported in chronological order.

1978—Jonestown Mass Murder/Suicide

During the 1970s Jim Jones, a charismatic preacher in San Francisco, gained popularity and power. In the end the cult Jones formed would come to represent the most terrible cult tragedy in American history. Now simply referred to as "Jonestown," this horrific mass murder/suicide claimed the lives of more than nine hundred people, including more than two hundred children.[5] The murders at Jonestown took place on November 18, 1978. The public struggled to understand how so many lives were claimed so suddenly under the influence of a single charismatic leader.

How could a church and a pastor, both once greatly admired, end in such infamy?

In the beginning there seemed to be little to fear from Jim Jones. A well-established Protestant denomination called the Disciples of Christ ordained him in 1964. Jones set up two churches, the main one in San Francisco and another one in Los Angeles. The organization was called People's Temple, and at its peak there were as many as eight thousand members.

Jim Jones, though now known as a notorious cult leader, was once a popular and trusted community celebrity. He could routinely turn out thousands of his people for an event. During the 1970s Jones appeared with many prominent politicians including the state assemblyman Willie Brown. In 1976 the mayor George Moscone gave Jim Jones a seat on the San Francisco Housing Authority Commission. Governor Jerry Brown was seen attending services at People's Temple.[6]

Negative press reports began to surface about Jim Jones in the summer of 1977. In response to criticism, Jones ultimately decided to move a core group of his followers to British Guyana in South America, effectively isolating them from the outside world. The intentional community or cult compound he created was named "Jonestown."[7]

Controversy concerning Jones's behavior continued despite his departure from California. Complaints from former members and concerned families led to an official investigation. The US congressman Leo J. Ryan of California, with permission from Jim Jones, visited the isolated Guyana community compound on November 17, 1978. Ryan toured the settlement and met with Jim Jones. During the congressman's visit, residents of Jonestown passed notes to the visitors, requesting to leave. Representative Ryan agreed to take some of them back with him.

It seems that Jim Jones was unwilling to let anyone leave, so he ordered an armed attack on Ryan and others at the airstrip. On November 18, as they prepared to leave, the congressman and four others in his party were murdered.

According to an affidavit dated June 15, 1978, by one-time Temple member and Jonestown resident Deborah Layton, "Jones…claimed that he was the reincarnation of…Lenin [and] Jesus Christ [and]…had divine powers." Layton further stated that Jones "appeared deluded by a paranoid vision of the world. He would not sleep for days at a time and talk[ed] compulsively about the conspiracies against him." The compound "was swarming with armed guards…No one was permitted to leave unless on a special assignment." Layton detailed Jones's warning "that the time was not far off when it would become necessary for [his followers] to die by [their] own hands." Layton described what was called the "White Night" or "state of emergency," which was often declared at the compound. It was within this supposed context of crisis that the group had rehearsed mass suicide.[8]

On November 18, 1978, anticipating the end of his ministry and certain arrest, Jones ended the rehearsals. He ordered his final "state of emergency." Cyanide was mixed with Flavor Aid punch, which was perhaps described erroneously in press reports as "Kool-Aid."[9] Everyone was commanded to drink the mixture. Most of the adults obediently complied and took the poison. Those who weren't cooperative were shot or forced to drink the cyanide to fulfill what Jones labeled an act of "revolutionary suicide."

Twenty years later, in 1998, the mayor of San Francisco Willie Brown explained, "Jonestown was a tragedy of the first order, and it remains a painful and sorrowful event in our history. Not a year has gone by that I have not stopped to remember San Francisco's terrible loss."[10]

In 2011 nearly two hundred people gathered at Oakland's Evergreen Cemetery at a mass grave, the final resting place for more than four hundred victims of Jim Jones. They came to dedicate a memorial composed of granite slabs inscribed with the names of the 917 who died at Jonestown. The controversial memorial included the name of Jim Jones, though he wasn't buried at the cemetery. A storm of both protests and litigation ensued, led by Rev. Jynona Norwood, a minister who lost twenty-seven relatives at Jonestown. She questioned the propriety of the inscription, "It is OK to honor a mass murderer?" Norwood pointed out that the inclusion of Jones's name on the controversial memorial was the equivalent of including Osama bin Laden on a memorial honoring those lost on September 11, 2001.[11]

Sadly, Jonestown was only the beginning of what would become an episodic nightmare of repeated cultic tragedies. The media, public, and authorities would seemingly rediscover this issue again and again whenever another cult tragedy occurred. Interest and focus, however, would eventually wane with each news cycle until the next sensational cult story emerged.

Authors Flo Conway and Jim Siegelman interviewed many former members of the People's Temple for *Snapping: America's Epidemic of Sudden Personality Change*, their seminal book about cults. They sadly observed, "We say that each new report of cult abuses and criminal offenses will stir a major advance in public opinion and await the moment when policymakers in government become aroused to action. But, on reflection, it seems to us that even the carnage of People's Temple may fail as a warning."[12]

In the wake of Jonestown, "drinking the Kool-Aid" would become a pop culture expression to describe becoming so brainwashed that you cannot think independently. This sad metaphor is a legacy of Jonestown.

1978—Synanon Attempted Murder

Just one month before the tragedy at Jonestown, in October 1978, California attorney Paul Morantz reached into his mailbox and found a deadly rattlesnake. Members of a drug rehabilitation community, known as Synanon, had put it there. The lawyer had been litigating against the group on behalf of former members, and the group's leader had ordered him eliminated.[13]

Morantz survived the attack, but Synanon didn't. Criminal prosecutions and litigation soon unraveled the community, which had started in 1958. Founded by Charles Dederich Sr. as a self-help group, Synanon eventually became a church in 1970.

The story of Synanon is a cautionary example of a group that may have initially begun with good intentions but nevertheless degenerated into a destructive cult. It's the story that won the small California newspaper *Point Reyes Light* a Pulitzer Prize in 1979.[14]

Charles Dederich was born in 1913 in Ohio. His father died in an auto accident when he was four. He lost his younger brother to influenza a few years later. Dederich's adult life was also unhappy. After two failed marriages he moved to California and ended up as a destitute drunk. In 1956 he discovered Alcoholics Anonymous.[15] AA changed Dederich's life. He became a true believer in its twelve-step program and eventually tried to help others. Subsisting on unemployment and donations, Dederich became a full-time proponent of AA and held small gatherings after local meetings. These sessions evolved into seminars that were highly confrontational. This process devised by Charles Dederich was described as a kind of "attack therapy" but was known within the group as "the game."[16]

Charles Dederich is said to have coined the saying "Today is the first day of the rest of your life."[17]

The life Dederich ultimately gave to his Synanon faithful, however, was one based on absolute obedience, total submission, and servitude. His reach even included control over infants in what was called the "hatchery." Eventually Dederich decided that children were a waste of time and money. Men were told to get vasectomies, and women were to get abortions. Childbirth was dismissed as "crapping a football."[18] In 1977 Dederich ordered 280 married couples in his community to divorce.[19]

Synanon was also a business empire, which by 1980 was worth between $33 million and $50 million.[20] This wealth included real estate holdings, gas stations, and apartment buildings as well as a fleet of trucks, automobiles, twenty-one boats, and ten airplanes. Synanon even had its own airstrip and beach resort.[21] Dederich had no meaningful accountability but managed to gain tax-exempt status. In 1975 he moved to a lavish retreat above Visalia, California, amid "pools, spas, art works and newcomer slaves" who served him.

Those who left Synanon were labeled "splitees," and many members were purged from the group through a process Dederich called the "squeeze"—like "squeezing rotten fruit from the trees."[22] It was some of that "rotten fruit" who sought the help of Paul Morantz and led to the attempt to end the lawyer's life.

In 1980 Charles Dederich pleaded "no contest" to the charges that he and two of his followers had plotted the murder of Paul Morantz. Dederich, then frail and in poor health, was given five years of probation, fined $5,000, and ordered by the court to cease in his participation at Synanon.[23] Government officials condemned Synanon for its policies of "terror and violence," and the organization was stripped of its tax-exempt status. After that it continued to decline until it ceased to exist.

Charles Dederich Sr. died in Visalia in 1997 at the age of eighty-three, but the legacy of Synanon lives on. Reportedly "no fewer than 50 programs can trace their treatment philosophy, directly or indirect-ly, to [the] anti-drug cult called Synanon." Synanon is credited with spawning the so-called tough love philosophy prevalent in many of the programs targeting troubled teens, such as controversial "teen boot camps."[24]

1978—US Congressional Investigation of the Unification Church ("Moonies")

During the 1970s there was enough interest in groups called "cults"— and specifically in the Unification Church of Rev. Sun Myung Moon— that the US Congress took note.

Representative Charles H. Wilson of California said, "I should like to say a few words, and introduce into the record some material regarding the controversial religious leader, the Reverend Sun Myung Moon, a man who has induced thousands of our young people to join his cult." The congressman then explained, "Unfortunately, there are always those who would take advantage of the American system, people who would take advantage of our laws safeguarding civil rights, and our laws insur-ing religious freedom. Such a person, in my estimation, is the Reverend Moon...who also seems to profit by it himself enormously, while his converts, our youngsters, are begging for him in the streets."[25]

Weeks before the tragedy at Jonestown, a congressional investiga-tion of Moon and the Unification Church (UC) concluded with the following:

> (1) The UC and numerous other religious and secular organiza-tions headed by Sun Myung Moon constitute essentially one international organization. This organization depends heav-ily upon the interchangeability of its components and upon its ability to move personnel and financial assets freely across in-ternational boundaries and between businesses and nonprofit organizations.

(2) The Moon Organization attempts to achieve goals outlined by Sun Myung Moon, who has substantial control over the economic, political, and spiritual activities undertaken by the organization in pursuit of those goals.

(3) Among the goals of the Moon Organization is the establishment of a worldwide government in which the separation of church and state would be abolished and which would be governed by Moon and his followers.

The congressional report stated that a "task force should address itself to the following issues."

(a) Whether there have been systemic and planned violations of U.S. immigration laws and regulations in connection with the importation of large numbers of foreign nationals for purposes of fundraising, political activities, and employment in the Moon Organization business enterprises.

(b) Whether there have been systematic and planned violations of U.S. currency and foreign exchange laws in connection with the movement of millions of dollars of cash and other financial assets into and out of the United States without complying with appropriate reporting requirements.

(c) Whether U.S. tax laws have been violated through large cash transfers to individuals which were characterized as loans.[26]

In July 1982 Moon and an associate, Takeru Kamiyama, were convicted by a jury of intentionally failing to pay taxes on the interest earned from more than $1.7 million. Reportedly this involved a "massive" and systematic effort to defraud the government and obstruct justice. After exhausting the appeals process, Moon served an eighteen-month prison sentence for tax fraud.[27]

In a pattern that would repeat itself endlessly concerning the criminal prosecution of a purported cult leader, Moon claimed he was being "persecuted." A subsequent book characterized his trial and conviction as an "inquisition."[28] Critics of the book noted that the author had ties to the UC and was less than objective.

Family members forcibly took at least four hundred members of Moon's church, whom they deemed "brainwashed," to undergo involuntary "deprogramming" interventions, which took place from 1973 to 1986.[29]

It should be noted that Moon had friendly relationships with presidents Richard Nixon, Ronald Reagan, and George H. W. Bush.[30] Moon donated $1 million to the presidential library of the first President Bush. Prominent people were also paid to appear at Moon-linked events, including presidents Bush and Ford, Mikhail Gorbachev, and the former US congressman and housing secretary Jack Kemp.[31]

In 2002 Moon paid for advertising in forty-five newspapers across the United States claiming that religious leaders in the "Spirit World" had had a meeting to confer special heavenly status on him. This assemblage had included Martin Luther, Karl Marx, Confucius, Jesus, and God—who supposedly had unanimously decided that Moon should be proclaimed the "Savior, Messiah and King of Kings of all humanity."[32]

Moon controlled substantial investments around the globe. He reportedly dominated the American wholesale sushi market[33] and bought the *United Press International* (UPI) wire service[34] and the *Washington Times*.[35]

In August 2012 Moon was hospitalized in Seoul, South Korea, suffering from pneumonia.[36] His condition worsened, and he was later moved to a church-owned hospital near his home in Gapyeong.[37] The UC website announced in September that Moon had died.[38] Moon is survived by his wife and ten children,[39] and his children now control his business and religious empire.[40] Kook-Jin, forty-four, known as Justin Moon, runs the Tongil Group, which is the church's business arm. Hyung-Jin, known as Sean Moon, born in New York in 1979, is now head of the UC.[41]

Reportedly, there are currently about one hundred thousand members of the UC worldwide,[42] with no more than five thousand remaining adherents in the United States.[43] In 2008 Moon's personal wealth was estimated at $980 million.[44]

1984—Bhagwan Shree Rajneesh Bioterrorism Attack

In 1984 the cult followers of Indian guru Bhagwan Shree Rajneesh spread salmonella in the salad bars of ten restaurants in the town of The Dalles, Oregon, sickening 750 residents. It was the first bioterrorism attack in modern American history.[45]

Rajneesh had once been a professor of philosophy at Sagar University in Jabalpur, India. He began to develop a cult following after delivering a lecture titled "From Sex to Super-consciousness" in the 1960s. The guru eventually presided over an ashram in Pune, India, and later led his followers to Oregon in 1981.[46]

During 1981 Rajneesh moved almost seven thousand of his disciples, called "Rajneeshies," to a one-hundred-square-mile ranch near The Dalles to form a community compound. The Rajneeshies effectively took over the nearby small town of Antelope. Eerily reminiscent of Jonestown, the newly incorporated city was called "Rajneeshpuram." And like Jim Jones, Rajneesh had his own heavily armed security force.[47]

Hoping to exercise more political power in the region, the Rajneeshies planned to take over Wasco County judgeships and the sheriff's office. The salmonella poisoning was part of an organized effort to incapacitate voters who would vote against Rajneesh's designated slate of candidates. Cult members ultimately hoped to contaminate The Dalles water supply. The poisoning of local salad bars was done as a preliminary test.[48]

Bhagwan Shree Rajneesh reportedly bragged about bedding hundreds of women, which earned him the title of "sex guru." He was also said to be addicted to drugs such as Valium and nitrous oxide. Rajneesh was a self-proclaimed "rich man's guru." Wealthy disciples bought the guru expensive gifts, including a fleet of more than ninety Rolls-Royce automobiles. When asked why he needed so many cars, Rajneesh replied that his goal was to have 365, a Rolls-Royce for each day of the year.[49] He often rode the cars during ceremonial parades at Rajneeshpuram.[50]

Meanwhile, reportedly about 87 percent of the residents of Rajneeshpuram had a sexually transmitted disease. And when women became pregnant, the guru told them to have an abortion and be sterilized. One woman, Jane Stork, was enthralled by Rajneesh for many years. It wasn't until she was jailed due to her involvement in the group's criminal activities that Stork finally broke free from Bhagwan. She later told the press, "He used to speak so lovingly about children, yet behind the scenes everybody's getting sterilized. There were no children born in the ashram." Both Stork and her teenage daughter were sterilized.[51] Jane Stork eventually came to realize the destructive nature of the group. "To come to terms with that much self-delusion is really difficult." She said, "It's a long, slow, painful process." Insisting on taking the blame herself, Stork said she had "brainwashed" herself.

In 1986 two Rajneeshies pleaded no contest to the salmonella poisoning. More than twenty cult members including Stork were criminally indicted. Jane Stork, also known as Catherine Jane Stubbs and Ma Shanti Bhadra, pleaded guilty to plotting the murder of federal prosecutor Charles Turner in 2005.[52] She served two years in prison.[53]

Bhagwan Shree Rajneesh was fined $400,000 for immigration fraud and deported. After his expulsion from the United States, Rajneesh tried to relocate to twenty-one countries without success. He finally returned to India in 1987.[54] Rajneesh died in Pune on January 19, 1990. Rajneesh's remaining disciples now market an international business based on his legacy of five thousand recorded lectures through Osho International, based in New York City. Osho is a name Rajneesh chose to use not long before his death. [55]

A bronze statue of an antelope stands in front of the Wasco County courthouse, donated by the town of Antelope, Oregon. It is inscribed with the following words: "In order for evil to prevail, good men should do nothing."[56]

1990—Yahweh ben Yahweh Murders and Terrorist Bombings

Hulon Mitchell Jr. was born on October 27, 1935, the eldest child of a Pentecostal preacher who fathered thirteen children. His sister Leona would grow up to become an acclaimed operatic soprano and perform at the Metropolitan Opera. Hulon Mitchell Jr. would make his mark as the "cult leader" of a black supremacist group. But Mitchell, unlike many cult leaders, was well educated.

A graduate of Phillips University, he also studied law at the University of Oklahoma.[57] After moving to Chicago, Mitchell assumed the name Hulon Shah and was involved in the Nation of Islam. He received the blessings of Louis Farrakhan. Mitchell then reportedly earned a master's degree in economics from Atlanta University. Hulon Shah became "Father Michel" and moved to Florida, where he was also known as "Brother Love."

Finally Mitchell settled in Miami and took the name of Yahweh ben Yahweh (meaning "God, the son of God"). Like the Reverend Moon he also proclaimed himself to be the "messiah." Ben Yahweh's followers reportedly numbered in the thousands, and by 1979 he also controlled a multimillion-dollar business empire, which included schools, stores, and valuable real estate holdings.[58]

Yahweh said he was the "original Jew" and preached a doctrine of racism. He ranted against "white devils."[59] Despite this fact, Yahweh, like Jim Jones, garnered political connections and influence. In 1987 the Miami Urban League gave him its highest humanitarian award and proclaimed that he was "an inspiration to the entire community." In 1990 Xavier L. Suarez, the Miami mayor, declared a "Yahweh ben Yahweh Day."[60] One month later Yahweh was indicted on racketeering and conspiracy charges. He was eventually linked to fourteen murders, two attempted murders, and a terrorist-style bombing.[61]

Members of Yahweh's inner circle—called the Brotherhood, according to the indictment—were expected to murder someone white and produce a severed head or an ear as proof of the kill.[62]

During his 1992 criminal trial, Yahweh was exposed as a totalistic leader who controlled every aspect of his followers' lives. This control included their clothing, food, and intimate sex lives. He also used young women in the group for sex.[63]

Robert Rozier, Yahweh follower and former NFL football player, confessed to killing seven people.[64] He was a witness for the prosecution.[65]

Hulon Mitchell Jr. ("Yahweh ben Yahweh") was ultimately convicted of conspiracy to commit murder. He was sentenced to eighteen years in prison. After serving nine years of his sentence, Mitchell was paroled in 2001. A primary condition for his parole was that Mitchell could have no contact with his followers.[66] He reportedly became a landscaper and lived alone. In May 2007 he died of cancer.[67]

1995—Aum "Supreme Truth" Poison Gas Attack of Tokyo Subways

In March 1995 a Japanese cult called "Aum Supreme Truth" released deadly sarin gas in the subways of Tokyo. Four people died immediately, and thousands were rushed to hospitals. This unprovoked attack profoundly changed the Japanese perception of cults and shocked the world.[68] People later learned that this was not the first violent act of the cult. In 1989 Shoko Asahara, Aum's leader, had ordered the abduction and murder of an anti-Aum lawyer, his wife, and his infant son.[69] In June 1994, less than a year before the Tokyo gas attack, Aum members released deadly sarin gas in Matsumoto, killing seven residents.[70]

Chizuo Matsumoto, who assumed the name Shoko Asahara, was born into a poor family living in the Kumamoto Prefecture of Japan. Visually impaired, he went to a special school for the blind. Not unlike other cult leaders, Asahara saw himself from childhood as a great leader and later fostered political ambitions. Tokyo University rejected Asahara. In his late twenties he made a spiritual trek through India, supposedly seeking and then receiving enlightenment while in the Himalayas. At thirty-five he returned to Japan, and in 1984 he founded his religious society.[71]

Aum, like many cults, is a composite reflecting the idiosyncratic beliefs of its leader. Asahara combined his interpretations of Yoga, Buddhism, and Christianity along with the writings of Nostradamus. In 1992 he published a book declaring himself "Christ," Japan's only fully enlightened master, and also took the title "Lamb of God." His purported mission was to take upon himself the sins of the world. Asahara claimed that he could transfer spiritual power to his followers as well as take away their sins and bad Karma.[72]

Like Jim Jones and the infamous cult leader Charles Manson, Asahara saw dark conspiracies everywhere. He spoke of evil plots concerning Jews, Freemasons, and rival Japanese religions. He also named the

United States as the "Beast" from the book of Revelation in the Bible and claimed America would eventually attack Japan.[73]

Asahara, like many cult leaders, predicted a doomsday scenario. His prediction specifically included a third world war. In an effort to bring on that event, Asahara ordered his followers to kill. That is why they planned and executed the poison-gas attack in Tokyo; they believed it would somehow initiate a chain of events and culminate in a nuclear Armageddon. Asahara's last taped broadcast to his followers called on them to rise up and carry out his plan for salvation and to "meet death without regrets."[74] Humanity would end except for an elite few.[75]

Aum's recruitment efforts included proselytizing aimed at professionals in the Japanese scientific community. These highly educated recruits became the basis for the development of the cult's chemical and biological weapons. Aum's search for weapons of mass destruction included a "medical mission" in 1992 to Zaire, supposedly to help fight an outbreak of the Ebola virus, but actually devised to obtain a strain of that virus for use in biological warfare.

Two days after the Tokyo gas attack, twenty-five hundred police and military personnel raided Aum's Kamukuishiki complex and simultaneously two dozen more of the cult's properties across Japan. Large stockpiles of gas-making chemicals and related equipment were found. Aum members and the cult's leader were arrested.[76] At court proceedings in January 2000, Aum members finally admitted that Shoko Asahara had planned and ordered a series of crimes, ending in the 1995 Tokyo subway sarin gas attack.[77] As the Japanese judicial system slowly proceeded against Aum, thirteen members were sentenced to death by hanging.[78]

Nevertheless, some in the academic community have defended destructive cults like Aum. Academics J. Gordon Melton and James Lewis, for example, flew to Japan shortly after the gas attack to investigate charges of "religious persecution." In subsequent press conferences while they were in Japan, the pair suggested that the cult was innocent of criminal charges and instead a victim. American attorney Barry Fisher accompanied Melton and Lewis and reportedly claimed that Aum couldn't have produced the poison gas based on photos the cult provided him. Aum paid all expenses for the trio to visit Japan.[79]

The exiled Dalai Lama of Tibet, the Nobel Peace Prize winner, also lent credibility to Asahara. The guru donated forty-five million rupees, about $1.2 million, to the Dalai Lama.[80] Seemingly in exchange for the cult leader's generosity, the Dalai Lama consented to several high-level meetings, including photo opportunities. Even after the gas attack in Tokyo, the Dalai Lama insisted that Asahara was his "friend, although not necessarily a perfect one."[81]

Shoko Asahara was sentenced to death in February 2004.[82] He remains in prison, and his lawyers claim he is "mentally incompetent." Asahara is reportedly confined to a wheelchair; he is incontinent and unable to respond to anyone in an intelligible manner. Despite this fact the guru continues to garner the devotion of many remaining followers who still insist he is a "spiritual being."[83]

Aum was stripped of much of its assets through claims filed by victims of its gas attack. In January 2000 the cult claimed to have changed and now has the new name Aleph. Aleph reportedly has about eleven hundred members[84] and is led by Fumihiro Joyu, a former subordinate of Asahara.[85] Aleph continues to perpetuate many of the conspiracy theories Asahara promoted and still considers him a "master."[86] It has been recently reported that Aleph is recruiting under the guise of a "yoga school."[87]

Former BATF director Steven Higgins explained in 1995 why law enforcement must respond to criminal behavior and the danger posed by destructive cults. Higgins said, "I can only say: Remember Jonestown or remember the members of the sect in Canada and Switzerland who committed mass suicide. Or look at what happened in the subways in Japan, where a group whose presence was known and considered potentially dangerous by government officials allegedly uncorked a deadly nerve gas [later conclusively proven]. The day has long passed when we can afford to ignore the threat posed by individuals who believe they are subject only to the laws of their god and not those of our government."[88]

1996–2002—Hare Krishna (ISKON) Racketeering and Child Abuse

In 1996 the International Society of Krishna Consciousness (ISKCON) leader Kirtanananda accepted a plea deal from prosecutors for racketeering related to a $10 million fund-raising scam. The charge was tied to the murders of two Krishna devotees. The killer, a follower of Kirtanananda, testified that the guru had ordered the murders.[89] The conspiracy to commit murder charge was dropped as part of the plea arrangement. One of the men killed had apparently intended to expose the guru. He reportedly claimed that Kirtanananda "condoned child abuse and sexual molestation."[90] Kirtanananda received a twenty-year prison sentence.

Prabhupada, an Indian businessman turned guru founded ISKCON, which has often been called a "cult," in 1966. We should note that the guru once reportedly said, "The Krishna consciousness movement has nothing to do with the Hindu religion."[91]

Keith Hamm, later known as Kirtanananda, became an ISKCON devotee in 1968. During the 1970s he built a lavish temple called "New Vrindaban" in West Virginia, which was to serve as a palace for Prabhupada. The building was lavishly decorated and painted in gold leaf. Tons of imported marble and onyx were used in its construction. It was not completed until 1979, two years after Prabhupada's death.

Kirtanananda was once one of the most powerful gurus within the ISKCON hierarchy; he was released from prison in 2004 after serving eight years of his sentence. ISKCON banned him. The disgraced guru wasn't allowed to return to the "Palace of Gold," known as "the crown jewel of the Krishna movement in America,"[92] he had built. Kirtanananda died in 2011 at the age of seventy-four.

In February 2002 ISKCON declared bankruptcy. This was done in response to a $400 million class-action lawsuit filed in 2000 against the organization. Ninety-two plaintiffs claimed sexual, physical, and emotional abuse during the 1970s and 1980s as children within ISKCON boarding schools.[93] The Chapter 11 bankruptcy took place before the scheduled trial and effectively forced the plaintiffs to accept a settlement. The court ordered a settlement plan of $9.5 million, which hundreds of children abused in ISKCON ultimately shared. This settlement included schools the group maintained both in the United States and in India.[94]

Prabhupada, the founder of ISKCON, wanted all children of his devotees sequestered in boarding schools, beginning at the age of five. This step freed parents to work unencumbered at such things as selling books for the organization and other fund-raising efforts.[95]

Children were reportedly "terrorized" within Krishna facilities. Young girls were given as "brides" to older men who donated generously to the group. Children were also deprived of medical care, at times scrubbed with steel wool until their skin bled, and prevented from leaving.[96] One plaintiff in the litigation told the *Los Angeles Times* that as a minor child, she had to "fend off sexual advances of gurus, teachers and other devotees in a Dallas boarding school" and that she "was frequently beaten." She also saw other Krishna children "put inside gunnysacks and barrels as punishment...[and] locked in closets and told that rats would attack them if they moved."[97] Another plaintiff, who spent time in the ISKCON schools, said that as a child he was "beaten," "starved," and "raped." When he was asked about the settlement, he said, "It kind of feels like a cop-out. They have a lot more money, but they were basically crying, 'We're poor, we're poor.'"[98]

Alfred B. Ford, an heir to the Ford Motor Company fortune, however, announced that he would build a multimillion-dollar "religious complex" at ISKCON's headquarters in India. He dubbed the project a future "spiritual Disneyland."[99] Ford, the great-grandson of Henry Ford and a longtime ISKCON devotee, had previously announced a $10 million donation to the organization in 2002.[100]

In 2005 attorneys for both sides said the final settlement payouts to the abused ISKCON children generally ranged from $6,000 to $50,000.[101]

2000—The Movement for the Restoration of the Ten Commandments, Mass Murder/Suicide

On March 17, 2000, more than five hundred members of the African "Movement for the Restoration of the Ten Commandments" entered their small church in Kangngu, in the western region of Uganda. They sang for hours before the small wooden building was set on fire from inside. The doors were locked, and windows were boarded and nailed shut. Everyone inside the church perished. Authorities later found their charred bodies, including those of eleven children.[102]

Africa reeled in shock as Ugandan police found hundreds more the cult had murdered. According to pathologists who examined their remains, some were poisoned, and others were strangled; many had stab wounds and/or fractured skulls. Their bodies had been hidden under houses or thrown down wells and latrine pits. The death toll ultimately reached 780,[103] though some reports placed the final number at more than 1,000.[104] Many bodies may not have been recovered. Possibly this cultic mass murder or suicide surpasses Jonestown.[105]

Joseph Kibwetere founded the Movement for the Restoration of the Ten Commandments in the late 1980s; at one time it may have included as many as five thousand members. The sixty-eight-year-old, self-styled "bishop" was once a prominent Roman Catholic and was active in Ugandan politics. Kibwetere was hospitalized due to a mental illness.

"He had an affective disorder. A cyclical thing. Up and down. Like manic depress[ion]," Dr. Fred Kigozi, executive director of Kampala's Butabika Hospital, told reporters.[106]

Like Shoko Asahara, Kibwetere also claimed a special and pivotal position in human history by divine mandate. He made grandiose claims based on his visions and said he had also overheard conversations between Jesus and the Virgin Mary.[107] Kibwetere told his followers that the Virgin Mary complained about the world's sin and departure from the Ten Commandments and said he had been commanded to restore them and announce a coming apocalypse in the year 2000.[108] The cult leader authored a handbook, which predicted a litany of coming calamities that would destroy most of the world's population. He said only those who obeyed the commandments and followed him might be spared within his church, which he called the "ark."[109]

Joseph Kibwetere's special revelation led to his expulsion and eventual excommunication from the Roman Catholic Church. The past bishop of Mbarara Diocese said, "Kibwetere claimed that he could talk to God, which was unacceptable."[110]

Joseph Kibwetere merged his leadership with a woman. His soul mate was a former prostitute named Credonia Mwerinde, often called the "programmer." Some say Mwerinde, who claimed to have met the Virgin Mary, ultimately eclipsed the cult's founder in both real importance and power. Fr. Paul Ikazire, a priest and former cult member, said she dominated the group and that "Kibwetere was just a figurehead." He characterized Mwerinde as "a trickster, obsessed with the desire to grab other people's property." It was the "Virgin Mary," as channeled through Mwerinde, who supposedly determined all the group rules.[111] Mwerinde preached that personal possessions were evil. She encouraged cult members to sell everything and surrender all their assets to her. Eventually Mwerinde became rich and accumulated farms, houses, and cars. Ikazire recalled, "She would come in and say things like: 'The Virgin Mary wants you to bring more money.'"[112]

Kibwetere and Mwerinde kept their followers isolated. Any contact with outsiders, labeled as "sinners," was strictly monitored and frequently forbidden. Cult members were predominately poor and former Catholics. They were encouraged to be celibate, swore to a vow of silence, and were unable to speak unless in prayer. They often relied on sign language.[113] The movement's members rose at dawn, prayed until noon, and worked long hours in the fields before going to bed, usually at 10:00 p.m. Though newcomers were fed well, the regular members largely subsisted on beans. They were hungry, tired, estranged from family, and largely cut off from the outside world.

Doomsday predictions the cult leaders made were pushed forward again and again.[114] Kibwetere's manifesto handbook, titled *A Timely Message from Heaven: The End of the Present Time*, was mailed out by the thousands. The date of the final event was set for December 31, 2000.[115] When that day passed as yet another unfulfilled prophecy, some disgruntled members apparently wanted to leave and have their property returned.

On March 15, 2000 (two days before the church fire), Kibwetere issued a "farewell" letter to government officials. The letter spoke of the imminent end of the current generation and the world. Similar sentiments had been expressed in a previous communication, which said, "God sent us as a movement of truth and justice to notify the people to prepare for the closing of this generation, which is at hand." One official, reflecting on Kibwetere's last letter, recalled, "The person who brought the letter bid farewell to the…staff. It was premeditated suicide."[116]

Joseph Kibwetere's family says he is dead. His body hasn't been positively identified, but a ring believed to be Kibwetere's was found on a finger amid the rubble of the burned church.[117]

There are conflicting claims regarding Credonia Mwerinde. At one point the police claimed to have identified her body, but some speculate she is still alive.[118] Cult survivors claim Mwerinde killed the other leaders before fleeing. One local businessman stated that just days before the church fire, she had talked to him about selling cult property, which included large tracts of land, vehicles, and buildings. A documentary, later produced for African television, concluded that "money and greed" motivated Mwerinde to initially help form the cult and ultimately led her to destroy it.[119]

An international law enforcement hunt for the leaders of the Movement for the Restoration of the Ten Commandments has so far produced no meaningful results. No leader has yet been located or arrested.

2001—Al-Qaeda Terrorist Attacks

On a September morning in 2001, nineteen members of a militant extremist group called al-Qaeda ("the base"), led by Osama bin Laden, hijacked four American passenger jets and crashed them into the World Trade Center towers and the Pentagon. On that day 2,977 lives were lost.[120] Osama bin Laden later arrogantly boasted, "These events were great by all measurement."[121]

Bin Laden's followers believed their criminal acts were part of a "holy war" or "jihad," which cast them as "martyrs," and those they despised and would destroy were "infidels." Jack Straw, Britain's foreign secretary, compared the cult of personality built around Osama bin Laden to Adolf Hitler and said it was "similar to the Nazi phenomenon."[122]

Al-Fadl, once an active bin Laden devotee, told a jury about the culminating event, which effectively marked the conclusion of his indoctrination. He was instructed to "follow the rule of the emir."[123] The rule was clarified through a secret rite, an oath of allegiance to Osama bin Laden and al-Qaeda called the "bayat." This oath signified not only each recruit's submission to al-Qaeda but also dependence on bin Laden himself for guidance. Stephen Kent, a professor of the psychology of religion at the University of Alberta, concluded, "The common refrain of former cult members is that they would've died for their leader. Suicide for a holy cause is not as mysterious as it first seems."[124]

Mohamed Atta, the suspected leader of the hijackers, appeared to enter into a trancelike state through a constant repetition of prayers before stepping onto the plane. Jim Siegelman, coauthor of the book *Snapping: America's Epidemic of Sudden Personality Change*, explained, "Saying a prayer a thousand times—that's just a way of jamming anything human from coming into his brain."[125] Al-Qaeda devotees often videotaped their own suicides. On such tapes the suicide bombers can be seen listening to audiocassettes of chanted praises, given to those willing to die, before boarding trucks loaded with TNT. Flo Conway commented that such thought-stopping techniques could potentially compromise a person's ability to think. She said, "The hardest thing to understand is that the mind itself can be captured and made into a machine."[126]

Bin Laden, like other cult leaders, told his followers they would reap supernatural rewards if they were willing to commit suicide. Bin Laden promised they would receive "a martyr's privileges…guaranteed by Allah." In a 1996 decree, bin Laden claimed that fighting the United States would "double" those supernatural rewards and told Americans that his followers would "enter paradise by killing you."[127]

Al-Qaeda eerily echoed the beliefs and behavior of a destructive cult from the distant past led by Hassan i Sabbah (1034–1124), a religious mystic and terrorist. Hassan's Order of Assassins, like al-Qaeda, deployed suicide killers. And the group believed that through this ultimate sacrifice they would enter the gates of heaven. Hassan, like bin Laden, allowed his followers to experience pleasures on earth before their deadly missions.[128] The assassins drank wine, used hashish, and enjoyed sex with courtesans. Centuries later, al-Qaeda's hijackers drank heavily and sought prostitutes before their suicide attacks.[129] Both bin Laden and Hassan used their followers like puppets to fulfill their own agenda.

Osama bin Laden didn't share the same humble beginnings of many cult leaders. He was the son of a billionaire from Yemen, who built a business empire based in Saudi Arabia. Osama's mother, a Syrian, was his father's fourth wife. But like other cult leaders before him, he may have felt estranged and isolated. A family friend explained, "In a country that is obsessed with parentage, with who your great-grandfather was, Osama was almost a double outsider."[130] According to his half-brother, Yeslam bin Laden, there are fifty-four siblings in the bin Laden family, which ultimately included twenty different mothers. Each wife was given a separate house. And because Osama bin Laden was the only child of his mother, he had very little contact with his extended family. Ironically, bin Laden's mother was not an Islamic fundamentalist but rather a sophisticated and well-traveled woman who refused to wear a burka (enveloping outer garment worn by some Muslim women) and instead favored Chanel suits.[131] Like many Arab children of his class, bin Laden enjoyed an early life filled with nannies, tutors, and servants. In 1968 bin Laden's father died, leaving his thirteen-year-old son $80 million.[132] Eleven years later he graduated from King Abdulaziz University with a degree in civil engineering.[133] As a young man he was known to frequent nightclubs in Beirut and enjoy free spending. According to one acquaintance, he was "a heavy drinker who often ended up embroiled in shouting matches and fistfights with other young men over an attractive night-club dancer or barmaid."[134]

But bin Laden would eventually become completely fixated on religion, first through Wahhabism, a very strict Islamic sect prevalent in Saudi Arabia. Later he created his own idiosyncratic amalgam of beliefs much like other cult leaders. Osama bin Laden also saw himself as someone on a divinely mandated messianic mission. His holy war against the "infidels" began in Afghanistan. First, he fought the Russians, and a mythology soon developed around him. The former playboy was now cast as a heroic figure. However, bin Laden spent most of the war as a fund-raiser in relative safety. "He was not a valiant warrior on the battlefield," according to one source, who said bin Laden actually "fought in only one important battle."[135]

According to the Cult Information Center of Great Britain, al-Qaeda indoctrinated its members and formed a closed, totalitarian society.[136] This was accomplished by putting recruits through months spent at isolated training camps.[137] These camps served much like cult compounds, which have historically produced brainwashed followers after periods of isolation and information control coupled with rigid indoctrination. One captured al-Qaeda member, Al-Owhali, testified that he was first trained within an al-Qaeda camp in Afghanistan for a month and then was moved to a "jihad camp." Only after the conclusion of his training was the possibility of a "mission," discussed, one that might lead to his "martyrdom."[138] This evolving process of training coincides with the often-deceptive pattern of coercive persuasion used by groups called "cults." Initiates may not come to know the group's ultimate goals and their role in that agenda until the group has manipulated their thinking and molded a new mind-set.

Osama bin Laden once admitted this fact to his supporters in a discussion recorded on videotape. He said that the men who conducted the 2001 World Trade Center attack only knew that it was "a martyrdom operation" in America. Bin Laden said, "We did not reveal the operation to them until they are there and just before they boarded the plane."[139]

Much like the way Jim Jones used Christianity, bin Laden operated through a facade of "Islamic beliefs" and the cause of "liberation." His disciples were told that Muslims were under attack and that Islam itself was in danger. "The snake is America," bin Laden told al-Qaeda members, "and we have to stop them. We have to cut the head of the snake."[140] But the establishment in Saudi Arabia rejected bin Laden's brand of religion. In 1991 the Saudi royal family officially expelled and denounced bin Laden. And he was stripped of his Saudi citizenship in

1994. From 1991 to 1996, he lived in Sudan until that country also asked him to leave.[141]

Islamic scholars have denounced the religious premise of bin Laden's violent beliefs. "It violates the very foundations of Islamic law," said Imam Yahya Hendi, Muslim chaplain at Georgetown University.[142] The grand mufti of Saudi Arabia, Sheik Abdulaziz bin Abdallah al-Sheik, also questioned what the al-Qaida leader taught his flock. "Jihad for God's sake is one of the best acts in Islam, but killing oneself in the midst of the enemy, or suicidal acts, I don't know whether this is endorsed by Sharia [Islamic law] or whether it is considered jihad for God. I'm afraid it could be suicide."[143]

Islamic scholar Bernard Lewis of Princeton wrote in a 1998 article for *Foreign Affairs* that at no point do basic Islamic texts even consider "the random slaughter of uninvolved bystanders." Sheik Muhammad Rafaat Othman, who teaches Islamic law at the most prestigious Islamic school in the Middle East, Cairo's Al-Azhar University, stated emphatically, "You can expose yourself to a situation where you might get killed. But you can't knowingly take your life. Attacking innocent, unarmed people is forbidden. Prophet Muhammad demanded that we not kill women, children or the elderly. Attacks should be against soldiers and armed civilians. I don't see any evidence of exceptions to this rule."[144]

Despite the established beliefs of Islam, bin Laden, like Shoko Asahara, created his own spin on religion. In a video distributed among his supporters, he said, "Yes, we kill their innocents and this is legal religiously and logically." He then referred to the World Trade Center's twin towers as a "legitimate target" and his hijackers as "blessed by Allah."[145]

Four al-Qaeda members were later found guilty of staging the 1998 suicide bombings of US embassies in Kenya and Tanzania, killing 224 people. Bin Laden was charged in the 308-count indictment as the leader of the conspiracy. A $5 million reward was offered for infor-mation leading to his arrest.[146] Ultimately Afghanistan would become both bin Laden's refuge and new home. When the fanatical religious sect known as the Taliban needed money, bin Laden gave its leader, Mullah Omar, $3 million.[147] He had basically bought himself a safe haven for planning and launching terrorist attacks.

After 9/11 Osama bin Laden was a hunted man. Pinpointing his exact loca-tion took the CIA years, but finally in 2011, he was found inside Pakistan. The al-Qaeda leader was living comfortably in an affluent suburb of Islamabad within a walled villa. A military operation was organized, and an elite American military group (Navy SEALs) raided the compound by helicopter at night. Osama bin Laden "resisted," and a bullet to the head killed him. A military detachment then buried him at sea.[148]

2002—Nuwaubian Child Sexual Abuse

In May 2002 federal agents arrested Malachi York, the founder and leader of an African-American separatist group called United Nuwaubian Nation of Moors, in Georgia for "transporting minors across state lines for sex."

The 116-count indictment a Georgia grand jury handed down against York included 74 counts of child molestation, 29 counts of aggravated child molestation, 4 counts of statutory rape, 1 count of rape, 2 counts of sexual exploitation of a minor, 1 count of influencing a witness, and 5 counts of enticing a child for indecent purposes. Four of the children York had victimized tested positive for sexually transmitted diseases.[149]

York, once called the "Master Teacher," was convicted on multiple criminal counts and received a 135-year prison sentence.[150]

Like other cult leaders before him, Malachi York made exaggerated, egotistical claims. He said he was "the supreme being of this day and time, God in the flesh."[151] York also had a penchant for titles, such as "the Imperial Grand Potentate" and "the Grand Al Mufti Divan."[152]

Malachi York, once known as Dwight York, Melki Sedec Isa Muhammad, and dozens of other aliases, was born on June 26, 1945, in Boston, Massachusetts.[153] He started his Nuwaubian group in Sullivan County, New York, during the 1970s. The group was then called the Ansaru Allah Community in Brooklyn just before it moved to Georgia. The York group was exclusively African-American and observed some Muslim traditions. York wove science fiction into his religious belief system. He told his followers he was an extraterrestrial from "the planet 'Rizq.'"[154]

York also had a criminal record. He had served three years in prison in the 1960s for resisting arrest, assault, and possession of a dangerous weapon.

According to former members, the abuse began long before York created his compound in Georgia. In New York children were brutally beaten, and living conditions were horrible. A young woman described her childhood in the group. "We slept on floors. We had to eat with our hands. We ate what [York] wanted us to eat."[155] And York had sex with "whomever he chose." In Georgia he chose children. One witness at his criminal trial said York began sexually abusing her when she was eight. He called it a "religious ritual."[156]

Many of York's followers and even his victims have defended him despite his criminal behavior. Former group member Saadik Redd explained, "The ultimate success of a con man is to make the person who's being conned make excuses for the con man. If I can get you to deny reality, then I have in fact controlled your mind."

Using the free labor of his followers to create businesses and accumulate assets, York became wealthy. At the time when his home and the group compound were raided in 2002, authorities found $430,000 dollars in cash. The 476-acre Nuwaubian compound was valued at $1.7 million. York also maintained a private residence in an affluent neighborhood in nearby Athens, Georgia.[157] The York house was later sold for $695,000 at auction.[158]

US attorney Maxwell Wood, who prosecuted Malachi York, pronounced the convicted felon a "con man."[159] York's son, Malik, seemed to confirm this description in an interview. His son said that York told him, "I don't believe any of this [expletive]. If I had to dress up like a nun, if I had to be a Jew, I'd do it for this kind of money." [160]

Malachi York (inmate 17911-054) is currently incarcerated at the US Penitentiary in Florence, Colorado. His projected release date is April 2122.[161]

2005—Polygamistic Child Abuse

In June 2005 an Arizona grand jury indicted Warren Jeffs, leader of the Fundamentalist Church of Jesus Christ of the Latter-Day Saints (FLDS), on charges of sexual misconduct with a minor and conspiracy to commit sexual misconduct with a minor. Jeffs was accused of arranging a marriage between a teenage girl and an older man.[162] Some polygamistic groups, such as the FLDS, have been called "cults."[163]

The FLDS is believed to be the largest organized polygamistic group in North America, with an estimated membership of ten thousand primarily located in the twin towns of Hildale, Utah, and neighboring Colorado City, Arizona.[164]

Jeffs went into hiding after his indictment. Arizona authorities then charged him with unlawful flight to avoid prosecution. Meanwhile the attorney general of Utah froze the assets of the FLDS, valued at $110 million. A judge appointed a fiduciary to manage the FLDS trust, called the United Effort Plan (UEP), which controls its holdings. Utah and Arizona authorities then announced a $10,000 reward for information leading to Jeffs' arrest. He would be named one of the FBI's "Ten Most Wanted" criminals.[165]

In August 2006 the Nevada Highway Patrol apprehended Warren Jeffs near Las Vegas. He was traveling as a passenger in a 2007 Cadillac Escalade. Inside the vehicle officers found more than $60,000 in cash, fourteen cell phones, a radar detector, two GPS units, three wigs, a laptop computer, several knives, three iPods, multiple credit cards, and seven sets of keys.[166] Mark Shurtleff, Utah attorney general, called Jeffs' arrest a victory for his victims, "who had the courage to stand up against a man some consider God on Earth." He added, "The message is nobody is above the law."[167]

But the FLDS and other polygamist groups had been able to operate with relative impunity, seemingly "above the law," for decades. It wasn't until 1998, when a badly beaten sixteen-year-old girl escaped the fifteen-hundred-member polygamistic Kingston Clan, known as "The Latter-Day Church of Christ," that the general public began to realize the extent of child abuse within these secretive groups. The teenager testified in court that her father had brutally whipped her for refusing to marry her uncle. "10 licks for every wrongdoing," she said. After twenty-eight lashes across her back and thighs, she reportedly lost consciousness. The judge called the treatment she endured "torture." The Kingston Clan reportedly controls a $150 million financial empire in Utah and Arizona.[168]

In Utah alone there are reportedly fifty thousand polygamists, and many of them proudly trace their ancestry back to the early days of the Mormon Church (LDS), which officially banned the practice of polygamy in 1890. At that time Wilford Woodruff, the president and officially proclaimed prophet of the Mormon Church, said he had received a revelation to end polygamy. But many Mormons disagreed with that edict and left the church, creating splinter churches and communities led by their own self-proclaimed "prophets."[169]

Lawmakers and law enforcement have often seemed ambivalent about these Mormon splinter groups, which often refer to themselves as "Mormon fundamentalists." For example, Utah Senator Orrin Hatch, who has expressed some sympathy for polygamists, is the great-grandson of polygamist and former Utah governor Michael O. Leavitt.[170]

The FLDS faction Warren Jeffs has ruled over has a long history in Arizona going back more than sixty years. Jacob Lauritzen, a cattle rancher, founded the town of Short Creek, which is now called Colorado City, in Arizona in 1913. It eventually became a stronghold for what was known as the Lee's Ferry polygamists. The LDS Church excommunicated this group in 1935 after they refused to sign an oath against polygamy. The Lee's Ferry polygamists liked the location of the group, largely due to its isolation. It is buffered by the Grand Canyon and a hundred miles of barren desert between the polygamists' town and the nearest law enforcement in Kingman, Arizona. Being so close to the state border also afforded the polygamists easy refuge in Utah if there was trouble with the Arizona authorities.[171]

There was trouble in Short Creek in 1953. Howard Pyle, Arizona governor, hired private detectives to investigate the community and concluded, "Here is a community...dedicated to the wicked theory that every maturing girl child should be forced into the bondage of multiple wifehood with men of all ages for the sole purpose of producing more children to be reared to become mere chattels." Pyle ordered a police raid. Polygamist men from Short Creek were jailed in Kingman, while their plural wives and children stayed behind. Arizona officials took days trying to sort through the families and determining who was related to whom. The raid became a public relations nightmare for Pyle when people saw newsreels of distressed children separated from their parents. The net result was only one year of probation for twenty-three polygamist men. The bad press and political fallout helped the Arizona polygamists avoid interference from law enforcement for many years to come.[172]

Perhaps it was because of the failed raid in 1953 that more than forty years later the Kingston and FLDS polygamist groups believed they would also ultimately prevail. David Ortell Kingston, however, was sentenced to five years in Utah State Prison for having sex with his sixteen-year-old niece. Rowenna Erickson, a former Kingston bride, said, "Their whole structure is beginning to quake, it's like a low-level earthquake."[173] The FLDS would also feel those reverberations.

Warren Jeffs succeeded his father, Rulon Jeffs, as the "prophet" and absolute leader of the FLDS shortly after Rulon's death in September 2002. Only a month later authorities revealed that they had been extensively investigating underage marriages within the FLDS communities.[174] That investigation would eventually lead to sex charges against numerous men and Warren Jeffs. They would face sex charges in both Utah and Arizona.[175]

Jeffs ruled over his FLDS kingdom like a ruthless tyrant. He threw out more than one hundred men, stripping them of wives and children, whom he then reassigned to other men who were loyal to him. Jeffs banned school and forbade the color red and use of the word *fun*. He also banned television, rock music, short sleeves for men, and trousers for women. Jeffs, like other purported cult leaders, sought to control every aspect of FLDS life. He controlled the homes of all FLDS members through the UEP trust.[176] The police of Colorado City and Hildale were his loyal followers.[177] When asked to explain the dynamics of the group, Warren Jeffs' nephew, Brent Jeffs, told a news correspondent, "The entire cult, as I would put it, is run by complete fear. Everything they do is run by fear. They control the women and the children all by fear...The men in there that have brainwashed these women and children, have convinced them ever since they were babies that this is right. Because they think in their minds they have nowhere else to go."[178]

As authorities began to close in on Jeffs, the polygamist leader sought a special refuge. In November 2003 David S. Allred, acting as a surrogate for Warren Jeffs, bought a remote 1,691-acre ranch in western Texas near the small town of Eldorado. Locals were initially told it was to be a "hunting compound," but it wasn't long before massive construction began and the "Yearning for Zion" (YFZ) FLDS stronghold took shape. Three three-story houses, each comprising ten thousand square feet, were quickly completed and would become dormitories. Soon there was a cheese factory, medical clinic, grain silo, commissary, and sewage treatment plant. The perimeter included watchtowers, infrared night-vision cameras, and walls encircling the compound, topped with spikes. A huge limestone-clad temple would become the centerpiece of the new, completely contained polygamist community populated by hundreds of FLDS members Jeffs had handpicked.[179]

The people of Eldorado recalled that another rural compound in Texas, run by a cult leader named David Koresh near the town of Waco, had ended in tragedy. They shuddered to think that the same situation might develop again in their own area. Like Koresh, Warren Jeffs had made a doomsday prediction that Armageddon was coming in 2005. Local rancher Lynn Meador, sixty-two, said, "Those people came under false pretenses to our area…I think people deep down were afraid this thing would end up like Waco. We were all just waiting for the other shoe to drop."[180]

The anticipated corresponding response finally came during April 2008. Authorities descended on the polygamist compound in a massive, well-planned, and carefully coordinated raid, the largest law enforcement action concerning polygamists since the Arizona raid of Short Creek in 1953. Hundreds of agents, including the FBI, the Texas Rangers, and the San Angelo police, highway patrol, and sheriff's department, converged on the YFZ ranch. Authorities used an armored vehicle for personnel, K9 dog units, and multiple ambulances.

After six long days of searching the compound, agents walked away with a collection of computers, photographs, and various records, all of which would prove to be pivotal evidence in coming criminal prosecutions.[181] Authorities removed more than four hundred children from the polygamist compound. This move included children ranging in age from infants to teenage mothers. "In my opinion, this is the largest endeavor we've ever been involved with in the state of Texas... This is about children who are at imminent risk of harm, children we believe have been abused or neglected," Child Protective Services (CPS) spokeswoman Marleigh Meisner explained.[182]

But in June a judge in San Angelo, Texas, ordered CPS to return all the children. Judge Barbara Walther stated in her order that Texas officials had exceeded their authority by removing the children from the compound.[183] The raid and ongoing expenses regarding the children's care and related litigation had cost the state of Texas more than $14 million. Questions were raised about this expense to taxpayers and the net results of the action. Krista Piferrer, deputy press secretary to the governor, responded, "Any action taken to protect children is never misguided."[184] The raid did lead to the prosecution of polygamist leaders. Authorities seized almost a thousand boxes of evidence and six terabytes of digital files, which provided overwhelming evidence in the subsequent criminal cases. All eleven men arrested at the YFZ were convicted of child sex and bigamy charges, and all received prison sentences.[185]

During the sentencing phase of the Texas trial of Warren Jeffs, the jury heard testimony from Jeffs' nephew that his uncle had raped him when he was five. The little boy had been told the rape was "God's will." Jeffs also had sex with twelve- and fifteen-year-old girls he took as his so-called celestial wives.[186] Warren Jeffs was sentenced to a term of life plus twenty years in prison. The Texas Third District Court of Appeals later denied his appeal in 2012.

Many FLDS members have disavowed Jeffs due to his criminal convictions.[187] Warren Jeffs, however, remains the official leader of the FLDS and, acting from prison, has ordered FLDS members excommunicated and exiled. Jeffs has purged perhaps as many as one thousand

FLDS members over loyalty issues since his incarceration.[188] In one of his most bizarre edicts from prison, Jeffs said fifteen remaining loyal men were "appointed...procreators" for the entire FLDS community, while others should be seen as simply "caretakers." After Jeffs' pronouncement was read, three hundred FLDS members walked out of the meeting in protest.[189]

Meanwhile, additional prosecutions of key polygamist leaders and lawsuits have been filed against the FLDS. The US Department of Justice has filed a major civil rights lawsuit, accusing FLDS-dominated police and utility companies in Colorado City and Hildale of religious bias against nonmembers.[190] The FLDS appears to be gradually dissolving through a death by a thousand cuts.

Dr. Bruce Perry is the senior fellow of the Child Trauma Academy in Houston and an adjunct professor at the Feinberg School of Medicine of Northwestern University in Chicago. He has researched the impact of trauma, specifically trauma concerning children in groups called "cults." Perry treated the children released from the Davidian compound in Waco before its fiery end, and Texas authorities also consulted him regarding the minor children of polygamists—minor children taken into custody. In an interview the researcher explained that children raised in such an environment may not understand their situation and may simply think, "My parents are right." Perry, however, noted the state's compelling legal interest. "You cannot have sex with 12-year-olds."[191]

2005—Children of God ("The Family") Suicides of Child Abuse Victims

In January 2005 Ricky Rodriquez stabbed to death his former nanny, fifty-one-year-old Angela Smith, in Tucson, Arizona. The twenty-nine-year-old then drove to Blythe, California, where he committed suicide in his car. Rodriquez and Smith both had ties to a notorious religious sect known as the Children of God (COG), which later changed its name to Family International.[192]

Before Rodriquez killed himself, he made a video explaining his actions. In what would become his final testimony, the young man recalled years of sexual abuse and parental alienation, which he endured as a child growing up in the COG. His wife told the media that Smith "was one of his nannies and she sexually abused him."[193] Rodriquez explained in his video, "It happened to thousands of us—some worse than others. My mother is going to pay for that. If I don't get her...I will keep hunting her in the next life."[194] "How can you do that to kids? How can you do that to kids and sleep at night?" he asked.[195]

Rodriquez's mother, Karen Zerby, was the wife of David Berg, the founder of the COG. Berg, who became Rodriquez's stepfather, was known to his followers as "Moses David, God's Endtime Prophet." He supposedly received revelation "directly from heaven."[196] Witnesses, however, said Berg was a pedophile and voracious sexual predator who molested children, including members of his own family. Karen Zerby was also reportedly seen having sexual intercourse with her son, Ricky Rodriquez, when the boy was only eleven.[197]

David Berg explicitly taught his followers to sexualize their children. COG members also reportedly engaged in group sex. Women in the group were encouraged to raise money and recruit new members using sex as a lure, which COG called "flirty fishing." This activity provided a path eventually leading to prostitution. COG sent out women as "God's whores" or "hookers for Jesus" to raise money for the group.[198]

After Berg's death in 1994, his widow became the official "prophet" or "Queen" of the group, she was often called "Mama Maria." According to Claire Browik, an official spokesperson for Family International, at the time of Rodriquez's death, Family International included "4,000 children and 4,000 adult members" who lived in "718 communal houses" within "100 countries."[199]

The systemic sexual abuse David Berg mandated within COG is well documented through the published group literature, which contained

Berg's instructions and teachings. This paper trail included what was known as the "Mo Letters," letters of communication from David Berg.[200] COG would later send out "purge notices," instructing its members to destroy any potentially damaging evidence its previous publications had provided. Much of this literature, however, remains intact.[201]

Throughout the 1990s authorities in Argentina, Australia, France, and Spain repeatedly investigated COG. Some of its members were jailed, but there were no convictions of top leaders.[202] Frustration with the failure of authorities to stop the Family haunted Ricky Rodriquez. "There's this need that I have. It's not a want. It's a need for revenge. It's a need for justice, because I can't go on like this," he said.[203]

The legacy of COG includes many suicides and shattered lives. The Rodriguez murder/suicide effectively served to focus attention on the group's sordid history and on the young lives its practices destroyed. A former member told the press, "We're dropping like flies," and recounted twenty-five second-generation members of the Family International/Children of God who had allegedly committed suicide in recent years. Another ex-member raised in the group said Rodriquez "was the poster child for us kids."[204] Another said, "I understand why children who grew up in the Family would want to kill themselves and why they would want to kill their mothers."[205] This statement keenly reflects the emotional ambivalence of many COG kids concerning their parents, who had initiated and/or raised them in the group.

Children in COG were reportedly put through a "detention and retraining program involving sleep deprivation, starvation, manual labor, silence restrictions and forced isolation."[206] Many who left COG expressed anger and resentment regarding the actions or continuing group loyalty of their parents. "It's a war now between ourselves and our parents," one second-generation former member said.[207]

Some ex-members of COG fell into substance abuse as an apparent means of numbing their psychological and emotional pain. Ricky Dupuy left the sect in 1992 and died of an intentional drug overdose in 1996. He wrote in a journal before his death, "What have I done with my life? Wasted it in the insanity of some maniacal bunch of pathological deviates...Some things are worse than death, and my continued existence in this unspeakable state is one of them."[208]

The most reported-about death of a second-generation ex-member was the demise of Oscar-nominated actor River Phoenix, the brother of actor Joaquin Phoenix. He died of a drug overdose in 1993 at the age of twenty-three.[209] Details Magazine reported that River Phoenix said he lost his virginity in COG at the age of four. "I blocked it all out," he said and later claimed that "I was completely celibate from 10 to 14." The Phoenix family reportedly left the group before River Phoenix turned seven.[210] After his death Phoenix was posthumously quoted, offering his opinion of COG. "They're disgusting...They're ruining people's lives," the actor said.[211]

COG has repeatedly claimed that it abandoned its abusive practices. In 2007 a spokesperson for the group said its "policy for the protection of minors was adopted in 1986. We regret that prior to the adoption of this policy, cases occurred where minors were exposed to sexually inappropriate behavior between 1978 and 1986."[212] In a 2005 news report, however, ex-members raised in the group refuted such claims. Kristina Jones, who was twenty-eight in 2005, stated, "By the time I was 12, I'd had sexual relations, against my will, with about 20 men and older boys. I was told it was 'sharing God's love.' That's how life was for me—adults having sex with children. It was the cult's Law of Love policy, the only life I'd ever known, and I didn't question it." Other former members provided similar testimony of the ongoing sexual abuse of minor children after 1986.[213]

Andrew Stone, a former member of the Family, explained, "This is essentially an organization that to this day is still composed of people who committed crimes against children." Former members say the Family has also established front organizations to launder its money. Stone claimed that leaders like Rodriquez's mother, Karen Zerby, live in the "lap of luxury."[214]

In a 1995 British court ruling that involved child custody tied to the group, Lord Justice Alan Ward wrote that the leaders of the Family must "denounce David Berg." Ward further wrote that they should "acknowledge that through his writings [Berg] was personally responsible for children in The Family having been subjected to sexually inappropriate behavior; that it is now recognized that it was not just a mistake to have written as he did but wrong to have done so; and that as a result children have been harmed by their experiences."[215]

The Family leadership has never officially denounced David Berg publicly.

2005—Colonia Dignidad Arrest of Cult Leader for Child Abuse

In March 2005 the former leader of a "German-Chilean religious cult" was arrested in a fashionable suburb of Buenos Aires, Argentina. The eighty-three-year old German citizen was Paul Schaefer, a convicted pedophile, who had been a fugitive hiding from Chilean authorities for eight years. Schaefer had been convicted in absentia in 2004 for the sexual abuse of more than two dozen minor children in Chile. Twenty-two members of the cult were also criminally convicted for covering up that abuse.[216]

Paul Schaefer was born in Sieberg, Germany, and was once a member of the Nazi youth movement. During World War II he served as a medic in the German army. In 1959 the Nazi turned preacher was fascinated by the teachings of controversial American Pentecostal preacher William Branham, a charismatic speaker who had gained popularity in the United States during the 1940s.[217] Schaefer's following grew in Germany, and he created a charitable organization that included an orphanage. It wasn't long, however, before Schaefer was accused of sexually abusing children under his care.

Schaefer fled Germany with many of his followers and ended up in Chile. In 1961 Jorge Alessandri, the Chilean president, granted Schaefer permission to create a tax-exempt organization called the Dignidad Beneficent Society.[218] Within a massive fifty-five-square-mile property near the town of Parral, at the foot of the Andes Mountains, Paul Schaefer created his own kingdom called Colonia Dignidad. He preached an "apocalyptic, anti-Communist and anti-Semitic creed," and hundreds of disciples "worshipped him as a god."[219]

Within his isolated domain Schaefer, known as Permanent Uncle, controlled virtually every aspect of daily life. He approved every engagement, managed every marriage, and required the group to collectively raise children. Men, women, and children were segregated and forced to live in separate dormitories in the Dignidad compound. According to court records, Schaefer also chose the children he sexually abused, which were typically boys between the ages of eight and twelve.[220]

Members of the community were forced to take daily doses of tranquilizer drugs. They weren't allowed to listen to the radio, read newspapers, or even walk alone. They always walked in pairs. According to Schaefer, Satan created women, but God made men. No one was allowed to have sexual relations except Schaefer. The boys' housing was conveniently situated next to his private cottage. Schaefer's daily routine included choosing one of the boys to spend the night with him.[221]

The three hundred members living in the compound typically worked eighteen hours a day for little more than room and board. "Most of us did not know what money was until Schaeffer ran away," one of his victims told the press.[222] The people were "programmed like robots and were treated as slaves, robbed of their own human rights," said psychiatrist Luis Peebles, who was once held within the compound as a political prisoner during the 1970s. Human rights groups say Schaefer cooperated closely with Chilean dictator General Augusto Pinochet and that political prisoners of the Pinochet regime like Peebles were held in dungeons below the Dignidad compound.[223]

For more than thirty years, Schaefer ruled over his cult kingdom. Lawsuits filed against the Dignidad organization or Schaefer for tax fraud, kidnapping, and the rape of minors were repeatedly dismissed due to "lack of evidence." Officials ignored the testimony of ex-members for decades. Paul Schaefer reportedly relied on a powerful network of judges, politicians, officials, police, military commanders, and businessman, who benefited from him or his organization in some way. Reportedly that network repeatedly protected its own as well as Schaefer's interests.[224]

When Chile returned to democratic government, Schaefer's corrupt network of influence slowly began to crumble. Finally in 1998 the grievances of families who lived near Colonia Dignidad were heard. Paul Schaefer was charged for sexually abusing twenty-six boys, who had been lured into the community by its free school and clinic.[225] Permanent Uncle then quickly vanished. He delegated his power over the compound to subordinates.[226]

In June 2005 Chilean officials found a cache of machine guns and rocket launchers at the Dignidad compound. Interior minister Jorge Correa said, "What's been discovered so far is of a dimension that can only be explained in a military context. We're talking about a large arsenal and I must stress that it's going to end up being the largest ever found in private hands in the life and history of Chile."[227] In August of the same year, Chilean officials took over the assets of the Dignidad organization, and control of the group compound was handed over to a court-appointed attorney.[228]

In 2006 former followers of Paul Schaefer published a full-page apology in the prominent Chilean newspaper *El Mercurio*. They asked for forgiveness for forty years of abuses and human rights violations. The apology read in part, "Since we have been liberated from the domination of Paul Schaefer we have come to understand that our community lived its religious faith as a hermetic sect, which accepted the transformation of the personalities of its members and made them incapable of making decisions contrary to his wishes as sole leader. Soon after we started and amid confessions of sin only to him, Schaefer came to know each of us completely, and he took advantage of that to dominate the community. Cutting us off from the outside world and forcing us to sever relations with our families and relatives, he was able to establish absolute control." A copy of the apology was also sent to Michelle Bachelet, the Chilean president.[229]

The following month, in May 2006, Paul Schaefer was sentenced to twenty years in prison and ordered to pay reparations to his victims. A lawyer for the victims said that the cult leader's conviction was the end of "40 years of impunity and [meant] justice for all the victims who, at the time, had no way to tell how they had been victimized."[230] Schaefer was later sentenced to three more years in prison for weapons violations in 2008.[231]

Paul Schaefer died in a prison hospital in April 2010. He was eighty-nine.[232]

In February 2013 six former leaders of Colonia Dignidad surrendered themselves to Chilean authorities. A month earlier Chile's supreme court found Gerard Mucke Koschitzke, Kurt Schnellenkamp Nelaismisckies, Gunter Schaffrik Bruckmann, and Dennys Alvear Henríquez, members of Schaefer's "iron circle," guilty of "various crimes of sexual abuse, rape of minors and abduction of minors." The men will serve eleven-year prison sentences. Judge Hernán González of the Talca Court of Appeals announced that a total of nineteen individuals convicted of cult-related crimes in January must surrender and serve their sentences.[233]

Allegedly Hartmutt Hopp, reportedly Schaeffer's "right hand man," escaped Chile and fled to Germany with millions of dollars taken from the Dignidad community. Chilean authorities have applied for his extradition. More than one hundred members of the Dignidad group eventually drifted back to Germany. Others remained behind in the Chilean compound, which is now called "Villa Baviera." They hope to eventually turn it into a financially viable community again. Just like many of the former members of the Children of God, second-generation survivors of Dignidad are reportedly deeply traumatized because of the horrible childhood Schaefer imposed on them.[234]

By the conclusion of the twentieth century and now in the twenty-first century, the damage done by destructive cults has become increasingly evident. Collective awareness about them has largely increased through media reports, criminal arrests, and court trials.

Groups called "cults" often fit a particular pattern, which may include a seemingly encapsulated or cocooned state of being. In this sense the people in cults appear to function within their own alternate reality. But when that alternate reality comes into conflict with mainstream society, some groups have imploded or exploded. The occurrence of such tragic events brings into sharp focus what Dr. Bruce Perry calls "the fracture lines in our culture."[235]

---

[1] Michael D. Langone, "Terrorism and Cultic Dynamics," *ICSA Today,* Volume 6, No. 1 (2015) p. 14.

[2] U.S. Constitution, First Amendment (Religion, Speech, Press, Assembly, Petition) 1791.

[3] Eric Nagourney, "John Clark, 73, Psychiatrist Who Studied Sects," *New York Times*, October 18, 1999.

[4] Tom Long, "Dr. John Clark, 73," *Boston Globe*, October 9, 1999.

[5] "Jonestown Suicides Shocked the World," *Associated Press*, March 27, 1997.

[6] Michael Taylor, "Jones Captivated San Francisco's Liberal Elite," *San Francisco Chronicle*, November 12, 1998.

[7] Ibid.

[8] Deborah Layton Blakey, "Affidavit of Deborah Layton Blakey," June 15, 1978 http://jonestown.sdsu.edu/wp-content/uploads/2013/10/04-24-BlakeyAffidavit.pdf

[9] Chris Higgins, "Stop Saying 'Drink the Kool-Aid,'" *Atlantic*, November 8, 2012.

[10] Taylor, "Jones Captivated San Francisco's Liberal Elite," November 12, 1998.

[11] "Nearly 200 Gather to Dedicate Jonestown Memorial," *Associated Press*, May 29, 2011.

[12] Flo Conway and Jim Siegelman, *Snapping: America's Epidemic of Sudden Personality Change*, 2nd ed. (New York: Stillpoint Press, 2005), 252.

[13] Lawrence Van Gelder, "Charles Dederich, 83, Synanon Founder, Dies," *New York Times*, March 4, 1997.

[14] Dave Mitchell, "Light to Celebrate 25th Anniversary of Its Pulitzer," *Point Reyes Light* (Point Reyes Station, CA), April 15, 2004.

[15] Paul Morantz and Hal Lancaster, *Escape* (Los Angeles: Figueroa Press, 2012), 91.

[16] Ibid., 92.

[17] Michael D. Clark, "Her Life with 'One Big Brother,'" *San Jose Mercury News*, March 19, 1999.

[18] Morantz and Lancaster, *Escape*, 95.

[19] Ibid.

[20] Lawerence Van Gelder, "Charles Dederich, 83, Synanon Founder, Dies." *The New York Times*, March 4, 1997.

[21] Morantz and Lancaster, *Escape*, 93–94.

[22] Ibid., 95.

[23] Van Gelder, "Charles Dederich, 83, Synanon Founder, Dies." March 4, 1997.

[24] Maria Szalavitz, "The Cult That Spawned the Tough-Love Industry," *Mother Jones*, August 7, 2007.

[25] Rep. Charles H. Wilson, California (Information about Rev. Sun Myung Moon and the Unification Church entered into the Congressional Record), 94th Congress, United States House of Representatives, 2nd session (January 28, 1976) Congressional Record Volume 122 Part 2 1390–1392.

[26] *Investigation of Korean-American Relations Report of the Subcommittee on International Organizations: Conclusions and Recommendations*, United States House of Representatives Committee of International Relations 95th Congress 2nd Session (October 31, 1978) 387, 390.

[27] Betty Fletcher, "Rev. Moon to Serve Jail Time," *Pantagraph* (Bloomington, IL), May 14, 1984.

[28] Carlton Sherwood, *Inquisition: The Persecution and Prosecution of Rev. Sun Myung Moon* (Washington, D.C.: Regency, 1991).

[29] Daniel J. Wakin, "Rev. Sun Myung Moon, Self-Proclaimed Messiah Who Built Religious Movement, Dies at 92," *New York Times*, September 2, 20012.

[30] Hyung-Jin Kim, "Unification Church founder Reverend Sun Myung Moon Dies at 92," *Associated Press*, September 3, 2012.

[31] Wakin, "Rev. Sun Myung Moon, Self-Proclaimed Messiah Who Built Religious Movement, Dies at 92," , September 2, 20012.

[32] Peggy Fletcher, "A Moonstruck Heaven Taps Favorite Son," *Salt Lake Tribune*, July 12, 2002.

[33] Monica Eng, Delroy Alexander, and David Jackson, "Sushi and Rev. Moon," *Chicago Tribune*, April 11, 2006.

[34] Yuki Noguchi, "Washington Times Owner Buys UPI," *Washington Post*, May 16, 2000.

[35] Ian Shpira, "Moon and Fired Executives Buy Washington Times for $1," *Washington Post*, November 3, 2010.

[36] "Unification Church Founder Rev. Sun Myung Moon, 92, Treated for Pneumonia South Korean Hospital," *Associated Press*, August 16, 2012.

[37] "Unification Church Plans to Move Founder to Its Own Hospital after His Condition Worsens," *Associated Press*, August 31, 2012.

[38] Wakin, "Rev. Sun Myung Moon, Self-Proclaimed Messiah Who Built Religious Movement, Dies at 92," , September 2, 20012.

[39] Kim, "Unification Church Founder Reverend Sun Myung Moon Dies at 92," September 3, 2012.

[40] "Moon's Rising Son Spells Change for the Unification Church," *BBC News*, March 24, 2012.

[41] Foster Klug, "Rev. Moon Oversaw Large, Often Bickering Brood," *Associated Press*, September 4, 2012.

[42] Hyung-jin Kim, "Rev. Moon Turning Over Unification Church to Sons," *Associated Press*, October 12, 2009.

[43] Monica Eng and David Jackson, "Despite Controversy Moon and His Church Moving into Mainstream," *Chicago Tribune*, April 11, 2006.

[44] "The Rev. Sun Myung Moon, Who Has Died Aged 92, Was the Soi-Distant Messiah and Savior of the Universe Who Founded the Unification Church, Popularly Known as 'The Moonies,'" *The Telegraph* (Kent), September 3, 2012.

[45] Gillian Flaccus, "Oregon Town Never Recovered from Scare," *Associated Press*, October 19, 2001.

[46] "Glimpses into the Life of the Controversial 'Guru,'" *The Times of India* (Haryana), December 21, 2002.

[47] Ibid.

[48] Ibid.

[49] Tallis Saule Archdeacon, "Oh No It's Osho: A Villain Speaks from Beyond the Grave," *The Baltic Times*, February 6, 2008.

[50] Ibid.

[51] "Escaping the Bhagwan," *The Age* (Sydney, Australia), April 11, 2009.

[52] "Cult Member Admits Murder Plot," *SBS TV* (Sydney, Australia), September 27, 2005.

[53] "Escaping the Bhagwan," April 11, 2009.

[54] "Glimpses into the Life of the Controversial 'Guru,'" December 21, 2002.

[55] Dennis McCafferty, "Old Bhagwan, New Bottles," *Salon*, October 20, 1999.

[56] Gillian Flaccus, "Oregon Town Never Recovered From Scare," *Associated Press*, October 19, 2001.

[57] Douglas Martin, "Yahweh ben Yaweh, Leader of Separatist Sect, Dies at 71," *New York Times*, May 9, 2007.

[58] Ibid.

[59] Ibid.

[60] Ibid.

[61] Ibid.

[62] Ibid.

[63] Ibid.

[64] Amy Westfeldt, "Ex NFL Player Charged in NJ Murder," *Associated Press*, March 23, 1999.

[65] "Convicted Killer, Former Football Player, Says He's Sorry for Slaying," *Associated Press*, March 6, 1999.

[66] Martin, "Yahweh ben Yaweh, Leader of Separatist Sect, Dies at 71," May 9, 2007.

[67] Ibid.

[68] Murray Sayle, "Nerve Gas and the Four Noble Truths," *New Yorker*, April 1, 1996.

[69] Ibid.

[70] Ibid.

[71] Ibid.

[72] Ibid.

[73] Ibid.

[74] Ibid.

[75] Ibid.

[76] Ibid.

[77] "Aum Blames Asahara," *Mainichi Shimbun*, (Tokyo) January 19, 2000.

[78] Yoree Koh, "Death Penalty Confirmed for Sarin Gas Attack Chemist," *Wall Street Journal*, February 15, 2011.

[79] T. R. Reid, "Tokyo Cult Finds Unlikely Supporter," *Washington Post*, May 5, 1995.

[80] Christopher Hitchens, "His Material Highness," *Salon Table Talk*, July 13, 1998.

[81] Tilman Müller, "The two faces of the Dalai Lama," *Stern* (Germany), August 30, 1995 38/95 126.

[82] "Tokyo High Court Rejects Plea for Asahara Retrial," *Japan Times*, (Tokyo) April 5, 2012.

[83] Ibid.

[84] "Aum Followers Number 1,151 up 11 from August," *Kyodo News Service*, November 15, 2000.

[85] "Faith in Aum Guru Resurges as Joyu Moves to Form His Own Group," *Asahi Shimbun* (Tokyo) February 3, 2007.

[86] "Young People Easily Get Sucked into Aum Shinrikyo Spin-off Aleph," *Japan Today* (Tokyo), August 28, 2012.

[87] Ibid.

[88] Steven Higgins, "The Waco Dispute: Why the ATF Had to Act," *Washington Post*, July 2, 1995.

[89] Mark Houser, "New Vrindaban Rebuilding Its Temple," *Pittsburgh Tribune-Review*, April 30, 2006.

[90] "'Guru' Did Jail Time," *New York Post*, March 25, 2005.

[91] "Can It Be That the Hare Krishnas Are Not Hindu?" *Hinduism Today*, October 1998.

[92] Corey Pickett, "Swami Banned," *Wheeling News-Register*, June 18, 2004.

[93] "Hare Krishna Plan OK'd by U.S. Court," *Associated Press*, May 24, 2005.

[94] Ibid.

[95] Hector Becearra, "Krishna Payouts Begin," *Los Angeles Times*, June 24, 2005.

[96] Ibid.

[97] Ibid.

[98] Ibid.

[99] "Ford Scion Plans 'Spiritual Disneyland' in Bengal," *Indo-Asian News Service*, February 19, 2004.

[100] "Ford Great-Grandson to Donate US $10 Million to Hare Krishna Temple," *Associated Press*, December 29, 2002.

[101] Ibid.

[102] Paul Busharizi, "Charred Corpses Piled in Uganda Suicide Site," *Reuters*, March 19, 2000.

[103] "Ugandan Police Say Final Death Toll 780," *Reuters*, July 20, 2000.

[104] Alfred Wasike, Matthias Mugishi, and agencies, "Kanunga Toll Reaches 1,000," *Africa News Online New Vision* (Uganda), April 3, 2000.

[105] "Ugandan Death Toll Surpasses Jonestown," *Reuters*, March 31, 2000.

[106] "Doomsday Leader Could Be a Mental Case," *African News Online* (Uganda), March 31, 2000.

[107] Adrian Blomfield, "Ex-prostitute May Have Ordered Uganda Cult Deaths," *Reuters*, April 2, 2000.

[108] Joshua Hammer, "An Apocalyptic Mystery," *Newsweek*, April 3, 2000.

[109] Ibid.

[110] "Catholic Church Had Excommunicated Kibwetere," *Africa News Online* (Uganda), March 21, 2000.

[111] Blomfield, "Ex-prostitute May Have Ordered Uganda Cult Deaths," April 2, 2000.

[112] Ibid.

[113] John Kakande, "NGO Board Confirms Receiving Kibwetere Farewell Message," *Africa News Online New Vision* (Uganda), March 23, 2000.

[114] Hammer, "An Apocalyptic Mystery," April 3, 2000.

[115] Karl Vick, "Prophecy's Price," *Washington Post*, April 1, 2000.

[116] Kakande, "NGO Board Confirms Receiving Kibwetere Farewell Message."

[117] Todd Pitman, "Family Says Ugandan Cult Leader Once Loving Father," *Reuters*, April 1, 2000.

[118] Lara Santoro, "Priestess of Death," *Newsweek International*, August 6, 2000.

[119] Daniel E. Martin, "Did Mwerinde Kill Other Kanungu Cult Leaders?" *Africa News Service*, December 10, 2000.

[120] Liz Glazier, "Lost Lives Remembered during 9/11 Ceremony," *Rocket* (Slippery Rock, PA), September 11, 2008.

[121] David Bamber, "Bin Laden: Yes I Did It," *The Telegraph* (Kent), November 11, 2001.

[122] "Straw: Bin Laden Is Psychotic," *CNN*, November 15, 2001.

[123] Mark Fineman and Steven Braun, "Life inside Al Qaeda: A Destructive Devotion," *Los Angeles Times*, September 24, 2001.

[124] Thirty Umrigar, "Experts Explain Terrorist training," *Akron (OH) Beacon Journal*, October 24, 2002.

[125] Ibid.

[126] Ibid.

[127] Michael Dobbs, "Inside the Mind of Osama bin Laden," *Washington Post*, September 20, 2001.

[128] Mary Ann Siegart, "The Cult Figure We Could Do Without," *Times* (London), October 26, 2001.

[129] Ibid.

[130] Mary Anne Weaver, "The Real bin Laden," *New Yorker*, January 24, 2000.

[131] Ibid.

[132] Ibid.

[133] Ibid.

[134] Ibid.

[135] Ibid.

[136] Siegart, "The Cult Figure We Could Do Without," October 26, 2001.

[137] Fineman and Braun, "Life inside Al Qaeda: A Destructive Devotion," September 24, 2001.

[138] Ibid.

[139] Simon Jeffrey, "We Were Overjoyed When the Plane Hit the Building," *The Guardian* (Manchester), December 13, 2001.

[140] Fineman and Braun, "Life inside Al Qaeda: A Destructive Devotion."

[141] Weaver, "The Real Bin Laden," January 24, 2000.

[142] Kenneth L. Woodward, "A Peaceful Faith a Fanatic Few," *Washington Post*, September 24, 2001.

[143] Alan Zarembo, "A Merger of Mosque and State," *Newsweek*, October 15, 2001.

[144] Ibid.

[145] Ken Hamblin, "Farrakhan a Dupe of Terrorists," *Denver Post*, November 18, 2001.

[146] Fineman and Braun, "Life inside Al Qaeda: A Destructive Devotion," September 24, 2001.

[147] Weaver, "The Real bin Laden," January 24, 2000.

[148] Ewen MacAskill, "Osama bin Laden: It Took Years to Find Him but Just Minutes to Kill Him," *The Guardian* (Manchester), May 2, 2011.

[149] Rob Peecher, "Indictments Allege More Than 100 Criminal Acts," *Macon Telegraph*, September 1, 2002.

[150] "Sect Leader Gets 135 Years for Molestation," *Associated Press*, April 22, 2004.

[151] Matthew L. Pinzur, "Nuwaubians, Who Are These People?" *Macon Telegraph*, May 15, 2000.

[152] Rob Peecher, "Nuwaubian Leader York Working on His Public Image," *Macon Telegraph*, July 22, 2001.

[153] Andrew Moran, "Who Is Dr. Malachi York?" *Digital Journal*, June 23, 2010.

[154] Ibid.

[155] Rob Peecher, "York's Accusers Describe Years of Sexual Abuse," *Macon Telegraph*, September 1, 2002.

[156] Ibid.

[157] Rob Peecher, "Government Seeks York's Money Properties," *Macon Telegraph*, July 23, 2003.

[158] Joe Johnson, "Nuwaubian Leader Jailed, but the Sect Carries On," *Athens Banner-Herald*, January 25, 2009.

[159] Terry Dickson, "Nuwaubian Leader Guilty," *Athens Banner-Herald*, January 24, 2004.

[160] Joe Kovac Jr., "New Book Asks Provocative Questions about Dwight York," *Macon Telegraph*, May 20, 2007.

[161] Federal Bureau of Prisons website (inmate locator). http://www.bop.gov/inmate-loc/ (accessed May 16, 2014).

[162] "Warren Jeffs Timeline," *Deseret News* (Salt Lake City), August 29, 2006.

[163] John Quinones, "FLDS Prophet's Nephew Testifies against Polygamists," *ABC News*, April 18, 2008.

[164] Bill Hanna, "Polygamist Sects Purchase of Texas Ranch Worries Residents," *Fort Worth Star Telegram*, July 11, 2004.

[165] Ibid.

[166] Brooke Adams and Nate Carlisle, "Police Share Details of Jeffs Capture," *Salt Lake City Tribune*, August 29, 2006.

[167] Ibid.

[168] Ray Rivera, "16-Year-Old Girl Testifies of Beating," *Salt Lake Tribune*, July 23, 1998.

[169] Charlie LeDuff, "A Holdout Polygamist, 88, Defies the Mormons," *New York Times*, February 23, 2002.

[170] Ibid.

[171] Tom Zoellner, "Polygamy: Throughout Its History, Colorado City Has Been the Home of Those That Believe in the Virtues of Plural Marriage," *Salt Lake Tribune*, June 28, 1998.

[172] Ibid.

[173] Ray Rivera, "Kingston Gets Maximum Term, Lecture on Incest," *Salt Lake Tribune,* July 10, 1999.

[174] Dennis Wagner and Mark Shaffer, "2 Polygamous Towns Investigated," *Arizona Republic*, October 2, 2012.

[175] Daphne Bramham, "Warren Jeffs: Prophet or Monster?" *Vancouver Sun*, September 8, 2007.

[176] Ibid.

[177] Nate Carlisle, "Arizona Boots Polygamist Town Cops," *Salt Lake Tribune*, September 19, 2007.

[178] Quinones, "FLDS Prophet's Nephew Testifies against Polygamists."

[179] Todd Lewan, "How a Hunting Ground Became Polygamous Nightmare," *Associated Press*, April 19, 2008.

[180] Ibid.

[181] Ibid.

[182] Emily Ramshaw and Paul Meyer, "CPS Takes Custody of 401 Youths from Polygamist Ranch," *Dallas Morning News*, April 8, 2008.

[183] Greg Flakus, "Texas Court Orders All Children from Polygamous Cult Returned to Parents," *Voice of America*, June 2, 2008.

[184] John Mortiz, "Texan's Tab for YFZ Ranch Roundup Tops $14 Million," *Fort Worth Star Telegram*, June 14, 2008.

[185] Paul J. Weber, "$4.5M Spent on Texas FLDS Prosecution," *Associated Press*, April 3, 2012.

[186] Nate Carlisle, "Nephew Alleges Jeffs Raped Him, Claimed It Was God's Will," *Salt Lake Tribune*, August 6, 2011.

[187] Greg Botelho, "Warren Jeffs' Appeal Denied; Another Sect Leader Convicted of Bigamy," *CNN*, March 30, 2012.

[188] Ben Winslow, "As Many as 1,000 May Be Exiled from the FLDS Church," *Fox News 13* (Salt Lake City, UT), January 2, 2012.

[189] Ben Winslow, "Jeffs Revelation Reportedly Names 15 Men as 'Fathers' to FLDS Children," *Fox News 13* (Salt Lake City, UT), June 18, 2012.

[190] Lindsay Whitehurst, "As Lawsuits Loom, More Kicked Out of FLDS," *Salt Lake Tribune*, June 28, 2012.

[191] Hilary Hylton, "The Future of the Polygamist Kids," *Time*, April 15, 2008.

[192] Lupita Murillo, "Man Kills Former Nanny, Then Kills Himself," *KVOA Tucson TV News*, January 10, 2005.

[193] Lupita Murrillo, "Man Kills Former Nanny,Then Kills Himself," *KVOA-TV News* (Tucson, AZ), January 10, 2005.

[194] Don Lattin, "On Tape, Son of 'Prophet' Declares War on Mother," *San Francisco Chronicle*, January 20, 2005.

[195] Craig Malisow, "Family Ties," *Houston Press*, November 17, 2005.

[196] Don Lattin, "Daughter of Family's Founder Renounces His Teachings," *San Francisco Chronicle*, February 14, 2001.

[197] Randi Kaye, "Young Man's Suicide Blamed on Mother's Cult," *CNN*, December 5, 2007.

[198] Malisow, "Family Ties," November 17, 2005

[199] Laurie Goodstein, "Murder and Suicide Reviving Claims of Child Abuse in Cult," *New York Times*, January 15, 2005.

[200] Esther Namugoji and Henry Lubega, "Sex Cult Claims It Is Living by the Law of Love," *Sunday Vision Uganda*, February 23, 2008.

[201] Goodstein, "Murder and Suicide Reviving Claims of Child Abuse in Cult," January 15, 2005.

[202] Ibid.

[203] Ibid.

[204] Don Lattin, "Ex-sect Members Fear New Violence," *San Francisco Chronicle*, January 17, 2005.

[205] "The Little Girl Seduced in the Name of God," *Evening Standard* (London), March 9, 2005.

[206] Don Lattin, "Deaths in the Family," *San Francisco Chronicle*, January 27, 2005.

[207] Lattin, "Ex-sect Members Fear New Violence," January 17, 2005.

208 Lattin, "Deaths in the Family," January 27, 2005.

209 Ibid.

210 Sherryl Connelly, "The Book 'Last Night at the Viper Room' Tells of River Phoenix's Life Before it was Cut Short at 22," *The New York Daily News*, October 5, 2013.

211 Tad Friendly, "River with Love and Anger,"*Esquire*, April 1994 121(3):108-110.

212 Randi Kaye, "Young Man's Suicide Blamed on Mother's Cult," *CNN*, December 5, 2007.

213 "The Little Girl Seduced in the Name of God," March 9, 2005.

214 Malisow, "Family Ties," November 17, 2005.

215 Ibid.

216 Ignacio Badal, "Cult Leader Arrest Stirs Joy in Chile," *Reuters*, March 12, 2005.

217 Stephen Brown and Oliver Ellrodt, "Insight: German Sect Victims Seek Escape from Chilean Nightmare Past," *Reuters*, May 9, 2012.

218 Cecilia Espinosa, "New Book on German Sect Says Abuses Were an Open Secret," Inter Press Service News Agency, May 3, 2005.

219 Badal, "Cult Leader Arrest Stirs Joy in Chile," March 12, 2005.

220 Larry Rohter, "Guru of Sadism, Safely in Jail, Leaves Cult to Fend for Itself," *New York Times*, May 16, 2005.

221 Marcelo Mackinnon, "Inside Chile's Colony of Terror," *Ohmy News* (South Korea), February 1, 2007.

222 Ibid.

223 Ibid.

224 Espinosa, "New Book on German Sect Says Abuses Were an Open Secret.," May 3, 2005.

225 "Cult Leader Must Pay Victims," *News 24* (Cape Town), May 25, 2006.

226 Rohter, "Guru of Sadism, Safely in Jail, Leaves Cult to Fend for Itself," May 16, 2005.

227 "Chile Discovers Weapons Cache on Cult Grounds," *Reuters*, June 16, 2005.

228 "Chile Officials Take Over Colony," *BBC News*, August 27, 2005 http://news.bbc.co.uk/2/hi/americas/4189920.stm (accessed May 16, 2014).

229 "Former German Cult in Chile Apologizes for Abuses," *Reuters*, April 19, 2006.

230 "German Cult Leader in Chile Gets 20-year Sentence," *Deutsche Welle*, (Germany) May 25, 2006.

[231] "Ex-Nazi Soldier Gets More Prison Time in Chile," *Associated Press*, March 26, 2008.

[232] Alexei Barrioneuvo, "Paul Schaefer, German Guilty of Chile Child Abuse, Dies at 89," *New York Times*, April 24, 2010.

[233] Charlotte Karrlsson-Willis, "Former Leaders of Chilean Cult Turn Themselves In," *The Santiago Times*, (Santiago, Chile) February 19, 2013.

[234] Sandra Weiss, "Its Horrific Past Exposed, A Notorious Sect Lingers on in Central Chile," *Die Welt*, (Germany) August 17, 2011.

[235] Hylton, "The Future of the Polygamist Kids," April 15, 2008.

CHAPTER 2

SMALL BUT DEADLY

Most of the destructive cults reported about around the world are actually quite small, often with less than one hundred members. Nevertheless, these small groups have greatly contributed to the history of cult tragedies. Unlike the larger organizations or movements, these smaller groups are typically very tightly wound around an ever-present charismatic leader. The tight-knit nature of small cults often means leaders more readily influence and control members.

Because small cults are so tightly wound, their members seem to be more subject to the mood swings and delusions of their leaders. Historically, mental health professionals have described some leaders of destructive cults as psychopaths, deeply disturbed individuals, or both. Within the environment of a tightly controlled small cult, there is what can be characterized as an almost symbiotic relationship between the leader and his or her followers. This close relationship in some cultic situations has become the basis for tragedy.

Members of small cult groups typically become largely dependent on the leader to determine the parameters of reality. In such a relationship, they may also feel unable to leave the group because of what they perceive as "exit costs." Exit costs in destructive cults, as described by sociologist Benjamin Zablcoki, can range "from financial penalties, to relational commitments to various sorts of cognitive and emotional dependencies."[236]

In such small cults, when the leader is delusional, progressively loses his or her grasp upon reality, or both, group members are often influenced to think, feel, and behave the same way. This situation can become a formula for tragedy. The consequences of such leader-driven, delusional thinking can be catastrophic and cause small cults to either implode or explode as we can see through the following historical overview.

1969—Charles Manson Murders

In the summer of 1969, a horrific cultic story would indelibly imprint itself on popular American culture, and its images would persist for decades to come.

During the morning hours of August 9, 1969, at a mansion located in an exclusive enclave of Los Angeles known as Benedict Canyon, five people were murdered. Among those found dead was actress Sharon Tate, the pregnant wife of film director Roman Polanski. Scrawled in blood at the scene were the words "Death to Pigs."[237]

Later that night another multiple murder shook Los Angeles. A prominent couple, Rosemary and Leno LaBianca, were found stabbed to death in their home at the edge of Hollywood.

The investigation of what became known as the "Tate-LaBianca murders" culminated in the arrests of members of a small cult group calling itself "The Family" or the "Manson Family," led by Charles Manson.

Manson had a history of manipulating and controlling others as well as a list of mental health issues, including schizophrenia and a paranoid-delusional disorder.[238] He had spent most of his youth in public institutions, and other than brief paroles, he had been locked up for most of the 1950s and 1960s. Manson studied Scientology and Buddhism. In 1967, at the age of thirty-two, he was released from prison for the last time.[239]

The small cult of followers Manson assembled, which never numbered much more than one hundred, was fixated on his dark vision of a coming apocalypse. In his twisted mind Manson imagined that the Tate-LaBianca murders would be a pivotal point in an apocalyptic drama. Manson saw these senseless slayings as somehow becoming the ignition point of a race war, which would engulf society and lead to the fulfillment of his destiny.

What followed instead was a sensational ten-month trial that transfixed the media and morbidly fascinated the public.

The mindless devotion of the Manson Family members was unsettling, and it was recorded and broadcast on television. The glassy eyes and eerie smiles of the cult leader's disciples were noticeable and deeply disturbing. His followers appeared totally disconnected from reality and completely enthralled by, and obsessed with, Manson.

Even though Charles Manson hadn't been physically present at the murders, he was nevertheless found guilty of the crimes. The prosecution proved, to the satisfaction of the jury, that Manson had been so totally in control of his group members that they had essentially become his weapon of choice.

Prosecutor Vincent Bugliosi pointed this out to the jury at trial during his summation. He said, "The Family at Spahn Ranch was Charlie Manson's Family, ladies and gentlemen. He controlled every single facet of their daily existence." The prosecutor explained, "Charles Manson's

Family preached love but practiced cold-blooded, savage murder. Why was that so? Because Charles Manson, their boss, ordained it. If Manson had wanted his Family to be singers in a church choir, that is what they would have been." Bugliosi concluded, "Manson is guilty of all seven counts of murder under the vicarious liability rule of conspiracy." [240]

Charles Manson and his followers—Susan Atkins, Leslie Van Houten, Patricia Krenwinkel, and Tex Watson—were all found guilty of murder and sentenced to death. But when California briefly abolished the death penalty in 1972, their sentences were commuted to life imprisonment.

Undue influence did nothing to mitigate the sentencing of Manson's cult disciples despite the premise of their leader's conviction. And after more than forty years, they remain in prison and are repeatedly denied parole.

"Everything that was good and decent in me I threw away," Leslie Van Houten has said. It was her father, she explained, who ultimately helped her realize during his prison visits "what had happened, and the monster I became."[241]

"They were brainwashed in a cult," explained Simon Fraser University professor Karlene Faith.[242] Faith, who teaches in prison, has been friends with Van Houten for years. Van Houten is the focus of Faith's 2001 book *The Long Prison Journey of Leslie Van Houten: Life beyond the Cult*. When asked during her twentieth parole board hearing to explain her past actions in the Manson cult, Van Houten replied, "I feel that at that point I had really lost my humanity and I can't know how far I would have gone. I had no regard for life and no measurement of my limitations."[243] Van Houten was once again denied parole after forty-four years in prison at the age of sixty-three. At the hearing Patrick Sequiera, the Los Angeles County deputy district attorney, offered the opinion that the Manson murders were so heinous that they might warrant an exception excluding the legal guarantee that provides for the possibility of parole.[244]

Charles Manson continues to be an object of morbid fascination and has become the ultimate icon of evil. Manson reportedly receives more mail than any other prison inmate in the United States.[245]

1974—SLA Abduction of Patty Hearst

In February 1974 a small political cult known as the Symbionese Liberation Army (SLA) abducted Patty Hearst, the nineteen-year-old heiress to a newspaper fortune in California.

Escaped convict Donald DeFreeze, who called himself "Field Marshall Cinqu," led the Berkeley-based group of self-styled revolutionary radicals.

The SLA declared Hearst was a "prisoner of war," who was taken to avenge the crimes of her wealthy parents.[246] She was terrorized, physically abused, and held confined in a closet for weeks.[247]

Subjected to a combination of nonstop indoctrination and coercion, Hearst eventually collapsed psychologically and emotionally, embracing a new name and group identity. She became Tania, the name of a woman who had died fighting with Che Guevara in Bolivia. Hearst, an unlikely revolutionary, even posed for photos as her new persona while holding a machine gun. The heiress wore a beret cocked on her head, emulating the original Tania. Hearst was also photographed during a bank robbery with the SLA.

In May 1974 DeFreeze and five SLA members died in a final shootout with police.

Hearst was finally found in September 1975 and arrested.

Patty Hearst's defense at her trial for bank robbery was that she had been brainwashed. But despite her abduction and abuse by the SLA, Hearst was found guilty. After serving almost two years in federal prison, President Jimmy Carter commuted her sentence. President Bill Clinton later pardoned her in 2001. "The pardon represents an act of ultimate understanding for which she is thankful," her lawyer said.[248]

Patty Hearst married her bodyguard, a San Francisco police officer, in 1979. The couple raised two children.

Looking back during an interview in 2002, Hearst said, "It's something that affects you so deeply that in a way you can never really trust people again. You know that you have to and you know that not everybody is like this, but it changes your perception of people for the rest of your life. And in a way it's sad to lose that kind of innocence, but in another way, you get a strength from it. And you can help other people."[249]

A key component in Hearst's recovery was the counseling psychologist Margaret Singer provided. Hearst said, "I had a psychologist who was incredibly good [Margaret Singer]…but you realize on your own that you don't have to [think] the things that they've been telling you to think. You don't have to participate in the disciplining of your mind."[250]

1985—MOVE and the John Africa Standoff

Vincent Leaphart, known to his followers as "John Africa," led the Philadelphia-based group known as MOVE. MOVE was based on the teachings of John Africa as set down in a book titled *The Guidelines*, which became the group's bible. [251] Africa preached against technology and for equality with animals.

In 1978, when a policeman went to evict the communal group from its residence, he was killed. Nine MOVE members were later convicted of murder.[252]

MOVE members adopted the same surname as their leader, Africa, and adhered to a diet of raw food. But their relationship with the community around them was often strained. MOVE's interaction with the outside world slipped away until its members became largely socially isolated, and they were "limited to the physical space of a 15-foot wide Philadelphia row house."[253] This little row house became the equivalent of a compound. Neighbors complained to authorities about MOVE, who used bullhorns to preach the group's political message and reportedly lived in "unsanitary" conditions.[254] Some MOVE members were criminals wanted for crimes ranging from parole violations and possession of illegal firearms to terrorist threats.[255]

MOVE behaved in a way that would historically repeat itself as the essential root cause of "cult standoffs" with authorities. That is, Africa and his followers largely refused to acknowledge the authority of virtually anyone other than their leader and saw law enforcement as an unwarranted intrusion.

When warrants were served on MOVE members in 1985, the group opened fire on police officers. In response to the group's resistance and intransigence, a police helicopter dropped a "percussion" or "concussion" bomb on the house, which the mayor of Philadelphia referred to as a "stun device,"[256] hoping to end the standoff. The explosion started a fire, which destroyed sixty-one houses. Within the MOVE row house, five children and six adults were found dead.[257]

The city of Philadelphia spent $42 million in the aftermath of the MOVE tragedy through settlements, investigation, and rebuilding efforts.[258]

MOVE continues to be a controversial group in Philadelphia. In 2002 a former member, thirty-four-year-old John Gilbride, was found dead in his car. Gilbride had been locked in a contentious custody battle with John Africa's widow, Alberta Wicker Africa. Two weeks before his death, a court had granted Gilbride time with his son. But just hours before the unsupervised visit would have taken place, Gilbride was found dead. The murder remains unsolved.[259]

1989—Jeffrey Lundgren Murders

In the spring of 1989, cult leader Jeffrey Lundgren murdered Dennis and Cheryl Avery and their three teenage daughters. But their bodies weren't found until January 1990 when they were discovered buried in a barn.

Lundgren recruited his followers primarily from the Reorganized Church of Jesus Christ of Latter-Day Saints, an offshoot of Mormonism. The cult leader had once been a tour guide at the denomination's historic, original temple.

Lundgren claimed that God wanted him to lead a revolution in Kirtland, a small town twenty miles from Cleveland, Ohio. Like Charles Manson, Jeffrey Lundgren convinced his followers that they were fulfilling a special and chosen role in human history. God's plan was for the group to seize the historic temple in Kirtland. Eventually Lundgren changed the plan and said the Avery family must be murdered to satisfy God as a sacrifice.

After the killings Lundgren's followers seemed mystified by their cult experience. "We were supposed to help the hungry. We were supposed to help the poor. Of course, none of that happened. I still don't know what happened...something went terribly wrong," said former cult member Susan Luff.[260]

At times Lundgren demanded money from his followers at gunpoint. He told Luff to dance nude for him, explaining it was "the way of God." Cult members described a life so controlled that almost anything they did could potentially be labeled as a "sin." For example, Lundgren somehow considered sinful such things as eating too much garlic or keeping your own money.

Jeffrey Lundgren was criminally convicted and sentenced to death. He was executed on October 24, 2006.[261]

Unlike the followers of Charles Manson, who have either died in prison or remained confined to this day, five of Lundgren's followers who were sentenced to prison have been released on parole.[262] But Jeffrey Lundgren's wife, son, and Susan Luff's husband, Ronald, remain in prison, serving minimum sentences that exceed one hundred years.[263]

1989—Roch Thériault Murders

The same year as the Lundgren group murders, a Canadian survivalist, cult leader Roch Thériault, was also arrested for murder. Thériault, like David Berg, used the name of Moses and ruled over a commune that included his "concubines," twenty-two children, and other followers located near Burnt River, Ontario.

In 1989 social workers and police were investigating complaints of abuse and torture in Thériault's group when they found the bodies of an infant and an adult. Solange Boislard had been brutally murdered and partially disemboweled as part of a purported "cult ritual."[264]

Thériault engaged in both the physical and sexual abuse of his followers, including the amputation of the hand of one woman, Gabrielle Lavallee. Lavallee later wrote a book about her experience and explained, "The first step that I took was to use writing, to apply myself to deprogramming. Because we were brainwashed. And during the catharsis I was able to recreate the personality that I had before I endorsed his ideology."[265] The French film *Savage Messiah*, based on the book by Lavallee, was released in 2002.[266]

Thériault pled guilty to second-degree murder and in 1993 was sentenced to life in prison. During his imprisonment three of Thériault's still-devoted "wives" were allowed conjugal visits, and the cult leader fathered more children. [267] Two of Thériault's children wrote a book about their lives while growing up in the cult.[268]

Another prison inmate killed Roch Thériault, and he was found dead in his cell in February 2011.[269]

1993—David Koresh and the Waco Davidian Standoff

Vernon Howell (also known as David Koresh) was the son a single mother. After dropping out of school in the ninth grade, he moved to Tyler, Texas, and joined a Seventh-day Adventist church at eighteen. Howell, however, had repeated conflicts with church members and left the Adventist church. He then went to Waco, where he found an obscure Seventh-day Adventist splinter group known as the Branch Davidians.[270]

Originally founded by an excommunicated member of the Seventh-day Adventist church named Victor Houteff, the Branch Davidians were a relatively benign and peaceful group.[271] Lois Roden was leading the small community when Howell arrived. The young man cultivated a close relationship with the aging leader and after her death assumed control of the group.

Howell's rule over the Davidians soon led to violence. He launched a gun battle in 1987 with Lois Roden's son, George Roden Jr., who opposed him. Howell and seven heavily armed followers attacked Roden, but he survived. Vernon Howell was tried for attempted murder. The jury ended up deadlocked, and prosecutors chose not to request a new trial. At the time Denise Wilkerson, the Texas prosecutor, warned that Howell "was building an arsenal."[272]

Vernon Howell later changed his name to David Koresh, which he claimed reflected his special prophetic role in human history. *David* symbolized the restoration of the Davidic kingdom of Israel, and *Koresh* was supposedly the Hebrew pronunciation of the name of the Babylonian king Cyrus, who allowed the Jews to return to Israel.[273] Koresh told his followers that the final conflict and judgment of the earth were coming soon. According to financial records, in preparation for that conflict, Koresh spent $199,715 on weapons and ammunition in the seventeen months immediately preceding a Bureau of Alcohol, Tobacco, Firearms, and Explosives (BATF) raid on the Davidian compound, which was called "Ranch Apocalypse."

A standoff between the Waco Davidians and federal law enforcement began in February 1993 when BATF agents tried to serve David Koresh with a warrant. Like MOVE in Philadelphia, the Davidians responded with gunfire. Four BATF officers were slain, and sixteen were wounded. Koresh refused to surrender. The FBI (Federal Bureau of Investigation) then assumed control of the perimeter around the compound and began negotiations with the cult leader. Koresh repeatedly broke promises to come out peacefully. A frustrated and exhausted FBI tried to end the fifty-one-day standoff by gassing the compound. Koresh decided that death in his compound was preferable to certain criminal prosecution, and like Jim Jones he chose death not only for himself, but also for his followers. On April 19, 1993, David Koresh, the self-proclaimed "Lamb of God," ordered the compound burned to the ground. Eighty Davidians, including twenty-five children, were found dead in the rubble.

Mental health experts categorized Koresh as a malevolent psychopath much like Charles Manson.[274]

Remnants of a huge arsenal were later found in the ruins, including grenades, gas masks, more than a million rounds of ammunition, body armor, Kevlar helmets, and at least forty submachine guns. Also found were lathes, milling equipment, and other tooling machinery most probably used for the illegal conversion of assault rifles and the manufacture of crude "grease guns."[275]

Five surviving Branch Davidians were convicted of voluntary manslaughter and weapons charges, and three more were convicted on weapons charges. A federal judge sentenced most of those convicted to long prison terms; however, the US Supreme Court later overturned their sentences, which were subsequently reduced. Thirteen years after the cult mass suicide, six Davidians were released from prison.[276]

Antigovernment conspiracy theories swirled around the Waco Davidian standoff. And it was such conspiracy theories that motivated Timothy McVeigh in 1995 to bomb the Murrah Federal Building in Oklahoma City as a supposed act of retaliation for Waco. That bombing claimed 168 lives.[277] McVeigh was sentenced to death and executed on June 11, 2001.[278]

The US Congress held hearings about Waco in 1996. The official Republican report concluded the following:[279]

- "Who fired the first shot on February 28th cannot decisively be resolved given the limited testimony presented to the Subcommittees. It appears more likely, however, that the Davidians fired first as the ATF agents began to enter the residence."

- "Koresh sexually abused minor females at the residence."

- "Koresh employed severe physical punishments as a means of disciplining the children."

- "On April 19th multiple fires began in different places inside the Branch Davidian residence and that they were deliberately set by the Davidians themselves."

- "Opportunity existed for the Davidians to safely leave the structure had they wanted to do so."

Nevertheless, surviving Davidians and relatives of deceased members of the group filed a wrongful death lawsuit against the government. The plaintiffs alleged that the government was responsible for the deaths of

Davidians in the compound. The trial concluded in July 2000. After two hours of deliberation, the jury found against the plaintiffs.[280]

During 1999 John Danforth, the former US senator, conducted an independent investigation of the Waco Davidian standoff. After conducting ten months of interviews with about nine hundred witnesses and examining more than 2.3 million pages of documents, Danforth said with "100 percent certainty" that the FBI didn't start the fire. He further stated, "There are no doubts in my mind," and concluded, "The blame rests squarely on the shoulders of David Koresh."[281]

Since the Waco Davidian standoff and through other standoffs with cultlike groups, authorities have learned and employed more nuanced strategies. The specific dynamics in cults make such special consideration necessary. Cult followers represent a unique and different mindset apart from common criminals, terrorists, or both.

1994—Luc Joret and the Solar Temple Suicides

Some academics and others have attempted to blame the government, cult critics, and former cult members for tragedies like Jonestown and Waco. They have opined that if cult groups were just left alone, there would be no such tragedies. History has repeatedly proved this theory wrong.

In October 1994 an obscure cult with members in Canada, France, and Switzerland became committed to self-extermination despite the fact that no one was "persecuting" or investigating them. Fifty-three members of a group known as the Solar Temple were found dead at two locations in Switzerland near Geneva. Almost all had been shot in the head (some shot as many as eight times), and others had been repeatedly stabbed. An elaborate system had been designed and set in place to subsequently burn all their remains. Twenty-two bodies were found at one Swiss site and twenty-five at another. Those dead included at least five children.[282] As authorities uncovered the charred remains of the cultists in Europe, five more dead devotees of the group were found in Canada forty-five miles from Montreal. This discovery included a Swiss man, his British wife, and their three-month-old son.

Luc Joret, a forty-six-year-old self-styled guru and supposed homeopathic healer, led the Solar Temple. He lectured about his various theories concerning nutrition and parenting. Joret, like David Koresh, told his followers about a coming apocalypse. He explained that this would occur through environmental disasters and that only the elect would survive.[283]

Joret was born in the Belgian Congo, now known as Zaire. He immigrated to Brussels in the 1970s to study acupuncture and homeopathy; later he joined a French group called Reformed Catholicism. The group's leader was a former Nazi Gestapo officer. The group practiced an eclectic mix of yoga and alchemy, suffused with supposed, arcane Christian rituals. After the leader died in 1981, Joret took over and set up a network of clubs to attract and recruit new members.[284] Joret publicly urged his followers to stockpile weapons. Originally the group was based in Canada. In 1993, however, Joret fled Canada after pleading guilty to charges of attempting to illegally obtain guns with silencers.[285]

Under the influence of Joret, the group's adherents came to believe in what they called "death voyages," which would supposedly allow them to be reborn on a star named Sirius.[286]

Luc Joret and Joseph Di Mambro, a prominent member of the group, lived lavishly and may have gathered a fortune of as much as $93 million from their followers' surrendered assets. Di Mambro's final words stated that he had simply "decide[d] to leave this terrestrial plane."[287] Luc Joret's body was identified along with the bodies of other Solar Temple members in Switzerland.

After the initial round of Solar Temple suicides in Europe and Canada, the death toll of the group continued to climb. In 1995 there were sixteen Solar Temple-related suicides in France. During March 1997 five more remaining devotees committed suicide at a retreat near Quebec City in Canada.[288] By 1999 seventy-four deaths were linked to the Solar Temple.

In early 1998 Spanish police arrested a German psychologist reportedly only hours before she allegedly planned another group suicide involving twenty-nine of her followers. This group included twenty-eight Germans, who were located in the Canary Islands. The group was believed to be an offshoot of the Solar Temple.[289]

In January 2002 Switzerland opened a public information center exclusively focused on religious cults. This was done largely in response to the Solar Temple members who had died in Switzerland.[290] Gérard Ramseyer, Geneva's cantonal justice minister, said, "Those seventy-four coffins, especially the eleven children's coffins, are still fresh in my mind."[291] Geneva's justice department estimates that there are between 150 and 180 fringe religious groups in French-speaking Switzerland. The center helps cult victims and generally educates the public.[292]

1997—Marshall Applewhite and the Heaven's Gate Suicides

In March 1997 thirty-nine people, twenty-one women and eighteen men, were found dead at a mansion in the exclusive neighborhood of Rancho Santa Fe near San Diego in the United States. They ranged in age from twenty-six to seventy-two and came from nine different US states. The thirty-nine bodies were identified as members of a cult group known as Heaven's Gate.[293]

Again, like the Solar Temple, the small group had not been subjected to intense scrutiny or what some might label "persecution"; rather it had remained relatively obscure and unnoticed.

The bodies of the cult members were found dispersed in the mansion on cots and mattresses. All but two had shrouds of purple covering their heads and shoulders. Most had died of suffocation, induced by plastic bags placed over their heads after they took a concoction of phenobarbital and alcohol. Found among the dead was Marshall Herff Applewhite, the sixty-five-year-old leader of the group.

Applewhite had a troubled history. In 1970 he checked himself into a psychiatric hospital after hearing voices. He also hoped to find a cure for his "homosexual urges."[294] Marshall Applewhite never resolved his mental illness. After discontinuing his psychiatric treatment, Applewhite had himself castrated, it appears in an effort to resolve his sexual conflicts. Videotapes of Applewhite's final statements were shown to Louis Jolyon West, professor of psychiatry at the University of California at Los Angeles. Dr. West concluded that the tapes demonstrated Applewhite was "delusional, sexually repressed and suffering from clinical paranoia."[295]

Applewhite taught his followers that he was a messenger from an "Evolutionary Kingdom Level Above Human." He claimed that periodically this higher kingdom sent messengers to earth and that one such previous visitor was Jesus. Applewhite believed he had once been Jesus in an "away team" and had been "incarnated again in…[a] mature (adult) [body] that had been picked and prepped for [his] current mission." He advised his followers that if they studied with him, he would become their pivotal link to this higher level. He said that only through him would it be possible for them to eventually evolve and shed their human "containers," which were only temporary "vehicles" for this supposed journey.

Applewhite's group evolved over the years, beginning in the 1970s. The group was known by successive names including The Two (Applewhite and his platonic companion, Bonnie Nettles), Human Individual Metamorphosis (HIM), Te and Do (Nettles was Te, and Applewhite was Do), and then Total Overcomers Anonymous.[296] Finally, Applewhite chose the name Heaven's Gate.

Applewhite required his "class" to give up virtually everything. This included their families, friends, and sex. Five of his male followers also had themselves surgically castrated, following their leader's example. Members of Applewhite's "crew" surrendered and renounced all their worldly possessions. They were told that they must overcome and do battle spiritually with dark forces known as the "Luciferians" and those they influenced. Luciferians became a negative label that could be applied to anyone or anything outside the group Applewhite saw as negative or threatening.

Through a process of rigid regimentation, Applewhite was able to ultimately purge his followers of their individuality and influence them to fully accept and embrace his teachings. Members also often suffered from sleep deprivation through a schedule of periodic prayers that punctuated the night. They ate the same food, called "formulas," at the same hours, which were referred to as "fuel for the vehicle." They all had the same haircuts and wore identical clothing. Their uniform appearance often included gloves, which they seemingly used to avoid physical human contact, contamination, or both. Work was divided into twelve-minute intervals indicated by audible beeps. They were also given new names, which further broke down their sense of individual identity and connection to their past lives. Applewhite also controlled information; his followers weren't allowed to watch television or read anything by choice. Rather they were given lists of designated literature. Each member was assigned a partner and encouraged to travel in pairs. One former devotee recalled that this step was an important facet of group control "to keep [members] in the mindset. The partner was there, if [a member was] falling out of what [he or she] had to do, so [he or she] wouldn't fall out. It was part of the mind control."[297] Communication was at times limited to simply saying, "Yes," "No," or "I don't know."[298] This process persisted to the end. All cult members ordered exactly the same last meal and ended their lives almost completely alike in virtually every detail. [299]

According to Marshall Applewhite the world was merely a "stepping stone" to "the true Kingdom of God." He said planet Earth was about to be "recycled" or "spaded under" because its inhabitants had refused to evolve according to Applewhite's prescribed process. Only those bound together through his teachings could survive the coming end by traveling to the next level with him.[300] The group's suicide might seem logical in this mind-set, since Applewhite insisted that "the Truth can be retained only as one is physically connected with the Next Level, through an Older Member."[301] Therefore, without Applewhite there was no assured hope of transition to the next "Evolutionary Level." When he elected to die, his followers were thus obliged to do likewise. Death was the only sure way they could retain "The Truth" and move through the final necessary step to enter "the true Kingdom of God."

2001—Elizabeth Smart Kidnapping

On June 5, 2002, Elizabeth Smart was kidnapped at knifepoint from her home in Salt Lake City. The fourteen-year-old girl was missing for nine months.[302] Police later found her walking along a road in a suburb of Salt Lake City with two adults on March 12, 2003. The story that emerged would prove to be eerily reminiscent of the saga of Patty Hearst. Hearst's attorney J. Albert Johnson observed that his former client "underwent the very same brutal ordeal as Elizabeth Smart."[303]

Elizabeth Smart was one of six children within a wealthy, tightly knit Mormon family. Her father, Ed Smart, was in the midst of remodeling the family home when he hired a drifter named Brian Mitchell as a handyman. Mitchell, an excommunicated Mormon and self-proclaimed "prophet," called himself Emmanuel. Mitchell became fixated on Elizabeth Smart as his next "wife." Already enthralled with the erratic homeless man was the woman who would become Smart's surrogate mother, Wanda Barzee.[304]

After Brian Mitchell abducted her, Elizabeth Smart was held captive in isolation. Mitchell threatened the girl's life and the lives of the

Smart family; he also raped her.[305] At the end of this reign of terror, a strange metamorphosis occurred. Smart, like Patty Hearst, took on a new identity and completely submitted to Brian Mitchell.

At first when police confronted Smart, she repeatedly denied her identity and said her name was "Augustine." She also told officers that the two adults with her were her parents. When police insisted that she was Elizabeth Smart, the girl responded eerily in stilted, seemingly biblical verbiage. "Thou sayest," she said, apparently denying her own name.[306] Robert W. Butterworth, a California psychologist, said, "They were well along in stripping away her identity. She was dressing differently, hearing nothing but their pseudo-religious talk. It was very much like the Taliban in Afghanistan."[307]

In the months before her rescue, various witnesses saw Elizabeth Smart, veiled and in a white robe resembling a hospital gown, with Brian Mitchell and Wanda Barzee at a party. A photographer named Dan Groeder took pictures of the odd trio. He said, "She could have just walked away or said something. She definitely had the opportunity to walk away."[308]

On numerous occasions Mitchell, Barzee, and Smart were seen walking together in public, eating together at a restaurant, and entering stores. They also stayed at the apartment of a Mitchell acquaintance for a week. At no time did Smart make any effort to get help. One witness told the press, "He must have really done a job on her, because all she would have had to do was to say her name."[309]

After his daughter's rescue, Ed Smart concluded, "I can just tell that he did an absolute brainwashing job on her."[310] Her grandfather, Charles Smart, a retired surgeon, explained, "She had no ability to control her life" and "was completely controlled by Emmanuel [Mitchell]."[311]

After the rescue of Elizabeth Smart, Patty Hearst commented in an interview that she could easily empathize with the teenager. Hearst said, "You come to a point where you believe any lie your abductor has told you. You don't feel safe. You think that either you will be killed if you reach out to get help. You believe that your family will be killed. You're not even thinking about trying to get help anymore. You've, in a way, given up. You have absorbed this new, you know, identity that they've given you. You're just surviving. You're not even doing that, really. You're just living while everything else is going on around you."[312]

Elizabeth Smart recovered and like Patty Hearst successfully moved on with her life. She testified in court against Brian Mitchell, describing her time with him as "nine months of hell."[313] Confronting her former captor in court, Smart told Mitchell, "No matter what you do you will never affect me again." She saw letting go of her hate as a meaningful component of her recovery. "It's just not worth holding on to that kind of hate; it can ruin your life. Nine months of my life had been taken from me, and I wasn't going to give them any more of my time," she told the press.[314]

Brian Mitchell was convicted of kidnapping and sentenced to life in prison. Mitchell's accomplice, Wanda Barzee, received a fifteen-year prison term in a plea arrangement with prosecutors. She cooperated in their case against Mitchell.[315]

In 2012 twenty-four-year-old Elizabeth Smart married Matthew Gilmour in Hawaii. At the time the bride was a senior attending Brigham Young University.[316]

2008—1 Mind Ministries and Child Abuse Death

The remains of eighteen-month-old Javon Thompson were found in a suitcase behind a Philadelphia home in the spring of 2008. A religious cult, including the child's mother, Ria Ramkissoon, had beaten and starved the baby to death. At the time of her son's death in the spring of 2006, Ramkissoon was nineteen years old.[317] Baltimore police identified the cult group as 1 Mind Ministries, led by Toni Ellsberry, age forty, known to her followers as "Queen Antoinette." Ramkissoon, Ellsberry, and three other members of the group were charged with first-degree murder. Ramkissoon was held in a psychiatric ward.[318]

Ria Ramkissoon's family insisted that the young woman was under undue influence. "She had no control over that situation at all," stepfather Craig Newton said. Ramkissoon's mother agreed. "My daughter was a victim, just like my grandson."[319] She explained that her daughter had been coerced. "The leader of the cult—Queen Antoinette—made the decision. She was the one that said, 'Do not feed him,' and would beat Javon and put him in a back room." According to her mother, Ria Ramkissoon had undergone a radical transformation. Once "a lively, jolly person," she had changed to "an empty shell." Family communication became largely nonexistent for two years.[320] Describing her daughter as "brainwashed," Ramkissoon's mother said after her arrest, "I was shocked. I didn't even recognize her voice…It's not the same person."[321]

The group 1 Mind Ministries never had more than a dozen members.[322] And like MOVE of Philadelphia, the cult lived in a single residence. At times the behavior of the group drew the attention of neighbors. Nearby residents in West Baltimore reportedly complained about "shouting and screaming" coming from the home. "You'd hear it in the middle of the night—loud noises and chanting. They were real strange—they'd wear all white or camouflage and talk about demons and devils all the time. People just left them alone," one neighbor said.[323]

Danielle Smith, a former member of 1 Mind Ministries, testified at trial during 2010, "Queen Antoinette made people believe that [living with her] would be a better situation for you. She just said that God spoke to her and told her how to live in her household." The prescribed rules included fasting and only wearing the colors tan, blue, or white. Smith too was cut off from her family, and Queen Antoinette turned her against them. Smith was told that they didn't properly follow the

Bible and that her mother was a "witch." Danielle Smith was also not allowed to be alone with "outsiders." Antoinette also didn't need "to abide by certain laws of the land," Smith testified, because as a "Queen" she was accountable only to God.[324]

Queen Antoinette ordered the starvation of Javon Thompson because the child reportedly failed to say "amen" after meals. "His body got weaker, he got thinner, his lips got dry…Everybody saw him," Ramkissoon testified. But no one helped Javon Thompson because Antoinette forbade it, prosecutors said.[325] Subsequent to the little boy's death, the cult leader told her followers to pray, and Javon Thompson would be resurrected. But when the child's body began to decompose, she decided that his remains would be moved and hidden.[326]

Maryland prosecutors didn't see Ria Ramkissoon as a murderer. Instead, they understood that she was a victim, as her mother described. A plea from Ramkissoon was agreed on in exchange for her testimony against cult members. Ria Ramkissoon pled guilty to one count of child abuse resulting in death, with the understanding that she would receive a sentence of probation. According to that agreement, if her son, Javon, did rise from the dead, she would withdraw her plea. Her attorney, Steven D. Silverman, told the press, "This is something that she absolutely insisted upon, and this is indicative of the fact that she is still brainwashed, still a victim of this cult," he said. "Until she's deprogrammed, she's not going to think any differently."[327] As a condition of Ramkissoon's probation, prosecutors required that she submit to treatment, including sessions with an expert on cult behavior.[328]

Cult leader Toni Ellsberry, known as Queen Antoinette, was sentenced to fifty years in prison. Her daughter, Trevia Williams, and another cult member, Marcus Cobbs, were sentenced to twenty-five years for second-degree murder and child abuse, with all but fifteen years suspended. The judge said they showed no remorse in court.[329]

Ria Ramkissoon spent months in a faith-based residential treatment center per the terms of her probation. Her lawyer said, "She's come to realize that she was misled." The judge commended Ramkissoon for making "great strides" and hoped she would "be one of our few true success stories."[330] In 2011 Ria Ramkissoon explained in an interview that she had once feared eternal damnation if she didn't obey Antoinette. "Those were the fears that I dealt with, no matter how ridiculous they may be to somebody else," she said. Commenting about her son's suffering and death, she told the press, "It is difficult, because I don't think it's settled, fully, the weight of what was lost."[331]

2010—Mohan Singh, Sexual Predator and Rapist

Michael Lyons used the name Mohan Singh and claimed to be a spiritual man focused on helping people. He said he was a trained "naturopathic" healer, whom celebrities often sought out. He said he was "chiropractor to the Queen" and an osteopath who treated the Dalai Lama of Tibet. But authorities described Lyons as a sexual predator who mesmerized and exploited women, creating an international cult composed of female followers who treated him "like a god." Lyons may have attacked hundreds of women before British police finally arrested him.[332]

In 2010 a London court sentenced Michael Lyons to seven years in prison for raping one woman and three more years of confinement, to run consecutively, for assaulting another. The court also heard the testimonies of five women, whom Lyons had raped in the United States.[333] Prosecutor Philip Katz described Lyons as a "sexual predator masquerading as a guru and a healer," someone who seemed "charismatic, charming and reassuring" but was in fact "controlling, aggressive and sinister."[334]

The counterfeit guru convinced his followers that he could cure cancer, and the women who followed Lyons lavished gifts and cash on him. He lived in a luxurious penthouse apartment in North London, liked to wear expensive, flowing robes, and was driven around in vehicles made by Bentley, Mercedes, and Roll-Royce. Lyons jetted around the world, visiting Miami, Paris, and India, methodically creating a network of women who would do his bidding. His female followers, called "The Friends of Mohan," would recruit or lure other women, whom the guru would then abuse. "It is about psychological and emotional control, brainwashing and isolation from families," investigating officer Detective Sergeant Nick Giles explained.[335]

Lyons's exaggerated persona was a cover for humble beginnings. He was born in Jamaica, and his parents moved to England in the 1960s. Lyons grew up in a poor neighborhood in Manchester. He began his group, The Friends of Mohan, while visiting India during the 1980s. The self-styled guru started frequenting gyms and yoga studios, promoting himself as a practitioner of "alternative therapies." "His victims [tended] to be highly intelligent with an interest in spirituality, but at a point in their life where they are searching for answers," Detective Giles said.[336]

The guru also reportedly used such methods as sleep deprivation as well as psychological and peer pressure to persuade women to obey him.[337] The women Lyons raped were alternately told that he would somehow enlighten them with his "organic penis" or that he was "feeling" their "energy pulse" and that this behavior was "unblocking" their "chakras."[338] Some of the women suspected they were drugged.[339]

Women who followed Lyons were deeply devoted. New initiates were "smothered in attention."[340] Many contributed substantially to their guru's cash revenue, often paying as much as [$625.00] a month into his personal bank account. Detective Giles told reporters, "When he was first charged the movement managed to put up his [$468,300.00] bail incredibly quickly."[341] One die-hard devotee even testified in his defense at trial despite the fact that her parents strongly opposed the guru and had cooperated with the prosecution.[342]

After appearing in court as a witness for the prosecution, one of Michael Lyons's victims told the press, "It was an incredibly liberating experience. Looking at him in court I felt disgusted by him. I can't believe that a master manipulator like him walked the streets for so long and I'm just glad that he will no longer be able to take advantage of other vulnerable people."

2012—Faith Healing Deaths

During 2012 there were multiple criminal convictions in the United States tied to the deaths of minor children due to medical neglect. This focused public attention on the faith healing beliefs of certain small religious groups and somewhat larger but not widely known churches.

In May 2012 Jacqueline Crank and her "spiritual father," Ariel Ben Sherman, were found guilty of misdemeanor neglect resulting from the 2002 death of Crank's fifteen-year-old daughter, Jessica. Under Sherman's influence Crank decided not to pursue medical treatment for a growing tumor in her daughter's shoulder. By the time authorities intervened, it was too late to help the girl. The conviction of the pair occurred only after years of legal wrangling and proceedings in the state of Tennessee. Tennessee law allows parents to choose between faith and medicine, even in a medical emergency. The law, however, states that their faith must be a "recognized church or denomination."[343] Apparently Crank's mentor, Sherman, didn't meet this criterion. Instead, he led a very small group that included the Cranks and about six other members. They lived together in a six-bedroom house. After their conviction Crank and Sherman were sentenced to probation, but despite this they both promised to appeal the court decision.[344]

Ariel Ben Sherman had a history of legal troubles. The itinerant preacher previously led a religious commune in Oregon during the 1980s. He was charged in Oregon with five counts of child abuse but fled prosecution.[345]

Susan Grady of Oklahoma didn't find refuge in any special provision under the law as Jacqueline Crank did. In 1983 the Oklahoma state legislature specifically ended the use of religious faith as a defense in the event of a child's death due to medical neglect.[346] In May 2012 Grady was found guilty of second-degree manslaughter in the death of her son, Aaron. The nine-year-old boy died in 2009 of complications from diabetes. Grady is a member of a controversial religious group known as the General Assembly Church of the First Born. The group has a long history of legal problems due to its beliefs about modern medicine. Susan Grady didn't receive probation. Instead she was sentenced to two and a half years in prison.[347]

The General Assembly Church of the First Born reportedly has no ministers[348] and is instead led by elders. Tom Nation, a fourth-generation elder of the group, has characterized its legal troubles as "persecution." "The people that lift their voice and persecute you the most are the people that don't know nothing about you...Maybe some of them would stone us if they thought they had a chance," he told the press.[349] The group's faith healing practices are reportedly "rooted in [the] elders' interpretation of specific Bible verses."[350] And they rely on the New Testament portion of James 5:12–16, which reads in part, "Is any sick among you? Let him call for the elders of the church; and let them pray over him, anointing him with oil in the name of the Lord." This biblical recitation doesn't explicitly prohibit medical care, but according to Nation, those who visit doctors are wrong. "As far as we're concerned, they're in violation of the word of the Lord...They're going to have to answer for it," he said.[351] Susan Grady seemingly agreed. She chose to disobey the law rather than her elder's teaching.

In October 2011 Dale and Shannon Hickman were sentenced to six years in prison for second-degree manslaughter. It was the harshest sentence yet doled out regarding medical neglect connected to faith healing beliefs. The Hickmans, both members of a group known as the Followers of Christ, were criminally convicted for the death of their infant son, David. The boy was born prematurely with underdeveloped lungs but almost certainly would have survived if he had been taken to a hospital. Relying instead on their faith, the parents allowed the baby to suffer and die. In 2011 Oregon, like Oklahoma, eliminated its legal exemption providing for a faith healing defense. Commenting on the couple's sentence, Robert D. Herndon, the presiding judge, said, "This is a sentence you have justly earned…a modest penalty for causing the death of a vulnerable person…This was so preventable."[352]

Walter White, known as a powerful, charismatic preacher, established the Followers of Christ. White's followers considered him to be an absolute authority and "apostle." "Walter became a Christlike figure…People believed the only way to get to God was through Walter White," a former member once told the press.[353] White was criticized for his use of intimidation. The preacher was known to rebuke people from the pulpit, and he frequently created fear through predictions about the end of the world. White created what some called a "cultlike" environment.[354] The fiery preacher died in 1969, but critics say "cultlike pressures" within the twelve-hundred-member group still persist. The Followers of Christ, like General Assembly Church of the First Born, is now led by elders. The group can be seen as socially isolated, largely living apart from outsiders and shunning defectors. Leroy Worthington, a lifetime member ostracized for expressing dissenting views, told the press, "I know there is a cult in this church." Terry Gustafson, the Clackamas County district attorney, described the mentality of the group. He said, "They think the world is out to destroy the church…This is what Walter [White] predicted."[355]

Together, the Followers of Christ and the General Assembly Church of the First Born are responsible for more minor children dying due to medical neglect in recent history than any other similar groups in the United States.[356] Historically, though, within the United States there have been other religious groups responsible for many needless deaths, notably Faith Assembly in Indiana, led by Hobart E. Freeman.

Faith Assembly, which once included approximately as many as two thousand members, was deemed responsible for ninety deaths in eight states. These deaths included mostly children and women in childbirth.[357] In 1984 Freeman was criminally indicted on conspiracy charges for encouraging parents to deny their children medical care. He died of congestive heart failure and bronchial pneumonia before the case went to trial.[358] Without Freeman, Faith Assembly, which was often called a "cult,"[359] disintegrated and faded away.

Another purported cult historically linked to the issue of medical neglect is Meade Ministries, also known as End Times Ministries led by Charles Meade. Meade was once closely associated with Hobart Freeman, who influenced his faith healing beliefs. But the two preachers parted ways in 1984.[360] Much like the other dominating leaders discussed, Meade had a long list of prohibited evils including TV, chewing gum, earrings, and Dr. Seuss books. Most notably he preached that sickness was "the work of the devil" to be healed by faith rather than by doctors.[361]

Joni Cutler, a former member of Meade Ministries, delivered her daughters at home according to Meade's teachings. But due to complications and the ministry directive against doctors, one of Cutler's babies died.[362] It was a breach birth, and the infant struggled for two days. "Libby quit breathing again and turned blue…We needed help, but I could hardly get out of bed," Cutler recounted in a press interview. Her mother-in-law suggested medical help, and she agreed but was overruled. "They told me if you think like that, that's what could kill her," Cutler said. The autopsy report stated that the cause of death was "pneumonia." Her daughter would have had a 99 percent chance of survival if she had been brought to a hospital.[363]

Cutler later divorced her husband and left Meade Ministries in Florida. She moved with her four remaining daughters back to South Dakota, where she completed law school and was later elected a state senator. Joni Cutler received an award in 1990 for helping her state become the first to eliminate religious immunity laws concerning medical neglect.[364] Cutler recalled in an interview, "For 10 years I did everything they told me to do…I lost the ability to think critically for myself. I had no idea that something that looks so much like a church could be so cultlike."[365]

Charles Meade died in 2010 at the age of ninety-three.[366] Meade Ministries subsequently changed its name to Mountaintop Ministries Worldwide Inc.

Rhode Island pediatrician Dr. Seth Asser published a study of the deaths of 172 children due to what he called "religion-based medical neglect." According to that study, 140 of the children had a 90 percent chance of survival, while 18 others had a 50 percent chance of survival if they had received proper medical care. "Most were ordinary illnesses that no one dies from—appendicitis, pneumonia…And many of them died slow, horrible deaths, without the benefit of [pain-relief] medicine," Asser said.[367] Child advocate Rita Swan worked with Asser on the study project. Swan left Christian Science, a church known for its faith healing beliefs, after her youngest son died without medical attention while a Christian Science practitioner prayed over him. Swan explained, "We're not against prayer…Parents have a right to pray for divine healing. But when parents see the situation is critical, they have a responsibility to seek medical help in addition to prayer."

---

236 Benjamin D Zablocki, "Exit Cost Analysis: A New Approach to the Scientific Study of Brainwashing," *Nova Religion* 2, no. 1 (1998): 219.

237 Linda Deutsch, "30 Years Later, Manson Cult Thrives," *Associated Press*, August 9, 1999.

238 "Charles Manson Denied Parole," *CNN*, April 12, 2012.

239 Charlie Gillis, "Charles Manson Still Casts a Long Shadow," *Macleans*, (Canada) April 23, 2012.

240 State of California v. Charles Manson (January 15, 1971) Closing Argument of Vincent Bugliosi, http://law2.umkc.edu/faculty/projects/ftrials/manson/manson-summation.html (accessed May 16, 2014).

[241] Linda Deutsch, "Charles Manson Follower Krenwinkle Denied Parole," *Associated Press*, January 11, 2011.

[242] Sarah Netter, "Leslie Van Houten Denied Parole for Role in Manson Murders," *ABC News*, July 6, 2010.

[243] "Youngest Manson Family Member Denied Parole," *Sky News*, (UK) June 6, 2013.

[244] Ibid.

[245] Gillis, "Charles Manson Still Casts a Long Shadow," April 23, 2012.

[246] William Schiffman, "Hearst Abduction Riveted the Nation," Associated Press, February 4, 1999.

[247] Don Oldunberg, "Stressed to Kill: The Defense of Brainwashing," *Washington Post*, November 21, 2003.

[248] "Media Heiress Patty Hearst Pardoned," Associated Press, January 2001.

[249] Patricia Hearst, interview by Larry King, *Larry King Live CNN*, January 22, 2002.

[250] Patricia Hearst and members of the Smart family, interview by Larry King, *Larry King Live CNN*, March 13, 2003.

[251] Johanna Saleh Dickson, *Pamphlet Architecture 23—Move: Sites of Trauma* (Princeton, NJ *Princeton Architectural Press*, 2002), 14.

[252] "Philly Radicals Fortifying House," *Associated Press*, September 17, 2002.

[253] Dickson, *Pamphlet Architecture 23*, 20.

[254] "Philly Radicals Fortifying House," September 17, 2002.

[255] Frank Trippett, Kenneth W. Banta, and Joseph N Boyce, "It Looks Just like a War Zone," *Time*, May 27, 1985.

[256] "Percussion or Concussion, It Was Still a Bomb," *Los Angeles Times*, May 18, 1985.

[257] "Philly Radicals Fortifying House."

[258] "1985 Bombing in Philadelphia Still Unsettled," *USA Today*, May 11, 2005.

[259] Monica Yant Kinney, "Father Grieves as Cold Case Simmers," *Philadelphia Inquirer*, September 26, 2006.

[260] "Cult Slayings Still Haunting Ten Years Later," *Associated Press*, April 11, 1999.

[261] "Cult Leader Loses Execution Appeal," *Irish Examiner* (Cork), October 24, 2006.

[262] David W. Jones, "Four More People Being Paroled in Kirtland Cult Killing Case," *News Herald* (Cleveland), November 11, 2010.

263 Ibid.

264 "Killer Cult Leader Is Denied Parole," *The Canadian Press*, July 12, 2002.

265 "Quebec Cult Leader's Chilling Story Told in New TV Movie *Savage Messiah*," *The Canadian Press*, June 19, 2002

266 Ibid.

267 "Killer Cult Leader Is Denied Parole," July 12, 2002.

268 "Cult Leader Roch Theriault Dead in Jail," *The Canadian Press*, February 26, 2011

269 Ibid.

270 Barbara Kantrowitz et al., "Secrets of the Cult: The Messiah of Waco," *Newsweek*, March 15, 1993.

271 Ibid.

272 Ibid.

273 Ibid.

274 Wendy Cole and Richard Woodbury, "In the Grip of a Psychopath" *Time*, May 3, 1993.

275 "Files Details Evidence of Huge Cult Arsenal," *Dallas Morning News*, May 26, 1993.

276 "Six Branch Davidians Due for Release 13 Years after Waco Inferno," *Associated Press*, April 19, 2006.

277 Nolan Clay, "Papers Show McVeigh Had Little Remorse," *Oklahoman*, December 30, 2007.

278 "Oklahoma Bomber Confessed to Catholic Priest," *Universe Catholic Newspaper*, August 18, 2006.

279 Committee on Government Reform, *The Tragedy at Waco: New Evidence Examined* (1996) House Report 106-1037 106th Congress 2nd Sess, Washington, D.C. Printing Office 1-89 http://www.gpo.gov/fdsys/pkg/CRPT-106hrpt1037/html/CRPT-106hrpt1037.htm (accessed May 16, 2014).

280 "Jury Finds U.S. Not to Blame in Waco Case," *Reuters*, July 14, 2000.

281 "Final Report from John C. Danforth, Office of Special Counsel, Waco Investigation," *PR Newswire,* November 8, 2000.

282 Michael S. Serrill, "Remains of the Day," *Time*, October 24, 1994.

283 Richard Lacayo, "Cults: In Reign of fire," *Time*, October 17, 1994.

284 Ibid.

285 Ibid.

[286] Rudolphe Landais, "French Police Fear Collective Suicide in Sect," Reuters, September 3, 2002.

[287] Serrill, "Remains of the Day," October 24, 1994.

[288] "1997: Solar Temple Cult Claims Five More Lives," *CBC Digital Archives*, 1997.

[289] "Spanish Cops Arrest Sect Leader," Associated Press, January 8, 1998.

[290] Roy Probert, "Geneva Seeks to Temper Influence of Cults," *Swiss Info*, November 3, 2001.

[291] Ibid.

[292] Ibid.

[293] "List of Mass Suicide Victims," *New York Times*, March 29, 1997.

[294] Jonathan Broder, "Marshall Applewhite's Cry for Help," *Salon*, March 31, 1997.

[295] Marc Fisher and Sue Ann Pressley, "Founder Sought to Purge Sexuality via Cult," *Washington Post*, March 29, 1997.

[296] Frank Bruni, "The Cult's Two-Decade Odyssey of Regimentation," *New York Times*, March 29, 1997.

[297] Ibid.

[298] Ibid.

[299] Joshua Bearman, "Heaven's Gate: The Sequel. Ten Years after the 39 Suicides, the Sole Survivor Is Back—and He Has Something Urgent to Tell Us," *LA Weekly*, March 29, 2007.

[300] Marshall Applewhite, "Final Offer from the Evolutionary Level Above Human," *USA Today,* March 27, 1993 http://culteducation.com/group/968-heaven-s-gate/9560-final-offer-150-from-the-evolutionary-level-above-human.html (accessed May 16, 2014).

[301] Marshall Applewhite, "Last Chance to Advance beyond Human," Heaven's Gate website, January 16, 1994 http://www.heavensgate.com/misc/lastchnc.htm (Accessed May 16, 2014).

[302] Dan Whitcomb and James Nelson, "Police Say Smart Girl Mentally Joined Captors," *Reuters*, March 13, 2003.

[303] Tom Mashberg, "Experts: Teen Was 'Brainwashed,'" *Boston Herald*, March 3, 2003.

[304] Ibid.

[305] Stephen Hunt, "Elizabeth Smart Tells Story of Her Survival," *Salt Lake Tribune*, November 8, 2010.

[306] Rebecca Boone, "Smart Returns Home a Changed Girl," *Associated Press*, March 14, 2003.

[307] Mashberg, "Experts: Teen Was 'Brainwashed.'"

[308] Timothy Egan, "In Plain Sight, a Kidnapped Girl behind a Veil," *New York Times*, March 14, 2003.

[309] Ibid.

[310] Mark Hume and Stacey Burling, "Elizabeth Smart Was 'Brainwashed,' Father Says," *Ottawa Citizen*, March 15, 2003.

[311] "Smart Was Brainwashed, Family Says," *Baltimore Sun*, March 17, 2003.

[312] Patricia Hearst; friends, members of the Smart family, interview by Larry King, *CNN*, March 13, 2003 http://transcripts.cnn.com/TRANSCRIPTS/0303/13/lkl.00. html (accessed May 16, 2014).

[313] James Nelson, "Elizabeth Smart's Kidnapper Gets Life in Prison," *Reuters*, May 25, 2011.

[314] "Elizabeth Smart Opens Up to *People*," *Deseret News* (Salt Lake City), June 12, 2008.

[315] Nelson, "Elizabeth Smart's Kidnapper Gets Life in Prison," May 25, 2011.

[316] "Elizabeth Smart Marries at Hawaii Temple," *Associated Press*, February 19, 2012.

[317] "Toddler 'Starved to Death by Cult,'" *Press Association*, August 12, 2008.

[318] Ibid.

[319] Ibid.

[320] Marcus Baram, "Cult Murder Suspect's Mom—It's Not Her Fault," *ABC News*, August 12, 2008 http://abcnews.go.com/US/story?id=5565557 (accessed May 16, 2014).

[321] Ben Nuckols, "Family: Cult 'Brainwashed' Mom Charged with Murder," *Associated Press*, August 16, 2008.

[322] Ibid.

[323] Baram, "Cult Murder Suspect's Mom—It's Not Her Fault," August 12, 2008.

[324] Tricia Bishop, "Witness: Accused Cult Leaders Had Her Committed to Keep Quiet," *Baltimore Sun*, February 26, 2010.

[325] Tricia Bishop, "Cult Steals a Daughter's Love, a Grandson's Life," *Baltimore Sun*, March 7, 2010.

[326] Nuckols, "Family: Cult 'Brainwashed' Mom Charged with Murder."

[327] Ben Nuckols, "Maryland Mom's Starvation Plea Pegged to Resurrection," *Associated Press*, March 31, 2009.

[328] Ibid.

[329] Ben Nuckols, "Mom Who Starved Son Praised By Judge," *Associated Press*, August 4, 2010.

[330] Ibid.

[331] "Cult Members Made Me Starve My One-Year-Old Boy," *Daily Mail* (London), September 5, 2011.

[332] Lucy Ballinger and Colin Fernandez, "Rapist 'Guru' in a Bentley Cast His Spell on Hundreds of Terrified Young Women," *Daily Mail* (London), July 27, 2010.

[333] Ibid.

[334] David Sanderson, "Self-Styled Guru Accused of Raping Seven Vulnerable Women," *Times* (London), April 8, 2010.

[335] Ballinger and Fernandez, "Rapist 'Guru' in a Bentley Cast His Spell on Hundreds of Terrified Young Women," July 27, 2010.

[336] Ibid.

[337] Kyle Munzenrieder, "Michael Lyons, Cult Leader That Raped Female Followers, Might Have Victims in Miami," *Miami New Times*, July 27, 2010.

[338] "Michael Lyons May Have Raped Dozens More Women," *The Telegraph* (Kent), July 26, 2010.

[339] Ballinger and Fernandez, "Rapist 'Guru' in a Bentley Cast His Spell on Hundreds of Terrified Young Women," July 27, 2010.

[340] David Sanderson, "Self-Styled Guru Accused of Raping Seven Vulnerable Women," *Times* (London), April 8, 2010.

[341] Ballinger and Fernandez, "Rapist 'Guru' in a Bentley Cast His Spell on Hundreds of Terrified Young Women," July 27, 2010.

[342] Munzenrieder, "Michael Lyons, Cult Leader That Raped Female Followers, Might Have Victims in Miami," July 27, 2010.

[343] Jamie Satterfield, "Mother 'Spiritual Father' Convicted in Faith Healing Case, but Questions Remain," *Knoxville News Sentinel*, May 8, 2012.

[344] Ibid.

[345] Syan Rhodes, "Religious Leader Facing Charges," *WBIR Knoxville News*, August 6, 2002 http://www.culteducation.com/group/1150-new-life-tabernacle/19248-religious-leader-facing-charges.html (accessed May 16, 2014).

[346] Teri Bowers, "Family Says Church Allowed Woman to Die Following Childbirth," *KTUL Tulsa News Channel 8*, November 1, 2005 http://www.culteducation.com/group/921-general-assembly-church-of-the-first-born/7054-family-says-church-allowed-woman-to-die-following-childbirth.html (accessed May 16, 2014).

[347] Kevin King, "Jury Delivers Verdict in Faith Healer Manslaughter Trial," *ABC News 8*, May 25, 2012 http://www.culteducation.com/group/921-general-assembly-church-of-the-first-born/7069-jury-delivers-verdict-in-faith-healer-manslaughter-trial.html (accessed May 16, 2014).

[348] Jean Torkelson, "Church Holds Fast to Healing Beliefs," *Denver Rocky Mountain News*, July 30, 2000.

[349] Scott Hall, "Church Elder: Faith Cures Sick People, Not Doctors," *Daily Journal* (Franklin, IN), August 23, 2000.

[350] Ibid.

[351] Ibid.

[352] Steve Mayes, "Dale and Shannon Hickman Receive Six-Year Sentence, the Harshest Ever for Faith Healing Church," *Oregonian* (Portland, OR), October 31, 2011.

[353] Mark Larabee and Peter D. Sleeth, "Followers' Roots Reveal Numerous Splinters," *Oregonian* (Portland OR), July 6, 1998.

[354] Mark Larabee, "Doubt, Secrecy Circle Followers of Christ," *Oregonian* (Portland, OR), June 28, 1998.

[355] Ibid.

[356] Bill Sherman, "Faith-Based Healing Reviewed," *Tulsa World*, December 31, 2010.

[357] Mark Larabee, "The Battle over Faith Healing," *Oregonian* (Portland, OR), November 28, 1998.

[358] Ibid.

[359] David Wedge, "Attleboro Group Not the First Questioned," *Boston Herald*, September 3, 2000.

[360] Todd Lewan, "Meade, the Self-Styled Prophet: A Man Cloaked in Lore and Mystery," *Associated Press*, April 17, 2005

[361] Todd Lewan, "A Self-Styled Prophet, a Legion of Followers, and a 'Promised Land' in Florida," *Associated Press*, April 16, 2005.

[362] Jon Walker, "The Preacher and His Flock," *Argus Leader* (Sioux Falls), May 11, 2005.

[363] Ibid.

[364] Larabee, "The Battle over Faith Healing," November 28, 1998.

[365] Ibid.

[366] Jackelyn Barnard and Dave Wax, "Family: Leader of Lake City Meade Ministries, Endtimers Has Died," *First Coast News* (Jacksonville), April 13, 2010.

[367] Sherman, "Faith-Based Healing Reviewed," December 31, 2010.n

CHAPTER 3

FAMILY CULTS

Some small cults can largely comprise the members of a single family or blended family led by an all-powerful—usually patriarchal—figure. In the book *Captive Hearts, Captive Minds*, Madeleine Tobias and Janja Lalich explain, "In addition to the larger, more publicized cults, there are…'family cults,' where the head of the family uses deceptive and coercive persuasion and control techniques."[368] The bonds within this particular type of cult are quite strong, strengthened by loyalty that is expected through family ties. Children raised within such an environment may know of no other life, and for this reason they accept without question what the outside world would regard as bizarre behavior. The following historical examples of family cults illustrate these points.

Within such closely tied family groups, the so-called DDD syndrome may develop, which summarizes a cultic situation that includes "debility, dependency and dread." A publication of the American Sociological Association first described this syndrome.[369] Psychologist Michael Langone later adapted DDD for the American Family Foundation (AFF), now known as the International Cultic Studies Association

(ICSA). Langone witnessed the additional factor of deception in the recruitment practices of some cults as well, so he included deception in his adapted version of DDD.[370]

In family cults a combination of deception, control of the environment, and socialization may debilitate those victimized. This is enforced through stringent rules and relative isolation. That is, those held within a family cult environment are expected to express dutiful submission and commitment to parental authority. Langone described people in destructive cults as "vulnerable" and influenced by authority figures who deceptively appeared to be both "benevolent" and beneficial. This role of authority, when assumed by a parent, can be particularly deceptive and debilitating to children.

Through varying degrees of relative isolation, members of family cults come to depend on the leader of the group, usually a father figure, who essentially becomes their sole source of confirmation or validation. Langone, explaining the wider context of destructive cults, says, "Because by definition the group is always right," the seemingly logical result is that any "'negative' thinking is unacceptable" and within a family cult functionally inexcusable.

It is within this environment, contained by absolutes, that whenever or whatever failures occur, they cannot be attributed to the leader. The members of family cults must therefore learn to suppress their "doubts and criticisms." They inhabit a world of shame and submission where their leader is "actively encouraging escalating dependency."[371]

Status within the family cult is contingent on agreement with a form of "black and white" thinking that allows little, if any, room for ambiguity. As psychiatrist Robert Jay Lifton noted, within such an environment, "nothing human is immune from the flood of stern moral judgments. All 'taints' and 'poisons' which contribute to the existing state of impurity must be searched out and eliminated."[372] As Langone elaborates about the wider world of destructive cults, there is an ongoing "subtle undermining" of self-esteem. And the group may also strengthen and/or sustain dependence by "threatening or inflicting punishment."[373]

It is the dread of disequilibrium, physical punishment, or some imagined terrible future retribution that often further solidifies control within a family cult. As Langone generally concludes concerning deceptive cults, "The result of this process, when carried to its consummation, is a person who proclaims great happiness but hides great suffering."[374]

The following historical examples of family cults offer vivid illustrations of this suffering, which people often endure silently and mainstream society doesn't readily see.

2002—Winnfred Everett Wright Murders

In February 2002 a man and four women faced criminal charges connected to the death of a nineteen-month-old boy due to malnutrition. The four adults lived with thirteen children in a small house near San Francisco. DNA tests subsequently proved that the man, Winnfred Everett Wright, forty-five, had fathered all the children.[375]

Wright and three of the women were indicted for second-degree murder. All five were also charged with involuntary manslaughter and child endangerment. The remaining children, ages eight months to sixteen years, were placed in foster care and "treated for varying degrees of malnutrition and neglect," Fred Marziano, the Marin County sheriff detective, told the press.[376]

The adults and children involved were described as a "cultlike family" ruled over by Wright, who manipulated "the bible's Book of Revelations or astrological charts" as a means of influence. He also reportedly "used a mixture of charm and psychological coercion to make the women stay." Drugs evidently played a role in the situation.[377] Wright simply referred to the women and children he dominated as "The Family."[378]

Psychologist Margaret Singer interviewed the mother of the dead child at the request of police. "What I found strange about it, it was not a great big deal to her," she said. Singer explained that Wright, an African-American, used "white guilt" to manipulate the women, who were Caucasians. "They [were told by Wright that they] had karma they had to work off because white men had been so cruel down through the ages to black men, that white women should come, live with him, take care of him, minister to him." Singer compared Wright to Charles Manson, calling his family a "cult based on conceit."[379]

Wright had a "Book of Rules," and if those rules were somehow broken, he expected "the kids to be ceremoniously whipped with belts and force-fed spicy jalapeno peppers." One little girl was reportedly "tied to a playpen for two weeks when, during an enforced fast" she ate something. At times "the children's mouths were taped shut for violating the 'rules.'" [380] Punishable infractions included "sneaking food" or "answering the front door of their home."[381]

A consulting psychologist who saw one of the women said the woman "suffered psychological regression and dependence" but was "ready to begin the therapeutic process necessary to rebuild her psychological stability." The women seemed to improve once they were removed from Wright's influence and control.[382] Two women from the Wright group requested that a judge allow them to be temporarily released for treatment at Wellspring Retreat in Albany, Ohio. Wellspring is a licensed mental health facility specifically focused on the treatment and recovery process of former cult members. The judge granted bail and release for one of the women to receive care at Wellspring.[383]

Winnfred Wright was sentenced to sixteen years and eight months in prison, which was the maximum allowed under his "plea deal" with prosecutors.

But the judge was lenient regarding the women Wright had influenced. One woman received a ten-year prison sentence, which was four years less than the maximum allowed. Another received seven years and four months, also about four years below the maximum. One of the Wright women died from leukemia while in custody. One had her charges dismissed.[384]

When the last woman from the Wright family was sentenced, she addressed the court and said, "Mind control is a reality." She also expressed "great sorrow" over the harm done to the children and said she would be "ashamed the rest of her life."[385]

The Wright women were granted parole in 2005 and 2007.

Winnfred Wright was granted closely supervised parole in November 2010. One of his children specifically requested that Wright not be paroled in the Marin County area near family members. That request was granted, and Wright was specifically required to serve his supervised parole four hundred miles away.[386]

2004—Marcus Wesson Murders

On March 12, 2004, the worst mass murder in the history of Fresno, California, occurred. Nine bodies were found. Three of the victims were toddlers, four were children younger than nine, one a teenage girl, and one was a twenty-four-year-old woman. All were found shot dead.[387] Charged with murder was Marcus Wesson, the fifty-seven-year-old patriarch of a family "cult" and "master manipulator."[388]

Wesson taught his family he was "God's messenger" and that the "end times" were "close at hand." The family was reportedly heavily "indoctrinated by Marcus Wesson's 'bastardization' of religion." Wesson wrote his own version of the Bible, and he insisted on daily "bible studies."[389] The Wesson family included seventeen children, seven nieces and nephews. A stern disciplinarian, Marcus Wesson dictated everything, including diet, dress, and home schooling. He didn't have a regular job but instead managed whatever money those in his household earned.

According to Wesson's son Dorian his father was "psychotic, delusional and narcissistic." Another son Adrian said, "He was God. That's just the way it was." Punishments were often brutal. One of Wesson's children recalled being beaten with wire for twenty minutes for simply sneaking a spoonful of peanut butter. "It felt like being in a prison. Very depressing—like, hopeless. And you felt trapped...nowhere to go," his daughter Gypsy Wesson told *ABC News*.[390] In private, individual conversations Wesson convinced each of his daughters that the Bible mandated incest.[391] He fathered eighteen children with seven women, including his daughters and nieces. At times Wesson fed his family from trash cans, while he ate hamburgers and junk food.[392]

Born in Kansas, Marcus Wesson, was raised by a "devout Seventh-day Adventist" mother and "alcoholic father." His family wandered from state to state, moving from Missouri to Kansas, to Indiana, to California, and then to Washington.[393] Wesson served in the army during the Vietnam War as an ambulance driver in Europe. He returned to the United States in 1968. In 1971 he moved into the home of single mother Rosemary Solorio in San Jose, California. Solorio had children, and one of her daughters, Elizabeth Solorio, married Wesson during 1974. He was twenty-seven, and she was fifteen. By the 1980s Marcus and Elizabeth Wesson had a family of nine children.[394] At various times the family lived in a tent, on a boat, on a bus, and on "bare land," according to court documents. In 1981 Wesson managed to buy a home with a loan of $60,000. In 1990 he was convicted of welfare fraud and perjury.[395] The family occupied a succession of homes purchased by various family members.[396]

Wesson began to sexually touch his daughters when they were eight and nine years old. "I didn't know anything else and I thought it was all right," Kiani Wesson told *ABC News*. "Such was his control over their minds that he could even send them out into the world and they didn't blow the whistle," commented psychiatrist Edward Hallowell, director of the Hallowell Centers in New York and Boston.[397]

According to testimony in court, Wesson was fascinated with cult leader David Koresh. And like Koresh he often characterized the authorities as "Satan."[398] Prophetically he warned his family that one day "the devil with a badge and a blue uniform would show up at their door."[399] His response on that fateful day of reckoning was that death would be preferable to family separation.[400]

Despite these dark predictions and what Hallowell described as a "crucible of fear" that effectively debilitated family members, two of Wesson's nieces managed to escape. But they left children behind. When they returned for their children, Wesson refused to give them up. The police were called, and when they arrived at the scene, Wesson seemed cooperative at first. However, after he disappeared into the house, the officers heard gunshots. It is believed that Marcus Wesson's twenty-five-year-old daughter, Sebhrenah, fired the gun that killed her son, sister, nieces, and nephews. "I think that he had her take everybody, and then he took her life," said Kiani Wesson, one of the mothers.[401]

Marcus Wesson was charged with nine counts of murder and fourteen counts of sexually abusing his daughters and nieces. He was the father of all the murdered children. Some of the children were the result of incestuous relationships with his daughters. "They were exterminated, one after the other," Lisa Gamoian, the prosecutor, said at Wesson's trial in 2005. "In this family, he was Christ himself, the ultimate authority figure who determined life and death. But for his suicide pact, for his teachings, none of this would have happened," Gamoian concluded.[402]

The jury found Marcus Wesson guilty on all counts. He was sentenced to death on June 27, 2005, and now resides on "death row" at San Quinton State Prison in California.[403]

Surviving members of the Wesson family have struggled to heal from the years of manipulation and abuse they endured. Both of Wesson's two nieces, Kiani and Gypsy, who lost their children in the mass murder, have new daughters. "It does get better...Counseling and talking to friends and loved ones helps," Kiani Wesson said in a 2009 interview.[404]

The house where Marcus Wesson molested and murdered his children stood abandoned and empty for years before it was finally demolished in 2006.[405]

2004—The Trial of Karen Robidoux

In 2004 Karen Robidoux was on trial in Massachusetts, charged with the second-degree murder of her baby boy, Samuel. The child was denied solid food for fifty-one days during 1999 and died before his first birthday. The suffering of Samuel Robidoux was demanded through a "leading," supposedly a revelation "God" had given to his aunt, Michelle Mingo.

Robidoux and Mingo belonged to an Attleboro religious group largely composed of Robidoux's family members and their relations, known as "The Body," which renounced modern medicine.[406] Mingo declared that her nephew, Samuel, must subsist only by being breast-fed, while her sister-in-law, Karen, consumed nothing more than almond milk. This was a punishment for her vanity. The young mother was then also pregnant, but she struggled to obey the dictates of the group. Charlotte E. Denton, a Department of Mental Health forensic psychologist, testified that Robidoux breast-feed Samuel every hour, twenty-four hours a day. However, the mother watched helplessly as her son deteriorated and died due to starvation.[407]

The defendant's lawyer, Joseph Krowski, explained that "evil" people around her had so controlled his client that she was incapable of saving her child. But Karen Robidoux's "vile, deranged, evil" father-in-law,

Roland Robidoux, led the group. "It was about power. It was about mind control. It was about brainwashing," Krowski said.[408] Psychologist Ronald Ebert examined Karen Robidoux through twelve meetings beginning in 2002. He testified in court that Robidoux believed that "if she wasn't good, God would take her baby. She had to do what they told her to do." Ebert concluded, "It's my opinion that she was not able to leave the group."[409]

Robidoux was twenty-eight at the time of her trial. She had joined the group at the age of fourteen and was wed to Jacques Robidoux, the leader's son. Karen Robidoux was described as successfully "deprogrammed" before her trial. According to press reports she "cut off all the group members" during her confinement. It was within this period that she was "deprogrammed." Shortly before trial she reportedly "finally emerged from the fog of the brainwashing sect that swallowed 14 years of her life."

The leader of that sect, Roland Robidoux, was a door-to-door salesman who had left the Catholic Church after listening to sermons by Herbert W. Armstrong on his car radio. Armstrong was the founder of the Worldwide Church of God (WWCOG), a controversial group that has been called a "cult."[410] After his radio conversion Robidoux attended WWCOG feasts and festivals with his wife and five children. In 1978 Robidoux left WWCOG, claiming God had called him to start his own church. His church was first named Church of God of Mansfield, later Church of God of Norton, and finally The Body, but it never had more than seventy members.[411]

A former associate described Robidoux as the "sole authority" of his group and someone who was "not being questioned." Robidoux "believed that he had the truth." His truth was hard on his family, which became socially isolated. Robidoux wanted to control everything. He exercised "absolute power over his family," said his former son-in-law, Dennis Mingo, who eventually left the group. One year he decided the family should eat only meat. The next year he ordered everyone to become vegetarians and then later to eat only organic food. The family always obeyed Robidoux's edicts.[412]

Robidoux then discovered a book by Carol Balizet, a former nurse who claimed seven impure systems in the world: education, medicine, government, banking, schools, entertainment, and commerce. Balizet said true believers should never seek medical care and should give birth only at home. Her website stated, "No matter what the result, we must do what God says. We mustn't fall into the trap of trying to figure out which choice will work best for us: God or the medical system. Our response to God must be based on obedience, not on outcome."[413] Robidoux incorporated Balizet's views into his own teachings.

Roland Robidoux's children then began to have their own "revelations." His son, Jacques, who became an elder in the group, heard orders from God telling him to give up a business, so he shut it down. His daughter Michelle said God had forbidden eyeglasses. Later God supposedly forbade shorts, cosmetics, and photo albums. In November 1998, Jacques said God had commanded them to throw away their books. Members of the group eventually told relatives there would be no further communication. Roland Robidoux even ended contact with his eighty-four-year-old mother, who lived next door, after she dropped out of his group. Finally in March 1999, after her marriage to Dennis Mingo had fallen apart, Michelle Mingo received the ominous revelation concerning her nephew, Samuel. Karen Robidoux was told God was testing her.

In 2004 a jury cleared Karen Robidoux of murder charges, but she was convicted of assault and battery for starving her son. The young woman was then sentenced to a prison term of two and a half years but was set free at the time of the verdict due to the time she had already spent in custody, primarily in a psychiatric hospital. After her release Karen Robidoux said, "I don't think I could ever have true peace, because there is a hole in my heart that's very big."[414]

Karen Robidoux's husband, Jacques, was found guilty of first-degree murder and was sentenced to life imprisonment for his role in the death of their son, Samuel. He later appealed that conviction on the grounds that he too had been "brainwashed" and therefore "was not competent at the time of his trial."[415] However, his appeal was denied.[416]

In 2004 Michelle Mingo pled guilty to being an accessory after the fact of assault and battery on a child. She was released after spending four years in jail.[417]

After a lengthy illness Roland Robidoux died in 2006. He was never charged with any crime. Paul Walsh Jr., Bristol County district attorney, said state law in Massachusetts limited the responsibility of care concerning a child only to parents.[418]

2009—Jaycee Lee Dugard Kidnapping

What might Elizabeth Smart's life had been like if she had never been found? That question may be answered in part by the story of Jaycee Lee Dugard, which emerged during 2009.

In June of 1991 eleven-year-old Jaycee Dugard was kidnapped while walking home from school on a neighborhood street in South Lake Tahoe, California. Her kidnapper was Phillip Garrido, a man already on parole for a rape and kidnapping conviction.[419] His previous victim, whom Garrido abducted in Las Vegas in 1976, described him as "a monster."[420]

But unlike either Garrido's last victim, who was soon rescued, or Elizabeth Smart, who was found after nine months, Jaycee Dugard was under her kidnapper's control for eighteen years. Dugard was discovered living in the backyard of Phillip Garrido's home in Antioch, California, east of San Francisco. And she was the mother of two children ages eleven and fifteen, whom Garrido had both fathered.

The convicted rapist had created a family he completely controlled. Dugard and her children lived in a makeshift compound accessible through a maze of tarps and sheds. "All of the sheds had electricity by cords, rudimentary outhouse and shower, as if you were camping," said Fred Kollar, El Dorado County sheriff.[421]

Jaycee Dugard's formal education effectively ended at the time of her kidnapping. Dugard's two daughters never attended school. A source close to the investigation told the press, "Some type of brainwashing clearly occurred." Similar to the situation of Elizabeth Smart, Duggard seemed physically able to escape. "There were moments in the 18 years when she could have called attention to who she was. She hadn't forgotten her real identity. In fact, she remembers a remarkable amount about her old life," a source told the press. But like Elizabeth Smart and Patty Hearst, the same source attributed "mind games" as the cause of Dugard's inaction and seeming inability to escape. "It sounds simplistic, but the real prison was her brain," a source told reporters.[422]

Phillip Garrido, like Brian Mitchell, had a female accomplice. Her name was Nancy Bocanegra, and she married Phillip Garrido in Leavenworth, Kansas, when he was still an inmate in prison. Garrido served eleven years for the kidnapping and rape of his previous victim. He was released in 1988. Nancy Garrido was with her husband when he kidnapped Jaycee Dugard, and she was criminally charged like Wanda Barzee, Mitchell's accomplice. Nancy Garrido was also a certified nurse assistant, which probably explains how Phillip Garrido managed to deliver two babies and provide some level of medical care for Dugard and her children, without seeing doctors.[423] Garrido's brother, Ron, described Nancy Garrido as "a robot." He said in an interview, "She would do anything he asked her to…It's no different from [Charles] Manson."[424]

Many who knew Phillip Garrido gave him the nickname "creepy Phil," but examining psychologists found him to be "very coherent."

He owned a print shop, where Jaycee Dugard and her children worked. Customers described the mother and daughters as "polite" and "well mannered," though one customer commented, "Obviously, there was some brainwashing going on." Dugard went by the name "Alissa," and her two children were called "Angel" and "Starlet." "They were not dressed like average teenage girls. They were dressed very conservatively," one print shop customer remarked.[425] Phillip Garrido later told police, "We raised them right. They don't know anything bad about the world."[426]

Like Brian Mitchell, Garrido believed he was special and chosen by God. He was prone to rant about his religious beliefs and at times gave "impromptu sermons." Garrido once blogged, "The Creator has given me the ability to speak in the tongues of angels." He would also talk about government conspiracies and "mind control."[427] One day when Garrido was handing out flyers announcing a religious event on the University of California's Berkeley campus, he came to the attention of authorities.[428] He was accompanied by Dugard's two minor children, and police were concerned. They said the girls seemed "robotic" and that Garrido was "very controlling."[429] Police talked with Garrido and decided to run a background check on him, which revealed his criminal history. Garrido was still on parole, and his parole officer interviewed him. That interview also included Nancy Garrido, and Jaycee Dugard attended it with her two children. After the interview Phillip and Nancy Garrido were arrested. According to the sheriff, the couple "had information only the kidnappers could have known."[430]

Phillip Garrido was ultimately sentenced to 431 years in prison.[431] He is housed in the Corcoran California State Prison's Protective Housing Unit, the same unit that holds Charles Manson. Officials don't believe Garrido or Manson would be safe living in the general prison population.[432]

Nancy Garrido was sentenced to thirty-six years to life in prison.[433] She is housed at the Central California Women's Facility in Chowchilla.[434]

Jaycee Dugard was reunited with her family, but her stepfather said, "We don't know if she'll ever be able to recover from this."[435] Ernie Allen, president of the National Center for Missing and Exploited Children, observed, "Despite the 18 years that have been lost, despite the theft of Jaycee's childhood, she's alive. She's young, and she has hope for the future."[436] The state of California paid Jaycee Dugard $20 million dollars in an out-of-court settlement for repeated mistakes by parole agents who were responsible for Phillip Garrido. Dugard now lives in seclusion with her two teenage daughters. She says, "I want my girls to have a normal life as much as possible. I think in time as they get older, they'll know how to deal with it better, and that would be the time that we would come out." Jaycee Dugard has had no contact with Phillip and Nancy Garrido since their arrest.[437]

2010—The Arrest of Goel Ratzon

"Nothing like this has ever happened before in Israel," said Menachem Vagashil, deputy director-general of the Ministry of Welfare and Social Services. The Israeli official referred to a coordinated team of 150 social workers, child welfare officers, and experts who took part in the six-month undercover investigation that ended with the arrest of fifty-nine-year-old cult leader Goel Ratzon in Tel Aviv for suspected sex crimes.[438] In January 2010 police raided three apartments Ratzon used and found seventeen women and thirty-nine children. Ratzon claimed that he had fathered eighty-nine children by more than thirty women.

Goel Ratzon's female followers were expected to observe restrictions regarding communication, associations, diet, and personal conduct, which were explicitly set down within a written rulebook, including fines for infractions.[439] One rule specifically stipulated, "No conversation is permitted in rooms other than the living room."[440] The children all had the name Goel, which means "savior" in Hebrew. And they were taught to kiss Ratzon's feet whenever he visited.[441]

Ratzon called his polygamist family a "cooperative."[442] He sent the women out to work, while others stayed at home as caregivers and did housekeeping.[443] A neighbor described them as "isolated" and said, "They never say hello, and always bow their heads if you go by. One mother would take seven kids to school, [and] then go to work. Another would stay at home with the smaller ones. When Goel would arrive he would get out of his car like he was a king, and they would run behind him carrying bags, clothes, even furniture."[444]

In a televised documentary before the police raid, Goel Ratzon claimed to be "perfect" and said, "I have everything a woman wants, all the qualities a woman wants. I give women the attention they want. It's made of many things, but fortunately, I have everything." Women in the group tattooed his image on their bodies with words such as "Goel Ratzon, my love forever" and "To Goel, with love." A Kabbalah teacher and supposed healer, Ratzon took on supernatural significance to his followers. One woman in the group claimed, "He's the Messiah that everyone talks about. The day he decides to reveal himself, this country will see it."[445] Private investigator Asher Wizman said Ratzon preyed on troubled young women. Once they were within the group, those women invited sisters, cousins, and friends to join. Ratzon was also known to recruit within Tel Aviv shopping malls.[446]

The woman who finally exposed Goel Ratzon and his crimes to police said, "I was in that house from the age of 5. I had no freedom of choice." At nineteen she began to have doubts, but didn't finally run away until she was twenty-two. "He started to disgust me. I couldn't stand his smell and his caresses made me shudder," she said.[447] Inbar Yehezkeli-Blilious, legal consultant for the Association of Rape Crisis Centers in Israel explained, "Ratzon put pressure on his wives and they submitted because he had the status of a guru…Even if these women agreed to the actions, they did it because of the illusion of special powers they attributed to the man. From past experience, they probably knew of the harm being done to their girls, but lacked the strength to object."[448] Dr. Hanita Zimrin, founder and director of the Israel Association for Child Protection, told the press, "This was not a normal family. The children were educated to worship a man and prevented from growing up in a normal environment, and each of their mothers was a victim. They grew up in an environment both emotionally and developmentally harmful."[449]

A twenty-five-page indictment in February 2010 charged Goel Ratzon with "rape, sodomy, molestation and enslavement."[450] In spring 2010 an Israeli judge ruled that Ratzon would remain in custody until all court proceedings against him had concluded. "[Ratzon] poses a great danger in every possible way. Thus I believe there is no other alternative," Judge Hayuta Kochan wrote in her decision.[451] Ratzon was subsequently sentenced to 30 years in prison.[452]

The wives of Goel Ratzon and his children began a lengthy process of rehabilitative treatment. Gabi Zohar, a social worker with years of experience caring for cult victims, talked about the "brainwashing" Ratzon's victims went through and advised, "Family members should help the victims build a new reality, meet new friends, and create a new life. It is a difficult task, which requires a lot of patience."[453] One former Ratzon follower, adjusting to her new life, said, "Today, I'm free to wear jeans, talk to my parents, meet friends, buy myself a cup of coffee without getting Goel's permission."[454]

In 2011 the Welfare Ministry of Israel called for legislation concerning cults. An official task force report also recommended focused public education about cults, intervention, and rehabilitative services concerning the problem and suggested a national cult hotline.[455]

2011—Peter Lucas Moses Jr. and the "Black Hebrews" murders

In June 2011 cult leader Peter Lucas Moses Jr. was charged, along with six of his followers, in the death of Antoinetta Yvonne McKoy, who had been reported missing months earlier.[456] Twenty-seven-year-old Moses led a small, obscure group called the "Black Hebrews," which included less than a dozen African-American adults, excluding children.[457] Moses and his followers claimed they were the descendants of ancient tribes of Israel[458] and reportedly believed a coming race war would end with black domination.[459] The group practiced polygamy, and the women had sexual relations with Moses. They lived together in a rented house in Durham, North Carolina. The women were treated as wives, and Moses fathered seven of the eight children who lived with the group.[460] Women and children in the group called Moses "Lord" and reportedly feared him.[461]

A former member informed police that one of the women, Antoinetta McKoy, had tried to run away from the group, but two members had brought her back. Moses then beat McKoy throughout the day[462] and handed a handgun to Vania Sisk, ordering her to kill McKoy.[463] Two of Moses's women buried the body, which was found after the group had vacated the rental property.

Police later learned that Jadon Higganbothan, Sisk's four-year-old son, had also been slain. Authorities recovered and identified the child's remains.[464] Higganbothan was the only child within the group Moses hadn't fathered. Moses, who reportedly has bipolar disorder, came to believe the child was gay, because his father was gay and because the child had hit another boy on the bottom. "Homosexuality was frowned on" by Moses and his followers, said Tracey Cline, district attorney.[465] Moses took Jadon Higganbothan into a garage and shot him in the head. What happened next was reminiscent of 1 Mind Ministries; the boy's lifeless body was stuffed into a suitcase and stored in the house until the odor caused Moses to have the remains buried.[466]

Willie Harris, the father of Lavonda Harris, one of the Black Hebrews charged with murder, told the media that Moses made communication difficult between his daughter and her family. After her arrest Harris spoke with his daughter and said she seemed "programmed." "She was very withdrawn and very sad…She's in denial about whether Moses had anything to do with the murders," he said.[467]

In June 2012 Peter Lucas Moses Jr. entered a guilty plea to avoid the death penalty. He also agreed to testify against his followers.[468] Moses was finally sentenced during June of 2013 and received two life terms in prison.[469]

Charges against two Black Hebrews, Sheila Moses and Sheilda Harris, were dropped, and the women were released from jail. Lavada Harris and Vania Sisk both entered guilty pleas, Sisk for second degree murder and Harris as an accessory after the fact of murder. Sisk was sentenced to two consecutive prison terms of fifteen to nineteen years each. Harris was sentenced to two consecutive terms of between six to eight years.[470]

In February 2013 LaRhonda Renee Smith pled guilty to second-degree murder, kidnapping, and conspiracy charges related to the deaths of Antoinetta McKoy and Jadon Higganbothan. Smith agreed to cooperate as a witness for the state but was sentenced to eleven to fifteen years in prison.[471]

The harm inflicted and the suffering endured in family cults have been horrendous and often seem unimaginable to the general public. For this reason they are often realized only through sensational media reports. But the fact that that this type of abuse exists is historically undeniable.

Within the larger context of destructive cults, the relatively small fraction that constitutes family cults is perhaps the most unsettling. This is because the leaders doing harm are parents. The idea of fathers—and in some cases, mothers—becoming cult leaders and using their parental power to physically, psychologically, and emotionally damage their children is a deeply disturbing reality. But what we can see through the case histories recorded in this chapter are the death and destruction family cults have wrought.

Parental rights have been repeatedly challenged in courts across the United States and around the world when the welfare of children is threatened and abuse allegations are investigated. The leaders of family cults have been criminally prosecuted and held legally accountable. These prosecutions have shocked communities when a family household within a residential neighborhood is exposed as a destructive cult.

---

[368] Madeleine Tobias and Janja Lalich, *Captive Hears, Captive Minds: Freedom and Recovery from Cults and Abusive Relationships* (Alameda, CA: Hunter House, 1994), 17.

[369] I. E. Farber, Harry F. Harlow, and Louis Jolyon West, "Brainwashing, Conditioning and DDD (Debility, Dependency and Dread)," *Sociometry* 20, no. 4 (December 1957): 271–285.

[370] Michael Langone, "Deception, Dependency and Dread," International Cultic Studies Association website http://www.csj.org/studyindex/studyconversion/study_recruitconvddd.htm (accessed May 16, 2014).

[371] Ibid.

[372] Robert Jay Lifton, *Thought Reform and the Psychology of Totalism* (Chapel Hill: University of North Carolina Press, 2012), 423.

[373] Langone, "Deception, Dependency and Dread," (accessed May 16, 2014).

[374] Ibid.

[375] "Five Californians Held in Toddler's Neglect Death," *Reuters*, February 11, 2002.

[376] Ibid.

[377] Justin Pritchard, "Cultish Family Used Lovers," *Associated Press*, February 15 2002.

[378] Kevin Fagan and Peter Fimrite, "Family Court Papers Describe Ritual Beatings and Target Practice," *San Francisco Chronicle*, February 22, 2002.

[379] "Picture of the Family Comes into Focus," *ABC-7 KABC News* (Los Angeles), July 11, 2002 http://www.culteducation.com/group/1235-the-wright-family/22304-picture-of-the-family-comes-into-focus.html (accessed May 16, 2014).

[380] Fagan and Fimrite, "Family Court Papers Describe Ritual Beatings and Target Practice."

[381] Gary Klein, "Judge Oks Cult Deprogramming," *Marin News*, March 3, 2003.

[382] Con Garretson, "Second Mother Wants Cult Therapy," *Marin News*, February 25, 2003.

[383] Klein, "Judge Oks Cult Deprogramming."

[384] Con Garretson, "Woman Sentenced in Death of Toddler," *Marin Independent Journal*, April 19, 2002.

[385] Ibid.

[386] Mark Prado, "Leader of Marin's 'Family' Paroled 400 Miles Away at Request of Victim," *Marin Independent Journal*, November 23, 2010.

[387] Carolyn Marshall, "All Nine Fresno Victims Died by Gunfire," *New York Times*, March 15, 2004.

[388] Jay Schadler and Elissa Stohler, "Family Brainwashed by Dad Struggles to Heal," *ABC* News *PrimeTime*, July 6, 2010 http://abcnews.go.com/Primetime/marcus-wesson-mass-murder-surviving-family-speaks-abuse/story?id=11089648 (accessed May 16, 2014).

[389] Ibid.

[390] Ibid.

[391] Harriet Ryan, "Family Massacre Trial on Question of Brainwashing," *Court TV*, May 9, 2005 http://culteducation.com/group/1225-the-wesson-family/21941-family-massacre-trial-may-revolve-on-question-of-brainwashing.html (accessed May 16, 2014).

[392] Cyndee Fontana, Barbara Anderson, and Donald E. Coleman, "The Many Portraits of Marcus Wesson," *Fresno Bee*, April 18, 2004.

[393] Pablo Lopez, "Jury Deciding Wesson's Fate Learns about His Family," *Fresno Bee*, June 24, 2005.

[394] Fontana, Anderson, and Coleman, "The Many Portraits of Marcus Wesson," April 18, 2004.

[395] Ibid.

[396] Ibid.

[397] Schadler and Stohler, "Family Brainwashed by Dad Struggles to Heal," July 6, 2010.

[398] Fontana, Anderson, and Coleman, "The Many Portraits of Marcus Wesson," April 18, 2004.

[399] Schadler and Stohler, "Family Brainwashed by Dad Struggles to Heal," July 6, 2010.

[400] Fontana, Anderson, and Coleman, "The Many Portraits of Marcus Wesson.," April 18, 2004.

[401] Schadler and Stohler, "Family Brainwashed by Dad Struggles to Heal," July 6, 2010.

[402] Juliana Barbassa, "Prosecution Says Marcus Wesson Carried Out Murder-Suicide Pact," Associated Press, June 2, 2005.

[403] Ibid.

[404] Elecio Martinez, "Wesson Family Massacre: Children Tell Story of Murder and Sexual Abuse," *CBS 48 Hours*, October 22, 2009 http://www.cbsnews.com/news/wesson-family-massacre-children-tell-story-of-murder-and-sexual-abuse/ (accessed May 16, 2014).

[405] "House Where Father Killed Children Is Razed," *Los Angeles Times*, July 11, 2006.

[406] Denise Lavoie, "Psychologist Says Mass. Woman Was in Sect," *Atlanta Journal-Constitution*, January 31, 2004.

[407] John Ellement, "Lawyer Says Mother Controlled by Evil," *Boston Globe*, February 3, 2004.

[408] Ibid.

[409] Lavoie, "Psychologist Says Mass. Woman Was in Sect," January 31, 2004.

[410] Jeff Robinson, "Once in Cult, Student Now Sees Importance of Knowing Theology," *Baptist Press* (Nashville), June 29, 2004.

[411] "The Sect: Led by a Father's Religious Zeal, Family Spurned Society's rules," *Boston Globe*, November 26, 2000.

[412] Ibid.

[413] Ibid.

[414] "Convicted Mother Describes Her Ordeal in Religious Sect," *Boston Globe*, March 4, 2004.

[415] David Linton, "New Hearing for Ex-leader of Cult," *Sun Chronicle* (Attleboro, MA), June 25, 2009.

[416] Robidoux v. O'Brien United States Court of Appeals, (First Circuit 10–1239 2011) http://www.plainsite.org/dockets/hexlmp4l/court-of-appeals-for-the-first-circuit/robidoux-v-obrien/ (accessed May 16, 2014).

[417] David Linton, "Sect Founder Robidoux Dies," *Attleboro Sun Chronicle*, May 18, 2006.

[418] Ibid.

[419] Sammy Rose Saltzman, "Jaycee Lee Dugard Kidnapped, Impregnated and Forced to Live in a Shed, Say Police," *CBS News*, August 27, 2009 http://www.cbsnews.com/news/jaycee-lee-dugard-kidnapped-impregnated-and-forced-to-live-in-shed-say-police/ (accessed May 16, 2014).

[420] Sharon Churcher and Peter Sheridan "Jaycee Lee Dugard's Prison: First of a Filthy Backyard Jail Where Religious Fanatic Held Kidnapped Girl" *Daily Mail* (London), August 30, 2009.

[421] Saltzman, "Jaycee Lee Dugard Kidnapped, Impregnated and Forced to Live in a Shed, Say Police," August 27, 2009.

[422] Churcher and Sheridan, "Jaycee Lee Dugard's Prison: First of a Filthy Backyard Jail Where Religious Fanatic Held Kidnapped Girl," August 30, 2009.

[423] John Simerman, "Wife Who Police Say Joined in Abduction and Rape of Jaycee Dugard, Worked as Contra Costa Nursing Aide," *Contra Costa Times*, September 2, 2009.

[424] "Garrido Bro: 'He Was Just like Manson,'" *The Sun* (UK), August 29, 2009.

[425] "Kidnap Victim's Daughters Lives Seemed Normal, Friend Says," *CNN News*, August 31, 2009.

[426] "Profile: Phillip Garrido," *BBC News*, September 1, 2009 http://www.bbc.co.uk/news/world-us-canada-13633403 (accessed May 16, 2014).

[427] Ibid.

[428] Saltzman, "Jaycee Lee Dugard Kidnapped, Impregnated and Forced to Live in a Shed, Say Police," August 27, 2009.

"Profile: Phillip Garrido," September 1, 2009.

[429] "Profile: Phillip Garrido," September 1, 2009.

[430] Saltzman, "Jaycee Lee Dugard Kidnapped, Impregnated and Forced to Live in a Shed, Say Police," August 27, 2009.

"Dugard to Remain in Hiding to Protect Daughters," *Associated Press*, March 14, 2012.

[431] "Dugard to Remain in Hiding to Protect Daughters," March 14, 2012.

[432] "Dugard Kidnapper Garrido to Be Held in Same California Prison Unit as Cult Killer Charles Manson."

[433] "Dugard to Remain in Hiding to Protect Daughters," March 14, 2012.

[434] "Dugard Kidnapper Garrido to Be Held in Same California Prison Unit as Cult Killer Charles Manson."

[435] Churcher and Sheridan, "Jaycee Lee Dugard's Prison: First of a Filthy Backyard Jail Where Religious Fanatic Held Kidnapped Girl," August 30, 2009.

[436] Erin Allday, "Experts: Kidnap Victim Faces Difficult Recovery," *San Francisco Chronicle*, August 30, 2009.

[437] "Dugard to Remain in Hiding to Protect Daughters," March 14, 2012.

[438] Ruth Eglash, "Welfare Officials Call This the Biggest Cult-Busting Operation Ever in Israel," *The Jerusalem Post*, January 14, 2010.

[439] Diane Moy Schaefer, "Israeli Cult Leader Goel Ratzon Arrested for Allegedly Keeping Harem of Women and Fathering Dozens," *New York Daily News*, January 15, 2012.

[440] "Jewish Cult Leader Turned a Profit," *Heeb*, January 15, 2010 http://heebmagazine.com/jewish-cult-leader-turns-a-profit/5060 (accessed May 16, 2014).

[441] Schaefer, "Israeli Cult Leader Goel Ratzon Arrested for Allegedly Keeping Harem of Women and Fathering Dozens," January 15, 2012.

[442] Dana Weiler-Pollak, "Experts: Polygamist Ran 'Family' as a Cult," *Haaretz* (Israel), January 17, 2010.

[443] "Jewish Cult Leader Turned a Profit," January 15, 2010.

[444] Weiler-Pollak, "Experts: Polygamist Ran 'Family' as a Cult," January 17, 2010.

[445] Matthew Kalman, "In Israel, the Messiah with More Than 30 Wives," *Time*, January 18, 2010.

[446] Amy Teibel, "Tel Aviv 'Savior' Accused of Enslaving Women," *Associated Press*, February 8, 2010.

[447] Yaniv Kubovich, "Woman Who Escaped from Cult Leader Accuses State of Neglecting Her Case," *Haaretz*, July 2, 2010.

[448] Yael Bronovsky, "Ratzon's Wives Begin Lengthy Treatment," *Ynetnews.com*, February 16, 2010. http://www.ynetnews.com/articles/0,7340,L-3849914,00.html (accessed May 16, 2014).

[449] Ibid.

[450] "Goel Ratzon Indicted in Tel Aviv," *The Jerusalem Post*, February 14, 2010.

[451] Ofra Edelman, "Polygamist Cult Leader to Be Held Until Case Ends," *Haaretz* (Israel), April 28, 2010.

[452] Yonah Jeremy Bob, "Head of Polygamist Cult Ratzon Sentenced to 30 Years in Prison," *The Jerusalem Post*, October 28, 2014.

[453] Bronovsky, "Ratzon's Wives Begin Lengthy Treatment," February 16, 2010.

[454] Teibel, "Tel Aviv 'Savior' Accused of Enslaving Women," February 8, 2010.

[455] Ruth Eglash, "Welfare Ministry Calls for Legislation to Fight Cults," *The Jerusalem Post*, May 24, 2011.

[456] Justin Quesinberry, "Seven Charged with Murder," *Herald Sun* (Durham), June 13, 2011.

[457] Ibid.

[458] Mitch Weiss and Renee Elder, "Polygamist Sect under Suspicion in Two Killings," *Associated Press*, April 6, 2011.

[459] Thomasi McDonald and Mandy Locke, "Additional Remains of Small Child Found at Durham House," *News Observer* (Raleigh), June 9, 2011.

[460] "Cult Leader Killed Boy He Thought Was Gay," *9 News* (Sydney), June 12, 2012 http://culteducation.com/group/1095-peter-lucas-moses-jr/15904-cult-leader-killed-boy-he-thought-was-gay.html (accessed May 16, 2014).

[461] "Fingerprint Links Accused Durham Sect Leader to Dead Bodies," *WRAL News* (Raleigh), February 8, 2012 https://www.google.com/search?q=WRAL+News&ie=utf-8&oe=utf-8&aq=t&rls=org.mozilla:en-US:official&client=firefox-a&channel=sb (accessed May 16, 2014).

[462] "Cult Leader That Forced His Three Wives and Nine Kids to Call Him 'Lord' Pleads Guilty to Murdering Woman, 28, Boy, 4, Because He Thought He Was Gay," *Daily Mail* (London), June 11, 2012.

[463] McDonald and Locke, "Additional Remains of Small Child Found at Durham House."

[464] Weiss and Elder, "Polygamist Sect under Suspicion in Two Killings."

[465] "Cult Leader That Forced His Three Wives and Nine Kids to Call Him 'Lord' Pleads Guilty to Murdering Woman, 28, Boy, 4, Because He Thought He Was Gay," June 11, 2012.

[466] "Cult Leader Killed Boy He Thought Was Gay," June 12, 2012.

[467] Justin Quesinberry, "Durham Murder Suspect's Father Describes Daughter's Cult Life," *WNCN NBC News 17*, (Raleigh) June 11, 2011 http://www.wncn.com/story/20884732/durham-murder-suspects-father-describes-daughters-cult-life (accessed May 16, 2014).

[468] "Cult Leader That Forced His Three Wives and Nine Kids to Call Him 'Lord' Pleads Guilty to Murdering Woman, 28, Boy, 4, Because He Thought He Was Gay," June 11, 2012.

[469] Carol Kuravilla, "Cult Leader Gets Two Life Sentences for the Murders of a Little Boy and One of His Wives," *New York Daly News*, July 5, 2013.

[470] Thomas McDonald, "Black Hebrew Cult Members Sentenced for Murders of Woman and Child," *News & Observer* (Raleigh), June 28, 2013.

[471] "Woman Pleads Guilty in Durham 'Cult' Killings," *WTVD-TV ABC News 11* (Raleigh), February 18, 2013 http://abc11.com/archive/8997075/ (accessed May 16, 2014).

CHAPTER 4

DEFINING A DESTRUCTIVE CULT

The definition of a cult has been debated, and it is frequently understood in a myriad of different ways from various perspectives. Many definitions have been offered over the years, including faith-based definitions derived from theology as well as behaviorally based models premised on interpersonal or group dynamics and structure. Some academics have tried to eliminate the word *cult* in favor of what they consider to be a more politically correct label, such as "new religious movements" (NRM).

Readers should understand, however, that many groups called "cults" aren't based on religion. For example, as explained in a preceding chapter, the cult known as Synanon began as a substance-abuse rehabilitation community. The Symbionese Liberation Army was a political group, and MOVE was also based on both political beliefs and concerns about the environment.

To demonstrate how the term *cult* can be potentially understood in popular culture, consider its definition. The *Merriam-Webster Dictionary* offers a broad range of meaning.[472]

1. : formal religious veneration:

2. : a system of religious beliefs and ritual; *also*: its body of adherents

3. : a religion regarded as unorthodox or spurious; *also*: its body of adherents

4. : a system for the cure of disease based on dogma set forth by its promulgator <health *cults*>
    a: great devotion to a person, idea, object, movement, or work (as a film or book); *especially*: such devotion regarded as a literary or intellectual fad
    b: the object of such devotion
    c: a usually small group of people characterized by such devotion

This dictionary definition could potentially include relatively benign organizations, fringe groups, fanatics, zealous devotees of the television series *Star Trek* (often called "Trekkies"), or even die-hard fans of the singer Elvis Presley. Some enthralled Elvis enthusiasts even established a church and this has been written about as a cultural phenomenon.[473] But a dictionary definition simply conveys the status of a word. It doesn't take into account research regarding the application of a word.

To define a destructive cult, distinctions are made based on behavior rather than on beliefs. A group may have seemingly unorthodox or spurious beliefs, but this fact doesn't mean the group is harmful or intrinsically destructive.

As the previous accounts demonstrate, destructive cults deliberately mandate harm, which is then practiced systemically in the group. For example, consider faith healing groups such as the Followers of Christ or the General Assembly Church of the First Born, which prohibits professional medical treatment and prescribed medications. Other examples include the Children of God and polygamist groups, in which minor children have been sexually abused as part of their group beliefs and practice. There are also groups like the Brethren, commonly called the "Garbage Eaters," led by Jim Roberts; these groups systematically demand family estrangement and relatively extreme social isolation. What all these groups have in common are mandated practices that do harm with corresponding demands for rigid conformity. This means that such groups by design, much like a machine, inherently and repeatedly produce the same destructive results.

As related in the previous historical profiles, the leaders of destructive cults appear in an array of incarnations, pitching everything from commercial schemes to racism. Cults have also been based on the premise of some form of meditation or yoga, therapy, martial arts, alternative healing, or philosophy. In addition splinter groups called "cults" have broken away from established religions such as Judaism, Christianity, Buddhism, Hinduism, or Islam.

Psychiatrist Robert Jay Lifton wrote the seminal book *Thought Reform and the Psychology of Totalism*,[474] which has been used as a guide or template to explain the techniques cults use to recruit and retain members. In his book Lifton breaks down coercive persuasion in detail and explains its mechanics. Lifton also wrote a closely related paper, titled "Cult Formation,"[475] that essentially condensed many of the attributes associated with destructive cults to three primary characteristics. These three criteria form what we can see as the nucleus of the definition for a destructive cult.

These three characteristic criteria are the following:

1. a charismatic leader who increasingly becomes an object of worship as the general principles that may have originally sustained the group lose their power;

2. a process I call coercive persuasion or thought reform;
3. economic, sexual, and other exploitation of group members by the leader and the ruling coterie.[476]

Lifton later reiterated his position regarding the definition of a cult. He said, "I am aware of the controversy surrounding the use of the word cult because of its pejorative connotation, as opposed to the more neutral new religion. I use both terms in this book, but as in past work I confine the use of cult to groups that display three characteristics: totalistic or thought-reform-like practices, a shift from worship of spiritual principles to worship of the guru or leader, and a combination of spiritual quest from below and exploitation, usually economic or sexual, from above."[477]

Psychologist Margaret Singer builds and expands on Lifton in her book *Cults in Our Midst*.[478] In her definition of a destructive cult, she includes elements based on behavior and structure. Singer says that when we evaluate a group, three primary areas should be our focus:

1. The origin of the group and role of the leader
2. The power structure or relationship between the leader[s] and the followers
3. The use of a coordinated program of persuasion, which is called thought reform

Singer's approach is essentially to scrutinize the reciprocal relationships between cult leaders and their followers. It is through such scrutiny that she explains why people may stay in a destructive cult, even when it doesn't seem to be in their own best interest.

The most salient single feature of most destructive cults is that an absolute, authoritarian leader essentially defines and controls them. A single leader is most often the sole authority, but at times an elite "ruling coterie" (a small group of leaders) function in that pivotal position of power. The group can therefore be seen as primarily personality driven and functionally defined by its living leader or leaders.

As cited in the previous descriptions of cult leaders, they can be highly charismatic and implicitly expect complete compliance and obedience from their followers. For example, Shoko Asahara ordered Aum devotees to attack the Tokyo subway system, and Bhagwan Shree Rajneesh demanded that his followers poison townspeople near his ashram to affect local elections in Oregon.

The followers of these leaders complied without resistance to their leader's wishes despite the fact that these were unlawful, criminal acts. Benjamin Zablocki, professor of sociology at Rutgers University, explains, "Charisma is not to be understood simply in terms of the characteristics of the leader, as it has come to be in popular usage, but requires an understanding of the relationship between leader and followers. In other words, charisma is a relational variable. Charisma is defined operationally as a network of relationships in which authority is justified."[479]

Singer explains the hierarchy of destructive cults this way: "In most cases, there is one person, typically the founder at the top…Decision making centers in him or her." Illustrating this type of group structure, Singer said, "Imagine an inverted T. The leader is alone at the top and the followers are all at the bottom."[480] In this sense the decision-making process is sequestered at the top, and the general membership at the bottom may not even know the details.

A destructive cult is typically totalitarian, and regardless of its stated purpose or belief system, "the overriding philosophy…is that the ends justify the means, a view that allows [such groups] to establish their own brand of morality, outside normal society bounds," Singer wrote.[481]

Many destructive cult leaders seem to be deeply narcissistic personalities, as historically characterized by the condition known as narcissistic personality disorder (NPD), according to the *Diagnostic and Statistical Manual of Mental Disorders* (DSM).[482] Mental health professionals use this tool to diagnose disorders. But it must be noted that these diagnostic criteria only provide basic guidelines and reflect a consensus rather than a definitive diagnosis, which would require specialized clinical training. The DSM in the past has identified the following pattern of behavior and collection of symptoms to denote NPD:

There is generally a pervasive pattern of behavior that reflects grandiosity, a need for admiration, and a lack of empathy. We can also see NPD through an accumulation of five or more of the following exhibited symptoms:

1. The person has a grandiose sense of self-importance (for example, he or she exaggerates achievements and talents, and expects to be recognized as superior without commensurate achievements).
2. The person is preoccupied with fantasies of unlimited success, power, brilliance, beauty, or ideal love.
3. The person believes he or she is "special" and unique and should associate with, or be understood only by, other special or high-status people (or institutions).
4. The person requires excessive admiration.
5. The person has a sense of entitlement (in other words unreasonable expectations of especially favorable treatment or automatic compliance with his or her expectations).
6. The person is interpersonally exploitative (in other words he or she takes advantage of others to achieve his or her own ends).
7. The person lacks empathy; he or she is unwilling to recognize or identify with the feelings and needs of others.
8. The person is often envious of others or believes others are envious of him or her.
9. The person shows arrogant, haughty behavior or attitudes.

Destructive cult leaders are frequently consumed with messianic visions and grandiose ideas about changing the world to suit their own purposes. Some have claimed to be an exclusive vehicle for enlightenment chosen by some higher power, a supposed "psychic" connected to historical figures, or even aliens from outer space. Waco Davidian leader David Koresh made such claims and said he was the "Lamb of God." Marshall Applewhite, leader of the cult known as Heaven's Gate, saw himself as the crucial link humanity required to reach a higher level of development.

Sociologist Stephen Kent has applied this description to L. Ron Hubbard, the founder of Scientology. Kent wrote, "Hubbard displayed traits of a particular form of the condition, malignant narcissism, in his reactions to perceived opponents, and…his personal reactions provided the impetus for Scientology's organizational policies of retaliation and vengeance. In essence, the corporate climate within Scientology largely is a reflection of Hubbard's narcissism and malignant narcissistic rage."[483]

Destructive-cult leaders often seem to be deeply delusional and even mentally ill. Many mental health professionals who have studied destructive cults have labeled some cult leaders "psychopaths." Psychiatrist Louis J. West, who was a professor of psychiatry at the University of California at Los Angeles medical school during the Waco Davidian standoff, saw David Koresh as a psychopath. He said, "The psychopath is often charming, bright, very persuasive. He quickly wins people's trust and is uncannily adept at manipulating and conning people."[484] After watching Marshall Applewhite's final statements on videotape, West said the cult leader was "delusional, sexually repressed, and suffering from a rare case of clinical paranoia."[485]

In his seminal book *Without Conscience*,[486] psychologist Robert Hare laid the groundwork for a better understanding of psychopaths. Hare studied prison inmates and developed a "psychopathy checklist" (PCL). The *Buros Mental Measurements Yearbook* referred to Hare's revised checklist (PCL-R) as the "gold standard" for measuring psychopathy. The PCL-R profile includes some personal characteristics that in part parallel or overlap a narcissistic personality.

Hare offers the following personality traits and lifestyle, which may reflect a psychopath.[487] He cautions that a qualified and credentialed clinician must administer his diagnostic tool to be properly definitive and valid.

Factor 1: Personality "Aggressive Narcissism"

- Glibness/superficial charm
- Grandiose sense of self-worth
- Pathological lying
- Cunning/manipulative quality
- Lack of remorse or guilt
- Shallow affect (emotion short lived and egocentric)
- Callousness, lack of empathy
- Failure to accept responsibility for own actions

Factor 2: Case History—"Socially Deviant Lifestyle"

- Need for stimulation/proneness to boredom
- Parasitic lifestyle
- Poor behavioral control
- Lack of realistic, long-term goals
- Impulsivity
- Irresponsibility
- Juvenile delinquency
- Early behavior problems
- Revocation of conditional release

What Lifton calls "thought reform" and what Singer refers to as a "coordinated program of persuasion" are what sociologist Richard Ofshe describes as "coercive persuasion."[488] Ofshe identifies "four key factors, which distinguish coercive persuasion from other socialization schemes."[489]

1. The reliance on intense, interpersonal, and psychological attack to destabilize an individual's sense of self to promote compliance

2. The use of an organized peer group

3. Applying interpersonal pressure to promote conformity

4. The manipulation of the totality of the person's social environment to stabilize behavior once modified

This process Ofshe, Singer, and Lifton describe is an intentional transformation of individuals through manipulation and control, which are used to gain undue influence. Coercive persuasion or thought reform leads to the breakdown of critical and independent thinking. It also causes those affected to become increasingly dependent on the group and its leadership to make value judgments for them, provide analysis, and in some situations determine the parameters of reality.

The net result of this process is that those affected often make choices that aren't in their own best interest but are typically and consistently in the best interests of the group and its leaders. For example, ingesting cyanide wasn't in the best interest of families at Jonestown, but it was what Jim Jones wanted. Committing suicide wasn't in the best interest for members of Heaven's Gate, but according to Marshall Applewhite, the time had come for them to shed their human "containers" or "vehicles" and attain what he told them would be the "evolutionary level above human."

But religious cults aren't the only groups who use brainwashing techniques. Sociologist Benjamin Zablocki noted in his study of cultic, coercive persuasion, "I do not mean to imply that there is anything about religion per se that is especially conducive to brainwashing or that brainwashing is not also to be found in political, psychotherapeutic, military or other totalist collectives."[490]

We should note that harm or exploitation by destructive cults, as Lifton described in his third criteria, varies by degree from group to group. That is, some destructive cults are more destructive than others. For example, only a small fraction of destructive cult leaders have ordered mass suicides or violence. Most seem largely focused on the financial exploitation of their followers through the surrender of their assets or free labor or both.

Otherwise destructive cults harm members psychologically through what can be seen as the intentional infliction of emotional distress. Damage is also done to family relationships through estrangement and sometimes divorce, which the group may mandate. Educational or career opportunities may also be ignored for years due to group influence and preoccupation with its activities. Years may go by before an affected individual eventually leaves the group and resumes such interests. This delay may result in fewer opportunities and diminished prospects for the future.

Psychiatrist Louis Jolyon West presented the following definition of a destructive cult at a conference, which the American Family Foundation (AFF), now known as the International Cultic Studies Association (ICSA), held at the University of California at Los Angeles (UCLA). The AFF/ICSA *Cultic Studies Journal* later published his definition. West was the director of the Neuropsychiatry Institute at UCLA and studied destructive cults for decades.

West stated, "A cult is a group or movement exhibiting a great or excessive devotion or dedication to some person, idea or thing and employing unethically manipulative techniques of persuasion and control (e.g. isolation from former friends and family, debilitation, use of special methods to heighten suggestibility and subservience, powerful group pressures, information management, suspension of individuality or critical judgment, promotion of total dependency on the group and fear of leaving it, etc.) designed to advance the goals of the group's leaders to the actual or possible detriment of members, their families, or the community."[491]

We can see West's definition as largely extending in more detail the three central criteria or themes found in destructive cults, as delineated so deftly by Lifton.

ICSA later condensed and somewhat refined its definition in an official handbook. The cultic studies organization stated, "A cult is characterized by an ideology, strong demands issuing from that ideology and powerful processes of social-psychological influence to induce group members to meet those demands. This high-demand, leader centered social climate places such groups at risk of exploiting and injuring members, although they may remain benign, if leadership doesn't abuse its power."[492]

Sociologist Janja Lalich and psychologist Michael Langone also provided a checklist of "social-structural, social-psychological, and interpersonal behavioral patterns commonly found in cultic environments," which is intended to be used as "an analytical tool."[493]

1. The group displays excessively zealous and unquestioning commitment to its leader and (whether he is alive or dead) regards his belief system, ideology, and practices as the Truth, as law.
2. Questioning, doubt, and dissent are discouraged or even punished.
3. Mind-altering practices (such as meditation, chanting, speaking in tongues, denunciation sessions, and debilitating work routines) are used in excess and serve to suppress doubts about the group and its leader(s).

4. The leadership dictates, sometimes in great detail, how members should think, act, and feel (for example, members must get permission to date, change jobs, marry—or leaders prescribe what types of clothes to wear, where to live, whether or not to have children, how to discipline children, and so forth).

5. The group is elitist, claiming a special, exalted status for itself, its leader(s) and members (for example, the leader is considered the Messiah, a special being, an avatar—or the group and/or the leader is on a special mission to save humanity).

6. The group has a polarized us-versus-them mentality, which may cause conflict with the wider society.

7. The leader is not accountable to any authorities (unlike, for example, teachers, military commanders or ministers, priests, monks, and rabbis of mainstream religious denominations).

8. The group teaches or implies that its supposedly exalted ends justify whatever means it deems necessary. This may result in members' participating in behaviors or activities they would have considered reprehensible or unethical before joining the group (for example, lying to family or friends, or collecting money for bogus charities).

9. The leadership induces feelings of shame and/or guilt in order to influence and/or control members. Often, this is done through peer pressure and subtle forms of persuasion.

10. Subservience to the leader or group requires members to cut ties with family and friends, and radically alter the personal goals and activities they had before joining the group.

11. The group is preoccupied with bringing in new members.

12. The group is preoccupied with making money.

13. Members are expected to devote inordinate amounts of time to the group and group-related activities.
14. Members are encouraged or required to live and/or socialize only with other group members.
15. The most loyal members (the "true believers") feel there can be no life outside the context of the group. They believe there is no other way to be, and often fear reprisals to themselves or others if they leave (or even consider leaving) the group.

This checklist, which Lalich and Langone offered, can also readily be linked to the three basic categories of criteria Lifton listed. That is, those points that directly deal with the nature of the leader and quality of leadership would fall under Lifton's first criteria pertaining to a "charismatic leader." The "mind altering practices" mentioned and various forms of manipulation cited would fit into Lifton's cited process of "coercive persuasion or thought reform." And the negative consequences or results of membership can be categorized under Lifton's third criteria, specifically denoting "exploitation of group members."

The Israeli Ministry of Welfare and Social Services seemed to largely follow Lifton's criteria in its report about cults in Israel. The ministry report sought to make distinctions in its determination of what constituted "harmful cults." The government agency stated, "Harmful cults are groups that are united around a person or idea, by the exercise of control of thought processes and patterns of behavior, for the purpose of creating an identity that is distinct from society and by the use of false representations. For the most part these groups encourage mental subservience to the leader of the cult and his objectives, exploit their members with a view to promoting the objectives of the cult, and cause mental, physical, economic and social damage (in one or more of these fields), to members of the groups, their families and the surrounding community."[494]

Ronald Enroth is a professor of sociology at Westmount College in Santa Barbara and the chair of its Department of Sociology. Westmount is an evangelical, Christian institution. His definition of a destructive cult specifically takes into consideration the fact that many groups called "cults," particularly those in the United States, claim to be "Bible-based" and therefore religious in nature. For example, both Ugandan cult leader Joseph Kibwetere of the so-called Movement for the Restoration of the Ten Commandments and Paul Schaefer, founder and leader of Colonia Dignidad in Chile, claimed that their respective groups were Christian and based on biblical authority.

Enroth makes distinctions about such groups from an evangelical, Christian perspective. Enroth's description of a destructive cult is largely religiously based and essentially an extension of what has been called the "counter-cult movement" (CCM). The CCM is mainly composed of "discernment ministries" that view Bible-based cults as aberrational and heretical religious groups that have deviated from what they define as a correct doctrinal Christian perspective. The Ontario Consultants on Religious Tolerance, a prominent website that is critical of the CCM, says it is "composed primarily of conservative Protestant Christian individuals, agencies, and para-church groups who attempt to raise public concern about religious groups which they feel hold dangerous, non-traditional beliefs."[495]

The CCM seems to have influenced Enroth's view of cults, though his position in the field of sociology has tempered it. He points out "that when the word 'cult' is used to describe a contemporary social phenomenon, it nearly always refers to groups seen as dangerous or destructive."[496]

Enroth lists the following four primary, defining features:

1. A charismatic, living leader
2. Claims of omniscience or divine descent for the leader

3. Absolute obedience to the leader
4. Social boundaries that separate and polarize members from mainstream society

These features again correspond to criteria Lifton established. Enroth also notes "nine common characteristics" and says that "all of the cults have some of these features; not all cults have all of them."[497]

1. Authoritarian—"A crucial dimension of all cultic organizations is authoritarian leadership. There is always a central, charismatic (in the personality sense), living human leader who commands total loyalty and allegiance." This would correspond to Lifton's description of charismatic leadership.
2. Oppositional—"Their beliefs, practices, and values are counter to those of the dominant culture. They often place themselves in an adversarial role vis-à-vis major social institutions." This characteristic would contribute to the social isolation of the group and eliminate any competing frames of reference.
3. Exclusivistic—"Related to the oppositional character of cults is their elitism and exclusionism. The group is the only one which possesses the 'truth,' and therefore to leave the group is endangering one's salvation." Again this contributes to continued isolation and control. Any information outside the group's control can be labeled as outside the "truth." This would also fit within the framework of Lifton's coercive persuasion process.
4. Legalism—"Tightly structured autocratic groups operate within a legalistic framework which governs both spiritual matters and the details of everyday living. Rules and regulations abound." This characteristic can be done through distorted biblical references, typically taken out of context, for the purpose of personal manipulation. Though this can be seen as a doctrinal issue of the CCM, it also contributes to the coercive persuasion process that locks people into a destructive cult.

5. Subjective—"Cultic movements place considerable emphasis on the experiential—on feelings and emotions. Subjectivism is sometimes linked to anti-intellectualism, putting down rational processes and devaluing knowledge and education." This might include excessive "speaking-in-tongues" and/or "strong prayer" used to still the mind. The special revelation of the group or leader can also become a subjective means of proving almost anything without the requirement of objective evidence. This again can be seen as a piece of Lifton's "thought reform" process.

6. Personal—Conscious—"Perceived persecution is one of the hallmarks of virtually all new religious movements." The claim of persecution can be used to reinforce social isolation and also be a means to dismiss critics or criticism. Those who criticize the group are "persecuting" it. Bible-based destructive cults have often equated bad press, litigation, and even criminal investigations with the persecution of Jesus at the hands of unbelievers and authorities. In this sense, despite its destructive behavior, the group may redefine reality by casting itself in the role of the victim and pointing out that any opposition or criticism is proof of its holiness.

7. Sanction Oriented—"Cults require conformity to established practices and beliefs and readily exercise sanctions against the wayward. Those who fail to demonstrate the proper allegiance, who raise too many questions, disobey the rules or openly rebel are punished, formally excommunicated or merely asked to leave the group." This characteristic is used as a tool of coercive persuasion to intimidate and threaten members through the threat of punishment.

8. Esoteric—"Cultic religion is a religion of secrecy and concealment. Eastern spirituality, especially, has been described by Brooks Alexander [research director of the Spiritual Counterfeits Project, a discernment ministry within the CCM] as 'split level religion, with an inner truth (the real truth) and an outer truth (an appealing, but limited and somewhat misleading face). This kind of esotericism,' Alexander continues, 'accepts the appropriateness

(and practical necessity) of a deliberately created gap between the picture that is projected to the general public and the inner reality known to the initiates."[498] Many destructive cults are deceptive. What the newly recruited member thought was the group's "truth" was only its outer shell shown to the world. The principle of "secrecy and concealment" can be used to play a game of "bait and switch." That is, the new initiate is first presented with an undemanding, pleasant picture of the group, which progressively evolves during his or her continued involvement into almost something else entirely. This is how people can be tricked into joining destructive cults without their informed consent.

9. Antisacerdotal—"Cults tend to be organizations comprised of laypeople. There are no paid clergy or professional religious functionaries like those in traditional groups. That is not to say that cults do not have spiritual hierarchies or titles applying to specific roles." This is a relevant issue for the CCM, but it also underlines the fact that many cult leaders are self-taught and self-proclaimed. They have often not been formally educated or sanctioned by an organization, through which they can be held accountable. They typically exercise absolute authority without any meaningful accountability.

Even though Enroth's nine characteristics include faith-based religious references, they also coalesce around the same three central themes based on behavior and structure, as Lifton established. Like Lifton, Enroth identifies the importance of a central charismatic leader who is an absolute authority and demands virtually total obedience. Enroth, like West, projects and expands upon the process of thought reform as identified by Lifton and understood by Ofshe and Singer in their descriptions. Enroth does this through his explanation of legalism and emphasis on subjective feelings, increasing isolation, exclusivity, perceived persecution, and the denigration of critical thinking. Enroth also notes the potential for related damage done through harsh sanctions and punishments as a consequence of disobedience.

The Ontario Consultants on Religious Tolerance website is quite critical of what it calls the "anti-cult movement" (ACM) and can be seen as an apologist for many groups called "cults." According to the website, the ACM "consists of individuals and groups who attempt to raise public consciousness about what they feel is an extreme danger. As they see it, the threat mainly comes from small, coercive, manipulative groups—mostly new religious movements—who use deceptive recruitment practices and...advanced psychological manipulative techniques to reduce their followers to near-zombie state."[499] Despite its apparent antipathy regarding the ACM, the Ontario Consultants on Religious Tolerance website includes a page titled "Common signs of destructive cults."[500] It lists there "a number of organizations that have lost membership through suicide or killing." The website has chosen to label such groups "doomsday destructive cults" and specifically includes the Solar Temple, Aum, the Waco Davidians, and Heaven's Gate. Noting the common attributes of such groups, the Ontario Consultants on Religious Tolerance say that doomsday cults "exhibit most or all of the following ten factors."

Apocalyptic Beliefs

1. The leader's preaching concentrates heavily on the impending end of the world.

2. The group expects to play a major, elite role at the end-time.

Charismatic Leadership

3. A single, male, charismatic leader leads them.

4. The leader dominates the members, closely controlling them physically, sexually, and emotionally.

Social Encapsulation

5. They are a small religious group, not an established denomination.

6. The group or at least the core members live together in an intentional community isolated from the rest of society.

7. There is often extreme paranoia in the group; members believe they are in danger and that governments or people outside the group are closely monitoring and heavily persecuting them. People on "the outside" are demonized.

8. Information and contacts from outside the cult are severely curtailed.

Other Factors

9. The group leadership assembles an impressive array of guns, rifles, other murder weapons, poison, or weapons of mass destruction. They may prepare defensive structures.

10. They follow a form of Christian theology (or a blend of Christianity with another religion), with major and unique deviations from traditional beliefs in the area of end-time prophecy.

Even though this definition narrowly focuses on so-called end-times or doomsday theology as its prerequisite, nevertheless it again conforms to the three categories of characteristics Lifton identifies. That is, the so-called doomsday cults are personality driven, and a charismatic leader dominates all of them. They also exhibit "social encapsulation" factors, which correspond to various aspects of the thought-reform process. And they have all done harm, which in the groups cited was so horrible that it became historically noteworthy.

Intentional Communities or Cultic Compounds?

We should note that thousands of counterculture communities were created and developed during the 1960s and 1970s.[501] Many of these intentional communities, or communes, have endured to the present. Benjamin Zablocki, professor of sociology at Rutgers University, broke down such communities into ten categories.[502]

- Alternative families
- Cooperatives
- Countercultural
- Egalitarian
- Political
- Psychological
- Rehabilitation
- Religious
- Spiritual
- Experimental

Zablocki studied hundreds of intentional communities, everything from an Israeli kibbutz to a Hutterite collective. He found that the dropout rate in many of these communities was approximately 25 percent. People who left often cited as a primary cause questions that arose concerning the group's internal dynamics; typically their concerns centered on the exercise of power and authority.[503]

Sociologist Stephen Kent, in his own study of the counterculture of the 1960s and 1970s, found that what was initially an idealistic movement focused on social and political activism in certain instances later contributed to various forms of spirituality or morphed into guru worship. This development could be seen in such groups as the Unification Church, Hare Krishna (ISKCON), and the Children of God.[504]

At times destructive cults with group compounds have tried to portray such heavily controlled environments as intentional communities or benign communes. A cult compound, however, can be differentiated from a benign community in the following three ways. These ways are noted in the handbook *Cults and Consequences*, which the Jewish Federation of Greater Los Angeles produced.[505]

1. Cults are established by strong and charismatic leaders who control power hierarchies and material resources, but communes tend to minimize organizational structure and to deflate or expel power seekers.
2. Cults possess some revealed "word" in the form of a book, manifesto, or doctrine, whereas communes vaguely invoke general commitments to peace and liberation freedoms and a distaste for the parent culture's establishments.
3. Cults create fortified boundaries, confining their membership in various ways and attacking those who leave as defectors, deserters, or traitors; they recruit sums of money; and they tend to view the outside world with increasing hostility and distrust as the organization ossifies.

Jayanti Tamm relates a firsthand account of life in a destructive cult in her book, *Cartwheels in a Sari: A Memoir of Growing Up Cult*.[506] Ms. Tamm became a visiting professor at Queens College in New York, but a New York group, which the guru Sri Chinmoy led, raised her. Her parents had been followers of Chinmoy before Tamm was born. It wasn't until she was an adult of twenty-five that Tamm left the community to begin a life of her own making outside the group. Eventually her parents also left some seven years later.

Tamm describes Sri Chinmoy's "masterful tactics of manipulation." The guru's group included more than one thousand followers, and he once had celebrity admirers, such as musician Carlos Santana, singer Roberta Flack, and Olympian Carl Lewis. Chinmoy died in 2007.[507]

Tamm offers the unique perspective of someone a destructive cult directly affected. She opines, "Perhaps it is more useful to discern what a religious movement is or what a cult is by comparing its impact upon members' lives: does it complement or control?"[508] Tamm says that cults "are surprisingly similar in their methods...tactics and techniques used to recruit and maintain and disown noncompliant" members; these tactics and techniques seem to be "pulled from a universal handbook."[509] She emphasizes the "absolute and unconditional control"[510] destructive cults express.

Again, the structure, methodology, and overall tactics Tamm describes can be largely grouped in Lifton's three general categories or criteria regarding cultic characteristics as follows:

The Nature of the Leader

Tamm points out, "Cults are fueled by and thrive on control," which comes from "excessive devotion to the leader and the leader's vision." She explains, "The leader's personal agenda is presented as a universal elixir, one that will eradicate both personal and global moral, ethical and spiritual maladies."[511] According to Tamm the leader is seen as "an agent used to unify a disparate collection of strong individuals." And he or she possesses "unquestioned, absolute authority over [group] member's lives."[512] The leader is also made to "seem infallible, to possess the answers, solution, the only route to salvation."[513]

The Group Process of Coercive Persuasion and Control

Tamm says that Chinmoy isolated and controlled members in his group by fostering a sense of spiritual elitism, which led to social isolation.

Tamm says, "There is a clear separation between those 'inside' and 'outside.' Members are holy, special, chosen; outsiders are unholy, ignorant[, and] toxic."[514] She also explains that the group became all encompassing. "Contact with the outside world—often including family—is discouraged, and family is redefined as the group itself...The group assumes all roles—family, friends, church, home, work, community," Tamm says.[515] She also explains that members in the group were influenced to subordinate their thoughts and emotions to the dictates of the leadership. Tamm explains, "Subjugation and subservience is expected and obedience and control demanded."[516] Tamm further recalls how the group emotionally manipulated its members. She explains, "Conformity is enforced through notions of guilt, shame and failure, by both the leader and other members."[517] This drive for conformity can be seen as part of Lifton's thought-reform process the group and its leader used to mold a mind-set.

Harmful Consequences

Tamm notes that the group diminished virtually anything that might reflect independence and promote self-esteem. She says, "Individual achievements [are] discouraged, downplayed and finally eradicated while the group's achievements are encouraged, celebrated and memorialized."[518] The net result was that members of the Chinmoy group continually concentrated their energy and efforts on the guru's goals, not their own. For example, Chinmoy "didn't want his disciples to get an education," Tamm said in an interview.[519] She says that the net result of involvement with the Chinmoy group produced "narrow, claustrophobic existences whose singular purpose is the cult itself" and that "logical reason and facts [became] blurry and nonsensical."[520]

Tamm's mother was reportedly once told to have an abortion and put the guru first. And when Tamm became disillusioned, she was "banished." Tamm says that Sri Chinmoy "sent a message to my parents that

I should be evicted and not be spoken to." Such family estrangements, which cult leaders order, can have devastating results. In Tamm's case she attempted suicide.[521]

Can destructive cults change?

After the death of the founding leader, many cults begin to disintegrate. Without their defining elements and driving forces, most cultic groups eventually fade away. But in some situations, especially when there is a large membership or substantial residue of remaining assets, the cult may continue under new leadership. Professor Benjamin Zablocki recognizes that some cults may evolve and eventually become generally accepted churches or denominations.

Zablocki has defined a cult as "an ideological organization held together by charismatic relationships and demanding total commitment."[522]

In his classic book *The True Believer*, Eric Hoffer writes about a similar progression for some mass movements. Hoffer said that such movements go through stages of development. He called the initial and most volatile stage of that development the "active phase" and observed "there is a natural point of termination once the struggle with the enemy is over or the process of reorganization is nearing completion."[523]

In this sense Hoffer, like Zablocki, provides for the possibility that controversial or revolutionary movements like destructive cults might eventually evolve into relatively reasonable and more mainstream movements. Hoffer notes, "The personality of the leader is probably a crucial factor in determining the nature and duration of a mass movement."[524]

In this light some cults have claimed that they have changed and ceased to behave destructively. The founding leader may have died or been deposed, and the organization claims it has gone through a reformation. Critics of such groups, however, have often expressed skepticism and at times urged caution when evaluating such claims.

When commenting on one group's claims of reformation, Michael Langone, executive director of the International Cultic Studies Association, said, "It seems very unlikely to me that the psychological abuse of members will end without eliminating the cultic dynamics that underlie it." Langone specifically points out the dilemma of "organizational leaders" the founder trained who are part of the historical hierarchy of the group. Though responsible for abuses, they still remained in positions of authority. In this sense Langone sees a kind of group "pathology," which a group founder or past leader develops and nurtures. This pathology is embedded in the group even after its originator is gone. Langone offers as an example of such an embedded pathology a "foundational structure of secrecy [that] probably set the stage for the manipulation and abuse."[525] Noting one group, Langone says that the "tree was rotten from inception. No amount of pruning will eliminate the poison in the seed."[526]

What we can see, based on the various definitions offered for groups called "cults," is that a nucleus for a definition exists and emerges from the various perspectives of researchers and experts. This nucleus has three central categories of characteristics, as Lifton identifies them, and they determine whether a group is a destructive cult. The lengthier definitions experts offer essentially expand upon those three central themes, which are based on the group's type of leadership; the group process of coercive persuasion, which largely shuts down critical thinking; and the inherent destructive nature of the group, which is directly related to its mandates and unchecked leadership.

---

[472] *Merriam-Webster* (Encyclopedia Britanica Company), "cult,"www.merriam-webster.com/dictionary/cult (accessed May 29, 2014).

[473] Hildebrand, Jamie (1994) "The Church of Elvis," *Totem: The University of Western Ontario Journal of Anthropology*: Vol. 1: Iss. 1, Article 4 Available at: http://ir.lib.uwo.ca/totem/vol1/iss1/4.

[474] Robert Jay Lifton, *Thought Reform and the Psychology of Totalism* (Chapel Hill: University of North Carolina Press, 2012).

[475] Robert Jay Lifton, "Cult Formation," *Harvard Mental Health Letter*, February 1981.

[476] Ibid.

[477] Robert Jay Lifton, *Destroying the World to Save It: Aum Shinrikyo, Apocalyptic Violence, and the New Global Terrorism* (New York: Metropolitan Books, 1999), 11.

[478] Margaret Singer, *Cults in Our Midst* (San Francisco, CA: Jossey-Bass, 1996), 7.

[479] Thomas Robbins and Benjamin Zablocki, *Misunderstanding Cults: Searching for Objectivity in a Controversial Field* (Toronto, Ontario, Canada: University of Toronto Press, 2001), 181–193.

[480] Singer, *Cults in Our Midst*, 8.

[481] Ibid., 9.

[482] Narcissistic Personality Disorder—Diagnostic and Statistical Manual of Mental Disorders, Fourth edition Text Revision (DSM-IV-TR), American Psychiatric Association (2000) as cited on the website BehaveNet http://behavenet.com/node/21653 (accessed May 19, 2014).

[483] Stephen A. Kent and Jodi M. Lane, "Malignant Narcissism, L. Ron Hubbard, and Scientology's Policies of Narcissistic Rage" (French journal Criminologie 41 No. 2 in 2008), 7.

[484] Wendy Cole and Richard Woodbury, "In the Grip of a Psychopath," *Time*, May 3, 1993.

[485] Marc Fisher and Sue Ann Pressley, "Founder Sought to Purge Sexuality via Cult," *Washington Post*, March 29, 1997.

[486] Robert D. Hare, *Without Conscience: The Disturbing World of Psychopaths Among Us* (New York: Guilford Press, 1999).

[487] Robert D. Hare, *The Hare Psychopathy Checklist*, rev. ed. (New York: Multi-Health Systems, 1991) .

[488] Richard Ofshe, "Coercive Persuasion and Attitude Change," *Encyclopedia of Sociology*, vol. 1 (New York: McMillan, 1992), 212–224.

[489] Ibid.

[490] Benjamin D Zablocki, "Exit Cost Analysis: A New Approach to the Scientific Study of Brainwashing," *Nova Religion* 2, no. 1 (1998): 216.

[491] Louis Jolyon West and Michael Langone, "Cultism: A Conference for Scholars and Policy Makers. Summary of Proceedings of the Wingspread Conference on Cultism," (lecture, American Family Foundation, Weston, MA, September 9–11, 1985).

[492] International Cultic Studies Association, *Psychological Manipulation, Cultic Groups, and Other Alternative Movements* (conference handbook, ICSA Annual International Conference, Denver, CO, June 22–24, 2006), 68.

[493] Janja Lalich and Michael Langone, "Characteristics Associated with Cultic Groups," rev. ed., International Cultic Association website, 2008, http://www.csj. org/infoserv_cult101/checklis.htm (accessed May 19, 2014).

[494] Ministry of Welfare and Social Services, "An Examination of the Phenomenon of Cults in Israel: Report of the Ministry of Welfare and Social Services Team," State of Israel 2011, http://www.culteducation.com/reference/general/ AnExaminationOfThePhenomenonOfCultsInIsrael.pdf (accessed May 19, 2014).

[495] "The Counter-Cult Movement (CCM)," Ontario Consultants on Religious Tolerance website 1997–2011, http://www.religioustolerance.org/ccm.htm (accessed May 19, 2014).

[496] Rachel Andres and James R. Lane, eds., *Cults and Consequences: The Definite Handbook* (Los Angeles: Jewish Federation of Greater Los Angeles, 1990), 14.

[497] Ibid., 12.

[498] Brooks Alexander, "The Rise of Cosmic Humanism," *Spiritual Counterfeits Project Journal* 5 (Winter 1981–82): 3–4.

[499] "The Anti-Cult Movement (ACM)," Ontario Consultants on Religious Tolerance website 1996–2011, http://www.religioustolerance.org/acm.htm (accessed May 19, 2014).

[500] "Factors Commonly Found in Destructive, Doomsday Groups," Common Signs of Destructive Cults, Ontario Consultants on Religious Tolerance website 1996–2011, http://www.religioustolerance.org/cultsign.htm (accessed May 19, 2014).

[501] Andres and Lane, *Cults and Consequences*, 9.

[502] Benjamin Zablocki, *The Joyful Community: An Account of the Bruderhof: A Communal Movement Now in Its Third Generation* (Chicago: University of Chicago Press, 1971).

[503] Benjamin Zablocki, *Alienation and Charisma: A Study of Contemporary American Communes* (New York: Free Press, 1980).

[504] Stephen A. Kent, *From Slogans to Mantras* (Syracuse, New York: Syracuse University Press, 2001).

[505] Ibid.

[506] Jayanti Tamm, *Cartwheels in a Sari: A Memoir of Growing Up Cult* (New York: Harmony Books, 2009).

[507] Brendan Brosh, "Child of Chinmoy Ministry Blasts 'Cult' in New Book," *New York Daily News*, April 24, 2009.

[508] Jayanti Tamm, "Cults Are Harmful and Extreme Religious Groups," *Cults: Opposing Viewpoints* (Farmington Hills, MI: Greenhaven Press, 2013), 26.

[509] Ibid., 23.

[510] Ibid.

[511] Ibid.

[512] Ibid.

[513] Ibid., 23–24.

[514] Ibid., 23.

[515] Ibid., 23–24.

[516] Ibid., 23.

[517] Ibid., 24.

[518] Ibid., 23.

[519] Brosh, "Child of Chinmoy Ministry Blasts 'Cult' in New Book."

[520] Ibid.

[521] Ibid.

[522] Benjamin Zablocki, "Cults: Theory and Treatment Issues" (lecture, International Cultic Studies Conference, Philadelphia, PA, May 31, 1997).

[523] Eric Hoffer, *The True Believer: Thoughts on the Nature of Mass Movements* (New York: Harper and Row, 1951) 142, 145.

[524] Ibid., 145.

[525] Michael D. Langone, "Reflections on the Legion of Christ 2003–2006" (lecture, International Cultic Studies Association, International Conference, Montreal, Canada, July 5-7, 2012).

[526] Michael Langone, "'By Their Fruits Ye Shall Know Them': How Good and Bad Works Can Deceive—the Case of the Legion of Christ," *ICSA Today* 3 (2012): 5.

CHAPTER 5

"CULT BRAINWASHING"

How do cult leaders convince people to become compliant and obey them? Is there some secret social skill they employ that renders their followers docile and suggestible? In news reports about destructive cults, a crucial element is often left out. How were people persuaded to join a cult group? And how did the cult subsequently convince them to comply with cult teachings and corresponding behavior?

News reports about cult tragedies may use the word *brainwashed* as a means of explaining the unsettling and seemingly mindless obedience of some cult members. This often seems to satisfy disturbing questions about the frequently self-destructive nature of cult behavior—for example, why parents in some faith healing groups have allowed their children to suffer and die needlessly or why followers of David Koresh preferred to be burned to death than to peacefully surrender to authorities at Waco.

Why do some cult members act against their own best interests while consistently behaving in accordance with the wishes of cult leaders? Again, the glib answer often reported is that they were somehow "brainwashed." Otherwise how could the people connected to

147

a reported cult tragedy be so completely persuaded to set aside their common sense, compassion, and priority of self-preservation?

Benjamin Zablocki, a professor of sociology at Rutgers University, did a study of cultic coercive persuasion. In it he has expressed concern regarding "the polarization that has occurred amongst scholars of new religious movements," which have often been called "cults." Zablocki argues that ongoing effort has been exerted to "block attempts to give the concept of brainwashing a fair scientific trial."[527] The researcher laments, "This campaign has resulted in distortion of the original meaning of the concept so that it is generally looked at as having to do with manipulation in recruitment of new members to religious groups." As Zablocki points out, however, the historic understanding of the term *brainwashing*, "on the contrary, should be in connection with the manipulation of exit costs for veteran members."[528]

Brainwashed or *brainwashing* is an imprecise and ambiguous description; nevertheless, it still has currency in contemporary popular culture. Journalist Edward Hunter first used the word *brainwashing* in an article he wrote for the *Miami News* in 1950.[529] Hunter worked as a propaganda specialist for the Office of Strategic Services (OSS) during World War II and later reported about psychological warfare used during the Cold War. Despite its ambiguity, *brainwashing* persists as the most universally understood generic means of expressing the sort of undue influence some extreme forms of leadership may exercise over others. Brainwashing has been used to explain why people enthralled with a particular cause, group, or leader will apparently act against their own interests and consistently in the best interest of those who have influenced them. This metaphorical description implies the existence of a process that can potentially wash the brain clean of its original individual thinking and then supplant and suffuse it with a new mind-set a group, movement, or leader prescribes.

The process is not, however, that simple. And there is a need to go beyond the catch phrases of popular culture to gain a better and more detailed understanding of the far more subtle process destructive cults have typically used to gain undue influence over members. What's also important to note is that brainwashing isn't exclusively used in a religious context. Zablocki says, "I do not mean to imply that there is anything about religion per se that is especially conducive to brainwashing or that brainwashing is not also to be found in political, psychotherapeutic, military or other totalist collectives."[530]

Researchers in the fields of mental health and sociology have developed or delineated a more precise terminology to describe the principal process of conversion destructive cults have used to engender obedience and conformity. Sociologist Zablocki defines brainwashing as "as an observable set of transactions between a charismatically-structured collectivity and an isolated agent of the collectivity with the goal of transforming the agent into a deployable agent. Brainwashing is thus a *process* of ideological resocialization carried out within a *structure* of charismatic authority."[531] Psychiatrist Robert Jay Lifton specifically called the process he observed "thought reform" in his seminal book *Thought Reform and the Psychology of Totalism.*[532] Psychologist and eminent cult expert Margaret Singer categorized the extreme methods cults have used to gain compliance as a thought-reform process, which she said was most often inherently deceptive.[533]

What these researchers have hypothesized, and in many instances confirmed, is that the human mind is far more fragile, persuadable, and malleable than we would like to think. Especially when people are in a state of distress or depression, are experiencing hardships, or are passing through major transition phases in their lives, they are typically more vulnerable to persuasion and other techniques of those who offer appealing answers and seemingly a way out of their difficulties.

Authors Flo Conway and Jim Siegelman presented a communication perspective based on the sudden personality changes and other cognitive alterations associated with cult mind control techniques, described in their book *Snapping: America's Epidemic of Sudden Personality Change.*[534]

They explained how many cults completely distort, manipulate, and control the process of communication in ways that may have a lasting impact on cult members' minds and give rise to a new category of cognitive disorders they termed "information disease." In their later book, *Holy Terror: The Fundamentalist War on America's Freedoms in Religion, Politics, and Our Private Lives*,[535] Conway and Siegelman went on to examine the ritual practices of emotional control cults and many religious groups use. They explained how specific messages and ritualized instructions tied to cult beliefs, scriptures, and images can be manipulated to suppress a person's bedrock emotional responses and everyday feelings in a systematic effort to promote obedience and compliance in the group. Conway and Siegelman's concepts of information disease and emotional control will be discussed in more detail later in this chapter.

This kind of information control was evident in the polygamist compound Warren Jeffs ran; there school and television were banned, and cult members' communication was also carefully regulated. Jeffs dictated everything his followers read and heard, including their music. He created a somber, cocooned, and controlled world where even the color red and the word *fun* were prohibited.[536] Another example of information control was the isolated community of Colonia Dignidad, which Paul Schaefer led. Within this self-contained compound, built at the foot of the Andes Mountains in Chile, no one was allowed to listen to the radio, read newspapers, or walk alone.[537]

Professor of psychology Robert Cialdini researched the basic techniques commonly used to influence people in everyday life.[538] Cialdini's groundbreaking book *Influence* specifically identified these techniques and explained how they could be used through venues as varied as advertising and political propaganda. A destructive cult can also use the same principles of influence in more deceptive and manipulative ways to gain undue influence over its adherents. Later in this chapter Cialdini's principles will be detailed and correlated more broadly with influence techniques cults use. Some cult leaders have researched influence techniques, including Jim Jones, who studied the methods of mind control George Orwell described in his book *1984*.[539] But most cult leaders appear to assemble and refine their methods through a process of trial and error.

Together programs of thought reform, coercive persuasion, and information control can produce the intensified modes of influence we see in destructive cults. This process of systematically applying manipulative techniques of influence, persuasion, and communication to produce persisting states of impaired thinking, feeling, and decision making in cult members has been widely recognized as one of mind control.

Not all forms of influence and persuasion are the same. Psychologist Margaret Singer made distinctions between various types of persuasion, such as education and advertising, and more manipulative coercive methods, such as propaganda, indoctrination, and thought reform.[540] Singer saw the process of thought reform as especially and uniquely rigid and distinctly different from other modes of persuasion. One example, Singer pointed out, is that thought reform effectively precluded any genuine or meaningful exchange of ideas and was instead "one sided" and actually expressed no sincere respect for differences.[541]

Perhaps the most notable distinction between the thought-reform schemes perpetuated by destructive cults, in contrast to other types of persuasion, such as education and advertising, is that they are frequently deceptive. Singer said such programs center "on changing people without their knowledge." She further explained that the structure of this coercive persuasion process takes an "authoritarian" and "hierarchical stance," with no full awareness on the part of the "learner."[542] And unlike advertising, which is persuasive but regulated, cultic thought-reform methods are unregulated, unaccountable, and devoid of respect for the individual.

The deceptive nature of such persuasion, combined with the group's hidden agenda of "changing people without their knowledge," means that people are often deceptively recruited into destructive cults without informed consent.

Michael Lyons, who went by the name Mohan Singh, lured followers into his group, Friends of Mohan, by using the guise of a "naturopathic" healer. He claimed he was "chiropractor to the Queen" and an osteopath.[543] Instead of healing, however, Lyons reportedly subjected his victims to "psychological and emotional control, brainwashing and isolation from families."[544] The Unification Church, commonly called "the "Moonies" and once led by Rev. Sun Myung Moon, has frequently been cited for its "deceptive tactics in recruiting followers."[545] Often targeting students on college campuses, the church operated through a number of front organizations such as the Creative Community Project, Students for an Ethical Society, and the Collegiate Association for the Research of Principles. Students who are initially approached might not even realize that the agenda of the group is religious.

Coercive Persuasion

The pioneering work of MIT professor Edgar Schein, who determined there are three basic stages of "coercive persuasion,"[546] summarized coercive persuasion. These stages are first "unfreezing" the person, then "changing" his or her perceptions, and finally "refreezing" the individual in the changed state. These parallel what many groups identify as the necessity of breaking people down before they can make them over or build them up again. This process can often be accomplished by creating an acute sense of urgency and/or crisis frequently through confrontational tactics and group pressure. This is one of the methodologies used to persuade the individual that change is necessary or imperative.

Later, sociologist Richard Ofshe sought to draw attention to and distinguish the persuasion techniques commonly employed by cults. He expanded upon Schein's earlier work in his study of coercive persuasion.[547] Ofshe built upon Edgar Schein's three stages of coercive persuasion,[548] and identified "four key factors that distinguish coercive persuasion from other training and socialization schemes."[549]

1. The reliance on intense interpersonal and psychological attack to destabilize an individual sense of self to promote compliance
2. The use of an organized peer group
3. The application of interpersonal pressure to promote conformity
4. The manipulation of the totality of the person's social environment to stabilize behavior once it has been modified

We can see an example of this process in practice in the rehabilitation community known as Synanon, led by Charles Dederich. Synanon used its seminars, which evolved into highly confrontational "attack therapy," to coerce its members. This coercion was called "the game."[550] During such sessions participants were surrounded by peers, who barraged them with criticism and berated them. This attack ultimately caused people caught in the game to collapse and readily accept suggested change. Subsequently Synanon members became submissive and compliant in conforming to the group's norms. In this way the community coercively controlled everything, including relationships and even infants in what was called the "hatchery."[551] Nothing was immune from Synanon's process of coercive persuasion. Hundreds of couples were even induced to divorce on demand.[552] In a ritual practice he called the "squeeze," this same group process was used as a tool to purge those members who somehow managed to harbor doubts about Dederich.[553]

Singer expanded on three basic steps of coercive persuasion, which Schein had outlined.[554]

1. "Unfreezing" or what Singer described as "the destabilizing of a person's sense of self." This process often includes "keeping the person unaware of what is going on and the changes taking place. Controlling the person's time and if possible their physical environment. Creating a sense of powerless covert fear and dependency. And suppressing much of the person's old behavior and attitudes."

2. "Changing" or what Singer explained as "getting the person to drastically reinterpret his or her life's history and radically alter his or her worldview and accept a new version of reality and causality."

3. "Refreezing," or as Singer said, "Put forth a closed system of logic; allow no real input or criticism." Ultimately this culminates in what Singer described as a person frozen or "dependent upon the organization…a deployable agent."

Thought Reform

Robert Jay Lifton first explained these basic building blocks of the cult-control process in detail in his eight criteria for identifying the existence of a thought-reform program.[555] Lifton said, "In identifying, on the basis of this study of thought reform, features common to all expressions of ideological totalism, I wish to suggest a set of criteria against which any environment may be judged, a basis for answering the ever-recurring question: 'Isn't this just like 'brainwashing'?"[556]

Lifton's eight defining criteria are as follows:

1. "Milieu Control," which Ofshe later interpreted as "the control of communication" within an environment.[557] This may include virtually everything a person might potentially see, hear, or read—as well as his or her personal associations. By controlling whatever enters the mind, destructive cults can largely control the mind itself.

2. "Mystical Manipulation," which Ofshe interpreted as "emotional and behavioral manipulation" That is typically accomplished in the guise of group beliefs and practices and often uses elements of deception in the controlled environment. This step could potentially be done by manipulating the daily news, anecdotal information, meditation, or religious writings in an effort to influence the thinking and feelings of group members.

3. "The Demand for Purity" or what Ofshe described as "demands for absolute conformity to behavior as prescribed and derived from the group ideology."[558] People subject to such demands may in a sense take personal inventory and relentlessly categorize their thoughts, emotions, and behavior per the group or leader's dictates. Lifton called this a "spurious cataloguing of feelings," which reflects the "peculiar aura of half-reality" within a "totalist environment" such as a destructive cult. The net result of this criterion is often "black and white thinking" or pushing people into a position where they feel they must pick between what the group labels "good" or "evil."

4. "The Cult of Confession" or what Ofshe sees as "obsessive demands for confession." This confession may be done on an individual basis, group basis, or both. The underlying assumption or premise is that there really is no individual right to privacy and that whatever is known must be disclosed. This also constitutes what Lifton calls "symbolic self-surrender" to the absolute authority of the leadership. In groups where confession is strongly emphasized, people may confess in an exaggerated sense to what they have done or, as Lifton says, "to crimes one has not committed." In the drug-rehabilitation community known as Synanon, group confession was formalized in what was called "the game." An individual was seated in the center of the group on what was known as the "hot seat" and bombarded with confrontational questions and criticism until he or she was broken. Many destructive cults have historically used a format of breaking sessions based on confession.

5. "The Sacred Science," or what Ofshe explains as "agreement that the group ideology is faultless" or that it is essentially perfect. Lifton describes this as an "ultimate vision for the ordering of all human existence." Whatever the leader or group determines is right must be right, and whatever is labeled wrong is wrong. People influenced by such a "Sacred Science"

will routinely subject their value judgments to its narrow rules. Within the world of Sacred Science, as in the Demand for Purity, there is no space for ambiguity or shades of gray.

6. "Loading the Language" or what Ofshe describes as the "manipulation of language in which clichés substitute for analytic thought." Lifton has characterized this as "thought terminating clichés," which are "brief, highly reductive, definitive-sounding phrases" that become insider verbiage the group frequently uses. Many groups or subcultures have their own insider jargon, but Lifton draws distinctions between that verbiage and what he describes as "totalist language," which "is repetitiously centered on all-encompassing jargon, prematurely abstract, highly categorical [and] relentlessly judging." And rather than being used as a means of communicating individual ideas and personal opinions, Lifton sees it as "the language of nonthought."

7. "Doctrine Over Person," as Ofshe explains, is the "reinterpretation of human experience and emotion in terms of doctrine" or as seen through the lens or the group mind-set and its world view. Everyone and everything must be subjected to, and fitted in, this doctrinal framework, including those who use it.

8. "The Dispensing of Existence," which Ofshe interprets as the "classification of those not sharing the ideology as inferior and not worthy of respect." These criteria can create a sense of elitism and social isolation. Lifton explains, "The totalist environment draws a sharp line between those whose right to existence can be recognized and those who possess no such right." The only means of validation is acceptance of the group and its beliefs. Lifton says, "Existence comes to depend upon creed (I believe, therefore I am), upon submission (I obey, therefore I am) and beyond these, upon a sense of total merger with the ideological movement." Under such influence cult members

may dispense with the existence of family, old friends, previous goals, and aspirations. Nothing has a right to exist unless it fits within the framework of the group and the Sacred Science, as its leadership has dictated.

Lifton notes, "The more clearly an environment expresses these eight psychological themes, the greater its resemblance to ideological totalism; and the more it utilizes such totalist devices to change people, the greater its resemblance to thought reform."[559] Sociologist Benjamin Zablocki observed, "It is probably not necessary to have every one of Lifton's eight structural characteristics of ideological totalism in place for [thought reform] to occur."[560]

These criteria may be expressed in varying degrees of intensity from group to group. Typically the more control a particular group seeks to exert over its members, the more it may intensify or express these eight criteria. For example, not all destructive cults maintain group compounds, but we may see the maintenance of such compounds as a more intensified means of exerting control over the environment, or what Lifton cites as "Milieu Control." Another understanding is that the more extreme the demands of the group are, the more extreme the controlling criteria may be expressed to meet those demands.

Not all individuals will respond in exactly the same way to such group controls. Some may become unhappy and leave due to conditions in the group environment, or leadership may reject them due to their lack of compliance. Likewise, each individual initially brings his or her own unique history and personality to the group experience, which to varying degrees provides the basis for his or her response to the leadership. Some may be more vulnerable than others due to their circumstances or individual history. The deceptive manner in which a destructive cult presents itself can also potentially affect people differently. For example, some may respond more readily to a group using a facade of religion as opposed to one of philosophy, politics, or pseudoscience, based on their personal interests and background. And individual interest or deference can account for an initial or ongoing acceptance of the group's imperatives, which are given in the guise of some religious, political, or otherwise relatable context.

This cult process of manipulation doesn't require overt physical coercion but may instead in part rely on sleep deprivation, dietary controls, intimidation, implied threats, or inducement of unreasonable fears. Sociologist Benjamin Zablocki notes, "Cult movements rarely retain their members by the use of physical force or constraint. But is the necessity of force or the threat of force required for true brainwashing? This widespread belief is based upon a misreading of Lifton and Schein. This misreading came about because, in fact, many (although by no means all) of the cases they studied were brought to a state of agency by real or threatened force."[561]

Zablocki, like Schein, sees this process in three phases, the third drawn from Lifton.

1. "The stripping phase: The cognitive goal of the stripping phase is to destroy prior convictions and prior relationships of belonging. The emotional goal of the stripping phase is to create the need for attachments. Overall, at the completion of the stripping phase, the situation is such that the individual is hungry for convictions and attachments and dependent upon the collectivity to supply them."

2. "The identification phase: The cognitive goal of the identification phase is to establish imitative search for conviction and bring about the erosion of the habit of incredulity. The emotional goal of the identification phase is to instill the habit of acting out through attachment. Overall, at the completion of the identification phase, the individual has begun the practice of relying on the collectivity for beliefs and for a cyclic emotional pattern of arousal and comfort."

3. "The symbolic death and rebirth phase: In the rebirth phase, the cognitive and the emotional tracks come together and mutually support each other. This often gives the individual a sense of having emerged from a tunnel and an experience of spiritual rebirth. The cognitive goal of the rebirth phase is to establish a sense of ownership of (and pride of ownership in) the new convictions."[562]

"Information Disease"

The long-term impact of the control and manipulation of information can be seen in a collection of symptoms Flo Conway and Jim Siegelman call "information disease."[563] They define this as "an alteration through experience of a person's everyday information processing capacities—his [or her] everyday powers of thinking, feeling, perception, memory, imagination and conscious choice." And that it "marks a lasting change of awareness at the most fundamental level of personality." We can see this in the suicides of Solar Temple members. Initially, there was a reported "mass suicide" in 1994, which included leader Luc Joret and more than seventy of his followers. But the lasting impact of Joret's influence and the group experience was evident in the continuing suicides of surviving Solar Temple members over the following three years. The last suicides linked to the group occurred in 1997.[564] The cult-related changes in thinking that occurred continued to dominate and animate the lives of surviving Solar Temple members until they ended them.

According to Conway and Siegelman, information disease can also result in part from physical causes such as "poor diet and lack of sleep,"[565] which have been reported in many cults, including the Unification Church, founded by the Reverend Moon.[566] Former members of that group allege that they were fed a low-protein diet and often slept only four to five hours a night. But the authors say information disease may also occur solely as the "result of information alone, especially from intense experiences that abuse an individual's natural capacities for thought and feeling." In the carefully managed confines of a Unification Church training retreat, potential recruits can see and experience only what the group wants according to its planned program. All access to information and personal associations is under tight group control. In this environment participants experience what has been called "love bombing," which is a term used to describe the seemingly unconditional affection church members direct toward them. However, this "love" is actually highly conditional and based on their growing acceptance of Unification Church principles and corresponding progress in the group. This contrived but intense experience in the context of a controlled group environment can produce the desired commitment.

After recovering from her experience under the control of the political cult called the Symbionese Liberation Army, the heiress Patty Hearst commented that she had been told how to think. Upon reflection Hearst compared the process she endured to something like "the disciplining of your mind."[567]

Conway and Siegelman notably include such practices as "group encounter, guided fantasy [and] meditation" as a means of implementation. The authors conclude, "By tampering with basic distinctions between reality and fantasy, right and wrong, past, present and future, or simply by stilling the workings of the mind over time, these intense communication practices may break down vital faculties of mind." The authors also point out that there is growing evidence that such abuses may ultimately "impair crucial working connections in the brain's underlying synaptic networks and neurochemical channels," which may potentially "destroy long-standing information processing pathways in the brain." [568]

Such changes in the brain were the focus of the book *Craving for Ecstasy* by professors Harvey Milkman and Stanley Sunderwirth, which examines how addiction and behavior affect the brain. Milkman and Sunderwirth, who specialize in brain chemistry, reinforce Conway and Siegelman's observations. They write, "Individuals can change their brain chemistry through immersion in salient mood-altering activities as well as through ingesting intoxicating substances." The researchers add, "If our synaptic chemistry changes dramatically we seem to possess altogether different personalities."[569] The authors specifically cite the power of "cults," which they say "may be used to short-circuit the usual course of an addictive process." They then offer "the tragic example of Jonestown, blind devotion to a religious cult," which "burned a path straight to the suicidal vortex."[570] The comparison of cults to chemical addiction may explain the seemingly addictive pattern of behavior often evident in cultic involvement. This analogy may also explain why discontinuing that involvement, especially after years of reinforcement, is frequently difficult.

Conway and Siegelman have identified "four distinct varieties of information disease" we can see by observing an affected individual.

1. "Ongoing altered state of awareness"—characterized as a "state of narrowed or reduced awareness." This can be brought on by an encapsulated environment controlled by a group and/or leader that virtually excludes any other focus or outside frame of reference.
2. "Delusional phase"—"vivid delusions [and] hallucinations" that lead to "irrational, violent and self-destructive behavior," which can be brought on through techniques of sensory deprivation and/or overload
3. "Not thinking"—"literally shutting off the mind"
4. "Not feeling"—"actively suppressing one's emotional responses" that may "ultimately numb a person's capacity for human feeling"[571]

Marshall Applewhite, the leader of the Heaven's Gate cult, prohibited his followers from watching television and strictly regulated their reading. Each member of the group had an assigned partner and was told never to be alone. These measures were taken "to keep [members] in the mindset." Communication was often limited to simply saying "Yes," "No," or "I don't know."[572]

"Emotional Control"

Conway and Siegelman succinctly explain in their first book, *Snapping: America's Epidemic of Sudden Personality Change*, how the mind can be stymied, sidetracked, and potentially subjugated by what it sees as "information disease." In their second book, *Holy Terror: The Fundamentalist War on America's Freedoms in Religion, Politics, and Our Private Lives*, they discuss the interlocking emotional control that controlling groups and leaders often use.

Conway and Siegelman write, "Because as human beings, beyond all differences of faith and culture, our feelings are our most important resource, our most complex and fully integrated and universal communication capacity. They may also be our most accurate monitor of personal morality—of what is right and wrong for each of us as individuals—and of the fairness of our conduct in relation to one another. When at that intimate level the wisdom of our feelings is stilled, distorted or thrown into confusion, our greatest strength may quickly be turned into our greatest vulnerability."[573]

The authors explain that such emotional control is achieved through "the reduction of individual response to basic emotions such as love, guilt, fear, anger, hatred, etc." This is accomplished by "means of suggestion" through "the indirect use of cues, code words, symbols, images and myths." For example, Bible-based groups may use the images of Jesus and Satan to emotionally manipulate members. In his book *Thought Reform and the Psychology of Totalism*, Robert Jay Lifton correlates the use of such imagery to the category of "ultimate terms" or "God terms" and "devil terms."[574]

This means of manipulation allows its practitioners to assign any action or feeling they perceive as negative or challenging to their authority in the category of "satanic" or "demonic" while simultaneously using the image of Jesus or God as a facade for their own authority. Within this box, whenever disobedience occurs or doubts surface, they are consigned to the devil or dark forces. Obedience to the leadership is correspondingly characterized as compliance to the will of God and heavenly authority.

In the family cult Marcus Wesson led, his children were taught that he was "God's messenger" and that the "end times" were "close at hand." One son said, "He was God. That's just the way it was."[575] Within the confines of this construct to obey Wesson was to obey God. Disobedience was, therefore, defiance of God. Those who opposed Wesson, such as the authorities, were characterized as "Satan."[576] Caught within this world of polarized imagery, one of Wesson's daughters said she felt "trapped."

But religious imagery isn't the only way such ultimate terms can be used. Secular symbols can easily be used, such as the popular principles and corresponding icons of business, art, philosophy, nationalism, political theory, psychology, philosophy, or virtually any field of interest.

Conway and Siegelman summarize that ultimately "the secret is surrender."[577] That is, surrender is not seen as giving in to the authority of a group or leader but rather as subordinating yourself to a supposedly higher cosmic power, honored purpose, or principle. It is by posing behind a carefully constructed facade of myths, symbols, and/or images that the practitioners of such indirect manipulation can effectively garner obedience, engender dependence, and ultimately solidify their control.

Powerful Suggestions

Certain suggestible states induced through hypnosis, trance induction, meditation, yoga, chanting, and various repeated physical exercises may also serve as a means of manipulation. These altered states of consciousness can potentially make people malleable. In such an altered state, techniques may be applied such as guided imagery, indirect directives, and peer pressure. Modeling of behavior can be used more effectively. If a licensed mental health professional uses such techniques, ethical concerns may arise, since the use of these techniques is most often done without informed consent.

The process of guided imagery has been used in hypnotherapy.[578] The subject is first in an induced state of deep relaxation or trance. This can be brought about through hypnosis, certain forms of meditation, yoga, chanting and breathing exercises. In this state of mind, a leader or therapist can then guide an individual or group to experience various feelings, an imagined environment, or sensations. Psychologist Margaret Singer observes, "A considerable number of different guided imagery techniques are used by cult leaders and trainers to remove followers from their normal frame of reference."[579] Wrapped within the mystique of a cult, such guided imagery can become a facet of what Lifton calls "Mystical Manipulation" and used to mold a mind-set and shape perceptions of reality to build an alternate cult reality.

The Indian professor of philosophy and self-styled guru known as Bhagwan Shree Rajneesh conducted what he called "Dynamic" and "Kundalini" meditation camps, in which his followers were transformed through the suggestible states of the experience.[580] One former devotee remarked, "I think I brainwashed myself" but observed, "Bhagwan had one line: the good disciple follows what the master says, the good disciple doesn't think."[581]

Indirect directives can also be an effective means of persuasion. Singer says, "Cult leaders who have become skillful at getting acts carried out through indirection and implication," rather than by directly ordering something to be done. That is, to "imply that something should happen, and it does."[582] This can also be achieved through the tone of voice, asking a question that prompts an action and offering other indirect suggestions that solicit compliance. Cult members often attempt to deflect accusations that they observe mindless obedience by offering the apology that no one directly orders them to do anything. Submission to authority and compliance, however, can be achieved indirectly.

Peer pressure and modeling, according to Singer, "[are] an effective means to get people to fit their behavior to group norms." This goal is achieved by noting "models around to imitate."[583] For example, those in a new environment created by a cult may observe the behavior, dress, and speech of others around them to understand the preferred way of living within that environment. Change largely occurs without direct demands being made; it occurs through the influence of the group environment. Singer explains, "The clever cult leader or mind manipulator manages to use the innate tendencies toward group conformity that we bring with us as a powerful tool for change."[584]

Influence Techniques

Robert Cialdini, professor of psychology at Arizona State University, lists "six principles of influence" within social environments.[585] These basic principles are inherently neither good nor bad; rather they exist as the foundational building blocks of influence.

1. "The rule of reciprocity," Cialdini says, is a "sense of future obligation according to the rule [that] makes possible the development of various kinds of continuing relationships, transactions, and exchanges that are beneficial to society. Consequently, virtually all members of society are trained from childhood to abide by this rule or suffer serious social disapproval." Expounding on this principle, Singer says cults can twist this basic rule regarding behavior. That is, the cult provides a sense of security, salvation, well-being, and love but implicitly expects its devotees to repay these benefits through obedience and behavioral compliance. Singer also points out

that this rule can be used to induce feelings of guilt and shame. She says, "If you have made a commitment to the group and then break it, you can be made to feel guilty" and by extension ashamed.[586]

2. "Commitment and consistency"—Cialdini points out that "people have a desire to look consistent through their words, beliefs, attitudes, and deeds," which are "highly valued by society." Singer explains that a destructive cult can use this rule to make its members feel guilty whenever they somehow fall short regarding their performance or are inconsistent in their duties and obligations as understood by the commitments they have made to the group.

3. "Social proof"—Cialdini says that the "means used to determine what is correct is to find out what others believe is correct. People often view a behavior as more correct in a given situation, to the degree that we see others performing it." Within a cult environment, Singer sees this as yet another means for achieving compliance. She explains, "If you look around in the group, you will see people behaving in particular ways. You imitate what you see and assume that such behavior is proper, good, and expected."[587]

4. "Liking," Cialdini says, is the principle that "people prefer to say yes to individuals they know and like." Singer elaborates that new initiates within a cult group may be the target of seemingly unconditional love, frequently called "love bombing." This may make members feel wanted and loved; therefore, it pushes them to reciprocate by liking the people in the group who "love" them. Now that they like members of the group, it follows that they should comply with their concerns. Singer says, "You feel you ought to obey these people."[588]

5. "Authority," Cialdini says, is characterized by "the strong pressure within our society for compliance when requested by an authority figure" and "that such obedience constitutes correct conduct." Singer explains that one can easily apply this ubiquitous tendency to respect authority to a cult leader who "claims superior knowledge, power, and a special mission."[589] In fact, members of destructive cults frequently see their leader as the ultimate authority, who may eventually come to supersede any other authority, such as the law, law enforcement, and government authorities.

6. "Scarcity," Cialdini says, is the simple principle that "people assign more value to opportunities when they are less available." Singer sees this principle as analogous to cult members who are told that "without the group they will miss out on living life without stress; miss out on attaining cosmic awareness and bliss; miss out on changing the world, gaining the ability to travel back in time; or whatever the group offers that is tailored to seem essential."[590] The group may also exemplify this rule through a claim of exclusivity, such as the claim that no other group exists that can offer the same or equal path of attainment and fulfillment.

Authority

There seems to be an innate human reliance on, and compliance with, authority. Yale University psychologist Stanley Milgram laid a foundation for this understanding in his seminal research, which made points other researchers later used in their work.[591] The Milgram experiment, done in 1961, was an examination of the predisposed human tendencies to obey authority figures, even when such obedience violated ethical concerns. This proclivity partly explains the subservience and submission of cult members under the influence of a perceived authority figure they have been persuaded to accept.

Milgram's experiment included student volunteers functioning in the roles of "teachers" or "learners," who were separated from each other in individual rooms. Teachers would question learners. When the answer was wrong, teachers administered an electric shock to the respondents. The shocks were supposedly increased incrementally until they became quite severe. What teachers didn't know was that learners were only actors pretending; no electrical shock was actually administered. The focus of the experiment was to see how compliant teachers would remain to authority, even when they witnessed increasing distress and pain from the learners. Whenever teachers hesitated, verbal prodding encouraged them. In the end, despite the learners' feigned screams of agony, 65 percent (twenty-six out of forty) of those functioning as teachers willingly administered shocks of up to 450 volts. [592]

Verbal prodding consisted of a succession of encouragement from the authority figure:

1. "Please continue."
2. "The experiment requires that you continue."
3. "It is absolutely essential that you continue."
4. "You have no other choice; you must go on."

Teachers were also told that they had no responsibility regarding the shocks administered.

Milgram summarized his experiment in an article titled "The Perils of Obedience"[593] as follows:

> The legal and philosophic aspects of obedience are of enormous importance, but they say very little about how most people behave in concrete situations. I set up a simple experiment at Yale University to test how much pain an ordinary citizen would inflict on another person simply because he was ordered to by an experimental scientist. Stark authority was pitted against the subjects' strongest moral

imperatives against hurting others, and, with the subjects' ears ringing with the screams of the victims, authority won more often than not. The extreme willingness of adults to go to almost any lengths on the command of an authority constitutes the chief finding of the study and the fact most urgently demanding explanation.

Milgram concluded,

Ordinary people, simply doing their jobs, and without any particular hostility on their part, can become agents in a terrible destructive process. Moreover, even when the destructive effects of their work become patently clear and they are asked to carry out actions incompatible with fundamental standards of morality, relatively few people have the resources needed to resist authority.

Milgram proposed two interpretations or theories pertaining to the ultimate meaning of his research experiment.

1. The theory of conformism is based on the Solomon Asch conformity experiments or what has been called the "Asch Paradigm."[594] That is, when someone feels unable or unqualified to make decisions, he or she is likely to defer to an authority, most especially in a crisis situation.
2. The agent state theory, Milgram says, is "the essence of obedience [that] consists in the fact that [people come] to view themselves as the instrument for carrying out another person's wishes, and they therefore no longer see themselves as responsible for their actions. Once this critical shift of viewpoint has occurred in the person, all of the essential features of obedience follow."

Milgram's explanations of behavior can also be useful in developing an understanding of the obedience cult members display in their responses to the often-extreme and destructive demands their leaders make. Cult members in such situations see themselves as the agents of some higher power or authority and are therefore exonerated of any personal responsibility for their actions. Moreover, if any doubts arise, they feel compelled to marginalize such concerns in deference to a higher authority and conform to whatever behavior their leader prescribes. Cult leaders may also create the perception of a crisis or impending catastrophe as a means of leveraging greater submission. Cult members must obey and conform to the leader's demands to gain a sense or assurance and safety. This is commonly expressed when leaders in many "doomsday cults" claim only their faithful flock will be protected from some final judgment or dispensation.

Philip Zimbardo, Stanford University professor of psychology, did additional research about the influence of authority and dynamics of group persuasion. He conducted what became known as the "Stanford Prison Experiment" in 1971. Zimbardo chose a group of students to play the roles of prisoners and guards in a simulated prison environment set up in the basement of the Stanford University psychology building. Zimbardo led a team of researchers and played the pivotal role as the "prison superintendent."[595]

What the prison experiment substantially demonstrated through largely anecdotal evidence was that a controlled authoritarian environment could potentially have a profound effect on the behavior of those involved. Zimbardo's prisoners became increasingly docile and obedient, while those playing guards became harsh and rigid. The Stanford Prison Experiment, much like the research of Stanley Milgram a decade earlier, offers compelling evidence that environment and authority can affect the way a person thinks and feels, and then influence his or her behavior. Zimbardo's research strongly suggests that in certain situations and environments, ordinary, ostensibly normal people can be influenced to do harmful things. This harmful behavior, which otherwise would seem objectionable, is nevertheless done under the influence of a perceived authority.

Similar patterns of behavior have been observed in destructive cults and often to a greater degree in the more tightly controlled environment of a cult compound. Certain members may be designated to roles of subordinate leadership or enforcement, while the general members frequently function in various degrees of subservience. Those in the role of enforcers often become increasingly harsh as they reinforce the rules or implement the edicts of leadership, even though their previous personal history may not reflect this type of behavior. In this sense the group dynamic of the cult has a profound effect on the personalities and behavior of those involved; the result is much like that of the Stanford Prison Experiment but over a much more prolonged period of time.

Personality Change

Flavil Yeakley, a researcher with a BA degree in psychology and MA and PhD degrees in speech communications, studied the effects of group influence on individual personality traits in a controversial church, which had been called a cult.[596] Yeakley comes from a distinctly evangelical Christian perspective in his book. His concern was that the group he examined was engaged in a kind of cloning process through its indoctrination and corresponding pressure tactics. Yeakley suspected that there was an effort to influence members of the group to think, feel, and behave the same way. He wrote, "A central element in the criticism that has been directed against the Boston Church of Christ [BCC], other discipling churches, and the discipling movement generally has been the charge that these churches employ methods that produce unnatural and unhealthy personality changes. Critics charge that discipling churches tend to make the members over after the image of the group leader, the group norm, or the group ideal."[597]

The "discipling" methodology Yeakley examined was based on a system of training through an ascending hierarchal structure of authority. Every member of the group was assigned to a discipling partner that became an advisor with implicit authority. The established chain of command continued, until it culminated in a single supreme leader at the top, named Kip McKean. What Yeakley's research suggests is that the group essentially developed and preferred a prototype largely based on the personality of Kip McKean. Yeakley came to this conclusion by testing nine hundred members of the group.[598] He used the Myers-Briggs Type Indicator (MBTI) as his preferred testing instrument.[599] The MBTI is a descriptive test sometimes used in psychological contexts. It is used as a tool to describe personality differences. Sixteen outcomes are possible in the MBTI; they reflect various combinations of personality traits.

Yeakley explained that the creators of the MBTI surmised, from their study of Swiss psychotherapist and psychiatrist Carl C. Jung's writings, "that some people prefer to deal with the world through a judging process (either thinking or feeling), while others prefer to deal with the world through a perception process (either sensing or intuition)... Those who prefer to extravert a judging process tend to be highly organized while those who prefer to extravert a perception process tend to be adaptable."[600]

Critics of the MBTI have noted, "Although we do not conclude that the absence of bimodality [functioning as more than one type] necessarily proves that the MBTI developers' theory-based assumption of categorical 'types' of personality is invalid, the absence of empirical bimodality in IRT [item response theory] based MBTI scores does indeed remove a potentially powerful line of evidence that was previously available to 'type' advocates to cite in defense of their position."[601] In fact, the accuracy of the MBTI depends on the honesty of the person who is being tested, since his or her chosen response to questions determines the results. In 1991 a committee of the National Academy of Sciences concluded that there was "not sufficient, well-designed research to justify the use of the MBTI in career counseling programs."[602] Self-reporting and psychometrically weak tests like the MBTI can confuse results when participants answer in socially desirable ways. The limitations of the MBTI should be taken into account when the results are interpreted.

Tested members of the BCC were asked to respond to the MBTI three times. Yeakley relied on their honesty in responding to questions. He explains, "One time the members were told to answer the questions the way they think they would have before their conversion [entrance into the BCC] or five years ago for the few who had been members that long. The members were also told to answer the questions the way they would at that present time. Finally, they were told to answer the questions the way they think they will answer them after they have been discipled [by the BCC] for five more years."

Yeakley noted "the degree of change in psychological type scores" and saw there was a "pattern of convergence in a single type." The MBTI personality profile ESFJ (i.e. extroverted, sensing, feeling judging) was the preferred and sought after point of convergence. Yeakley observed that "the past distribution [before entering the BCC] was the closest to population norms while the present and future distributions increasingly deviated from those norms."[603] Additional testing of other churches or organizations used as control groups appeared to show similar results.[604] Yeakley explains, "What was being investigated in this research was simply the overall group pattern. The focus was not on any individual, but on the dynamics of the group."[605]

We should note that Yeakley's testing results might also be attributed to the so-called halo effect or halo bias. [606] That is, those BCC members he tested may have tried to emulate qualities they attributed to their leader, Kip McKean, because he was perceived as an ideal person. Marty Wooten, a prominent group leader who worked closely with McKean, demonstrated this fact. Wooten said, "I cannot think of any virtue that Kip is not known for. There is no greater discipler, disciple, brother, husband, father, leader, and friend than Kip McKean. Some say it is dangerous to respect any one man that much. I believe it is more dangerous not to."[607] Another ranking leader in the BCC, Jim Blough, said, "Let me tell you my attitude towards Kip. Let me explain to you. You know, I may have a good quality here and there, occasionally. If you look hard enough, you can find one in almost everyone, you know. But I believe this. I believe if I could become exactly like Kip, I'll be a whole lot more useful to God than I am by myself."[608]

Based on his study, Yeakley interpreted and hypothesized the following:

1. "Most of the members of the Boston Church of Christ showed a high level of change in psychological type scores."
2. "There was a strong tendency for introverts to become extroverts, for [intuitive people] to become [sensing people], for thinkers to become feelers, and for perceivers to become judgers."
3. "This kind of pattern was not found among other churches of Christ or among members of five mainline denominations, but that it was found in studies of six manipulative sects."[609]

Interestingly, the "manipulative sects" Yeakley referred to with the same pattern of results as the BCC included the Unification Church, Scientology, Hare Krishnas (ISKCON), and the Children of God.[610]

What Yeakley hoped to demonstrate through his research was the process of personal manipulation, which he believed occurred through the discipleship training process within the BCC. His research results can be seen as a possible confirmation of the process of coercive persuasion Edgar Schein identified.[611] That is, the discipleship training appeared to employ a process of "unfreezing," "changing," and then "refreezing" people. Yeakley says, "To the extent that the members respond to that group pressure, the observed changes in psychological type scores are likely to become (or have already become) actual changes in the personality that is manifested."[612]

We should note that the results Yeakley achieved were descriptive and do not precisely explain why these changes occurred or whether they can be seen as permanent. Most probably without continuing group pressure and influence, the observed changes could crumble and ultimately dissipate. Yeakley's study can be helpful, though, in understanding how malleable people can be within a group environment that uses extreme pressure to manipulate and influence behavior. His study demonstrates that personality characteristics can be affected and shaped through high pressure tactics and then perhaps hardened in place.

Lifton also describes how people influenced by a thought-reform program strip themselves of anything objectionable or at variance with the preferred prototype of the true believer. He says, "Yet one underlying assumption makes this arrogance mandatory: the conviction that there is just one path to true existence, just one valid mode of being, and that all others are perforce invalid and false. Totalists thus feel themselves compelled to destroy all possibilities of false existence as a means of furthering the great plan of true existence to which they are committed." [613]

Yeakley's book warned of the potential consequences that could be linked to the "falsification of psychological type." He opined that it might produce detrimental results such as a "serious midlife crisis" and "major burn-out problems, serious depression, and a variety of other psychological…problems."[614]

One of the most reported cult personality transformations in history was Leslie Van Houten, a former follower of Charles Manson. Van Houten grew up in a comfortable middle-class neighborhood and was a high school cheerleader. But under Manson's influence, at the age of nineteen in 1969, she stabbed one of the cult's targeted victims fourteen to sixteen times in the back.[615] After decades of imprisonment, the former cult member said, "Everything that was good and decent in me I threw away." It was only through her imposed separation from the group through imprisonment and her father's visits that she apparently came to realize "what had happened."[616] Repeatedly denied parole, Van Houten tried to explain her alleged rehabilitation before a parole board hearing in 2003. She said, "I was raised to be a decent human being. I turned into a monster and I have spent these years going back to a decent human being." During her incarceration Leslie Van Houten became a model prisoner, earned college degrees, and worked for a prison supervisor.[617]

Less stigmatized and more sympathetic examples of radical cult transformations include Patty Hearst and Elizabeth Smart. Both women were kidnapped, and their captors radically transformed them. Only after leaving that influence did they both return to their normal lives. The cult persona Hearst and Smart had once been manipulated to embrace then became a historical anomaly.

Cognitive Dissonance

In his description of "Milieu Control," Lifton notes that such an environment "never succeeds in becoming absolute, and its own human apparatus can, when permeated by outside information—become subject to discordant 'noise.'"[618] The source of that outside information, which can permeate a controlled environment, could potentially be the Internet, television, radio, newspapers, or people outside the group, such as old friends and family. This influence could include anything that might provide an outside frame of reference.

How then do destructive cults bent on psychological and emotional control shut out or deal with uncontrollable "discordant noise," which can create profound internal conflict in the minds of their adherents?

Cognitive dissonance is a term used in psychology and is often included in the paradigm of cultic persuasion and control. This theory is frequently the basis for understanding how cult-involved individuals can continue to cling to beliefs even when facts contradict them. Cognitive dissonance theory explains that cult members can resolve such conflicts by essentially spinning or accepting rationalizations. It is this spinning process that then reconciles the dissonance between their cultic beliefs and reality. For example, a mother in a faith healing group may reconcile the needless death of her child by proclaiming that it was somehow "God's will" rather than admit the death was, in fact, the result of medical neglect.

Leon Festinger first used the description of cognitive dissonance in his book *When Prophecy Fails*. [619] The book tells the story of a UFO cult led by a woman named Dorothy Martin (1900–1992), also known as "Marian Keech," who predicted the end of the world but foretold that aliens from another planet would rescue her followers on a precise date (December 21, 1954). When her prophecy failed, members of the group, who had given up everything to follow Keech, nevertheless remained loyal and committed believers.

Festinger proposes five factors that provide a basis for cognitive dissonance to be successfully implemented to resolve such a failure, which he calls "unequivocal disconfirmation."[620]

1. There must be a deep conviction concerning the belief.
2. There must be commitment to this conviction.
3. The belief must be amenable to unequivocal disconfirmation.
4. Such unequivocal disconfirmation must occur.
5. Social support must be available after the disconfirmation.

Deep conviction is a common attribute among cult members. This commitment can be expressed through years of hard work, surrender of assets, isolation from family and old friends, and the renouncing of previously held goals and ambitions in favor of a group or leader's agenda. What this means is that cult members may have a considerable amount of literal and emotional equity in the group and its beliefs. It is because of this considerable personal investment that deeply committed members are likely to accept whatever rationalization or explanation is offered to obviate the "unequivocal disconfirmation" or some failure in the group.

Members frequently cling to such rationalizations rather than accept the more alarming alternative, which is that all their efforts and sacrifices may have been for nothing. Others in similar circumstances within the group will join them in their willingness to accept convenient apologies for failure and offer whatever social support is necessary to protect and secure the sense of equity and mutual sacrifice they share in common. This can also be seen as a refusal to bear the "exit cost" of leaving the group. Sociologist Benjamin Zablocki generally defines such "exit costs" cult members consider as "all disincentives for leaving." Zablocki includes "costs ranging from financial penalties, to relational commitments to various sorts of cognitive and emotional dependencies."[621]

In what is one of the most poignant examples of cognitive dissonance, Waco Davidian survivors Clive Doyle and Sheila Martin continue to cling to their beliefs about David Koresh despite the fact that the cult leader's prophecies led to death and destruction, not heavenly fulfillment. Eighteen years after the fire that claimed the lives of seventy-six Davidians, including Doyle's daughter who was one of Koresh's "wives" as well as Martin's husband and four of her seven children, their loyalty remains unshaken.

The two aging cult members support each other in their continuing commitment. Sheila Martin says God wanted the fire and destruction. "I don't expect you to understand," she told a reporter. But she admits, "We didn't have a plan for death. I wondered: Did someone change the plan without telling me?" Nevertheless Martin still insists,

"David is the messiah, and he's coming back…Now we just wait for the kingdom."

Clive Doyle explains, "When people ask why we still believe in David and what he preached, after everything, I think they are asking because they really do want to understand." Martin concurs. "I think they'll realize someday everything is under his order, and they'll understand that it's not really a choice."[622] Despite the historical facts the two cultists cannot face the disconfirmation of Koresh's demise and have decided instead to interpret the end in a way that allows them to continue as true believers. This response is most probably linked to the devastating losses they both suffered and the corresponding emotional equity they share. Admitting that David Koresh was a delusional cult leader and fraud would mean that all their sacrifices were for nothing. Rather than bear those exit costs, they have instead embraced what can be seen as cognitive dissonance.

"Psychology of the Pawn"

All these interlocking schemes based on information and emotional control, personality change, and influence techniques lead to an ultimate end result, which Lifton calls "the psychology of the pawn." Margaret Singer defined six conditions necessary to be "changed one step at a time to become deployable to serve the leaders" of a destructive cult.[623] She said, "The degree to which these conditions are present increases the level of restiveness enforced by the cult and the overall effectiveness of the program."[624]

1. "Keep the person unaware that there is an agenda to control or change the person." Few cultic groups or leaders readily or willingly admit their agenda or ultimate purpose. They may conceal certain teachings from new members and generally endeavor to rationalize anything that may potentially seem negative. No one intentionally joins a destructive cult.

2. "Control time and physical environment (contacts, information)"—These vary from group to group. Minimally they may mean becoming cocooned within a social environment that monopolizes time and constrains associations, but they can become as extreme as an isolated compound like Jonestown.

3. "Create a sense of powerlessness, fear and dependency"—This has been called "learned helplessness." Members are afraid to leave and become dependent on the group for a sense of security, safety, and purpose.

4. "Suppress old behavior and attitudes"—This is the breaking-down process of an individual personality.

5. "Instill new behavior and attitude"—This is a changing process to adopt more acceptable personality traits and corresponding characteristic behavior approved by the group.

6. "Put forth a closed system of logic"—This is based on what Lifton calls a "Sacred Science" that cannot be questioned. And this then becomes the basis of all value judgments.

In this role of "pawn" in a destructive cult, the victim of thought reform may largely feel helpless. As previously mentioned, that response has been called a type of "learned helplessness." This condition is often associated with battered women who develop a diminished "sense of mastery and self-esteem," and correspondingly this hinders their "ability to take active steps to change their situation."[625] Victims of both domestic violence and cults are often made to feel they can never be "good enough." This feeling renders them largely dependent on their controlling influence for validation of their self-worth and contributes to a belief that without that controlling influence, they would be largely "helpless." Lifton describes the helpless pawn, controlled by thought reform: "Unable to escape from forces more powerful than himself, he subordinates everything to adapting himself to them. He becomes sensitive to all kinds of cues, expert at anticipating environmental pressures, and skillful in riding them in such a way that his psychological energies merge with the tide rather than turn painfully against himself. This requires that he participate actively in the manipulation of others, as well as in the endless round of betrayals and self-betrayals which are required."[626]

Psychologist Margaret Singer sees this as the primary purpose of destructive cults—that is, through their "tactics of thought reform" they cast those under their sway in the role of pawns. She explains that this tactical process is used to "develop in the person a dependence on the organization, and thereby turn the person into a deployable agent of the organization."[627] Zablocki defines a deployable agent as "one who is uncritically obedient to directives perceived as charismatically legitimate. A deployable agent can be relied on to continue to carry out the wishes of the collectivity regardless of his own hedonic interests and in the absence of any external controls." He explains, "Deployability can be operationalized as the likelihood that the individual will continue to comply with hitherto ego-dystonic demands of the collectivity (e.g., mending, ironing, mowing the lawn, smuggling, rape, child abuse, murder) when not under surveillance."[628]

Many cults repeatedly claim that their members are "free to leave whenever they want." But the insidious tactics of thought reform often render its victims psychologically and emotionally unable to escape. This is what sociologist Benjamin Zablocki describes as "the paradox of feeling trapped in what is nominally a voluntary association."[629]

Zablocki has also answered the question: why isn't everyone exposed to cultic coercive persuasion and influence techniques trapped? He explains, "Often it is assumed that a demonstration that not all a cult movement's members were brainwashed is equivalent to proof that none were brainwashed. But why does this follow? No leader needs that many deployable agents. The right question to ask is not whether all Moonies [Unification Church members] are brainwashed, but whether any Moonies were brainwashed."[630]

Zablocki adds, "A common misconception about turnover data in cults stems from confusion between the efficiency of brainwashing and the efficacy of brainwashing...But nothing in the brainwashing conjecture predicts that it will work on everybody, and it says nothing at all about the proportion of recruits who will become agents." Zablocki points out, "For the system to perpetuate itself, the yield need only produce a sufficient number of deployable agents to compensate it for resources required to maintain the brainwashing process." Rather than seeing the dropout rate of destructive cults as somehow providing proof that brainwashing doesn't work, Zablocki observes, "In general, dropout rates tell us only about the rigor of the program, not about its effectiveness for those who stick it through to the end."[631]

What is commonly called "cult brainwashing" is actually a composite of coercive persuasion and undue influence techniques used in an interconnecting process. The various facets of this process and how its pieces fit together and enable each other are best understood through the detailed explanation of thought reform and coercive persuasion. Both information and emotional control are powerful tools used in this context. The foundation of the process is built on basic principles of influence and is continually reinforced in large part by the human tendency to defer to authority.

This chapter includes some of the seminal research done that forms the framework, but there is much more evidence that reflects an innate human vulnerability to such schemes when people are ignorant or unaware that they are being used. Again, some cult leaders have actually studied coercive persuasion and influence techniques in an effort to copy and craft their own version, while others have simply learned from experience how to control and manipulate their followers. A common operating principle seems to be that destructive cult leaders like what they control and don't like what they cannot.

Those outside the world of destructive cults often become unsettled and at times even horrified by the strange and seemingly mystical power cult leaders appear to possess. As previously pointed out, cults often use convenient masks to hide their true intentions and ultimate objectives. They may pose behind the facade of religion, philosophy, politics, business schemes, therapies, pseudoscience, and miscellaneous forms of exercise, nutrition, meditation, and martial arts. But the truth about destructive cults is that if you remove their outer veneer, they are in fact quite similar. That is, they most often have the same basic structure of authority and rely on virtually an identical process of persuasion and corresponding group dynamics to gain undue influence.

As outlined in a previous chapter regarding the definition of a destructive cult, it is not what the group believes but rather how it behaves that defines it. Destructive cults behave badly. They deceptively employ tactical thought reform, which quells independent thinking and engenders dependency in an effort to attain compliance. This is all done with little regard for collateral damage, which destructive cults rationalize as a necessary evil. Cult leaders instead seem to be relentlessly focused on their own needs and fulfillment; that is the hidden agenda of most, if not all, destructive cults.

---

[527] Benjamin Zablocki, "The Blacklisting of a Concept: The Strange History of Brainwashing Conjecture in the Sociology of Religion," *Nova Religion* 1, no. 1 (October 1, 1997): 91.

[528] Ibid.

[529] John Marks, *The Search for the Manchurian Candidate: The CIA and Mind Control* (New York: Times Books, 1979), 12–30.

[530] Benjamin Zablocki, "Exit Cost Analysis: A New Approach to the Scientific Study of Brainwashing," Nova Religion 2, no. 1 (1998): 216.

[531] Thomas Robbins and Benjamin Zablocki, *Misunderstanding Cults: Searching for Objectivity in a Controversial Field* (University of Toronto Press, 2001), 181–193.

[532] Robert Jay Lifton, *Thought Reform and the Psychology of Totalism* (Chapel Hill: University of North Carolina Press, 2012).

[533] Margaret Singer, *Cults in Our Midst* (San Francisco,CA: Jossey-Bass, 1996), 58–59.

[534] Flo Conway and Jim Siegelman, *Snapping: America's Epidemic of Sudden Personality Change*, 2nd ed. (New York: Stillpoint Press, 2005).

[535] Flo Conway and Jim Siegelman, *Holy Terror: The Fundamentalist War on America's Freedoms in Religion, Politics, and Our Private Lives* (New York: Doubleday, 1982).

[536] Daphne Bramham, "Warren Jeffs: Prophet or Monster?" *Vancouver Sun*, September 8, 2007.

[537] Marcelo Mackinnon, "Inside Chile's Colony of Terror," *Ohmy News International* (South Korea), February 1, 2007.

[538] Robert B. Cialdini, *Influence: Science and Practice* (Needham Heights, MA: Allyn & Bacon, 2001).

[539] Melissa Dittman, "Lessons from Jonestown," *Monitor on Psychology* 34, no. 10 (2003): 36.

[540] Ibid., 6.

[541] Singer, *Cults in Our Midst*, 58–59.

[542] Ibid., 59.

[543] Lucy Ballinger and Colin Fernandez, "Rapist 'Guru' in a Bentley Cast His Spell on Hundreds of Terrified Young Women," *Daily Mail* (London), July 27, 2010.

[544] Ibid.

[545] Steve Herman, "Unification Church founder Dies at 92," *Voice of America*, September 2, 2012.

[546] Edgar H. Schein, *Coercive Persuasion: A Socio-psychological Analysis of the 'Brainwashing' of American Civilian Prisoners by the Chinese Communists* (New York: W.W. Norton, 1971).

[547] Richard Ofshe, "Coercive Persuasion and Attitude Change," *Encyclopedia of Sociology*, vol. 1 (New York: McMillan, 1992), 212–224.

[548] Schein, *Coercive Persuasion: A Socio-psychological Analysis of the 'Brainwashing' of American Civilian Prisoners by the Chinese Communists*.

[549] Ofshe, "Coercive Persuasion and Attitude Change," 212–224.

[550] Paul Morantz and Hal Lancaster, *Escape* (Los Angeles: Figueroa Press, 2012), 92.

[551] Ibid., 95.

[552] Lawrence Van Gelder, "Charles Dederich, 83, Synanon Founder, Dies," *New York Times*, March 4, 1997.

[553] Morantz and Lancaster, *Escape*, 95.

[554] Singer, *Cults in Our Midst*, 62.

[555] Lifton, *Thought Reform and the Psychology of Totalism*, 419–437.

[556] Ibid., 420.

[557] Ofshe, "Coercive Persuasion and Attitude Change," 212–224.

[558] Ibid.

[559] Lifton, *Thought Reform and the Psychology of Totalism*, 435.

[560] Zablocki, "Exit Cost Analysis: A New Approach to the Scientific Study of Brainwashing," 222.

[561] Ibid., 231.

[562] Robbins and Zablocki, *Misunderstanding Cults: Searching for Objectivity in a Controversial Field*, 181–193.

[563] Conway and Siegelman, *Snapping: America's Epidemic of Sudden Personality Change*, 147.

[564] Sean Gordon, "Trial Highlights Canadian Cult Link," *Toronto Star*, October 1, 2006.

[565] Conway and Siegelman, *Snapping: America's Epidemic of Sudden Personality Change*, 189.

[566] Joe Schoenmann, "Unification Church 'Means Business' with Las Vegas facility," *Las Vegas Sun*, August 30, 2011.

[567] Patricia Hurst and members of the Smart family, interview by Larry King, *Larry King Live*, CNN, March 13, 2003.

[568] Conway and Siegelman, *Snapping: America's Epidemic of Sudden Personality Change*, 149–150.

[569] Harvey Milkman and Stanley Sunderwirth, *Craving for Ecstasy: The Consciousness and Chemistry of Escape* (Lanham, MD: Lexington Books, 1987), 6–7.

[570] Ibid., 173.

[571] Ibid., 150.

[572] Joshua Bearman, "Heaven's Gate: The Sequel. Ten Years after the 39 Suicides, the Sole Survivor Is Back—and He Has Something Urgent to Tell Us," *LA Weekly*, March 29, 2007.

[573] Conway and Siegelman, *Holy Terror: The Fundamentalist War on America's Freedoms in Religion, Politics and Our Private Lives*, (New York: Doubleday; 1st edition June 1982), 216.

[574] Lifton, *Thought Reform and the Psychology of Totalism*, 429.

[575] Jay Schadler and Elissa Stohler, "Family Brainwashed by Dad Struggles to Heal," *ABC News*, July 6, 2010.

[576] Cyndee Fontana, Barbara Anderson, and Donald E. Coleman, "The Many Portraits of Marcus Wesson," *Fresno Bee*, April 18, 2004.

[577] Conway and Siegelman, *Holy Terror*, 206.

[578] H. Leuner, "Guided Affective Imagery (GAI): A Method of Intensive Psychotherapy," *American Journal of Psychotherapy* 23, no. 1 (1969): 4–22.

[579] Singer, *Cults in Our Midst*, 157.

[580] "Glimpses into the Life of the Controversial Guru," *The Times of India* (Haryana), December 21, 2003.

[581] "Escaping the Bhagwan," *The Age* (Sydney), April 11, 2009.

[582] Margaret Singer, *Cults in Our Midst* (San Francisco, CA: Jossey-Bass, 1996), 160.

[583] Ibid., 167–168.

[584] Ibid., 168.

[585] Cialdini, *Influence: Science and Practice.*

[586] Singer, *Cults in Our Midst*, 170.

[587] Ibid.

[588] Ibid.

[589] Ibid.

[590] Ibid.

[591] Stanley Milgram, "Behavioral Study of Obedience," *Journal of Abnormal and Social Psychology* 67, no. 4 (1963).

[592] Ibid.

[593] Stanley Milgram, "The Perils of Obedience," *Harper's Magazine*, 1974.

[594] S. E. Asch, "Studies of Independence and Conformity: A Minority of One against a Unanimous Majority." *Psychological Monographs* 70, no. 416 (1956).

593 The Stanford Prison Experiment website (1999–2013) http://www.prisonexp.org/psychology/41 (accessed May 19, 2014).

594 Flavil R. Yeakley Jr., *The Discipling Dilemma: A Study of the Discipling Movement among Churches of Christ* (Nashville, TN: Gospel Advocate, 1988).

595 Ibid., 24.

596 Ibid.

597 Isabel Myers and Kathrine Briggs, "The Myers-Briggs Type Indicator" (Palo Alto, California: Consulting Psychologists Press, 1976).

598 Yeakley, *The Discipling Dilemma: A Study of the Discipling Movement among Churches of Christ*, 26.

599 T. L. Bess and R. J. Harvey, "Bimodal score distributions and the MBTI: Fact or artifact?" *The Annual Conference of the Society for Industrial and Organizational Psychology* (San Diego, 2001).

600 K. Nowack, "Is the Myers Briggs Type Indicator the Right Tool to Use?" *American Society of Training and Development*, Fall 1996, 6.

601 Yeakley, *The Discipling Dilemma: A Study of the Discipling Movement among Churches of Christ*, 40.

602 Ibid., 33–34, 42, 44.

603 Ibid., 30.

604 Edward L. Thorndike, "A Constant Error in Psychological Ratings," *Journal of Applied Psychology* 4, no. 1 (March 1920): 25–29.

605 Jerry Jones, "What Does the Boston Movement Teach?" Volume 1, (Bridgeton, MO: Mid-America Book and Tape Sales, 1990), 43.

606 Ibid., 38.

607 Yeakley, *The Discipling Dilemma: A Study of the Discipling Movement among Churches of Christ*, 39.

608 Ibid., 33.

609 Schein, *Coercive Persuasion: A Socio-psychological Analysis of the 'Brainwashing' of American Civilian Prisoners by the Chinese Communists.*

610 Yeakley, *The Discipling Dilemma: A Study of the Discipling Movement among Churches of Christ*, 38.

611 Lifton, *Thought Reform and the Psychology of Totalism*, 434.

612 Yeakley, *The Discipling Dilemma: A Study of the Discipling Movement among Churches of Christ*, 84.

[613] "Charles Manson Cult Member Denied Parole for the 15th Time," *Channel News Asia CNA* (Singapore), August 26, 2004.

[614] Linda Deutsch, "Charles Manson Follower Krenwinkle Denied Parole," *Associated Press*, January 11, 2011.

[615] "Judge to Hear Parole Plea of Manson Follower," *Daily (LA) News*, May 20, 2002.

[616] Lifton, *Thought Reform and the Psychology of Totalism*, 421.

[617] Leon Festinger, Henry W. Riecken, and Stanley Schachter, *When Prophecy Fails* (Minneapolis: Wilder, 2011).

[618] Ibid., 216.

[619] Zablocki, "Exit Cost Analysis: A New Approach to the Scientific Study of Brainwashing," 219.

[620] Ashley Frantz, "18 Years after Waco, Davidians Believe Koresh Was God," *CNN*, April 14, 2011.

[621] Singer, *Cults in Our Midst*, 59.

[622] Ibid., 64.

[623] Roger E. Mitchell and Christine A. Hodson, "Coping with Domestic Violence: Social Support and Psychological Health among Battered Women," *American Journal of Community Psychology* 11, no. 6 (1983).

[624] Lifton, *Thought Reform and the Psychology of Totalism*, 423.

[625] Singer, *Cults in Our Midst*, 69.

[626] Robbins and Zablocki, *Misunderstanding Cults: Searching for Objectivity in a Controversial Field*, 181–193.

[627] Zablocki, "Exit Cost Analysis: A New Approach to the Scientific Study of Brainwashing," 219–220.

[628] Ibid., 228.

[629] Ibid., 228–229.

CHAPTER 6

HISTORY OF CULT-INTERVENTION WORK

Professionals engaged in cult-intervention work have historically used many titles. Beginning in the 1970s, the first title used was "cult deprogrammer." This title is specifically linked to the process of deprogramming or unraveling a program a destructive cult used based on behavioral, emotional, and psychological control. The job description of the cult deprogrammer seems to be permanently etched on popular culture and may remain the most common label the general public uses and understands to describe cult-intervention work.

Ted Patrick

Ted Patrick was the first cult deprogrammer, and he originated the term *deprogramming* in the early 1970s.[632] Patrick said, "Deprogramming is like taking a car out of the garage that hasn't been driven for a year. The battery has gone down, and in order to start it up you've got to put jumper cables on it. It will go dead again. So you keep the motor running until it builds up its own power. This is what rehabilitation is. Once we get the mind working, we keep it working long enough so that the person gets in the habit of thinking and making decisions again."[633] This vivid analogy identifies the essential elements of cult-intervention work. Patrick also said that cults often use "fear, guilt, poor diet and fatigue" to recruit and retain members.[634]

The activities of a notorious group called the Children of God (COG), now known as Family International, founded by David Berg, initially drew Ted Patrick to the issue of destructive cults. The group, which is known for the sexual abuse of minor children,[635] tried to recruit Patrick's son.[636] As the head of community relations for San Diego and Imperial counties in California, Patrick also received complaints from distressed families about the group. He infiltrated COG in the summer of 1971 to investigate how it worked.[637]

Patrick, who attended public school for only ten years, developed his deprogramming approach by "trial and error," which he refined through many cases.[638] According to cult researchers Flo Conway and Jim Siegelman, who wrote about cults in the book *Snapping: America's Epidemic of Sudden Personality Change*, Patrick "probed with questions…until he found the key point of contention at the center of each member's encapsulated beliefs. Once he found that point, Patrick hit it head on, until the entire programmed state of mind gave way."[639] A man Patrick successfully deprogrammed confirmed, "Ted took me to the limits with a series of questions."[640] But Ted Patrick said he didn't promote a particular belief system in the context of his intervention work. "When I deprogram people I don't make any mention of a church or whether or not I even believe in God. That's beside the point. My intention is to get their minds working again and to get them back out in the world," he said.[641] Eventually others copied or adapted Patrick's method of intervention and began doing deprogramming across the United States.[642]

Psychologist Margaret Singer, a discriminating observer of cult-intervention work since its inception, interviewed many former cultists.

She later wrote, "Deprogramming is providing members with information about the cult and showing them how their own decision-making power had been taken away from them."[643] Singer's succinct description continues to be an accurate understanding of what actually forms the foundation for cult-intervention work and is a precise explanation of the basic process.

Ted Patrick did some involuntary deprogrammings based on court action with the cooperation of authorities. During the 1970s in some situations through legal proceedings, parents were granted temporary conservatorship over a cult-involved adult child; that is, using the judicial system, families were able to retrieve and deprogram cult victims. Some called this process "kidnapping by court order."[644] However, eventually such conservatorships were ruled unconstitutional.[645] The court noted that there might be "a compelling state interest in preventing fraud under the guise of religious belief" but ultimately cited constitutional protection concerning the freedom of religion, which effectively protected religious cults. Only when there were actions that posed "some substantial threat to public safety, peace or order" was there a legal basis for intervention. The court said, "We conclude that in the absence of such actions as render the adult believer himself gravely disabled as defined in the law of this state; the processes of this state cannot be used to deprive the believer of his freedom of action and to subject him to involuntary treatment."[646]

Ted Patrick nevertheless continued to do both voluntary and involuntary interventions regardless of court rulings, and he paid a price for his anticult activism. He was repeatedly arrested, criminally prosecuted, and imprisoned on kidnapping charges stemming from his involuntary deprogramming efforts. Patrick was also sued in various cult-related cases two dozen times for claims totaling $100 million.[647]

Ted Patrick was accused of violence. He said, "The cults tell them [cult members] that I rape women and beat them."[648] However, researchers Conway and Siegelman said, "No parent, ex-cult member or other reliable witness we talked to ever substantiated any of those charges."[649] Former cult deprogrammer Steve Hassan, who participated in involuntary cult interventions during the late 1970s, points out, "Deprogrammers were falsely portrayed as beating and raping people to force them to recant their religious beliefs. For the record, I know of no instance of deprogramming (and I've met hundreds of deprogrammees) that involved any physical abuse such as beating or rape. No family I have ever met would go to the extreme of rescuing a loved one through deprogramming and allow anyone to harm their child in any way."[650]

Legal Concerns

Concern developed among cult-intervention specialists and cult-watching organizations regarding the use of the word *deprogrammer*. Hassan notes, "By the late 1970s, the question of mind control had become intertwined in the public eye with the issue of forcible deprogramming. This occurrence was partly the result of public relations campaigns financed by certain major cults to discredit critics and divert the debate from the cults themselves."[651] Conway and Siegelman wrote that all the legal action taken against deprogrammers "brought a global chill" to the issue."[652] Hassan reflects, "The truth is that [in voluntary] deprogramming is extremely risky in legal terms."[653] For some time, however, Hassan continued to recognize the need for such involuntary interventions. He writes, "Forcible intervention can be kept as a last resort if all other attempts fail."[654] But Conway and Siegelman summarized the final situation: "In the new climate, judges were deaf to the pleas of the parents and families of cult members, and the precarious deprogramming profession was largely eclipsed by the efforts of the new generation of cult 'exit counselors.'"[655]

A succession of new titles and corresponding terminology emerged and evolved as many cult-intervention professionals in the United

States distanced themselves from the title "deprogrammer" and the term "deprogramming." This aversion has included titles such as "exit counselor," "exit counseling," "strategic interaction approach," "high demand group consultant," "cult information specialist," "thought-reform consultant," "cult mediator" and my own professional preference, "cult-intervention specialist."

Despite the proliferation of new labels used to describe cult-intervention work during the 1980s and 1990s, Margaret Singer remarked, "In fact, 'deprogramming' is in many ways a more accurate description of the process of getting the cult member to recognize what has happened to him or her, but since that word is now tinged with memories of the early snatchings and restraint, most people are reluctant to use it."[656]

However, a small group of cult-intervention specialists noted, "Not all deprogrammings were 'rescue and hold' situations. There were some where the group member was free to leave at any time and there were some where ex-members sought voluntary deprogramming."[657] Despite this fact many professionals still felt it was necessary to respond to well-financed cult propaganda and litigation by altering titles and adapting new terminology.

One group led by exit counselor Carol Giambalvo nevertheless tacitly recognized the reasoning and practical considerations that had historically prompted involuntary deprogramming. Families often based their decision to take such extreme action on "the fact that in some groups, members were zealously protected from parents, often having their names changed and moved from locations to location."[658] Sadly, this fact remains true today in some situations. The same concerns about involvement in destructive cults persist and may include such issues as financial exploitation, family estrangement, medical neglect, and physical and/or sexual abuse.

Deprogramming Court Cases

Ted Patrick went through a series of legal battles regarding his involuntary deprogramming work. In 1974 he was charged with kidnapping Kathy Crampton but was acquitted. The judge stated, "The parents who would do less than what Mr. and Mrs. Crampton did for their daughter Kathy would be less than responsible, loving parents. Parents like the Cramptons here, have justifiable grounds, when they are of the reasonable belief that their child is in danger, under hypnosis or drugs, or both, and that their child is not able to make a free, voluntary, knowledgeable decision."[659]

In 1980 Patrick was found guilty of conspiracy, kidnapping, and false imprisonment concerning an attempted involuntary deprogramming, which resulted in a one-year prison sentence.[660]

In 1990 Ted Patrick attempted to deprogram Elma Miller, an Amish woman who joined a splinter Amish group, which apparently drew the concern of her family. Criminal conspiracy charges were filed against Patrick, Miller's husband, and Miller's brother. Miller later requested that charges against her family be dropped, and the prosecutor subsequently decided to dismiss the criminal charges filed against Patrick.[661]

In 1992 New York cult deprogrammer Galen Kelly was arrested and prosecuted in a federal court in Virginia.[662] It seems that he grabbed the wrong cult member, which Kelly and his attorney believed had been a "set up."[663] Kelly was found guilty and served one year in prison before an appeal overturned his conviction.[664] The federal prosecutor in the Kelly case was later suspended amid allegations of prosecutorial misconduct.[665]

Cult deprogrammers Joseph Szimhart and Kenneth J. Paolini were acquitted of aiding and abetting a kidnapping in 1993. The kidnapping reportedly took place in early November 1991. The two men were hired to deprogram a member of the controversial Church Universal and Triumphant, founded by Elizabeth Clare Prophet. The deprogramming effort failed. Also charged was cult deprogrammer Mary Alice Chronalagar, who had once worked with Ted Patrick. The jury couldn't agree on a verdict for Chronalagar.[666]

My cult-intervention work, which began in 1982, has included the involuntary deprogramming of adults. In 1991 I assisted a mother in an attempt to rescue her eighteen-year-old son, Jason Scott. He was involved in a controversial fringe Pentecostal group located in Bellevue, Washington. This intervention effort failed, and I was charged and later prosecuted for unlawful imprisonment. My trial ended with a jury verdict of not guilty and acquittal.[667] Subsequently, Kendrick Moxon, a lawyer closely associated with Scientology, reportedly recommended to Scott that he file a civil lawsuit.[668] That lawsuit ended with a judgment against me for almost $3 million, which was subsequently settled largely for my consultation time and $5,000 in cash.[669] The settlement was concluded after Scott left the group, which had caused his mother concern, and he fired Moxon. Jason Scott later concluded that he had been used through the litigation."[670] "I was naïve. I just kind of rode the waves of what they wanted me to do," he said.[671]

Perhaps the most recently known example of an involuntary deprogramming took place in Canada during 2006. Parents in Burlington, Ontario, reportedly believed their twenty-two-year-old daughter was involved with a "cult" in Hamilton, Ontario. They abducted the young woman and held her for ten days before she escaped. The father, a family doctor, was later charged with kidnapping and forcible confinement. The mother, a secondary school teacher, was also charged.[672] Two of the couple's other children were also involved in the deprogramming attempt. US cult deprogrammer Mary Alice Chronalagar was involved but fled across the border and wasn't charged. Chronalagar later told a reporter, "I didn't come up there to take part in anything; I did come up there and talked to the family." She then reportedly refused to answer any other questions.[673] The charges against the parents and one sibling were eventually dropped at the daughter's request.

However, the young woman's older brother, a twenty-nine-year-old law student, entered guilty pleas to kidnapping and forcible confinement. He was sentenced to a fifteen-month term of house arrest and community supervision.[674]

I no longer do involuntary cult-intervention work with adults, though such an involuntary intervention for minor children remains completely legal in the United States when it is under the direct supervision of their legal guardian or custodial parents. But despite my decision to abandon involuntary intervention work with adults, I deeply sympathize with families and others concerned who may find themselves facing an extreme situation, in which voluntary interventions seem to be improbable, if not impossible, due to a lack of meaningful access as a direct result of cultic influence and manipulation.

After his acquittal in 1993, deprogrammer Kenneth J. Paolini said, "What pulls on you is when a parent calls and says, 'I'm desperate.'"[675] But today, regardless of how desperate the situation may be, due to legal concerns, cult-intervention professionals in the United States have abandoned involuntary intervention, with the possible exception of minor children under the direct supervision of a custodial parent or legal guardian.

Evolution of Deprogramming

What was once called "deprogramming" remains largely the same process used today for cult-intervention work, but it is done only with adults on a voluntary basis. Conway and Siegelman succinctly described the deprogramming process in their book *Snapping: America's Epidemic of Sudden Personality Change*. The authors wrote, "It appears to be a genuinely broadening, expanding personal change, it would seem to bear closer resemblance to a true moment of enlightenment, to the natural process of personal growth and newfound awareness and understanding, than to the narrowing changes brought about by cult rituals and artificially induced group ordeals."[676] Steve Hassan, himself a former member of the Reverend Moon's Unification Church, related about his own deprogramming, "I had the indescribable experience of my mind suddenly opening up, as if a light switch had been thrown." He concluded that this was like "rediscovering myself."[677]

In the second edition of Conway and Siegelman's *Snapping: America's Epidemic of Sudden Personality Change*, they explain that the "methods of voluntary deprogramming and exit-counseling, while far less controversial and much safer from a legal standpoint, prompted fewer cult members to experience a sudden 'snapping out' of their controlled states of mind."[678] Instead, as I discussed with the authors, what now most often occurs is a slower, less pronounced moment of emergence or "gradual 'unfolding' from the cults' ingrained altered states."[679]

From the time of Ted Patrick to today, cult-intervention work has evolved and changed. But the essential elements for a successful intervention remain largely intact and based on an educational model and process. The essential building blocks are the following: learning about the inherent dynamics and authoritarian structure of destructive cults; reviewing the systematic persuasion, influence, and control techniques evident in such groups; sharing historical information about the particular group or leader; and understanding the family concerns that led to the intervention.

The goal of cult intervention remains intrinsically the same—that is, to stimulate critical thinking and promote independence and individual autonomy. Such an intervention is an information-driven process centered on an examination of relevant research material within the context of an ongoing discussion or dialogue; this often pointedly questions the basic assumptions held within the group. The result should provide a factual basis for a more informed decision-making process in respect to the individual's further involvement with the group or leader.

This educational process requires the careful preparation of all concerned parties who will participate in the intervention. Much like an alcohol or drug intervention, a cult intervention typically occurs as a complete surprise to avoid outside interference and to ensure at least the initial participation of the person who is the focus of the intervention effort. Families and other concerned individuals go through a consultation or educational process, which may include relevant reading, preliminary discussion, and finally specially focused preparation immediately before the intervention begins. Today that preparation and intervention process is made much easier by accessing information through the Internet, educational DVDs, and e-mail. The advent of the Internet and expansion of the World Wide Web have greatly enhanced the deprogramming process, which has always heavily depended on information.

Steve Hassan

Steve Hassan, who became a professional counselor during his years as a cult deprogrammer, put together what many observers consider to be a viable approach to cult intervention. Hassan calls it the "strategic interaction approach" (SIA), which purportedly "emphasizes the value of meeting with trained consultants to be effectively guided and coached and also to plan and implement effective interventions." Hassan's approach incorporates aspects of family and individual counseling, personal coaching, and education. Hassan says, "In the SIA, each person has issues that should be addressed. One focus is on the growth and development of healthy relationships within the family. The safe and nurturing environment created by the SIA offers many opportunities to heal old wounds. As an integral part of the family system, the cult member is automatically included in the process."[680]

Hassan's hybrid approach to cult-intervention work has also drawn criticism. Other professionals working in the area of destructive cults have expressed ethical concerns about Hassan's melded methodology, which he initially termed "strategic intervention therapy."

Calling his approach "strategic intervention [sic] therapy," Hassan (1988) stresses that, although he too tries to communicate a body of information to cultists and to help them think independently, he also does formal counseling. As with many humanistic counseling approaches, Hassan's runs the risk of imposing clarity, however subtly, on the framework's foundational ambiguity and thereby manipulating the client.[681]

Dr. Cathleen Mann, a PhD in psychology, has been a licensed counselor for over eighteen years and has been court qualified as an expert witness in cult-related cases across America. Mann also provides training and supervision for other counselors and is a licensed provider of counseling and assessment for children, families, and adults affected by cults. In some situations she has also participated in cult-intervention efforts.

Mann, like Michael Langone, draws distinctions between counseling and cult-intervention work. According to Mann, "The very nature of counseling is persuasive. This is why informed consent must occur first. A counselor cannot be objective and subjective at the same time."[682] This is in stark contrast to a cult intervention, which like most interventions begins as a surprise. Mann further explains the ethical requirements of professional counseling. "The counseling relationship should be entered into openly by virtue of the informed consent process. Informed consent means that a client knows the methods and duration of counseling, what theories or techniques will be used, and what types of effects can be expected from counseling."

Hassan also engages in what he calls "covert interventions," which involve deception. He explains that this as "an attempt to counsel the cult member without his knowing that the family is trying to help him reevaluate his involvement." Hassan adds, "It is tricky to find a pretext to meet the individual and gain enough time to do much good."[683] However, Mann states, "The counseling relationship needs to be entered into voluntarily and not contain any coercion, deception, or manipulation. Counseling should always be a choice."[684]

Mann defines the boundaries of what she considers an ethical cult intervention. "In an intervention, information about a cult's deception and manipulation should be the sole focus." She warns, "It is destructive to provide counseling on personal or family issues when the sole reason the intervention was created was to focus on education and information, rather than trying to counsel family with a legion of existing problems, some of which may not be related to the cult issue." Dr. Mann, who has conducted many forensic evaluations for courts in child custody, fraud, and parental alienation cases, concludes, "It is a myth, and not supported by the research, that family pathology is the 'root' cause of cult involvement. People affiliate with cults because of deception, not because their families are dysfunctional."[685]

Ethical Concerns

Ted Patrick once mused, "Sooner or later, they're going to have to recognize deprogramming as a profession."[686] An effort to do just that took place in the late 1990s. Cult-exit counselor Carol Giambalvo, along with others who were formerly associated with deprogramming, launched a professional group called "thought reform consultants."[687] This small group tried to establish ethical standards for their profession based on an adaptation of the codes and standards of the American Association for Marriage and Family Therapy, the National Association of Social Workers, the Private Practice of Clinical Social Work, the American Psychiatric Association, and the National Academy of Certified Clinical Mental Health Counselors.[688]

As of this writing, however, their efforts fail to demonstrate that there are effective means of enforcing the group's stated ethical standards. A lawsuit filed against Patrick Ryan, a thought-reform consultant and coauthor of the group's ethical standards, highlighted this weakness.[689] The plaintiff claimed that Ryan was "verbally contracted...to provide counseling services" and that he had received $2,250 as a deposit for the services he would render. Shortly thereafter the arrangement was terminated, and it was allegedly agreed that the unearned deposit would be refunded. Ryan never refunded the money. A claim was subsequently filed in court. Carol Giambalvo was repeatedly asked to mediate the situation based on the group's published ethical standards, which specifically emphasized "the importance of clear understandings on financial matters with clients," [690] but she declined to do so.

Ryan later lost the lawsuit, and his former client was awarded a judgment of $2,000. He appealed the verdict but lost again, and the court increased the judgment to $2,400. After Ryan's second appeal, the plaintiff apparently tired of the litigation and failed to appear. The case was dismissed.[691]

The unhappy client who filed the lawsuit against Ryan had been referred to him by psychologist Steven K. D. Eichel.[692] Eichel later commented that he was "greatly pained by what [had] happened" and expressed "deep empathy and respect for the travails and tribulations of the client" who had sued Ryan. He noted that "most professional associations have mandated consequences when a member of that association breaches its ethics code" and that "an ethics code without some means of enforcement...is of educational value and little more." Eichel added that a "meaningful venue for enforcing an ethics code" is required, or a "'code of ethics' is simply a set of aspirations that has no bearing on actual behavior."[693]

Costs

In addition to legitimate concerns about the ethical standards of cult-intervention professionals, there is always concern about costs. Fees charged may vary widely from hundreds to thousands of dollars per day. For example, in 1988 Steve Hassan pointed out that the cost of deprogramming had become a serious consideration. He claimed that "a fee of from $18,000 to $30,000" was the range to be expected.[694]

In inflationary adjusted dollars, this would be $35,000 to $58,000 to-day. Fees currently range from less than a thousand dollars per day to teams that charge thousands of dollars daily. Hassan himself now reportedly charges fees ranging from $2,500 to $5,000 per day, not including expenses.

Declining Number of Professionals

In 1981 Margaret Singer identified ninety working cult-exit counselors. Roughly half were former cult members, and many had left their respective cults through deprogrammings conducted by one of the "early pioneers."[695] Over the years the ranks of cult deprogrammers and intervention specialists have dwindled. Today only a few people with substantial experience in this field are still working full time. These professionals are scattered around the world, with only a handful remaining in the United States.

[632] Flo Conway and Jim Siegelman, *Snapping: America's Epidemic of Sudden Personality Change*, 2nd ed. (New York: Stillpoint Press, 2005), 58.

[633] Ibid, 63.

[634] Ibid, 59.

[635] Matt Coker, "Child Custody Deal Favors 'Escapee of Notorious Cult 'The Family,'" *Orange Country Weekly* (Costa Mesa, CA),March 16, 2009.

[636] Conway and Siegelman, *Snapping: America's Epidemic of Sudden Personality Change*, 58–60.

[637] Ibid.

[638] Ibid., 61, 69.

[639] Ibid., 62.

[640] Ibid., 67.

[641] Ibid., 69.

[642] Ibid., 69.

[643] Margaret Singer, *Cults in Our Midst* (San Francisco, CA: Jossey-Bass, 1996), 285.

[644] John E. LeMoult, "Deprogramming Members of Religious Sects," (New York: Fordham Law Review Volume 46, Issue 4, Article 1, 1978), http://ir.lawnet.fordham.edu/cgi/viewcontent.cgi?article=2305&context=flr (accessed May 20, 2014), 629.

[645] Katz v. Superior Court (October 6, 1977) Court of Appeals of California, First Appellate District, Division One.

[646] LeMoult, *Deprogramming Members of Religious Sects*, 617.

[647] Conway and Siegelman, *Snapping: America's Epidemic of Sudden Personality Change*, 70–72.

[648] Ibid., 62.

[649] Ibid., 61.

[650] Ibid.

[651] Steven Hassan, *Combatting Cult Mind Control* (Rochester, VT: Park Street Press, 1988), 113.

[652] Conway and Siegelman, *Snapping: America's Epidemic of Sudden Personality Change*, 72.

[653] Hassan, *Combatting Cult Mind Control*, 113.

[654] Ibid., 114.

[655] Conway and Siegelman, *Snapping: America's Epidemic of Sudden Personality Change*, 72.

[656] Singer, *Cults in Our Midst*, 286.

[657] Carol Giambalvo, "From Deprogramming to Thought Reform Consultation," (lecture, American Family Foundation Conference, Chicago, IL, November 1998).

[658] Ibid.

[659] United States v. Patrick (December 11, 1974) *Transcript of Proceedings* appeal dismissed 9th Circuit (1976).

[660] Jack Jones, "Cult Deprogrammer Patrick Sentenced to Year in Kidnapping," *Los Angeles Times*, September 28, 1980.

[661] "Amish Woman Asks Prosecutor to Drop Charges on Kidnapping," *Madison Courier*, December 8, 1990.

[662] Conway and Siegelman, *Snapping: America's Epidemic of Sudden Personality Change*, 72.

[663] Bill Moushey, "Hiding the Facts," *Pittsburg Post-Gazette*, November 24, 1998.

[664] Conway and Siegelman, *Snapping: America's Epidemic of Sudden Personality Change*, 72.

[665] Charles W. Hall, "U.S. Seeks to Fire Prosecutor in Virginia for Alleged Misconduct in Cult Kidnapping Case," *Washington Post*, October 4, 1995.

[666] Melanie Threlkeld, "Jury Acquits Two in Deprogramming Case," *Idaho Statesman*, April 24, 1993.

[667] Kim Sue Lia Perkes, "Cult Deprogrammer Acquitted," *Arizona Republic*, January 21, 1994.

[668] Leslie Stahl, "The Cult Awareness Network," *60 Minutes*, CBS, December 28, 1997.

[669] Tony Ortega, "What's $2.995 Million between Former Enemies?" *Phoenix New Times*, December 19, 1996.

[670] Laurie Goodstein, "Plaintiff Shifts Stance on Anti-Cult Group," *Washington Post*, December 23, 1996.

[671] Susan Hansen, "Did Scientology Strike Back?" *American Lawyer*, June 1997.

[672] Paul Morse, "Woman Disappeared for 10 Days," *Hamilton Spectator*, August 31, 2006.

[673] Ibid.

[674] Barbara Brown, "Crown Drops Charges in 'Cult' Kidnapping," *Hamilton Spectator*, October 13, 2009.

[675] Threlkeld, "Jury Acquits Two in Deprogramming Case."

[676] Conway and Siegelman, *Snapping: America's Epidemic of Sudden Personality Change*, 63.

[677] Hassan, *Combatting Cult Mind Control*, 29.

[678] Conway and Siegelman, *Snapping: America's Epidemic of Sudden Personality Change*, 72.

[679] Ibid.

[680] Steven Hassan, "Frequently Asked Questions," Freedom of Mind website (2013). https://freedomofmind.com/Info/faq/sia.php (accessed May 20, 2014).

[681] M. D. Langone, ed., *Recovery from Cults*, 2nd ed. (New York: W. W. Norton, 1996), 174–175.

[682] Cathleen Mann, e-mail message to author, January 14, 2013.

[683] Hassan, *Combatting Cult Mind Control*, 123–124.

[684] Ibid.

[685] Ibid.

[686] Conway and Siegelman, *Snapping: America's Epidemic of Sudden Personality Change*, 71.

[687] Giambalvo, "From Deprogramming to Thought Reform Consultation."

[688] Carol Giambalvo et al., "Ethical Standards for Thought Reform Consultants," *Cultic Studies Journal* Volume 13, No. 1 (1996), 95-106.

[689] Detomi v. Ryan (2005) Philadelphia Municipal Court First Judicial District of Pennsylvania (SC-04-09-23-6469).

[690] Giambalvo et al., "Ethical Standards for Thought Reform Consultants."

[691] Detomi v. Ryan (2006) Court of Common Pleas, Philadelphia, PA. (Case ID 050301175 2005).

[692] Steve Eichel, Prepared Statement (October 26, 2005).

[693] Ibid.

[694] Hassan, *Combatting Cult Mind Control*, 112.

[695] Singer, *Cults in Our Midst*, 291.

CHAPTER 7

ASSESSING THE SITUATION

Here are some helpful suggestions and guidelines for families, friends, and others concerned about a suspected cult problem. Having a well-grounded and practical approach is important when identifying and assessing whether a particular group or leader might be "cultlike" or potentially unsafe. Typically groups or leaders who can be seen as potentially unsafe lack accountability and transparency through meaningful checks and balances, which create firm boundaries and safeguards. Questions should be asked and research done, as outlined in this chapter, to evaluate and assess this situation effectively.

The process for determining whether a particular group or leader may pose potential problems concerning the well-being of individuals involved should be based on behavior, not beliefs. That is, what is the objectively observable structure and dynamics of the suspected group? This question can be answered by both examining the group itself and observing how someone involved has been changed as a result of group influence. An examination of the group should focus not only on the leader but also on others involved in the group who may also influence or reinforce group behavior.

Don't panic. Your initial concern and suspicion may be wrong.

Before moving forward and considering a response, it is important to better understand and educate yourself about cults in general. What can you see as distinct differences between a destructive cult and a benign group? The key to understanding this difference is first recognizing that the "thought reform" process destructive cults use heavily relies on the control of information and communication. This is what psychiatrist Robert Jay Lifton has called "Milieu Control," which is based on control of the environment.

For example, we can see Milieu Control through such elements as tightly controlled housing arrangements, intentional communities, or what has often been referred to as cult compounds. But a state of relative isolation can also be achieved by simply keeping people so busy with group activities that there is functionally little, if any, meaningful time spent away from the group with the exception of work, school, or sleep.

A pattern of hyperactivity can effectively monopolize a member to the extent that it cuts him or her off from any meaningful outside frame of reference or objective feedback. Hyperactivity may also eliminate much of the time previously used for personal reflection and contribute to an eventual erosion of the desire for that process. Instead the group and associations in the group consume time, leading to isolation from family and old friends. Group activities may ultimately deprive members of sleep and effectively produce a state of sleep deprivation. Research suggests that prolonged periods of sleeplessness can produce hallucinations, delusions, and disorientation.[696]

Ultimately the net effect is the creation of a kind of group bubble, which encapsulates those involved. The group controls life in the bubble, which its devotees dominate and suffuse with its own perspective and agenda.

Warning Signs Based on Structure and Behavior

How can you recognize whether this invisible bubble exists? Here are some prominent warning signs you can use to identify a leader or regime controlling such an environment. Does the group or leader fit a familiar profile, which would tend to define a potentially unsafe group or destructive cult? Here are ten "warning signs" regarding leadership based on structure and behavior. These features are frequently associated with unsafe groups or cults.

1. The leadership of the group has absolute authority without any meaningful accountability. There is no genuine democratic form of governance that would offer any meaningful checks or balances to the power of the leadership through elections, a constitution, or bylaws.

2. There is no meaningful financial disclosure or transparency regarding the group's money or assets. There is no detailed and independently audited financial statement or budget published or distributed to the members or contributors annually, disclosing in detail all salaries, compensation, and expenses paid out from group funds. Only the leadership and its chosen few really know about the finances of the group in any depth.

3. Leaders define what is right and wrong, and group members are expected to essentially defer any meaningful value judgments of their own. A kind of learned dependence often develops regarding problem solving and conflict resolution.

4. There is notable and extreme hyperactivity in the group, which is completely centered on the agenda of the leadership, with little, if any, meaningful consideration for the goals of individual members or their interests.

5. The group deliberately isolates its members in a substantially controlled environment. Information is controlled by creating strict rules or guidelines regarding such things as books, outside reading, television, movies, radio, and music. Members may be prohibited contact with anyone who might express independent or opposing ideas, doubts, or negative feelings about the group. The group and its leaders are seen as absolutely necessary to filter out the contamination of the outside world.

6. There are no meaningful boundaries. There is no area of a member's life that appears to be private and therefore immune from the leadership's scrutiny.

7. The group promotes unreasonable fears about the outside world. This may be expressed through predictions of impending catastrophe, obsessions about evil conspiracies, or seemingly exaggerated claims and paranoid suspicions about the group's perceived enemies.

8. The group perpetuates an ethos of perfectionism. Members subsequently feel that they can never be "good enough" and are forever striving to further prove themselves.

9. The group devalues self-esteem and individual expression and considers them "selfish." Group members who try to question leadership or express ideas outside the group mind-set are characterized negatively with such labels as "ego driven," "rebellious," "suppressive," "demonic," or "satanic."

10. Former members once associated with the group often relate the same allegations of abuse by the leadership. This repetition reflects a continuing pattern of grievances.

The group leadership may possess some of these attributes, but when an increasing number of these characteristics are evident, they often indicate that the group is potentially unsafe. It is important to note the leader's communication style, such as the means used to convey his or her rules and orders. Always keep in mind that a recently recruited member of a controversial group may not know all the facts. Information in authoritarian groups tends to flow downward from the top, and often relatively new members at lower levels may be kept unaware of many of the more controversial practices, rituals, and lifestyle requirements those at higher levels know.

"Cultlike" Behavior

Another layer of warning signs relates to the behavior of someone suspected of cult involvement. Here are ten of the most commonly cited behaviors that lead to suspicion about cult involvement.

1. Growing obsessiveness regarding a group or leader, resulting in the exclusion of almost every practical consideration

2. The blurring of identities. The identity of the group, the leader, or some higher power increasingly ceases to be seen as distinct and separate. Instead identities become blurred and seemingly fused as involvement with the group continues and deepens.

3. Whenever critical questions arise about the group or leader, they are often dismissed and characterized as "persecution."

4. Uncharacteristically stilted and seemingly programmed repetitive verbiage and mannerisms that reflect a group mind-set or cloning of preferred group language and behavior

5. Growing dependence on the group or leader for problem solving and solutions, coupled with a corresponding decrease in individual analysis and reflection

6. Hyperactivity regarding the group or leader, which seems to inhibit or supersede previously held personal goals or individual interests

7. A dramatic loss of spontaneity and sense of humor

8. Increasing lack of communication and isolation from family and old friends unless they demonstrate an interest in the group or leader

9. Anything the group or leader says or does can be justified or rationalized, no matter how harsh or harmful it may appear.

10. Former group members are typically considered in a critical or negative light, and they are most often avoided. There seems to be no legitimate reason to leave the group. Those who leave are always wrong.

Some of these behaviors may be observed when individuals become involved in and excited about any new group or association. But when an increasing number of these behaviors are evident, coupled with the structural authority issues previously cited, there may be cause for serious concern.

Don't Blame the Victim

It's important at this point to dispel a common myth about cultic involvement. Many people believe there is a certain type of person who is vulnerable and becomes involved in a destructive cult. This assumption is based on the theory that somehow healthy, strong, intelligent, and well-educated people from good families don't become involved in destructive cults. Some people suppose that if someone is religious, he or she is somehow inoculated and less vulnerable to cults.

In my experience such theories and assumptions are not useful and are often quite misleading. There is no psychological research that definitively correlates a specific type of person or predisposition with cult involvement. When we keep this fact in mind, the focus for assessment should be not on the person the cult recruited but rather on the cult itself—its leaders and their behavior, such as recruitment and retention practices.

I have found that all types of people are potentially vulnerable to cults given the right set of circumstances. The members of destructive cults come from both strong and troubled family backgrounds. They are also often highly educated and intelligent people. In fact, I have deprogrammed five medical doctors.

Some cult members I have worked with over the years have come from troubled or problematic families, but this is not a required precondition likely to lead to cult involvement. Even though some cult members may have histories of psychological problems or substance abuse or both, these are not prerequisites either. Likewise, socioeconomic backgrounds are not that significant. I have met cult members from a very wide cross section of social, ethnic, and religious backgrounds. Because cult recruitment is so often inherently deceptive, there should be no blame placed on those who are recruited. Most cults don't want psychologically damaged, physically impaired, or dysfunctional people; they instead prefer emotionally healthy and high functioning people who can be useful and productive.

The process of cult recruitment is also often based on highly honed coercive persuasion techniques. The most established cults have carefully crafted and refined their process and techniques. People aren't generally prepared, either through specifically focused education about cults or through their own personal experiences. The people cults approach are most often ignorant concerning their methodology and how they really work, and individuals frequently overestimate the innate ability to resist such coercive persuasion and undue influence techniques. This lack of awareness then becomes a vulnerability cults can exploit.

Some notorious cults have historically used front organizational names to hide their actual identity and purpose. A religious cult may not even initially explain to a potential recruit that it has any spiritual or religious agenda. Groups with controversial leaders may likewise withhold information about their hierarchy and more radical beliefs. In many cults only after a recruit is under undue influence is this information genuinely shared.

Scientology, which has been called a "cult," often begins its pitch with a "personality test" or "stress tests."[697] These tests are done to supposedly identify areas of concern that can be improved or require further attention. Respondents are led to believe the purpose is self-improvement, not a measure of religious devotion. Scientologists may point out to a potential recruit that Jews, Protestants, and Roman Catholics are actively engaged in Scientology. Only after a person moves more deeply into Scientology's course curriculum and training, however, does he or she begin to realize more fully the demands of the organization and its distinct religious identity and status. No new recruit fully understands the responsibilities or full implications of total commitment, nor is he or she completely informed of the beliefs forming the basis for Scientology.

Falun Gong presents itself as a form of traditional Chinese exercise to improve physical health and promote "truthfulness, compassion and tolerance." However, much more controversial beliefs proposed by its founder lie behind the group practice, and these are not readily explained to a potential practitioner.[698] Initially, new recruits most probably don't fully understand the special importance of the movement's founder, Li Hongzhi. Later they learn about the fantastic supernatural claims of "Master Li" and his singular status as the "living Buddha."[699] The personality-driven nature of the group isn't completely evident at the beginning. But eventually, as the recruit becomes more deeply involved and his or her training progresses, he or she will learn that the supposed healing benefits of the group essentially depend on the supernatural powers of Li Hongzhi.[700]

Researcher Robert Cialdini, author of the book *Influence*, identified six basic principles of influence.[701] These principles of influence can be used as tools to persuade anyone about almost anything, through carefully crafted advertising, sales gimmicks and fund raising. For example, the high-pressure sales and investment schemes that employ a "bait and switch" approach. This occurs when a shopper is lured in with the promise of one thing but subsequently moved to buy something else. In much the same way, cults can attract attention and interest by presenting themselves deceptively to lure in a potential recruit and then switch to something else as the recruitment process is completed.

The unsettling truth about cults is that virtually anyone might be targeted and then successfully recruited. We are all more vulnerable and suggestible when we are suffering depression, feeling lonely, experiencing a difficult transition period, or trying to navigate in a new environment. This vulnerability is something most first-year college students experience. That is probably why many cults routinely target college and university campuses for recruitment.

We are all more vulnerable at particular times to persuasion techniques. Anyone experiencing a personal trauma or setback, such as a death in the family, relationship problems, or some other personal ordeal, may experience a certain level of temporary vulnerability. Cults often exploit such transitional difficulties as an opportunity for recruitment. In this sense destructive cults can be seen metaphorically as a kind of seeping ooze, penetrating people through the cracks in their lives. In a rapidly changing world, people sometimes feel overwhelmed and anxious.

Cults can present themselves as a solution or appear to respond to almost any dilemma. In this way they may pose as would-be providers of relief or the arbiters of certainty. Everyone at certain times wants assurance about difficulties and answers to perplexing questions. There is also a human need for security and sense of safety. Cults often feed on fear and insecurity, using such human frailties as a means of leveraging cult recruitment. Loneliness can also become a window of opportunity. The very human need for family, community, acceptance, and belonging can also be exploited as a vehicle for cult recruitment.

Former cult members I have spoken with frequently recount a particularly vulnerable time in their lives when someone first approached and recruited them. It may have been a coworker, a family member, or an old friend; it was someone they trusted. In that moment they didn't recognize what was happening, and they were in distress. What they initially felt was a sense of relief; that is, they had found someone to address their needs.

No one intentionally joins a cult. Few new recruits make what can be seen as a fully informed decision about their cult involvement. Given all these considerations, we see that blaming the victims of destructive cults for their predicament is neither meaningful nor productive. And it is important not to be angry or punitive with someone you are concerned about. An angry response to cult involvement will almost certainly not be the basis for any successful resolution of the problem.

Recognizing the Cultic Mind-set

Ultimately the cult milieu produces a type of mind-set that is essentially the by-product of the cult's systematic process of coercive persuasion. We can typically see this through the polarized "black and white" thinking cult members express. They exhibit a low tolerance of ambiguity and often express a relentlessly judgmental attitude. Cult members frequently develop something like the "jeweler's eye," a constricted, selective vision that searches out and finds the tiniest flaws and imperfections in anything or anyone outside the group. When viewing the group, however, the cult member's vision changes to a soft focus, which obscures almost anything negative. Correspondingly cult members often see almost everything in polarized oppositional terms, what can be seen as an "us" versus "them" world. The members' group, or "us," is cast as the ultimate good, and those outside the group, or "them," are frequently characterized as negative or even threatening.

This mind-set can produce seemingly arrogant feelings of superiority or spiritual elitism along with unreasonable fears, which often include exaggerated fears about "persecution" or annihilation or both. Almost any criticism of the group can potentially be characterized as "persecution." Unreasonable fears about the outside world closely correspond to feelings of anxiety about leaving the group. These fears may be based on conspiracy theories, prophecies, or predictions of an impending catastrophe the group or leader has propagated.

Members of destructive cults that have doomsday predictions can develop a crisis mentality about impending threats to their personal safety. Cult leaders may also warn their followers that if they leave the group, they will be in physical danger, contract an illness, or experience some eternal punishment. Leaders may tell stories about how the lives of those who left were negatively impacted or ended in tragedy. These stories may be grossly exaggerated, distorted, or just made up, but they reflect a simple purpose: to intimidate members through unreasonable fears in an effort to keep them in the group.

The cultic mind-set is often expressed through what Lifton refers to as "loaded language."[702] This is the stilted, repetitive jargon cult members use; it reflects its process of thought reform. This can be identified through repetition of "thought terminating clichés." Cult members frequently memorize such verbiage and often substitute it for critical thinking. These are the phrases that have been referred to as communication shortcuts and called "ultimate terms."

Cult members reciting slogans and chanting mantras may at times seem to drift into a kind of floating trance state, which can be seen in their blank or vacant expressions. Some who have observed this effect have speculated that it is tied to drug use. But it actually reflects the psychological and emotional control that is the by-product of the coercive persuasion process destructive cults use. In fact, most cult groups strongly discourage drug use and have rules that strictly prohibit the use of controlled substances, alcohol, and smoking. The net result of this cultic mind-set is impaired thinking. As a direct result, cult members can be seen making decisions that are not in their best interest.

Abusive or Controlling Relationships

It is also possible for a cult to be composed of only two people. This cult would include a leader with a single follower in what can also be seen as an abusive or controlling relationship. This may occur within romantic relationships, marriages, or domestic partnerships. Some authorities and researchers within the mental health profession have described the "battered woman's syndrome,"[703] which has been characterized as a form of undue influence and learned dependency.

Those dominated in abusive or controlling relationships may be so completely under the influence of another person that they appear to have lost the ability to think independently, much like the member of a destructive cult. The person under such control is also frequently isolated from family and friends and becomes increasingly dependent on the controlling and dominating partner. It may seem ironic, but initially in most abusive relationships, control and isolation may be seen as being treated "special." This feeling of being special can be intoxicating in the initial phase of a relationship, which might be called its "honeymoon" phase.

Research

Responding to suspected cult involvement without first educating yourself in some depth is unwise. You can and should focus on developing a better understanding of how cults work and also be educating yourself about the group or leader, the focus of your concern. Only after taking the time to accomplish this step will you be properly prepared to address the situation you face and be fully able to consider your viable options. As you gather information, it is important to create a file, which should include all the material you have assembled and whatever relevant notes you've compiled.

Numerous books can be helpful in gaining a better understanding of both the cult phenomenon and the coercive persuasion techniques destructive cults commonly use. Books have also been written about specific groups and movements that have been called "cults" or "cultlike," such as the Church of Scientology,[704], the Unification Church,[705] martial arts "cults,"[706] the Jehovah's Witnesses,[707] Landmark Education,[708] Transcendental Meditation,[709] the Children of God,[710] Amway,[711] and multilevel marketing in general.[712] This book includes an extensive bibliography.

Many cultic groups and their leaders have deeply troubled histories of bad press, complaints, and lawsuits. This may include related criminal prosecutions and personal injury lawsuits filed by former members. The group may also have a history of divorce disputes and custody battles. There may be records of court judgments, liens, and unpaid tax bills evident in public records. Substantial resources are accessible through the Internet for obtaining public records, making it relatively easy to find out if such background information exists.

Corporate filings may also be a source of meaningful information. The group or leader may have incorporated and filed disclosure documents in accordance with local, state, or federal requirements. These documents would include groups that have corporate nonprofit or tax-exempt status. Numerous resources are available through the Internet and state and federal government records to check the charitable status of individual organizations. Paper work you find may disclose such things as the governance of the group, its board of directors, and possibly some of its finances.

For example, a tax-exempt 501(c)(3) in the United States must make certain documents available to the public on request, such as its initial application for exemption. Anyone interested can request documents, which must be provided either immediately in person or within thirty days of a written request. The law providing for such disclosure includes 501(a), 501(c), and 501(d) tax-exempt organizations. The specific documents included for inspection are the Form 1023 and Form 1024. Depending on their status, certain organizations may also be required to disclose their Form 990, which is an Exempt Organization Business Income Tax Return.[713] Information concerning many tax-exempt organizations is also typically made available through various websites, such as Charity Navigator[714] and the Evangelical Council for Financial Accountability.[715]

In some circumstances hiring a private investigator to dig deeper may be useful, but such specialized help can be expensive. In most situations doing research through the Internet and through whatever access is available to public records and press reports is more cost effective. Internet searches may also provide easy access to archived media reports about the group or leader. Most newspapers and media outlets maintain such databases, which can be searched for information. Numerous websites also archive such information. The Cult Education Institute maintains one of the largest online archives about destructive cults, controversial groups, and movements on the World Wide Web.

There may also be websites created by the former members of a particular group. Such sites often have archived grievances, testimonies, and other relevant information, all of which are publicly available.

Most groups that are considered cults maintain their own websites, which typically include a mission statement as well as biographies and profiles of leaders. There may also be audio and video recordings or other materials archived at such a site. This source material can be quite helpful in developing a better understanding of the group's history and its stated purpose, practices, philosophy, and specific beliefs.

Group websites, however, can also be deliberately misleading or deceptive or both. Keep in mind that such sites are typically developed to recruit new members; therefore, they may not discuss or disclose information that might potentially discourage interest. If the group material appears to be disingenuous, it may be helpful in illustrating a deliberate pattern of deception.

When you research cults, it is important to recognize that cult groups and their apologists may also be misleading. The cult may have front groups that pose as neutral resources to deliberately mislead the public. There are also cult-controlled media and front organizations, such as the *Washington Times*,[716] run by Rev. Moon and the Unification Church, or New Tang Dynasty Television (NTD Television),[717] which is controlled by Falun Gong devotees. Some cults have also sponsored or funded academic research and studies.[718] Some cults have paid academics and others to professionally apologize for their behavior or attack unwanted criticism. Some academic apologists have insisted that there are no such things as cults and prefer to call such groups "new religious movements" (NRM). However, many cultic groups are not based on religious beliefs. Many of these same apologists have attempted to dismiss the personal accounts of former cult members by dismissively labeling them as "apostates." Keeping this in mind it is important to research the background of an academic source. Moreover, Michael Langone, counseling psychologist and Executive Director of the International Cultic Studies Association, noted that former cult members are "the best source of intelligence concerning what goes on in cults behind the scenes."[719]

Consulting with knowledgeable mental health professionals, educators, and clergy about cult concerns is meaningful. There are also helpful organizations within the United States and around the world that offer valuable resources. But before sharing any personal information about a specific situation, remember that understanding the organization's mission and history and its positions regarding cult issues is important. The Internet can be a useful tool to check almost any organization's background and history. Every contact should agree to keep any inquiry completely confidential. A leak through a breach of confidentiality could result in negative and perhaps punitive consequences. For example, cult leaders may inhibit or prohibit further communication with a cult member.

What's important to understand is that most destructive cults have extensive experience in dealing with concerned families and friends. Careful assessment and preparation are necessary before engaging such a group. Without pertinent facts and proper preparation, confronting the group or any of its members is unwise.

Family members who decide not to directly intervene nevertheless need focused education through specifically relevant and helpful information. Only in this way will they know how to best respond to a cult member and avoid the pitfalls.

Communication

If your suspicions of cult involvement have been proved correct, it is best to avoid escalating the situation by engaging in accusations and arguments. Doing so is neither practical nor productive. Before beginning a dialogue about cult involvement, you must first develop and then decide on a comprehensive strategy to address the problem.

During this period of assessment, avoiding confrontation is vitally important. Instead, stay as positive as possible and refrain from criticism. This strategy is necessary to maintain goodwill and ongoing communication. Only the most extreme cult groups completely isolate their members. In most situations cult members continue to live within the larger community, though the narrowness of their associations and constraints created by group demands may make them seem increasingly isolated.

Response

In some situations an intervention isn't possible due to a lack of access. Perhaps the cult member isn't communicating with family or old friends and is living in relative isolation, often in group housing. In such situations the only alternative may be to wait until there is communication and then gradually improve that communication until there is meaningful access—that is, family visits or visits with friends.

In some situations those who are concerned may find that they have a limited window of opportunity as communication diminishes and access becomes increasingly infrequent. Under these circumstances moving forward relatively quickly may be necessary if an intervention is to take place. An intervention is typically done only once. This means that the intervention should be carefully planned and coordinated to make sure the opportunity for success has been maximized as best as possible.

The key to dealing with destructive cults is to be as prepared as possible and very specifically focused on learning the facts, being educated about cults, and settling on a carefully considered strategy. In most situations there is adequate time to do this. An option is always to wait or not to respond. It is also important to recognize the personal limitations of those who might be potentially involved in an intervention, such as immediate health concerns and the emotional distress of undertaking such an effort. And there is always the possibility that the intervention won't work and may produce negative consequences, such as the cult-involved individual cutting off communication for an extended period of time.

The operating axiom that fits the process of deliberation is "When in doubt, don't." That is, when you are unsure of how to respond in a particular situation, it is often safer to refrain from an immediate response.

Keep in mind that there may be only one opportunity to stage an intervention. Careful planning will be crucial for any success to be realized. In some situations when an intervention fails, the returning cult member may experience an elevated status due to his or her demonstrated loyalty. This "halo effect" may enmesh the member deeper and may hinder the possibility of another intervention anytime soon. That is why a considered assessment process, including all the elements mentioned in this chapter, is of vital interest.

Choosing Someone to Conduct the Intervention

The choice of someone to conduct the intervention as the coordinator and facilitator is also a pivotal factor. That person could be a cult-intervention specialist with significant experience. But if no such person is readily available or affordable, there might be someone else, such as a trusted professional in the local area, who can function in that role. This person might be a family physician, psychiatrist, psychologist, professional counselor, attorney, or trusted mentor such as an old teacher or friend. The facilitator should be someone with good communication, organizational, and analytical skills who can effectively moderate such a dialogue and move it forward.

Everyone involved in the intervention must essentially agree on the reasons for concern, the goals of the intervention, and the range of possible outcomes. All must understand that there can be no physical restraint whatsoever during the intervention and that anyone is free to leave at any time, with the exception of a minor child under the supervision of a legal guardian. In most situations an intervention will take three or four days. The chosen moderator or facilitator will need to understand this expectation and have the time necessary to fully complete the process.

The person conducting the intervention must be someone who can effectively maintain a certain level of neutrality and objectivity when presenting the gathered information. For example, if the group being discussed is religious in nature, the moderator leading the intervention shouldn't take a specific religious position to promote a certain sectarian point of view. Proselytizing should never be part of the process. This same consideration would also apply to a group's particular philosophy or political views. No preferred alternate philosophy or political view should be specifically advanced during the intervention. The focus should be on how the cultic group behaves, not on what it believes. The facilitator involved in the intervention should avoid potentially manipulative or often-deceptive persuasion techniques such as neuro-linguistics programming (NLP) or hypnosis.

NLP is a strategic communication approach Richard Bandler and John Grinder created in California during the 1970s.[720] This approach involves the carefully planned use of subtle suggestions conveyed by certain chosen vocabulary and behaviors, which are strategically employed to influence people. NLP practitioners typically employ this approach without informed consent. It is therefore both deceptive and unethical to use such a manipulative and deceptive persuasion process in a cult intervention, which is based on education, not on deceptive manipulation.

Hypnosis is an altered state of consciousness one can use as a component of a manipulative persuasion process. Hypnosis takes place when a person in a hypnotic state of trance (the subject) is guided by another (the hypnotist) to respond to suggestions for changes in subjective experience or alterations in perception, sensation, emotion, thought, or behavior."[721] Some destructive cult leaders have used hypnosis and related techniques of trance induction to make their followers more suggestible and malleable.

It is unethical to use hypnosis within the context of a cult intervention; hypnosis could potentially manipulate the subject through the power of suggestion. Hypnosis places one person in a position of power and authority as the hypnotist and the other through the process in a subordinate position of suggestibility. This situation can easily lead to undue influence.

The goal of a cult intervention is to share information about deceptive and manipulative techniques of persuasion. This educational process is based on honest disclosure and dialogue. It is, therefore, wholly inappropriate and unethical to use deceptive techniques of communication and persuasion similar to those destructive cults use.

One of the most common excuses destructive cults offer to apologize for the deception or manipulation they may use is that "the ends justify the means." This apology is based on the idea that unethical behavior can be rationalized on the premise that it is justified if the ultimate goal of that behavior is good. But this is a "slippery slope" that has led many cults to essentially condone abuse. The use of deceptive persuasion techniques or psychological tricks shouldn't compromise the ethical integrity of a cult intervention if the goal is for an honest outcome. Instead, the basis for an ethical and effective intervention is an emphasis on independent decision making through a process of education that employs critical thinking and personal reflection.

If the chosen moderator or facilitator for the intervention is a mental health professional, there are certain additional professional boundary issues that would apply and must be considered. Typically a cult intervention isn't counseling but rather an information-driven process of education. A licensed mental health professional has very specific legal and ethical requirements when he or she engages in counseling, such as reviewing and completing a specially required consent form before beginning counseling. The boundaries for a licensed counseling professional should be clearly understood and firmly established beforehand if a licensed mental health professional is to be involved.

Due diligence in the selection of any professional should also include a detailed understanding of qualifications and expertise. How was that expertise obtained? Has the expertise of the person being considered been officially recognized? What is his or her specific area of focus linked to this expertise? And how can that particular focus and related background be helpful in the current situation?

All the issues and considerations listed above should be reviewed and explicitly understood and agreed on before initiating a plan for an intervention with anyone.

I advise you not to enter into any agreement with a professional unless it is a written agreement. A written agreement must disclose in detail all the fees and costs expected and explains exactly what professional services will be provided. No intervention professional can reasonably guarantee success, but it is reasonable to ask any professional for references regarding his or her relevant experience and past clients.

---

[696] John T. Brauchi and Louis J. West, *Journal of the American Medical Association* 171, no. 1 (1959): 11–14.

[697] Neille Illel, "Scientologists' Stress Test in Jackson Heights Raise Questions," *Queens Chronicle* (New York), February 3, 2005.

[698] Phillip Cunningham, "Sinister Motives May Lurk in Sect," *South China Morning Post* (Hong Kong), October 8, 2000.

[699] Peter Carlson, "For Whom the Gong Tolls," *Washington Post*, February 27, 2000.

[700] Ibid.

[701] Robert Cialdini, *Influence: The Psychology of Persuasion*, rev. ed. (New York: Quill, 1993).

[702] Ibid., 4.

[703] Lenore E. Walker, "Battered Woman Syndrome: Key Elements of a Diagnosis and Treatment Plan," *Psychiatric Times* 26, no. 7 (July 7, 2009).

[704] Janet Reitman, *Inside Scientology: The Story of America's Most Secret Religion* (Boston, MA: Houghton Mifflin Harcourt, 2011).

[705] Nansook Hong, *In the Shadow of the Moons: My Life in the Rev. Sun Myung Moon Family* (New York: Little Brown, 1998).

[706] Joe Smith, *Herding the Moo: Exploits of a Martial Arts Cult Legend of the Upside Down King* (Bloomington, IN: Trafford, 2006).

[707] Brenda Lee, *Out of the Cocoon: A Young Woman's Courageous Flight from the Grip of a Religious Cult* (Brandon, OR: Robert D. Reed, 2006).

[708] Steven Pressman, *Outrageous Betrayal: The Real Story of Werner Erhard from EST to Exile* (New York: St. Martin's Press, 1993).

[709] Geoff Gilpin, *The Maharishi Effect: A Personal Journey through the Movement That Transformed American Spirituality* (New York: Tarcher, 2006).

[710] Kristina Jones, Celeste Jones, and Juliana Buhring, *Not Without My Sister* (New York: Harper Collins Entertainment, 2007).

[711] Ruth Carter, *Amway Motivational Organizations: Behind the Smoke and Mirrors* (Winter Park, FL: Backstreet, 1999).

[712] Robert L. Fitzpatrick and Joyce K. Reynolds, *False Profits: Seeking Financial and Spiritual Deliverance in Multi-Level Marketing and Pyramid Schemes* (Harrisonberg, VA: Herald Press, 1997).

[713] "What Information Are We as a 501(c) (3) Required to Give Members?" *World Law Direct*, July 13, 2010 http://www.worldlawdirect.com/forum/nonprofit-law-issues/41003-what-information-we-503-c-3-required-give-members.html (accessed May 28, 2014).

[714] Charity Navigator website http://www.charitynavigator.org/ (accessed May 28, 2014).

[715] Evangelical Council for Financial Accountability website http://www.ecfa.org/ (accessed May 28, 2014).

[716] Ian Shapira, "Moon and Fired Executives buy Washington Times for $1," *Washington Post*, November 3, 2010.

[717] Diane Hartman, "Ties to Falun Gong and Controversy to the Chinese New Year Spectacular," *Los Angeles Times*, January 7, 2008.

[718] Stephen A. Kent and Theresa Krebs, "When Scholars Know Sin: Alternative Religions and Their Academic Supporters," *Skeptic Magazine* 6, no. 3 (1998).

[719] Michael D. Langone, "Terrorism and Cultic Dynamics," *ICSA Today,* Volume 6 No. 1, (2015) p. 15.

[720] P. Tosey and J. Mathison, "Introducing Neuro-Linguistic Programming," Centre for Management Learning & Development, School of Management, University of Surrey, 2006, http://www.som.surrey.ac.uk/NLP/Resources/IntroducingNLP.pdf (accessed May 28, 2014).

[721] J. P. Green et al., "Forging Ahead: The 2003 APA Division 30 Definition of Hypnosis," *International Journal of Clinical and Experimental Hypnosis* 53 (2005): 259–264.

CHAPTER 8

COPING STRATEGIES

Initial Response

Developing practical coping strategies when dealing with a cult situation is important. Learning a pragmatic but principled approach is in the best interest of those concerned. This includes what to say and what not to say in conversation with someone suspected of cult involvement.

A confrontational, critical, and argumentative approach can easily result in a breakdown of communication and estrangement. For this reason the first practical rule to learn is that words such as *cult* or *brainwashing* are not useful in conversation with someone involved in a destructive cult. It may seem obvious that the group is a cult to those on the outside looking in, but for insiders the term is likely to be perceived as derogatory or even hateful. Likewise, devoted members would probably perceive the word *brainwashing* to describe group influence in much the same way. Using these words would likely lead only to an argument and perhaps engender hostility. For this reason it's best to avoid using these words.

If someone believed to be in a cult becomes confrontational about his or her beliefs and demands a response regarding his or her validity, responding directly is usually unwise. Instead it's better to deflect, defer, or delay any direct response. For example, someone might respond by simply saying, "I am certainly willing to look at some of the literature, books, or materials from your perspective." Or, "Let's not have this discussion right now. I would like to have this discussion later when there is more time." Appearing serious and genuinely interested in learning more about the group is important.

We should note that any explanation of group beliefs and practices, as a relatively new member may explain, may not reflect the actual nature of the group, its complete teachings, or its actual intent. Destructive cults often selectively withhold information from new initiates until they reach higher levels in the group.

The point at this juncture is that early on most people don't have detailed information about the group or leader, and it's best to wait until whatever information can be obtained has been reviewed. Also, a deep discussion about the group might be the premise used for an intervention effort, which would need to be planned first in some detail. This is why it is more practical to initially defer and delay until information can be effectively gathered and options carefully considered. It is very important in this context to keep communication open and access viable. A confrontational conversation could easily escalate into an argument, which could result in diminished communication. This would then effectively narrow whatever options might be considered.

If a cult member becomes agitated and is increasingly insistent on receiving a more direct answer regarding his or her group and its beliefs, a measured response again might be, "I would rather not discuss this now, but I am willing to sit down and discuss this with you in more depth at another time." It may be difficult, but remaining calm and appearing positive is critical. But don't feign agreement with the group or its beliefs, which is being dishonest. Simply avoiding negative statements isn't lying and therefore is more appropriate. Remember that one of the criticisms of destructive cults is that they are deceptive. If and when the probable deception of the cult in question becomes an issue or focus of concern, it is best that those present at the intervention don't themselves have a history of making deliberately deceptive statements about the group or leader.

Likely, a cult member will cut off, or greatly reduce, communication if he or she is upset because of critical comments. Also, if the group or leader learns about such criticism, he or she may exert influence to end communication with critical family or friends. This is why it is important to carefully avoid appearing excessively negative or critical. For example, concerns about personal finances, health, diet, work, or education can be expressed in a reasonable tone without becoming shrill or punitive. For example, honestly raising questions when and if they are necessary regarding expenses, compensation, doctor's visits, or some other practical concern should be done courteously and without rancor.

Never allow such questions to escalate into an argument by pronouncing negative conclusions and leveling accusations. Instead, reasonably raise issues, such as fairness or safety, through questions without offering answers in a calm and subdued manner. Such questions may not be answered succinctly or satisfactorily, but arguing about the answers isn't best. Raising the questions is probably the best that can be done, and this may stimulate critical thinking. But defer any deeper discussion, which could potentially cause an argument and might be part of a planned intervention effort at some later date.

Regardless of what decision is made regarding how best to respond to a cultic situation, it is important to keep the lines of communication open and maintain meaningful access. Communication and access afford family and friends the continuing opportunity to reinforce love and friendship. They also allow those who are concerned the ability to collect additional relevant information and gain a better understanding of the group or leader. Cutting off communication due to a disagreement or unhappiness about cult involvement is never wise. This act could effectively surrender all influence to the group or leader. Continued communication provides the cult member with an outside frame of reference and alternate feedback, which can become the basis for critical thinking and reflection. This can ultimately broaden the basis of the cult members' intellectual and emotional life and affect their perspective.

In any contact with a cult member, remaining visibly calm is critical.

Everyone involved should be unified in this approach. Discuss coping strategies with other family members and others who are concerned to be sure everyone is acting appropriately in unison. Any strategy or planned response is best approached when everyone concerned is acting together in concert and is fully informed. Seeking a second opinion from someone outside the situation who can be more objective may be helpful. Ideally this should be someone who is specifically knowledgeable about destructive cults. If no such person is readily available in the local area, a professional who has experience dealing with or researching destructive cults should be sought out for advice. Such professionals exist in the fields of psychology, sociology, counseling, and academia. But before consulting such professionals directly, it's best to understand their specific work experience and read their published opinions regarding the issue of destructive cults. This due diligence should determine whether their experience and understanding of the issue are helpful and relevant to the circumstances.

One way to determine whether a helping professional might potentially be a good fit is to ask specific questions about his or her experience in dealing with the recruitment and retention techniques destructive cults use. If responses to these questions seem defensive or vague, likely he or she doesn't have much, if any, actual experience in the area. If a professional sees a cult problem as a "religious" or "family problem," that is a red flag. The issue isn't what the group believes but how it behaves, and there is no conclusive research to support the contention that cult involvement is a family-based problem. Few helping professionals have any specific experience dealing with destructive cults. But if a professional admits to such limitation and seems open and willing to learn, see this response as encouraging evidence that he or she might be helpful.

Continued Communication

Most cult groups will allow continued communication with family and old friends to some extent if they do not feel threatened—that is, if family and friends have seemingly remained neutral, not overtly critical and therefore not perceived as potential problems. Only the most extreme cults demand total isolation and cessation of all communication with those outside the group.

Continued communication is essential for two practical reasons. First, it demonstrates commitment, which ensures that the cult member knows someone outside the group still cares about him or her and that old relationships remain intact regardless of cult involvement. Second, through continued communication the cult member has a viable link to the outside world, and conversely those outside the group will be better able to understand what is going on inside. This access can become a crucial factor if and when the cult member begins to have doubts or fears about the group or is considering leaving. In this sense continuing communication allows outsiders to penetrate the cultic milieu and the group's control over the flow of information. This communication can also reinforce individual ideas and feelings.

We should understand that any conversation or information shared with a cult member may be recounted to other members of the group or its leaders. It is therefore important to be sensitive about what is said, keeping in mind that leaders in the group could later potentially scrutinize and somehow manipulate whatever is shared. Destructive cults often use such tactics to isolate members from those outside the group, including family and old friends, and to engender increasing dependency.

Every opportunity to communicate with a cult member is a chance to emotionally connect. This is why staying positive is so important. Find subjects of mutual interest in an effort to maintain or build on the existing relationship and rapport. Be affectionate, friendly, and reasonable. Look for areas of potential agreement.

Never be confrontational, combative, or argumentative. Never denounce the group's leader(s), beliefs, or practices. This doesn't mean, however, that anyone should be deliberately misleading, give false information, or act obviously out of character. It simply means to filter out negativity and criticism that might distress or upset the cult member. Again, never use the word *cult* or terms like *brainwashed* or *mind control*. If an uncomfortable situation arises, someone might say, "I would really rather not discuss that right now. Let's talk about something else. I don't want to argue." Or, "I am happy to have this time with you. I want this to be pleasant visit."

The more frequently a cult member is contacted, the better. This connection might include phone calls, letters, or personal visits. Concerned family members and friends might, to some extent, coordinate communication efforts, encouraging regular calls and visits from a number of people. But this should be done with the positive cooperation of the cult member. In other words reasonably respect the person's space and schedule. Visits or mail should include sharing photographs of family, friends, favorite pets, and places of interest. An occasional gift of some favorite food is a meaningful gesture. All this may stimulate fond memories of happy times.

Keeping cult members informed about contact information, such as changes of address and phone numbers, is crucial. Cult members should be kept up to date about family news and situations. This might include information about someone who is sick or hospitalized as well as births, deaths, weddings, graduations, engagements, and so forth. And they should always be sent invitations or announcements of such events. If there is a family emergency, they should be called. If the cult member doesn't have a phone or cell phone, some means of communication might be provided and paid for to ensure continued contact and access.

Never forget a cult member's birthday, special anniversary, or significant holiday. Send thoughtful gifts, cards, text messages, e-mail and special commemorative keepsakes but don't send money. All these considerations serve as important reminders not only of family and old friends but also of pleasant memories.

If at all possible, maintain health insurance coverage for a cult member through a family policy or provider. And if it seems meaningful, provide a car, without titling it in the cult member's name, along with the necessary required insurance. This gesture may serve as a means for maintaining contact and possibly visiting outside of the group.

Only the most extreme destructive cults, those living in group housing, censor incoming mail. But it may prove useful to keep a record of any communication through letters, cards, and sent gifts.

Considering the Cultic Mind-set

People who are in cults often develop what appears to be an alternate personality or mind-set, which is the result of group influence. The cult member may mimic certain behavior consistent with the qualities or attributes the group or leaders value. However, this isn't proof that a genuinely unique or different personality exists. It is rather a reflection of the undue influence of the group, which produces its preferred mind-set.

Often a particular leader may serve as a model or prototype of the ideal person. Members of a group may try to emulate the leader's perceived positive characteristics. This emulation might include certain verbiage, idiosyncratic expressions, and mannerisms. The cult member may behave oddly; this behavior might be confusing and perhaps unpleasant. But by recognizing that this affectation is the result of a group process rather than an independent individual choice, those who are concerned can put this behavior in its proper context. Understanding this can help the family and old friends of a cult member to be more tolerant and inform their responses.

Keeping in mind that the cult member's innate individual personality has only become obscured can enable family and friends to more easily avoid angry responses, unproductive emotional outbursts, and confrontations. For example, a cult member may be hypercritical, offer harsh judgments, or act negative or seemingly petty. Cult members in some groups may also seem insensitive or emotionally disconnected. These traits should most often be understood as the result of undue influence and not as an independent decision to deliberately hurt family and old friends.

Knowledge about the group's particular beliefs, demands, and practices in this context is very important. This awareness can provide the sensitivity necessary to avoid arguments and needless confrontation. For example, if cult members have a rigid diet, clothing requirements, or prohibitions against certain activities, such as watching television or reading newspapers, don't do anything to offend them. Insensitivity toward such issues may stimulate unreasonable fears instilled by the group and might abruptly end a visit, conversation, or general communication.

If at all possible, it is also important to develop some sensitivity to certain terms, phrases, or words a certain group or leader may teach. This is what psychiatrist Robert Jay Lifton has labeled "loaded language" or "thought-terminating clichés."[722] Certain words or references may be twisted and reinterpreted in some way to have special meaning or significance. For example, Scientologists often call those who are critical of Scientology "suppressive persons" (SPs). Amway frequently defines its critics as "dream stealers." Learning this language is important. You can accomplish this by reading articles and books about the group or reviewing the group's literature and materials. Be sensitive to the group vocabulary and the implications of its use.

Conversation

Whenever one converses with a cult member, it is very important to ask open-ended and thought-provoking questions without being accusatory or argumentative. For example, ask questions about the future such as, "What plans do you have for next year?" or "How do you imagine yourself in five years?" or "What will you be doing then?" If such questions are asked honestly and sincerely—and not in a condescending or patronizing manner—they may spark spontaneous ideas and stimulate consideration and critical thinking. This might provide the basis for the cult member to consider his or her role in the group, sense of security, or concerns about the future. It would also be meaningful to discuss any education plans, medical care, or even retirement. Keep in mind—and be sensitive to—unreasonable fears he or she may have developed through group denunciations of such things as higher education or prescribed medicine. Conversation must thus be limited within certain parameters to avoid conflict.

If unreasonable fears come up, try to put them into a more objective frame of reference by giving accurate feedback. For example, respond thoughtfully, "Why is that a serious concern?" Always allow the cult member to answer completely and listen courteously. Being a good listener is important. Don't interrupt or in any way belittle or ridicule his or her responses. Always remember that you are largely dealing with a cult-influenced person. Be aware that what you think or feel is reasonable, rational, and logical may not be considered the same within the group or by its leaders. Also keep in mind that cult members go through a process of change to adapt themselves to the group norm. This may result in alternating moments of clarity when they seem reasonable and receptive, but then this may suddenly shift to suspicion or fear. In this sense it is often difficult to determine how a cult member is likely to perceive and receive an outsider, since this may vary due to the group's ongoing influence.

Ask simple questions about daily life such as, "What did you do this week?" or more generally, "How are things going?" Demonstrate genuine interest in the group, its daily life and activities. Don't ask pointed questions that sound accusatory and never imply in any obvious way that something in a conversation might be wrong.

Encourage family members and old friends to keep in contact with and visit the cult member. Be sure everyone is aware of the boundaries and limits to this communication, as previously outlined. Generally, the more communication exists with people outside the group, the better the situation can be.

In any conversation with a cult member, connecting in some way with his or her past is meaningful. That is, mention things that occurred before his or her involvement with the group. This reminder can stimulate happy memories of life before group involvement, and these memories can be recalled and reinforced. You can do so by recalling happy times spent with family and friends, accomplishments at school, perhaps even old romantic interests. But this must be done without offending the group's sensibilities and/or breaking any of its rules. For example, the group or leader may have special rules regarding celibacy, celebration of holidays, or certain prohibited activities. Working within such a framework in conservation can be difficult, but it is important to demonstrate to the cult member through relatively passive and nonthreatening conversation that his or her past life did have some happiness, value, and meaning.

Never be aggressive or envoke punishments. Never try to induce guilt feelings through the recollection of family memories. A destructive cult or leader can easily turn this conversation around and use it as an indictment of family, old friends, and their intentions. Assume that anything said to a cult member will be repeated to leaders or others in the group and will be further scrutinized. That is why it is so important not to say anything negative; you do not want to provide the basis for the group and its leaders to discredit and dismiss family and old friends. Always be truthful, positive, and consistent; and make every effort to fulfill commitments.

Being a good listener leads to more effective information gathering about the group, its practices, living conditions, and whatever jargon the group may use. Try to keep notes about conversations whenever possible, including key points, certain words, and frequently used phrases. Note rules, practices, and diet standards that exist in the group. Many cults are so small and relatively obscure that there is little, if any, meaningful information readily available about them. The notes may prove to be invaluable in the future.

Only the most extreme groups discourage any expression of emotion or endearment. In most groups there is no prohibition against sincere feelings. As we keep this in mind, it's important to include words of love and regard in a conversation. Saying "I love you" and "It's always good to hear from you" or "I miss you" may be especially meaningful.

Life often becomes boring in a destructive cult. Repetitious and tedious tasks can lead to boredom. There is also often a shaming milieu that leads to low self-esteem. Many cults promote the general impression that no one can ever really be good enough. Members find themselves toiling endlessly to demonstrate that they are truly committed and to meet the expectations of leaders. In addition, cults are notorious for barely compensating members for their work and often simply exploiting them for free labor. Ultimately these conditions can make daily life in many cults dull and little more than drudgery. As time passes a cult member's memories of a better life before involvement in the group may begin to filter through and seem increasingly appealing despite the group's influence.

It is very important for cult members to know that they have family and friends on the outside who care. These people can be a constant reminder that there is a better life and that a safety net exists. The continuing, loving support of family and old friends can reinforce this reality. If a cult member considers leaving the group, this ongoing outside support may become a crucial factor in such consideration. By continuing to express love and commitment, family and old friends send the message that there is a way out and that the possibility of a better life still exists.

Personal Visits

Visiting and making face-to-face personal contact with cult members is important. Concerned family members and old friends should frequently try to make and encourage such visits. These visits could potentially include birthdays and special occasions such as anniversaries and holidays. Again, they must be done with sensitivity regarding the group's influence.

Most cult members don't live in isolated compounds, and doing personal visits is often relatively easy to do. If there is a history of arguments concerning the group or leader, it may take time to diminish the stress level that exists and resume more relaxed conversations and visits. Always remember that what is said and done has consequences. Consider this whenever communicating or visiting a cult member. That is, confrontational and negative behavior may lead to an end of communication.

Organizing visits with cult members away from the cultic group is always preferable. This could include visits at home or in a private residence, such as an invitation for a meal. Always remain courteous, even if rebuffed. Visits may include long descriptions of group activities and projects. Listen patiently but don't confuse courtesy with feigned feelings. Expressing support for the group and its activities isn't necessary. But be polite and attentive; if there's nothing positive you can honestly say, it's preferable not to comment.

Remember that every comment you make will be viewed through the lens of the group and could potentially be repeated to others in the group. That is why you should exercise caution when making comments. When you are in doubt about what to say and how to act, doing nothing is preferable. It is much easier to add comments later than to retract those you've already made.

Encourage happy memories or talk about things that can be seen as universally positive, such as someone who recovered from an illness or something as simple as good weather. If possible, try to draw on the cult member's known sense of humor to strengthen rapport. If possible, everyone should be encouraged to maintain contact through face-to-face visits. These visits may be the only meaningful personal contact and emotional connection the cult member has outside the group.

Hopefully the cult member can be courteous too. But if you aren't being treated respectfully, it's all right to offer a gentle reminder, such as, "I am doing the best I can to understand and be respectful. Please give me the same consideration." If during a visit the cult member becomes confrontational or argumentative, a considered response might be, "I am sorry you are upset, but I appreciate it when you express your feelings honestly." And if the visit becomes too stressful, it's all right to say, "Maybe this is not a good time for you." At that point, apologize and leave. Again it's almost always appropriate to add, "I love you" or "It's been really good to see you." It's best to avoid an argument that might negatively affect future communication and visits.

When invited to cult activities, such as a religious service or group program, be careful. Attending a public service or program to visibly demonstrate a reasonable attitude may be valuable, but participating in training sessions or intensive group programs designed for indoctrination would be unwise. Such a session or program could potentially become confrontational and volatile, and it could possibly lead to serious problems, such as arguments with leaders.

Public events are much safer and more likely to be basically passive encounters. Cults typically try to manage their public image and often use open events to recruit new members. In such circumstances leaders and members are far less likely to engage in provocative behavior or become confrontational. Instead they usually endeavor to appear benign and welcoming. It is also possible to be influenced and even recruited into a group through such exposure. The influence of group involvement, or what is called "participant observation," is recognized in the fields of sociology, anthropology, and communication. That is, the researcher's involvement in a group being studied can diminish his or her objectivity, may potentially lead to bias, and can substantially affect research results.[723]

Doubts

There may come a time when a cult member expresses doubts about the group, its leaders, or its practices. It's important to understand that this time of questioning may be only a temporary time and it may pass. Being mindful that this situation might pass is an important reminder not to comment too readily about how bad the group is or to say, "I always knew that leader was bad" or "wrong." Keep in mind that if the cult member later decides, often through the group or leader's influence, that his or her doubts were somehow misplaced and family or friends said something negative, it's likely that group members and possibly those in leadership will discuss their comments.

For this reason being circumspect when commenting about a member's doubts is best. A careful and considered response is to be a good listener and take no definite position. A cautious response might be, "That's interesting" or "I didn't know you felt that way." This response defers taking a definite position. If the member communicates repeated doubts and misgivings about the group through further conversations and visits, you may want to consider a more assertive response.

A measured response may be to tentatively test the situation by sharing some information—for example, documentation specifically gathered about the group. Depending on how that material is received, you may suggest additional information, such as books about cults and coercive persuasion techniques, when and if that opportunity seems suitable. But you should preface the sharing of such materials with, "I came across some information about the group or leader. Would you like to see it?" Or you may say, "Someone once suggested that I read books on the subject of undue influence and coercive persuasion techniques. Do you think those might be helpful?" It's important to be calm and conciliatory as opposed to aggressive. Allow the cult member space for comfort and personal reflection. If an offer of help is rejected, don't be persistent. A careful response might be, "That's all right; let me know if you change your mind. The information is here if you ever wish to review it."

At times it is much easier for cult members to recognize what is wrong with other groups than with their own. In this sense, depending on the situation, it may be better to offer material and books that do not name their group specifically but rather others with similar problems and practices. Again, allow space and time for the cult member to sort through such issues at his or her own pace. If this seems to be an especially unique opportunity or crucial juncture, consulting a knowledgeable professional might be best. This could potentially be a psychologist or counselor. Make a careful choice. The person should be someone who is sensitive to cult issues and experienced in counseling former cult members.

Some cult situations, however, may be so extreme that immediate action seems necessary. Certain group activities or practices may be illegal, potentially unsafe, or dangerous. In such circumstances families and those concerned often feel torn between preserving goodwill and communication with a cult-involved individual and informing the appropriate authorities and risking alienation. Cults often cut off communication after such an action is taken by the family or friends of a member. Leaders often feel threatened and may decide to isolate the group member. When one considers contacting the authorities or the media or both, keeping these possible consequences in mind is important.

What do you have to lose?

Would such action narrow your options in the future?

For example, if an intervention is a possible consideration for the future, increased isolation and lack of access may make that option impossible.

This is a decision that must be made very carefully. If the matter involves criminal activity such as child abuse, labor violations, or health or housing concerns, however, local authorities should be notified. If there is a legal or medical concern, it may also be necessary to call an attorney or medical doctor for his or her input and consultation.

If there is no evidence of criminal conduct and only the suspicion of possible illegal activity, always remember that one option is to wait, gather more information, and not act immediately. The operating axiom that fits is, "When in doubt, don't." That is, when you are unsure about how to respond in a particular situation, refraining from responding is safer. What is done cannot be easily undone. In most circumstances you can decide on some action after gathering information and doing careful deliberation.

But in the case of a suspected medical emergency, child abuse, or potential violence, time may be of the essence. It might be necessary to act immediately regarding suspected wrongdoing rather than take any risk. Anonymous reports can be made to authorities such as the police, child protection, and social services.

Support

Just as former cult members may need support, the families and old friends of cult members may also find support groups helpful. A relevant support group may be nearby. Specific support groups devoted to the families and friends of cult members are available in the United States. A support group can be helpful in handling and coping with a difficult ongoing situation that is both psychologically and emotionally draining. Counseling professionals with relevant experience may also prove to be a meaningful resource.

When dealing with the issue of cult involvement, some families may benefit from networking with others in similar situations, and by contacting knowledgeable professionals and former cult members. Some people find that such support helps to sustain them and also that such networking can be useful for gathering information and keeping current and informed about a cult group.

When participating in a support group and networking with others, being discreet and maintaining confidentiality are also important. Cult members may perceive such involvement as threatening or negative, and it may potentially affect whatever relationship and level of communication currently exist. Be sure that any contacted person or group understands the importance of privacy and confidentiality. Verifying that any support or networking group shares your concerns and is credible is also critical.

Cult Awareness

Some concerned parents, family members, and friends may become anticult activists. That is, they may become involved in publicly exposing a cult or cults in general by working with the media, law enforcement, public officials, or protection services to monitor a certain group and its activities. This step can produce positive results by protecting the public or cult members, such as children in a particular group who are at risk. Such action may also provide a release by "doing something" and creating a feeling of empowerment in what otherwise may seem like a powerless situation.

But there are possible consequences to anticult activism, and these need to be carefully weighed. Those considering activism should carefully consider their priorities in the context and status of their current situation. What is at stake? What can be lost? It isn't wrong for a family or concerned friends to feel that personal considerations outweigh the need for public education and greater awareness. But in some cultic situations, family and friends may feel they have nothing to lose.

Anyone considering such action should first consult trusted professionals, such as a family physician or attorney. Making such a critical decision quickly or without additional input from a professional perspective is unwise and needlessly risky.

Former Cult Members

Families and friends of cult members often suffer in relative silence for years, waiting for a loved one to leave a destructive group. This can be a long, painful journey. Some cult members may eventually decide to walk away from their respective groups. Leaders may ask some to leave due to some infraction or simply because they are no longer seen as useful or are somehow seen as a liability. Sadly, this exit may take place after years of exploitation.

Some cult refugees leave with little more than clothing and few personal effects despite years of devotion and personal sacrifices. Many cult members have experienced psychological, emotional, physical, and sexual abuse. Often cult members may also have lost relationships, been neglected, or ignored education or career opportunities. The problems of leaving a destructive cult are also compounded when children are involved.

When dealing with former cult members, unconditional love must be expressed when at all possible. Never say, "I told you so" or act in a punitive, guilt-inducing manner.

When someone leaves a cult, that exit isn't the signal to begin attacking the group and its members. It's important to understand that a cult experience isn't usually completely negative. The member's time in the group may have resulted in some positive changes and realizations. He or she may have ceased some self-destructive behavior or given up some form of substance abuse. It's important to scrupulously avoid sweeping generalizations and judgmental statements about the group and his or her experience. Again, be a good listener and try to be as positive as possible. Remember, cult leaders may be deeply destructive, but the people who follow them are most often decent, well intentioned, and idealistic. Leaving a cult often means abruptly ending significant and close relationships, and that loss can be very difficult for the departing member. Don't make the situation any more difficult than it already is.

There is research regarding "exit cost analysis," which sociologist Benjamin Zablocki defines as "the systematic study of all disincentives for leaving voluntary collectives." Zablocki explains, "There are many types of exit costs ranging from financial penalties, to relational commitments, to various sorts of cognitive and emotional dependencies." The sociologist concludes that these costs create "the paradox of feeling trapped in what is nominally a voluntary association."[724]

For example, if a member of Scientology is declared a suppressive person (SP), other Scientologists are reportedly likely to cut him or her off socially and cease meaningful contact.[725] If a Scientologist considers leaving the organization, this being cut off becomes a disincentive or exit cost that inhibits leaving. If employment or business ties could be severed, there may be a financial penalty connected to leaving the group.

There are mental health professionals who have experience helping former cult members. Some former cult members seek counseling from knowledgeable professionals, but many do not. Allowing former members the space to make their own decisions is important. Resuming individual decision making and becoming self-reliant are often crucial parts of the recovery process after leaving a controlling cult group. Be helpful but not controlling. Respect the former cult member's freedom of choice. Each individual will sort through the recovery process at his or her own pace.

If a former cult member seems to be in distress, those concerned might suggest seeking help from a professional. When picking a counselor for assistance, it is best to find someone who is warm and willing to learn. There are few professional counselors who have specific experience providing recovery assistance to former cult members. Beware of experts who cannot or will not explain in meaningful detail how they acquired their expertise. Ask for references before deciding on any counseling relationship.

Don't be critical of the former cult member's spirituality, idealism, or claimed awareness. The stated goals and ideals of the group may have been laudable despite any destructive behavior that may be evident. Don't try to convince a former cult member of what beliefs are best. Respect the person's process of recovery and personal discovery. The person will need to make his or her own choices in his or her own time and may require a period of rest before again exploring politics, philosophy, religion, or participating in some sort of support group.

---

[722] Robert Jay Lifton, *Thought Reform and the Psychology of Totalism* (Chapel Hill: University of North Carolina Press, 2012), 429.

[723] *Participant Observation: Becoming a Part of the Research* (About.com Sociology) M. L. Andersen and H. F. Taylor, *Sociology: The Essentials* (Belmont, CA: Thomson Wadsworth, 2009) http://sociology.about.com/od/Research/a/Participant-Observation.htm (accessed May 28, 2014).

[724] Benjamin D. Zablocki, "Exit Cost Analysis: A New Approach to the Scientific Study of Brainwashing," *Nova Religion* 2, no. 1 (1998): 219–220.

[725] Lawrence Wright, "The Apostate: Paul Haggis vs. the Church of Scientology," *New Yorker*, February 14, 2011.

CHAPTER 9

PREPARATION FOR AN INTERVENTION

Initial Information

After a family, spouse, or someone else who is concerned decides to do an organized and coordinated intervention effort, the first step in the general preparation process is to define the history of the situation. This can be done by disclosing the relevant background and history in detail through a written narrative. This step entails sharing thoughtful and helpful biographical information, which effectively illustrates whatever concerns exist about the specific situation.

In my work I have used a questionnaire with about fifty background questions. These are questions about the individual who might potentially be the focus of an intervention effort and the history of the situation that has prompted concern. The response to questions or the detailed written narrative discloses immediate concerns such as medical neglect, ongoing abuse, family estrangement, and/or personal exploitation.

This initial information is necessary to evaluate the situation—that is, for a chosen professional or agreed-upon facilitator to decide whether an intervention is necessary or possible. In some situations referring a family member or concerned party elsewhere may be necessary—for example, if there is a serious medical crisis or a history of mental illness. In such cases a medical doctor may be the best resource. In such situations I have worked under the supervision of psychiatrists and psychologists and sometimes in hospital settings when medical concerns were evident.

In some cultic situations there is severe isolation and lack of communication to the extent that an intervention may need to be postponed or may not be possible. That is, there is no current basis or effective opportunity for an intervention to take place. Until such time that these conditions change, the family or other concerned parties must wait until a meaningful opening occurs to make an intervention possible. During this period they can develop coping strategies to improve communication and better facilitate such an opportunity, as I explained in the previous chapter about coping strategies.

At this juncture we must acknowledge that if there is no meaningful access to the individual to provide the basis for an intervention, no covert attempt to employ deception is recommended. A covert approach is also not a realistically viable alternative. Specifically, a covert intervention would entail approaching an individual under false pretenses in an effort to somehow affect his or her continued cult involvement. This deceptive approach is unethical and poses substantial risk. Rather than offering a potential solution, it is more likely that such an effort will fail and not produce any meaningful results. And if a covert intervention effort is discovered and exposed, it is likely to produce distrust, alienation, and further isolation. It may also exacerbate communication. One of the most repeated criticisms of destructive cults is that they employ deception and trick people. Trickery cannot be the basis for ethical intervention work.

After all the background information has been obtained and evaluated, there may be follow-up phone discussions and e-mail exchanges between the designated facilitator or coordinator and those concerned so they may ask further questions to clarify the situation. In some instances face-to-face meetings may be more geographically convenient. In most situations, however, such meetings may not be easily done. In my work such face-to-face meetings usually occur only immediately before the intervention begins. This arrangement is much more practical and avoids unnecessary expense.

At this point it is important to note that all those concerned in the intervention must understand and agree upon reasonable confidentiality. That is, no information that specifically identifies the individuals or family members involved should be disclosed without their permission. The only exception would be if criminal activity is somehow discovered through the process of preparation or during the intervention. In such a situation there would be an obligation to report criminal activity to the authorities.

Preparing a File

When and if parties decide to move forward with an intervention, collecting more detailed information and organizing it in a file will be necessary. This file will be largely relied on during the intervention and will be used as a resource during the preparation process. This file may include information about the specific cultic group or leader as well as relevant research and educational material about cults, coercive persuasion, and related influence techniques.

Gathering information about some groups may prove difficult due to their small size and obscurity. Many groups or leaders are relatively new, and little information is readily accessible about them.

Any material the group or leaders have published or distributed may be potentially important and must be gathered for the file. Previously published literature or other material may be available somewhere on the World Wide Web. Many groups or leaders maintain websites, blogs, or an archive of literature or online videos. Social media may also be a meaningful resource through such sources as Facebook, message boards, or online discussion groups.

Court documents may also be useful. For example, the group or leader may have been involved in criminal or civil court proceedings. Documents that disclose in detail such prosecution or litigation may be meaningful points for discussion during an intervention and may therefore be valuable material for the assembled file. Other relevant material for the file might be financial records, corporate disclosure documents, and real estate records that disclose assets and income. News reports or documentaries might exist about the group or leader.

In some situations a private investigation has been paid for, and a private investigator may submit a prepared report with attached documentation. This may be particularly helpful if the group or leader is relatively unknown and obscure and little information is readily available. But Internet access to the World Wide Web has made public information increasingly easy to obtain. Various online services and search engines can be very effective tools for gathering needed information. For example, certain public records, such as criminal convictions, past addresses, and miscellaneous corporate disclosure documents, can be found online using the World Wide Web. But information gathered online must be carefully reviewed for accuracy and verified.

Again, all this material must be carefully organized so it will be on hand at all times during the course of an intervention. This material must also be reviewed during a preparation meeting with potential participants immediately before the intervention begins.

Preparation Meeting

In my experience having a face-to-face preparation meeting with all potential participants immediately before the intervention begins is essential. This meeting usually takes several hours to a full day. Ideally the meeting is scheduled the day before the intervention begins. This timing is ideal because the subjects discussed and information reviewed will be fresh in everyone's mind during the intervention. Also, from a practical perspective, there is no point in having a preparation meeting unless an actual intervention has been specifically planned and is imminent.

Before the meeting those involved must individually prepare by reading relevant material. This reading may include helpful books about cults and coercive persuasion, relevant news reports, research, and other related material in an effort to become better informed before the meeting. This educational process will provide a foundation and meaningful framework for the preparation meeting.

The Cult Education Institute for the Study of Destructive Cults, Controversial Groups and Movements has made the following two DVD presentations available, which generally cover such issues: *Cults: An Educational Volume*[726] and *In the Name of Love: Abusive Controlling Relationships.*[727]

This book and others listed within the attached bibliography can be helpful before and during the preparation process.

Understanding What Issues Will Be Discussed

The preparation meeting is built on an educational foundation. This includes a review of basic cult education issues, to be discussed during the intervention, which is of crucial importance. There is discussion about the basic research regarding the definition of a destructive cult and the specific type of coercive persuasion and undue influence techniques such groups and leaders use. Potential participants must have a solid understanding of these issues.

For example, there is the paper "Cult Formation" by psychiatrist Robert Jay Lifton.[728] This long-standing analysis must be discussed because it succinctly identifies the core characteristics or essential nucleus for the definition of a destructive cult. This analysis features the following three primary criteria:

1. a charismatic leader who increasingly becomes an object of worship as the general principles that may have originally sustained the group lose their power;
2. a process I call coercive persuasion or thought reform;
3. economic, sexual, and other exploitation of group members by the leader and the ruling coterie.

These principal characteristics become the focus of discussion with potential participants as part of the preparation process and meeting immediately before the intervention begins. We should note that in some situations, destructive cults somehow manage to survive despite the death of a charismatic leader, but many subsequently collapse. Potential participants are now asked how they see Lifton's three primary characteristics as being applicable to the current situation, which has drawn their concern.

Another educational tool to be used and understood is chapter twenty-two of Lifton's book *Thought Reform and Psychology of Totalism.* In this chapter Lifton details eight criteria to use to determine whether a thought-reform program is evident and ongoing.[729]

Other relevant research to be discussed includes the description of "coercive persuasion" by sociologist Richard Ofshe.[730]

Ofshe lists four key factors that define coercive persuasion:

1. The reliance on an intense interpersonal and psychological attack to destabilize an individual's sense of self to promote compliance
2. The use of an organized peer group
3. Applying interpersonal pressure to promote conformity
4. The manipulation of the totality of the person's social environment to stabilize behavior once it has been modified

These four factors will be points of discussion with potential participants during the preparation meeting. How do those concerned see coercive persuasion expressed, as these four factors outline, in the current situation? Do these factors provide a meaningful framework to understand the dynamics of a certain group or relationship? This review during the preparation meeting will help those involved focus on the relevant features and facts that will be discussed during the intervention.

Illustrating the distinctions between various forms of persuasion is also important and must be included.

Margaret Singer composed a chart in her book *Cults in our Midst* that demonstrates the distinctions between education, advertising, propaganda, indoctrination, and thought reform as varying forms of persuasion.[731] Also important is discussion about the six basic rules of influence as researcher Robert Cialdini defined in his classic book *Influence*.[732] This explains how people are influenced through the manipulation of such things as authority, commitment, a sense of obligation, likability, social environments, and the perception of scarcity.

Educational films can be shown during the preparation meeting to visibly demonstrate how destructive cults work and also to effectively illustrate the inherent power of influence and persuasion techniques.

The same films might be used during the intervention. Useful films are available in DVD format or are accessible on the World Wide Web.

Here are three suggested classics about cults and persuasion techniques:

- *Captive Minds: Hypnosis and Beyond* directed by Pierre Lasry and produced by the National Film Board of Canada.[733]

This documentary examines various forms of persuasion in detail. It begins with hypnosis or trance induction and culminates in an exploration of cultic control. The documentary starts with a stage hypnotist, whirling dervishes and also includes psychiatrists and a guru Bhagwan Shree Rajneesh, now known as Osho. The training at a US Marine Corps boot camp is examined. Jesuits and the Unification Church of Rev. Moon are also covered. Through this ongoing narrative, the film consistently demonstrates the power of coercive persuasion and the apparent fragility of the human mind. This documentary is now accessible online through the World Wide Web.

- *The Wave*. ABC initially did the first version as an after-school television special made for a younger audience.[734]

- *Die Welle* (*The Wave*), the second version, was done in Germany. It is now available with English subtitles and is more focused on an adult audience.[735]

The Wave is largely based on a true story. It is the dramatization of a classroom experiment an American high school teacher did in California.[736] In the story the teacher hopes to help his students understand how malleable people are and how almost anyone can be manipulated to support a dictatorship, such as Nazi Germany. What the experiment illustrates is how easily an authority figure can influence people in a controlled social environment. Both versions of *The Wave* are available on DVD and can be used to illustrate coercive persuasion and undue influence techniques.

- *You Can Go Home Again* is an educational video produced by the Union of American Hebrew Congregations (UAHC), now known as the Union of Reform Judaism (URJ).[737]

Though this video is more than thirty years old, it remains a compelling classic about cults. It features a discussion with former members of purported cults, who explain their experiences. Moderated by cult awareness pioneer Rabbi Maurice Davis, it illustrates repeated parallels between former cult members regardless of their different group background. The video offers compelling historical evidence that the key structural features and behavior defining destructive cults have remained the same.

Picking Participants

During the preparation process and ultimately by the conclusion of the preparation meeting, those concerned about the cult member must decide who will attend the intervention. That is, family members, friends, past mentors, and associates are the most respected and therefore would be the most effective at the intervention.

Who will be included in the intervention and why?

Who cannot be included due to some personal or potential conflict?

Everyone involved should be informed of the time commitment required to participate—that is, eight hours each day for three to four days. If someone cannot afford to contribute the time allotted, he or she must make this fact clear before the intervention begins. Some people may be able to make only a partial commitment. For example, someone might agree to participate on the first day but cannot continue beyond that point. Or someone may agree to come in at a later point after the first day of the intervention. Everyone involved should understand who will be involved and how much time he or she will be available.

On the first day too many people may cause excessive stress or embarrassment for the person who is the focus of the intervention. Another consideration may be that certain people will be more welcome and better understood at a later point in the intervention. For example, a former cult member may not initially be welcome, but after some discussion, he or she may be later introduced as a viable source of additional information.

An intervention cannot be done without the complete support of those directly participating in it. Anyone who expresses conflict or ambivalence about the intervention need not participate and must be excluded. Someone who lacks genuine commitment to the process can easily sabotage an intervention effort.

At this juncture of the preparation process, the net result is to determine who specifically will attend the intervention. Any scheduling conflicts must be considered, and ultimately all who plan to participate must agree on the set schedule and location for the intervention.

Defining Roles and Boundaries

During the preparation meeting it is important for all those participating in the intervention to understand the distinct boundaries involved and what their respective roles will be.

Meaningful boundaries must be understood. What is the role of the intervention specialist, facilitator, or coordinator who has been chosen? How will he or she run the intervention, and what are the respective roles of each attendee or participant? Each person's role must be clarified before beginning the intervention so there is no misunderstanding that might potentially create confusion or a disruption.

During the preparation meeting, one area of concern to be discussed, which the intervention poses, is the potential uncovering or disclosure of painful family problems or secrets. Everyone must understand that family issues aren't the focus of the intervention. Everyone must agree that if such issues arise during the intervention and interrupt its focus, taking a break may be necessary. At that time the leader or facilitator may privately point out to individuals that the discussion is losing its necessary focus and suggest other more appropriate alternative means and resources, which might be used at some future time.

The person chosen to lead the intervention is in the primary role and will lead the discussion. That person will essentially control the presentation based on the assembled and organized file, and will keep the dialogue focused on that material and research. Others attending the intervention cannot interfere with that organized presentation and will not needlessly divert attention to other topics that aren't directly relevant. He or she will present the main body of information. In this sense the intervention process can be seen in many ways as a kind of lecture series or ongoing educational seminar largely led by one person who has been primarily delegated with the responsibility of presenting the material.

An intervention isn't therapy or counseling. Therefore, an intervention isn't the time to bring up personal family disagreements or grievances. Such matters can easily disrupt and potentially terminate an intervention. Family, friends, and other concerned parties in attendance must also understand that making disparaging or derogatory remarks and engaging in personal arguments are detrimental and may easily sabotage the intervention effort. For example, asking, "How could you believe that?" or saying, "You are too smart to be taken in by this" serves no useful purpose and may instead seem to denigrate the individual. Such remarks also ignore the fact that intelligence, general education, and career experience don't somehow protect people specifically from coercive persuasion techniques.

During an intervention family members, friends, and other partici-pants must remain focused on two primary purposes. They will func-tion as eyewitnesses of the situation that has caused concern and as emotional anchors. The cult-involved individual must feel emotion-ally anchored and safe because of their presence. This is the primary reason why they will stay. Thus participants must help to create an atmosphere of mutual support and safety based on whatever historical trust and understanding exist. This is vitally important, because any intervention with an adult in the United States today must be done on a voluntary basis. This means the person who is the focus of the inter-vention must give his or her consent, and the intervention depends on his or her ongoing cooperation.

During the preparation process, participants should discuss likely sce-narios or potential situations that may occur. For example, how will those present respond if the person who is the focus of the intervention becomes belligerent, threatens to leave, or abruptly begins to exit? At this point who would be most effective at persuading him or her to stay? Who would be most effective at persuading the person to stop and re-consider? This step might necessitate following the person when he or she leaves and then privately discussing the matter of returning to the intervention. No physical coercion may be used—only moral suasion. Someone might quite literally need to pursue the person for such a dis-cussion. This possibility must be discussed in some detail to determine who the designated person will be to handle such a situation if it occurs.

What would the person say in that situation?

My advice in such a situation is to always underscore the purpose of the intervention, which is education and information—and that this educa-tional process and dialogue are done within a finite framework. That is, the cooperation being requested is only temporary and relatively brief. The intervention will end at an agreed-on point of time. The decision to continue with a group or leader ultimately remains an individual choice, and that decision will be respected. Those participating in the intervention are asking only for some designated time for discussing and sharing their concerns and helpful information. Education is helpful and useful in providing for an informed decision-making process.

As previously mentioned, family and friends gathered for the intervention can provide firsthand eyewitness information. They can explain what they have seen and observed regarding recent events or behavior that has caused them concern. At various points during the intervention, the person in focus may deny that any problematic situation has existed or continues to exist. But because family and friends have firsthand knowledge, they may at the appropriate time be able to share another perspective through their personal experiences. When instances of denial arise, addressing them immediately isn't always necessary. What's important is exercising patience and waiting for the appropriate time to address such issues. As more information is shared and discussed, the intervention leader will evaluate the best time to address such concerns; then he or she can moderate such input.

During the intervention family and friends in attendance should feel free to respond as the facilitator or discussion leader makes various points if they feel they have something directly relevant and pertinent to say. For example, they may offer their personal observations, corroborating points about manipulation, undue influence, or coercive persuasion techniques that appear to be evident.

Important Rules to Remember

Those participating must understand that they cannot demand declarative statements. They must never demand that the person who is the focus of the intervention make some type of definitive statement about his or her future commitment to the cultic group or leader. If and when that person decides to make a definitive statement, he or she will do so subject to his or her own timeframe.

The purpose of the intervention isn't to present a list of demands that require an immediate response but rather to solicit cooperation in an ongoing educational process based on sharing information. What this means is that those participating must refrain from making demands and function within previously described boundaries—only as emotional anchors and eyewitnesses, not as inquisitors.

If a professional intervention specialist or facilitator is present, he or she cannot stay at a family residence or at whatever venue is being used for the intervention. Preferably he or she should stay at a nearby hotel. Those involved may call the facilitator if an urgent situation arises between intervention sessions that may require advice and attention. This separation affords a level of privacy and rest for everyone concerned. This intervening time typically takes place overnight between daily eight-hour intervention discussions.

Establishing boundaries between a professional intervention specialist and other participants is critical. This measure not only allows everyone some space to ease tension but also serves to maintain the interventionist's separate and distinct role—that is, as someone who isn't personally invested in the process or outcome but rather is present to serve as an educational resource and facilitator for informational purposes.

The daily schedule for an intervention usually runs between about 9:00 a.m. to 5:00 p.m. and is usually an extended weekend. But this may vary depending on the needs and schedules of those involved.

Hours outside the intervention are for rest and relaxation. Nothing should be discussed regarding the intervention, the group, the leader who has drawn concern, or any related topic. Discussions of these issues could potentially escalate into a needless argument, which might subsequently explode and then effectively end the effort. Instead of discussing such potentially explosive subjects, everyone concerned can enjoy TV, watch a movie, or play games. But it is important to stay together.

Everything should be done to make the environment comfortable. Primary participants in the intervention typically stay with family or friends at the location of the intervention overnight. It's important to ensure that any promises made regarding communication with the group or leader are kept. There should be no telephone calls, Internet access, or outside visits.. Those staying together should seek to ensure that this commitment is honored. This agreement may mean keeping fairly close company. For example, depending on the severity of the situation, someone may sleep in the same room or near the person who is the focus of the intervention.

At the conclusion of the first day, the discussion will focus on an agreement to meet the following day. At this point obtaining a firm commitment is important. There should be an understanding that the intervention discussion may continue for at least two or possibly three more days. Such a commitment must include an understanding about communication with the cultic group or leader who has raised the concern. Specifically, there should be no communication during the intervention process with anyone associated with the cultic group or leader in any way, shape, or form. This must include phone calls, text messages, e-mails, physical contact, or other forms of communication. The reason for this stipulation is simple. Those involved must be assured that the person at the focus of the intervention is thinking independently and not being coached. The temporary cessation of any ongoing communication or interference specifically guarantees this assurance.

If someone protests such an agreement about communication, it is best to respond by pointing out that what is being requested is, in a practical sense, quite reasonable. First, quality time is necessary to discuss serious concerns without interruption or interference. Second, the person who is the focus of the intervention has probably spent considerable time exclusively devoted to the group or leader without interference from family or friends. Therefore, allowing family and friends some time to privately discuss their concerns seems only fair.

If and when an agreement to temporarily discontinue communication with the group or leader is effectively made, it may be a good idea to ask everyone to turn off his or her cell phones and disconnect all Internet access and phone lines at the location chosen for the intervention. Typically interventions take place at a private residence where those involved can stay together overnight. But in some situations it may be better to arrange for hotel accommodations. Expect the cultic group or leader to interfere if there is communication. In most situations, if someone contacts the cultic group or leader, the group or leader will make every effort to sabotage or end the intervention.

Again, no physical coercion may be employed to enforce an agreement to temporarily discontinue communication with the group or leader. But the person who is the focus of the intervention may be asked to temporarily surrender his or her cell phone, laptop, notebook, or any other means of communication; the device will then be stored away until the intervention ends. This step may also necessitate closely monitoring the person in focus to make sure he or she honors whatever commitments he or she has made regarding time allotted and ongoing communication. Again, someone may sleep in the same room to ensure the individual doesn't leave or try to contact the group or leader during the night.

But if the person makes an effort to leave or contact the group or leader, nothing can be done to physically restrain him or her. Ultimately all that can be done is moral suasion. This means family and other concerned parties may plead as persuasively as possible that whatever allotment of time and constrained communication were agreed on should be honored. The importance of the suggested close supervision simply allows those involved an opportunity to present their objections and remind the individual of their commitment when, or if, he or she tries to violate the agreement.

During the preparation process what must be emphasized is how important it is to consistently follow and maintain the rules, boundaries, and roles previously outlined and discussed.

Starting Out

Often families and others involved in intervention efforts are most concerned and nervous about the initial introduction and first few minutes. They must understand that such interventions, including substance abuse interventions, occur as a complete surprise. This is usually an imperative that is most especially necessary due to concerns about interference from the group or leader. Because of the unexpected nature of the intervention, participants frequently worry about the initial introduction. That is, how should they introduce an intervention specialist and explain the situation?

The introduction and explanation should be presented as simply and succinctly as possible. For example, they can say, "We are worried about you, and we want to have an open discussion about our concerns." Then they can add, "Frankly we feel a bit overwhelmed, and so we asked someone knowledgeable to help us." At this point the family members or those involved specifically introduce the cult-intervention specialist by name. Simply a first name is at least initially sufficient and nonthreatening. At this juncture an intervention specialist or leader assumes the role of facilitator. In other words the primary responsibility for the intervention has now shifted from the family and others attending the intervention to the designated facilitator or specialist. Going over this point and understanding each specific piece of the intervention process in detail are important steps during preparation and specifically during the preparation meeting.

The first day usually begins in the morning to allow the maximum amount of time before ending the first day of discussion; it then typically ends in the late afternoon or early evening. Explaining the goals for the first day is important.

At the end of the first day, it is unlikely that the cult-involved person will demonstrate particular progress or sudden new insights. The goal of the first day is simply to build a foundation and gain a commitment to continue to the second day. If that agreement, with the aforementioned prohibition regarding communication with the cultic group or leader, is achieved, then the first day is a success. Most failed interventions end on the first day.

Staying Focused

The preparation process is an opportunity for everyone to fully understand the basic structure of the intervention—that is, breaking down block by block how the intervention process will be structured. This includes the four basic blocks of discussion during the intervention, which are defining a destructive cult, understanding how coercive persuasion and influence techniques work, discussing specifically relevant and historical information about the group or leader, and addressing family concerns.

At this point it is important to understand the inherently fluid nature of an intervention, which may shift and turn during an ongoing dialogue and exchange of ideas. This means that the order in which the four blocks of the intervention proceed largely depends on the corresponding interest and concerns of the person who is the focus of the intervention.

Again, the four basic blocks or focal points of the intervention dialogue are the following:

1. What is the definition of a destructive cult or cultic relationship?
2. How does the process of coercive persuasion or thought reform really work?
3. What is the history of the particular group or leader who has drawn concern?
4. What are the concerns of those gathered for the intervention?

In my experience an intervention becomes increasingly positive as each day passes and more information is exchanged. The accumulation of information by the person who is the focus of the intervention provides him or her with an expanded body of knowledge, which can then become the basis of more informed decision making and critical thinking. As each day of the intervention is completed, there is that much more information delivered and potentially considered.

This is why some destructive cults may seek to sabotage an intervention if they become aware that it is taking place. This is also why some destructive cults will attempt to isolate their members or continuously moderate their contact with outsiders. Simply put, such groups and leaders like what they can control and don't like what they can't. Unfiltered exposure to an outside frame of reference may be perceived as a possible threat to their continued dominance and control.

Those involved should understand that as each day of the intervention progresses, there is usually some evidence of movement. This means the person who is the focus of the intervention will often begin to function more independently and exhibit evidence of critical thinking. For example, the person may raise his or her own questions about the behavior of the group or leader and related dynamics of relationships. Or he or she may begin to question such things as the lack of transparency regarding the group or leader's finances or what steps for accountability actually exist. Evidence of increased critical thinking is an indication of progress.

Conclusion

As an intervention continues to progress, those involved want to know whether the intervention is moving in a positive direction. What signs can they look for? In my experience the first thing to look for is whether the person who is the focus of the intervention is meaningfully engaged. That can be seen based on the level and depth of his or her participation. Is the person attentive and acting interested? Is he or she actively involved in discussion? The worst-case scenario is when someone is shut down, angry, sullen, and not meaningfully engaged in dialogue.

Families and those concerned need to understand that they cannot reasonably expect to receive any definitive or declarative final statement at the conclusion of the intervention. Some people who are the focus of an intervention may decide at some point to openly express their decision to leave the influence of the cultic group or leader who has caused concern. But others may not make such a direct or succinct statement. There cannot be any pressure to make such a statement.

No blame or guilt can reasonably be assigned to the person who has been the focus of the intervention regarding his or her history of involvement in whatever cultic situation has drawn concern. No one knowingly consents to such undue influence and is instead tricked as the victim of deception. It is wrong and ultimately not useful or productive to be critical about past cultic involvement—for example, asking, "How could you be so gullible?" or "Why did you hurt us like this?" Such remarks that attempt to assign blame or induce guilt are both factually wrong and totally counterproductive.

Attempting to induce shame or guilt might produce a backlash or effectively create an obstacle concerning consideration to leave the group or leader. That is, if leaving the group or leader must include ongoing confrontation, which induces guilt and shame, perhaps it is preferable to stay in the cultic group rather than endure such painful humiliation.

Instead of creating such obstacles, everyone concerned must understand that his or her role is to do everything he or she can to make leaving the group or leader as easy and painless as possible. This means doing nothing during the intervention that should induce remorse.

Instead, everyone concerned must express positive support that reflects care and common concerns for the welfare, security, and future happiness of the person who is the focus of the intervention. This can lead to meaningful consideration about viable alternatives to the group or leader. Everything must be done to allow for space without fear of embarrassment or some form of emotional retribution.

Families and others concerned often ask how they will know when the person who is the focus of the intervention has genuinely decided to move away from a group or leader's undue influence if he or she hasn't made a definitive declarative statement. In most interventions this decision becomes evident when the person who is the focus of the intervention begins to disclose previously unknown and potentially harmful information about the group or leader. He or she may share information that could somehow damage the group or leader. This might include hidden historical facts or examples of extreme and alarming behavior, unethical conduct, murky or improper finances, or criminal activities. He or she might also admit that the group or leader manipulated him or her; he or she might offer vivid examples based on criteria previously discussed during the intervention.

In my experience when people begin to disclose such potentially damaging information about the group or leader, they have probably decided to move on and leave. Again, no one must say or do anything to apply any pressure to make this declaration. And nothing should be said or implied that might make the individual feel ashamed about whatever information he or she has disclosed. Instead, those present at the intervention must do their best to express unconditional support and affirm the love and friendship they feel and value. The person has suffered enough and quite often, due to the manipulation and abuse of the group or leader, is in a fragile state. Everything must be done to sustain an atmosphere of support and safety, and deference must be given for the sake of the person's dignity. The goal of an intervention is education, which can form the basis of more independent and informed decision making. Nothing must be done to hinder that process by causing unnecessary emotional distress.

Families will frequently ask, "What comes next?" if the intervention is successful. Some former cult members express a desire to follow up through counseling, while others do not. This is an individual choice based on personal reflection and the varying needs of each former member. Family members and others involved must not put undue pressure on the former cult member to seek professional counseling. They may simply suggest that this is a potential possibility or future option. There are very few professionals who have specific experience counseling former cult members. Many former cult members seem to prefer education rather than counseling. That is, they may engage in further research about cults, coercive persuasion, and influence techniques to better understand their experience. Issues former cult members commonly face will be discussed in more detail in the chapter "Moving On."

An intervention is not a "magic bullet" or miracle solution that will somehow fix every problem. Typically, people who leave cults and abusive, controlling relationships will continue to have personal problems just like everyone else. The family and friends of a person who is the focus of an intervention must understand this truth and have reasonable expectations.

Net Result

The net result of the preparation meeting is that everyone who plans to participate in the intervention fully understands his or her role, specific boundaries and rules, and crucial points that will be covered during the intervention. He or she now has both a meaningful understanding of the process and realistic expectations. By addressing these issues in some depth and answering any related questions, the potential for misunderstandings, conflicts, and needless missteps during the intervention can be greatly reduced and hopefully avoided.

The preparation meeting is the time to clarify each participant's role and the framework of the intervention so everyone involved understands what will, or may, potentially unfold. The net result of a proper preparation meeting are focused and fully informed participants; this is the best basis to ensure the most positive results.

Some families and others involved may not be able to locate an intervention specialist to help them. In such situations they may decide to delegate this responsibility to someone else. They might decide on a highly regarded family member, a respected mentor, a long-standing and close friend, or a paid professional they feel can effectively fulfill this role. In such a situation this book may serve as a helpful resource by providing meaningful information and practical guidelines.

The person chosen to lead and facilitate an intervention must be well spoken, have good communication and organizational skills, and the time required to complete the task.

---

[726] Rick A. Ross, "Cults: An Educational Volume," DVD, Trenton, NJ: Cult Education Institute, 2001.

[727] Rick A. Ross, "In The Name of Love: Abusive Controlling Relationships," DVD, Trenton, NJ: Cult Education Institute, New Jersey, www.culteducation.com (2004).

[728] Robert Jay Lifton, "Cult Formation," *Harvard Mental Health Letter*, February 1981.

[729] Robert Jay Lifton, *Thought Reform and the Psychology of Totalism* (University of North Carolina Press, 2012), 419–437

[730] Richard Ofshe, "Coercive Persuasion and Attitude Change," *Encyclopedia of Sociology*, vol. 1 (New York: McMillan, 1992), 212–224.

[731] Singer, *Cults in Our Midst*, 58–59.

[732] Robert B. Cialdini, *Influence: Science and Practice* (Needham Heights, MA: Allyn & Bacon, 2001).

[733] "Captive Minds: Hypnosis and Beyond." Documentary. Directed by Pierre Lasry. Montreal: National Film Board of Canada, 1983. http://www.youtube.com/watch?v=mQC0nFfp2nc&index=1&list=PL2D64B3CB3D593ACF (accessed May 22, 2014).

734 Davison, Bruce, Lori Lethin and John Putch. "The Wave." DVD. Directed by Alexander Grasshoff. Thousand Oaks, CA: BN Publishing, 1980.

735 Lau, Frederick, Max Riemelt and Jennifer Ulrich. "Die Welle [The Wave]." DVD. Directed by Dennis Gansel. Munich, Germany: Constantin Video, 2008.

736 Todd Srasser, "The Wave," *Ember*, January 8, 2013.

737 Maurice Davis,. "You Can Go Home Again."DVD. Directed by Elliot Bernstein, New York: Union for Reform Judaism, 1982.

CHAPTER 10

THE INTERVENTION PROCESS

This chapter is devoted to explaining the process of cult intervention based on my many years of experience, which has included hundreds of such efforts while working with families across the United States and internationally. I'm not a mental health professional, but based on my experience and knowledge, the cult-intervention process is an information-driven educational dialogue. It is neither counseling nor family therapy, which requires personal disclosure and a different set of distinct boundaries. As cultic studies professional and psychologist Michael Langone noted, "Humanistic counseling approaches…[run] the risk of imposing clarity, however subtly, on the framework's foundational ambiguity and thereby manipulating the client."[738] In contrast an educational approach simply offers information, which ideally provides a basis for individual decision making without such manipulation.

Keeping ethical considerations regarding manipulation in mind, we can see that neither neuro-linguistics programming (NLP) nor hypnosis should be used in the context of a cult intervention. Both are techniques used to increase the suggestibility or manipulate the subject. NLP, which is a communication approach created in the 1970s, involves the carefully planned use of subtle suggestions conveyed by certain chosen vocabulary and behaviors, which are strategically employed to influence people.[739]

Typically NLP is done without informed consent and thus is a deceptive form of manipulation. Similarly, hypnosis can also be used to manipulate a subject "guided by another (the hypnotist) to respond to suggestions for changes in subjective experience, alterations in perception, sensation, emotion, thought or behavior."[740] These techniques cannot be components of an ethical process of education, which is based on informed consent and an honest exchange of information.

The most important single component, which is the foundation for any intervention effort, is meaningful access. That is, the person who will be the focus of the intervention still communicates with and visits family and old friends. Without such a level of meaningful access, there is no basis to initiate an intervention. For this reason many people considering an intervention may need to wait for the right opportunity, such as a family vacation, weekend visit, or event, that may potentially provide the time and privacy needed to stage an intervention.

This may require a period of slowly developing better rapport if there has been an estrangement or rupture in communication due to a past argument or ongoing criticism of the group or leader in question. A previous chapter suggests "coping strategies" that can help to develop better communication and more meaningful access. It is important to be consistent and patient. This period of development may take months or possibly longer. When communication is good and regular visits occur, the planning can begin for an eventual intervention.

An average cult intervention is typically a multiday process that doesn't include time for travel or preparation. Preparation with family members and other concerned parties who will participate in the intervention should normally consume about five to eight hours and take place on the day immediately before the intervention begins. A completed intervention should take approximately twenty-four to thirty-two working hours, which is spread out over three to four days at about eight hours each day, not including breaks. Structuring an intervention in this organized way ensures that adequate time will be spent on each category of concern and that nothing important will be missed. Limiting the duration of discussion to eight hours each day provides rest and relaxation time for everyone involved. People need to have proper sleep and private time to unwind and reflect. The schedule may vary according to the sleeping habits and responsibilities of participants.

There may be breaks allotted more frequently depending on specific needs. For example, someone involved in a cult may feel that frequent breaks are necessary due to the amount of information being shared. He or she may at times feel somewhat overwhelmed, and it is important to respect such considerations. A reasonable level of comfort for everyone involved in the intervention should be maintained. An intervention to extricate someone from a destructive cult should in no way replicate cultic manipulation, which frequently relies on sleep deprivation and information overload.

Most often the more time is spent on the intervention, the more likely it is that the cult member will leave the group. That is, the amount of time made available within the given multiday framework to explain and discuss concerns linked to destructive cult involvement directly corresponds to the likelihood that the cult-involved person will decide to leave the group or situation in question. The more information the cult member has to consider, the more potential there is to stimulate his or her independent critical thinking. This may be the reason some destructive cults have historically urged or often coached members to immediately leave any apparent intervention effort. Cults that have lost members through interventions seem to understand that the more time there is to share information, the more likely it is that the member won't return to the cult. But an intervention, including the necessary preparation time with participants, shouldn't exceed four to five days total.

Interventions require a fine balance between providing too much information too quickly, which might overload and distress the cult-involved person and cause him or her to leave, and discussing enough relevant information each day to keep him or her interested and engaged. It is also important to be receptive to the cult member's questions and particular interests. We make it clear from the beginning that any relevant questions are welcome and that if someone thinks a certain detail or issue hasn't been addressed sufficiently, it is all right to stop an ongoing segment of discussion to specifically address such concerns. Those setting the pace of the intervention and exchange should also be sensitive to the situation. It may be necessary to slow down or speed up the dialogue and exchange of information depending on the receptivity of the cult-involved person, the needs of those involved, and other circumstances.

Most of my interventions have been successful. That is, the individual who was the focus of the intervention decided to leave the cult, destructive group, or abusive and controlling relationship by the conclusion of the intervention process. I know of only a few occasions when people who decided to leave a group at the conclusion of an intervention later returned to that same group or situation. Conversely, some people who initially decided to stay with a group despite an intervention effort later left it, largely due to the information they had received during the intervention.

Most of my failures have occurred within the first day of the intervention. The person who was the focus of the intervention left abruptly, usually before the second day began. When someone indicates he or she wants to leave, family members and others participating in the intervention will try to persuade him or her to stay. At times when a cult-involved person leaves a family member, a friend or mentor will talk with him or her, and he or she will come back.

Only a very small fraction of cult members I have worked with for a period of three to four days chose to continue in the group. What this means is that as each day goes by and the hours spent on the intervention steadily accumulate, the likelihood that the cult member will decide to leave the group or situation increases proportionately.

If an intervention fails, it is important that every effort be made for it to end in positive terms. That is, despite any disagreement and stated concerns, the love, friendship, and ongoing communication of those concerned are reinforced and will continue. Following a failed intervention, the guidelines in the chapter about "coping strategies" should be followed as closely as possible.

An intervention is essentially an ongoing dialogue or discussion. During such a discussion, all those present offer their impressions, observations, and opinions as long as they do so respectfully. My role as an intervention specialist is to lead and facilitate that ongoing discussion, often directing and focusing attention on specific research material and emphasizing certain points by asking thought-provoking questions. I also organize and focus the discussion around specific points of interest based on categories of collective research or concern. The questions hopefully elicit reflection and stimulate critical thinking. Others attending the intervention contribute by offering their observations and insights as they become relevant to the points or topics being examined and discussed. This is an ongoing and fluid dialogue in what is usually a small group of three to five people including me, the cult-affected person, and his or her concerned family and friends who have agreed to participate.

If a particular family member or friend is repeatedly rude or disrespectful, interrupting him or her and reiterating the need for courtesy in the discussion may be necessary. In some situations such behavior may necessitate a time-out or break to individually discuss such behavior with the offending person. If this attempt to remedy the situation fails to correct the problem, the offending person may need to withdraw and cease participating in the intervention effort. Unchecked outbursts of anger, rudeness, or needlessly confrontational behavior can easily sidetrack the ongoing discussion and potentially lead to a breakdown that might ultimately end the intervention.

An intervention typically takes place in a private and quiet place where participants can dialogue and exchange ideas without interruptions. This most often occurs within a private residence. But at times I have worked in a hospital setting, a business office, hotel conference rooms, and resort retreats.

During the first day of the intervention, I ask everyone to agree to continue uninterrupted, which means shutting off cell phones, Internet connections, and other potential sources of interruption. I explicitly ask the person who is the focus of the intervention not to contact or have any communication with the group or leader who has caused concern during the intervention. This request includes anyone associated with that group or leader. At the end of the first day, plans to continue the discussion during the immediately following days are discussed and agreed on. This is done with active family participation. That is, family and others involved are quite actively engaged at this point in persuading the cult-involved person to stay and continue, as discussed during the previous preparation process.

During the intervention the cult-involved person will stay with family or friends participating in the intervention. This most often means staying at the house of someone involved or sharing a room at a hotel or at whatever venue has been chosen for the intervention. This is all done to rule out any interference from the cultic group or leader during the intervention. It is important that the cult-involved person not be coached and that his or her interaction and considerations are spontaneous rather than rehearsed. Of course, any adult is free to go at any time during the intervention, though family and friends may use moral suasion to urge the person to stay.

At times, depending on group influence and its level of the use of coercive persuasion and undue influence techniques, a cult member may drift in and out of altered states of consciousness or what has been called "floating." At such times it may be necessary to take a break and allow some time before becoming refocused and engaging in dialogue again. Taking an outdoor walk, playing with a pet, doing some exercise, or participating in some other physical activity may effectively interrupt such a state and also break up the day, offering a respite. If such floating states occur frequently, it may be meaningful to draw attention to this situation and specifically discuss it. If the cultic group or leader encourages trance states through daily meditation or some other practice, one should suggest that this routine be suspended during the time of the intervention.

In an intervention focused on the cult involvement of a minor child, the parents or legal guardian might decide not to allow the minor child to leave, which is his or her legal right. Parents may also legally forbid a minor child from contacting or communicating with a cultic group or leader. This prohibition could potentially be enforced by local law enforcement or a court-issued restraining order. A cultic group or leader would typically have no legal right to interfere with or supersede such parental authority.

Before taking such legally sanctioned action, those concerned should consult a local attorney. In some very rare and extreme situations, an involuntary intervention might occur if a cult-involved adult is being legally held in a treatment facility or is otherwise detained by authorities.

At the beginning of the intervention, the family should introduce the moderator or facilitator they have honestly chosen. I have typically been introduced as a professional consultant asked to participate due to my knowledge base and work experience. After being introduced, I then explain my work experience and answer any questions before starting the discussion. At this juncture honesty and courtesy are the best responses.

There should be no deception regarding why everyone has assembled. And the explanation offered for the surprise nature of the intervention is usually explained as follows: if the intervention had been announced in advance, the cult-involved person wouldn't have attended, the cultic group or leader would have told him or her not to participate, and he or she would possibly have been accompanied by someone from the group or otherwise influenced not to cooperate. In this sense a cult intervention is comparable to the same surprise usually employed in a substance-abuse intervention, with the notable exception that an outside group isn't typically an issue during an intervention about drug or alcohol abuse. What's also important during the introduction is assuring the person who is the focus of the intervention and agreeing with everyone present that no one will be rude or disrespectful and that there is no reason to be afraid of asking questions.

Four basic blocks or categories of discussion should be covered in the intervention. These four building blocks form the foundation needed to accomplish a successful discussion about areas of concern. These blocks might effectively be discussed in the order that follows, but the sequence may vary due to the fluid nature of an intervention, which reflects the interest and focus of the cult-involved individual.

The four blocks of discussion are the following:

1. What are the defining elements of a destructive cult?
2. How do destructive cults use identifiable persuasion techniques to gain undue influence over their members?
3. What is the history of the particular group or leader who has drawn concern?
4. What is the family's immediate and potential concerns regarding involvement with the group or situation that has led to the intervention?

First Block of Discussion: Defining a Destructive Cult

This segment of the intervention is a discussion specifically about the definition of a destructive cult and is largely premised on the simple, three-point definition psychiatrist Robert Jay Lifton offered in his paper "Cult Formation."[741] Lifton's definition forms the nucleus of most, if not all, definitions of destructive cults, which often simply expand upon these three primary characteristics.

This definition offers a basis to begin the discussion about destructive cults on an objective basis, which is based on behavior rather than on belief. It is important to avoid any appearance of attacking beliefs and instead focus on group behavior, dynamics, and the cult's hierarchal power structure. This block of discussion does to some extent enable the conversation to touch on the other blocks of the intervention process. That is, Lifton's criteria include coercive persuasion and exploitation, which may intersect issues such as group dynamics, family concerns, and the specific group or leader's history. But the discussion at this juncture should stay focused on defining a cult and not be tangentially pulled off track for too long.

Lifton states that

> cults can be identified by three characteristics:
>
> 1. a charismatic leader who increasingly becomes an object of worship as the general principles that may have originally sustained the group lose their power;
>
> 2. a process I call coercive persuasion or thought reform;
>
> 3. economic, sexual, and other exploitation of group members by the leader and the ruling coterie.

A Powerful, Charismatic Leader

The first criterion is that the group can be seen as essentially personality driven—that is, defined by a living totalitarian leader. He or she is the focus of the group, the locus of power, and its driving force. Whatever he or she says is right is right, and whatever he or she says is wrong is wrong. Members of the group, therefore, ultimately abdicate their ability to make many of their value judgments in deference to the leader.

At this point in the intervention, historical examples or profiles of destructive cult leaders are offered to specifically delineate and demonstrate how cult leaders operate. For example, well-known cult figures who can be cited and examined include Jim Jones, David Koresh, Shoko Asahara, and Charles Manson. The purpose here is not to needlessly frighten anyone by offering such extreme examples of destructive cults, but rather to establish the common traits and behaviors historical cult leaders share. Who they are and how their followers reportedly perceived them are commonly known. What did they have in common as personalities? What parallels are evident in the structure and dynamics of the groups gathered around these leaders?

At this juncture produce research material relevant to the discussion; this might potentially include news articles, book excerpts, documentaries, and news reports relevant to the history and behavior of well-documented cult leaders. The purpose of this block of discussion is to develop a consensus or agreement that there have been historical figures called "cult leaders" and that these leaders share some common, noteworthy characteristics. Discussion then can develop concerning how the particular group or leader, who is the focus of the intervention, might in some ways be similar to the historical profiles of past destructive cult leaders.

Important points in such a discussion might include a review of accountability in the group. What meaningful checks and balances effectively limit the power of leadership? Is there a form of democratically elected group governance, as mandated by corporate or constitutional bylaws? For example, is there an elected board that serves fixed terms and stands for reelection, as established by an existing set of bylaws? What government of the group exists, and how was it constituted? Is there meaningful financial transparency concerning group funds and the way those funds are handled? For example, this could be through an independently audited budget, which discloses in detail all salaries, compensation, and expenses paid from group funds. Is such a budget made available to all group members or contributors on a regular basis?

On an interpersonal level, what explicit boundaries exist regarding the leader's influence? For example, what areas of an individual's life remain private and personal and are therefore immune from the group or leader's questioning or scrutiny? Is the leader ever wrong? If the leader has been wrong, what examples can be cited to illustrate this point? Can the leader be meaningfully questioned or contradicted? If the leader can, in fact, be questioned and contradicted, what are some specific examples?

Has the leader become such a dominant figure that he or she can be seen as the focus and driving force of the group? Has the leader made personal or professional claims that can be seen as grandiose or self-important and self-serving—and that could potentially encourage admiration? Has the group become personality driven? At this juncture there might also be some discussion about narcissistic personalities and about how some of the statements historical cult leaders have made appear to parallel that personality profile.

Thought Reform

During this block of the intervention, discussion should focus on defining a destructive cult through the practice of what Lifton calls "thought reform." This is the second of Lifton's three criteria to define a destructive cult. But since this topic will be discussed later in far more depth in a succeeding block of the intervention, it is not necessary to delve into it too deeply at this juncture.

At this point a single salient feature or objective of thought reform may be offered. This might be confined to the basic pattern of corresponding behavior that demonstrates undue influence. That is, members of destructive cults often do things that are not in their own best interest but are consistently in the best interests of the group or leader. We can see this behavior as evidence of undue influence due to diminished independent and critical thinking.

Undue influence can also be seen in an increased dependence on the group or leader for problem solving, decisions, and value judgments. Some examples can be offered regarding historical cult groups, such as the Waco Davidians, Jonestown, or members of Heaven's Gate. What did members do that was not in their best interests but was dictated by leadership? These activities might include such acts as relinquishing parental rights, surrendering assets, providing free labor, suffering medical neglect, experiencing family estrangements, and participating in criminal acts on behalf of the group or leader.

Harm and Exploitation

The final criterion Lifton offers is that the group or leader does harm or exploits people. The point should be made that not all groups are identical in the level of harm they do; this area varies by degree from group to group. That is, some groups may be more destructive than others. The discussion here focuses on what specific harm groups have historically done and what potential for harm might be seen to exist in the group in question.

At this point research material and specific documentation should be shared to establish how various cults have exploited or harmed people. Material might include news reports, documentaries, and court records. It is important to establish a pattern of grievances and harm done and then use that information as a basis to determine whether a similar pattern might have occurred in the current situation. At this point friends or family members might briefly discuss some of their concerns, though this stage will be discussed more in depth later in the intervention.

The previous chapter, "Defining a Destructive Cult," can be used along with its cited research to support certain points during this first block of discussion. The Cult Education Institute archives and other research resources accessible through the Internet contain a many articles, reports, and other documentation. This material can be used to support and emphasize certain points. The gathered research material should include specific information about histories and profiles of known cult leaders coupled with cult behavior. The Cult Education Institute distributes a helpful DVD titled *Cults: An Educational Volume* that provides a synthesis of research regarding the basic attributes of destructive cults. This can be viewed along with news reports featuring various destructive cults. News reports about cults can often be seen through the Internet at various points on the World Wide Web.

Second Block of the Intervention: How Does the Process of Thought Reform Work?

This block of discussion focuses on thought reform, persuasion techniques, and influence. It is largely based on the writings of Robert Jay Lifton,[742] psychologist Margaret Singer,[743] sociologist Richard Ofshe,[744] and professor of psychology Robert Cialdini.[745] The writings of these experts form the basis of the discussion as cited along with other authors and experts listed in a previous chapter on "Cult Brainwashing."

You can see the interlocking research reviewed during an intervention by looking at the same phenomenon but from different perspectives and at times different fields of research. What those various perspectives offer and can potentially provide is a kind of three-dimensional imaging that demonstrates how destructive cults and cult leaders operate and how they use recognizable persuasion techniques—or what some might call "tricks" of manipulation to gain undue influence.

A basic guide to begin is contained in Ofshe's "Coercive Persuasion and Attitude Change." Ofshe offers what he calls the "four key factors that distinguish coercive persuasion from other training and socialization schemes":

1. "The reliance on intense interpersonal and psychological attack to destabilize an individual sense of self to promote compliance"

   Some questions should be raised regarding this point. For example, has the group or leader—the focus of this intervention—often been confrontational? If there have been confrontations, what level of critical feedback is tolerated in such a situation? What are the boundaries in such situations? And do people subsequently feel any pressure to change? Is there noticeable compliance in the group after confrontations take place? Is there a process of breaking people down that can be discerned from this group process?

2. "The use of an organized peer group"

   Some basic questions should be asked about group structure and dynamics. Do an identifiable group and framework exist? Is there a sense of group identity? How is the group organized? What is the schedule of the group? Answers to these questions should establish the existence of a peer group, its general focus, and expectations.

3. "Applying interpersonal pressure to promote conformity"

   Here questions should focus on how group interaction and relationships lead to accepting group norms. Do members of the group genuinely appreciate differences and meaningfully demonstrate tolerance of different opinions and behavior? If so, how is this tolerance specifically expressed? Do relationships in the group seem to become easier when there is agreement and harder when there is critical feedback and resistance? Does resistance or negative feedback to the suggestions of the group or leader cause serious problems? Can friendships in the group deteriorate due to such a conflict?

4. "The manipulation of the totality of the person's social environment to stabilize behavior once modified"

How much time is spent in the group and its related activities? How much time is spent away from the group? What old friendships, associations, and interests outside of the group remain as active as in the past and intact? Have old friendships, associations, and outside interests deteriorated since one became involved in the group? Has the group or leader encouraged the retention and maintenance of strong friendships, associations, and interests outside the group and its interests?

These basic factors, as Ofshe outlined, become the foundation for an expanded and more detailed discussion about thought reform as Robert Jay Lifton defined it. Lifton cites eight criteria to use to establish the existence of a thought-reform program, as outlined in his book *Thought Reform and the Psychology of Totalism.*[746] Lifton says that if six of these eight criteria are evident, then a thought-reform program exists and is ongoing.

1. "Milieu Control," Ofshe describes, is the "control of the environment and communication."

What environmental controls evident in the particular group have drawn concern? Are suggestions or restrictions stated or implied on reading materials, television viewing, communication, and relationships? Do group members live together? If so, what are these living arrangements like? Do they also work together for the same employer? Is that employer somehow associated with the group or leader? How much quality time do members of the group spend alone?

Answers to these questions can potentially demonstrate the existence of milieu control and lead to a better understanding of how group controls work in the environment. We should understand that some destructive cults or leaders exercise overt control, while others choose to exercise control in a more covert manner. Some groups can therefore achieve Milieu Control through a subtle process of implied rules and suggestions rather than overt demands. The choice of using a subtle process can nevertheless limit associations, control the allocation of personal time, and ultimately control the environment.

2. "Mystical Manipulation," Ofshe explains, is "emotional and behavioral manipulation" done through the guise of group beliefs and practices. Lifton also calls this "planned spontaneity."

What has the group or leader done that seemed spontaneous but was actually carefully planned? For example, were people knowingly targeted for recruitment in a deceptive manner? Is training or study undertaken in a specific way to obtain specific results without the knowledge of those affected? Are they led to believe such results are spontaneous? How has the leadership knowingly misled and manipulated group members?

3. "The Demand for Purity" is what Ofshe describes as "demands for absolute conformity to behavior as prescribed and derived from the group ideology." To some extent all destructive cults have an ultimate idealized prototype. This prototype is the required paradigm to measure each individual member's success or attainment of ideal purity.

What is the preferred profile or prototype of a perfected member of the group being discussed? What constitutes a member in good standing? Does the group tolerate ambiguity in this regard? Or does the group tend to express its ideal prototype in terms of black and white without any meaningful room for ambiguity? Specifically, how much room is there for individual, personal expression outside the rigid profile of an ideal member?

4. "The Cult of Confession" or what Ofshe sees as the "obsessive demands for personal and group confession," renders those involved increasingly vulnerable and transparent, and it diminishes any sense of real privacy.

What is actually allowed to remain private in the group or situation? Is there anything explicitly immune and off limits to scrutiny? Are those involved expected to answer virtually any question when asked? What group activities exist that would tend to promote or solicit personal disclosure? This might potentially include some type of group encounter session, a religious practice, a retreat observance, or some other mandated activity.

5. "The Sacred Science" is what Ofshe explains as "agreement that the group ideology is absolutely perfect, faultless" or what Lifton calls its "ultimate vision for the ordering of all human existence."

This criterion solicits questions about how the group or leader sees his or her role in society and the world. Does the group or leader believe he or she has the ultimate solutions or answers to virtually any problem? Or has the group or leader admitted there are many questions or problems he or she is unable to address or answer? Does the group or leader essentially express that his or her beliefs, ideas, or philosophy is the means for resolving just about any problem? Is this belief somehow expressed in the confidence and confirmation that the group or leader's answers represent a kind of "one size fits all" solution for virtually anything? Does the group or leader acknowledge that other groups and leaders are equally equipped to address problems with their answers and solutions? What can develop from these points being discussed is that the group or leader believes his or her philosophy and answers exclusively represent the only and ultimate set of solutions for everyone without any meaningful exceptions.

6. "Loading the Language," Ofshe explains, is the "manipulation of language often characterized by thought terminating clichés, which substitute for critical and analytical thought."

What specific insider language or terms typify the group or leader in question? Do members redundantly recite group terminology that reflects a particular world view or mindset? For example, are negative labels routinely applied to outsiders or those who offend the group? Are there similar clichés that label unwanted thoughts and feelings? Do members of the group tend to categorize people, things, thoughts, and feelings using the same verbiage? For example, Scientologists label those perceived as negative as suppressive persons or SPs. Bible-based cults often refer to themselves as "true Christians" while dismissively categorizing and labeling those outside their group as "lukewarm Christians" who are somehow not completely committed. Former members of such groups have also been derisively described as "backsliders."

7. "Doctrine Over Person," Ofshe describes, is the "reinterpretation of human experience and emotion as seen through the lens and according to the terms of group doctrine."

The following questions should be asked: Do members tend to categorize their thoughts and feelings in terms of either negative or positive, as determined by the group's beliefs? Do members likewise see those outside the group through a similar lens per their rules and beliefs? Thus can almost anything be potentially categorized in accordance with the group's doctrine?

8. "The Dispensing of Existence" is what Ofshe sees as the "classification of those not sharing the group's beliefs as inferior and not worthy of respect." This criterion represents the culmination of thought reform, and it explains how cult members can dismiss and ultimately eliminate family and old friends from their lives. For example, Scientologists are often encouraged to disconnect from so-called suppressive persons.

Has the group or leader in question somehow encouraged a similar pattern of behavior? Has anyone been cut off? Under what circumstances might this rejection potentially occur? Have any disagreements about the group or leader with family and old friends somehow diminished communication or led to estrangement? Has the group or leader caused individuals to disengage from the outside world? Has the group or leader somehow diminished former members? Has a disagreement or lack of compliance led to the diminishing of some members in the group in some way?

At this point distinctions should be made between the process of coercive persuasion or thought reform used by destructive cults and other forms of persuasion such as education, advertising, propaganda, and indoctrination. Psychologist Margaret Singer provides an excellent chart for this matter that draws distinctions between these various forms of persuasion and demonstrates those differences based on focus of body of knowledge, direction and degree of exchange, ability to change, structure of persuasion, type of relationship, deceptiveness, breadth of learning, tolerance, and methodology.[747] Discussing these distinctions, using Singer's chart on the next page, is important. Go over each form of persuasion one by one to clarify that thought reform is a unique and separate category of persuasion. For example, thought reform is coercive, intolerant of another frame of reference, and deliberately deceptive.

	Education	Advertising	Propaganda	Indoctrination	Thought Reform
Focus of Body of Knowledge	Many bodies of knowledge based on scientific findings in various fields	Body of knowledge concerns product, competitors, how to sell, and influence via legal persuasion.	Body of knowledge centers on political persuasion of masses of people.	Body of knowledge is explicitly designed to inculcate organizational values.	Body of knowledge centers on changing people without their knowledge.
Direction and Degree of Exchange	Two-way pupil-teacher exchange is encouraged.	Exchange can occur, but communication is generally one sided.	Some exchange occurs, but communication is generally one sided.	Limited exchange occurs; communication is one sided.	No exchange occurs; communication is one sided.
Ability to Change	Change occurs as science advances, as students and other scholars offer criticism, and as students and citizens evaluate programs.	Change is made by those who pay for it, based on the success of ad programs, based on consumer law, and in response to consumer complaints.	Change is based on changing tides in world politics and on the political need to promote the group, nation, or international organization.	Change is made through formal channels via written suggestions to higher-ups.	Change occurs rarely; organization remains fairly rigid; change occurs primarily to improve thought-reform effectiveness.
Structure of Persuasion	Uses teacher-pupil structure; logical thinking is encouraged.	Uses an instructional mode to persuade consumer or buyer.	Takes authoritarian stance to persuade masses.	Takes authoritarian and hierarchical stance.	Takes authoritarian and hierarchical stance; there is no full awareness on part of learner.
Type of Relationship	Instruction is time limited and consensual.	Consumer or buyer can accept or ignore communication.	Learner support and engrossment are expected.	Instruction is contractual and consensual.	Group attempts to retain people forever.

Deceptiveness	It is not deceptive.	It can be deceptive, selecting only positive views.	It can be deceptive and is often exaggerated.	It is not deceptive.	It is deceptive.
Breadth of Learning	Focuses on learning to learn and learning about reality; broad goal is rounded knowledge for development of the individual.	Has a narrow goal of swaying opinion to promote and sell an idea, object, or program; another goal is to enhance seller and possibly buyer.	Targets large political masses to make them believe a specific view or circumstance is good.	Stresses narrow learning for a specific goal: to become something or to train for performance of duties.	Individualizes target; there is a hidden agenda (you will be changed one step at a time to become deployable to serve leaders).
Tolerance	It respects differences.	It puts down competition.	It wants to lessen opposition.	It is aware of differences.	There is no respect for differences.
Methods	There are instructional techniques.	There is mild-to-heavy persuasion.	There is overt persuasion; sometimes it is unethical.	There are disciplinary techniques.	There are improper and unethical techniques.

Singer also expands on the three stages of coercive persuasion Edgar Schein, a professor at MIT, defined; these outlined the process of coercive persuasion in three basic steps.[748] Going over these three steps offers an opportunity to examine the dynamic process of coercive persuasion and how change in that process is obtained.

Condition (Singer)	Themes (Lifton)		Stages (Schein)
1. Keep the person unaware of what is going on and the changes taking place.			Unfreezing
2. Control the person's time and, if possible, physical environment.	1.	Milieu control	
3. Create a sense of powerlessness, covert fear, and dependence.	2.	Loading the language	
4. Suppress much of the person's old behavior and attitudes.	3.	Demand for purity	
	4.	Confession	

5.	Instill new behavior and attitudes.	5.	Mystical manipulation	Changing
		6.	Doctrine over person	
6.	Put forth a closed system of logic; allow no real input or criticism.	7.	Sacred science	Refreezing
		8.	Dispensing of existence	

1. "Unfreezing" is what Singer describes as "the destabilizing of a person's sense of self." This process includes "keeping the person unaware of what is going on and the changes taking place. Controlling the person's time and if possible their physical environment. Creating a sense of powerless covert fear and dependency. And suppressing much of the person's old behavior and attitudes."

   Did group members initially explain in detail what their ultimate goals were and what changes they expected from people? Did they completely explain what needed to be done to achieve those goals? What exactly was said, and did this genuinely constitute meaningful and detailed disclosure? How did the group or leader expect the daily schedule of new members to change as they became more involved? Was the group or leader critical of new participants? How exactly was this criticism expressed, and how did the criticized people respond? Did the group or leader do or say anything that caused people to feel fearful, apprehensive, or anxious about anything? Did fear of something in any way seem to motivate people to be more receptive to change?

2. "Changing" is what Singer describes as "getting the person to drastically reinterpret his or her life's history and radically alter his or her worldview and accept a new version of reality and causality."

   This definition raises relevant questions such as the following: As people became more involved with the group or leader, did they feel different about the meaning and direction of their lives? How did they express this change? Did people in the group express anguish or unhappiness about their past? In what context did such personal disclosures take place, and what seemed to be their net effect? How was unhappiness about the past sorted out within the group? Were there any comments or sentiments expressed about how the group contributed or helped people in a sorting-out process concerning past experiences? Were the subsequently expressed sentiments increasingly consistent with the group or leader's beliefs and world view?

3. "Refreezing," Singer says, is to "put forth a closed system of logic; [to] allow no real input or criticism."

As people in the group evolved and changed, did their schedules also somehow change? That is, did they spend increasingly more time with the group or leader? At meetings and in discussions with leaders, what level of overt and challenging criticism was allowed or tolerated? What specific examples can be given of such a free exchange of ideas the group or leader tolerated? When have long-term members of the group directly challenged authority or questioned the basic assumptions of the group? How was criticism of those outside the group viewed? Were people in the group discouraged in any way, shape, or form from associating with outsiders or those who expressed criticism? How did the group and its leaders view former members?

The answers to these questions can demonstrate that the group essentially represents a closed system, which is intolerant of an outside frame of reference. Group members are deliberately sealed inside this static system and strategically maintained in a type of stasis within a controlled environment.

Documentary DVDs may also be shown at this juncture in the intervention process to demonstrate these specific coercive persuasion techniques in action. These DVDs might include news reports about destructive cults that demonstrate their internal behavior and also research regarding the suggestible states achievable through hypnosis, trance induction, meditation, yoga, chanting, and various other exercises.

Questions at this point may focus on how such states of suggestibility can be manipulated through various techniques such as "guided imagery" and "indirect directives." For example, guided imagery might occur gently through a soft voice suggesting certain images and feelings to someone while he or she is in a hypnotic trance. This may have a lasting effect on both his or her perception of reality and emotions. An indirect directive might also be used, which is done to convey a directive without telling someone explicitly. That is, rather than through a direct verbal command, an indirect directive may rely on nonverbal clues evident through such things as body language, vocal inflection, or facial expressions. When employed, this technique affords the user the apology that no direct influence appeared to take place.

An excellent documentary titled *Captive Minds: Hypnosis and Beyond* can effectively illustrate these points.[749] This one-hour presentation explains how hypnosis works and describes the inherent suggestibility people experience while in trance states. The film also examines the activities of purported "cult" leaders such as Rev. Moon of the Unification Church and Indian guru Bhagwan Shree Rajneesh. It also explores the cloistered and controlled lifestyles of less controversial groups such as Roman Catholic monks as well as the rigid training used by the US Marines. What the documentary demonstrates is the vulnerability and apparent fragility of the human mind. It also features firsthand accounts by former participants in the various groups, who explain their personal encounters and experiences. The film can be an effective tool to vividly illustrate specific points regarding the various manipulative persuasion techniques used to gain undue influence, which have already been discussed.

The discussion should then focus on how the group in question may express these criteria and coercive persuasion techniques. Does the group use some form of hypnosis or trance induction through meditation, yoga, devotional activities, or some other routinely repeated exercise? Does the group or leader encourage this as an avenue or basis for change? What changes are solicited through such activities? Is there any evidence of guidance being given during or shortly after participants achieved altered states of consciousness? How have such exercises ultimately impacted, influenced, and shaped the group experience for those involved? What can be seen as the goal or end result of such experiences? Do such exercises somehow promote a particular point of view, a framework for gaining some insight or meaning? Those participating in the intervention can offer their perspectives on how they see that these points may be relevant to the situation.

Now a review of more general influence techniques should be discussed. This discussion is based on the writings of Robert Cialdini, author of the seminal book *Influence*.[750] In his book Cialdini, professor of psychology at Arizona State University, offers what he identifies as the "six principles of influence."

1. "The rule of reciprocity," Cialdini says, "requires that one person try to repay what another person has provided."[751] Singer explains that cults that take credit for, and seemingly provide, a sense of security, salvation, well-being, and love but expect to be repaid with obedience and compliance use this rule.

   Questions can be asked, such as the following: What has the group or leader objectively provided? Has the group or leader ever directly expressed that someone owed him or her consideration? How was this expressed exactly? Do members of the group ever express a sense of indebtedness? What examples can be given to clarify this? Can the group or leader legitimately take credit for something if he or she didn't directly or physically provide it? What is the nature and basis for any sense of well-being the group provides?

2. "Commitment and consistency," Cialdini says, are expressed by the "desire to be (and to appear) consistent with what we have already done."[752] Singer explains that a cult can turn this rule around and make members feel guilty whenever they fall short regarding their consistent performance of duties and obligations through commitments made to the group.

But can anyone completely or perfectly maintain his or her commitments with total consistency? On that basis do group members have unrealistic expectations? Do they feel they are good enough? Does a failure to be consistent in commitments frequently make people feel they haven't been good enough? Would a feeling of failure tend to increase or decrease a person's self-esteem? Are people with low self-esteem more or less sure of themselves? Are people with low self-esteem therefore more prone to look to authority figures to provide answers? Does this make them more or less easily influenced?

3. Cialdini describes "social proof" as "one means we use to determine what is correct is to find out what others believe is correct."[753] Within a cult environment Singer explains that "if you look around in the group, you will see people behaving in particular ways. You imitate what you see and assume that such behavior is proper, good, and expected." Singer further says that people then "assume that such behavior is proper, good, and expected."[754]

To what extent does the group environment promote and sustain similar patterns of behavior? Is the group or leader providing what can be seen as the dominant template or frame of reference in the situation? Do members of the group mirror this dominant template or prototype and exemplify an identical frame of reference? What has occurred when participants act or speak out in a discordant way that is inconsistent with that frame of reference? Is such discordance the reason why some members are asked to leave or have left the group? How are such departures later characterized? Are there examples of any former members who acted contrary to the group social norms but weren't characterized negatively? Is the group maintaining a consistent social environment as a means of manipulation and influence?

4. "Liking," Cialdini states, is the principle that "we most prefer to say yes to the requests of someone we know and like."[755] Singer explains that new initiates in a cultic group may be the target of seemingly unconditional love, which has been called "love bombing." This can soften people up by making them feel wanted and loved—and correspondingly less wary and defensive. This technique, which ultimately promotes reciprocal "liking," can make people feel obligated to comply with the concerns and suggestions of those they have come to like.

    The following questions should be raised: Is the love received from the group or leader really genuine and unconditional? Or is it instead highly conditional and dependent on continued compliance with the group's norms and expectations? Do members of the group still like or love former members who have left? Does the group or leader respond kindly to criticism? Is liking someone easier, or does it become more difficult if he or she disagrees with the group or leader? How can you objectively test whether someone is a genuine friend? What examples would you give of genuine and valued friendships or relationships? Do these examples reflect typical relationships in the group? How does the influence of the group and its leaders affect relationships? How are relationships in the group different from those outside of the group? How are they the same?

5. "Authority," Cialdini explains, means "we are trained from birth that obedience to proper authority is right and disobedience is wrong."[756] Singer says this tendency to respect authority can be easily applied to a cult leader who claims superior knowledge, power, and a special mission. Members may then accept the cult leader as an ultimate authority.

This issue raises the following questions: On what basis does the group or leader claim authority? Are other authorities recognized as equal and/or of similar importance? Can the group or leader's authority be questioned? What is the process for such questioning? Can specific examples be given of such questions being raised? Is the group or leader's authority somehow reinforced by a higher power? Is questioning the group or leader's authority tantamount to questioning that higher power? What distinctions does the group or leader make regarding a separation of authority concerning such a higher power? Is any authority outside the group given equal weight and importance? What examples can be given to show a sense of equal or recognized authority outside the group?

6. "Scarcity," Cialdini says, is when "we see that a less-available item is more desired and valued."[757] If cult members are told, Singer says, that without the group they will miss out on living life without stress; miss out on attaining cosmic awareness and bliss; miss out on changing the world; miss out on gaining the ability to travel back in time or whatever the group offers, that benefit is tailored to seem essential. The group may also exemplify this rule by claiming exclusivity; in other words, no other group exists that can offer the same or equal path of fulfillment.

This principle forms the basis for the following questions: Has the group or leader ever mentioned another path of fulfillment that is considered equal? If so, what is the precise name or identity of the group or leader that offers this alternative path? Does the leader or group denigrate anyone or anything outside the group that might offer an alternate approach or path to problem solving or fulfillment?

During this segment of discussion about coercive persuasion, undue influence techniques, and group behavior, it may be useful to review whatever published material or documentation exists about the group or leader. This might include official literature, website pages, message board posts, and video or audio presentations available online, including whatever examples exist that can be specifically credited to the group or leader and then used to demonstrate various discussion points.

Third Block of Discussion: What Is the Specific History of the Group or Leader?

At this point the specific history of the group or leader who has caused concern is closely examined. This may include information that has been gathered through research, a private investigation, or readily accessible documentation. In some situations those who are concerned have retained the services of a private investigator to develop a comprehensive file of information about a group or leader. Many prefer the more cost-effective alternative of gathering information themselves by accessing public records such as court documents, previously published news articles, and disclosure documents possibly filed with the relevant authorities. Easy access to the World Wide Web may provide information through various searched resources, which are readily available online.

Some groups or leaders may have a history that includes criminal prosecution and/or litigation—for example, the criminal tax-fraud conviction and subsequent incarceration of Rev. Sun Myung Moon.[758] In some situations there may have been a group member or leader who was professionally disciplined. This might be reflected in public records of someone such as a licensed professional with a history of complaints, a disciplinary record, or a suspension. Former members of the group may have filed lawsuits, and there may also be evidence of family estrangement or abuse through divorce or child-custody filings.

Corporate records may also disclose the finances of the group or leader. Such disclosure may be required if the group has tax-exempt, nonprofit status or is incorporated. Filing requirements vary, but some documents may be on file. These documents might detail, to some extent, the group's finances, general structure or delegation, and administration of authority. For example, a controversial group known as Eternal Flame disclosed in its corporate filings that about half of the more than $1 million collected in annual revenue from its supporters was spent on generous salaries and compensation. This included a $52,000-a-year housing allowance and use of a Cadillac and Land Rover for its three leaders.[759]

There may be evidence of alleged abuse, which one may see through publicly posted testimonies available at websites that are critical of the group or leader. This might include online video recordings former members made about the group or leader. For example, the personal accounts of past members of the Children of God detail childhood sexual abuse.[760] There may be legal PDF documents posted or related public records. Abuse allegations corroborated by historical documentation, such as public records and press reports, typically gain greater credibility and importance than those allegations made without such supporting material.

Another facet of the group's relative status and wealth might potentially be discerned through a review of real estate records. This may specifically reveal what property the group or leader owns and has progressively accumulated over a period of time. The value of those properties can also be deduced from recorded tax assessments and mortgage liens. For example, the homes Falun Gong founder Li Hongzhi purchased in New Jersey and New York represented a combined value approaching $1 million.[761]

All this background information can be used to construct a picture of the group or leader based on historical documentation. When reviewing this history, one should ask specifically relevant questions. What does the objective evidence indicate either negatively or positively about the group or leader? Does this evidence seem to expose a consistent pattern of behavior? Has the group or leader in some way been deceptive or intentionally misleading? Do the facts somehow contradict the popular or preferred image of the group or leader? Have events occurred that the group or leader might have deliberately slanted, falsely interpreted, or propagandized?

The discussion should also focus on how those present at the intervention view the gathered information. Those involved may add additional important firsthand impressions about what they see as noteworthy about the group or leader's historical record.

This process offers the cult member a unique opportunity to evaluate and critically examine the group and its history outside what may have been a largely controlled environment. Much of the information reviewed might otherwise be either unknown or somehow obscured by the group or leader to avoid or obfuscate its significance or importance. This cult member may also be exposed to various perspectives regarding the assembled information.

Fourth Block of Discussion: What Are the family's Specific Concerns?

At this juncture family members and those concerned may express why they feel the intervention was necessary and important. They explain in detail, based on their firsthand observations, why involvement with the group seems to be problematic and potentially unsafe or even dangerous.

Evidence might include medical neglect, sexual abuse, child abuse and neglect, suspected psychological and emotional damage, criminal conduct, financial exploitation, diminished and increasingly strained communication, escalating isolation, and substandard living conditions. Each person participating in the intervention has an opportunity to present his or her personal point of view and general perspective. This may include both anecdotal examples as well as concerns motivated by gathered historical information. This is often the most volatile, difficult, and emotional phase of the intervention.

My role through this process is to keep the discussion focused but with an appropriate level of flexibility. This might include focusing attention on how the cultic group may have caused, contributed to, and/or exacerbated certain personal problems or situations. All those present express their concerns regarding such issues as personal safety, quality of life, family relations, and reasonable expectations for the future. Those present may feel a sense of special urgency due to particular recent events tied to cult involvement. For example, there might be an anticipated marital separation or divorce, critical child custody or visitation dispute, expected bankruptcy or business failure, closely related criminal prosecution, or a serious illness that is not being properly treated.

This difficult part of the intervention and must be carefully moderated. Everyone present has been prepared by setting guidelines for this portion of the discussion during the previous preparation process. That is, no one should become punitive, angry, or needlessly emotional or confrontational. Instead, participants are encouraged to stay focused on the facts and connect their concerns to the well-documented details about the group or leader. Everyone is also encouraged to be both candid and precise about his or her concerns while also on balance expressing his or her continuing love and support. Every opportunity is afforded to allow the cult-involved individual a response to each concern. It is crucial for those concerned to participate meaningfully, and everything must be done to encourage that participation within the boundaries previously discussed during the preparation phase.

Conclusion

As the intervention ends, there should be a review of what has been learned, including the major points of exchange regarding certain concerns. Again this would focus first on the definition of a destructive cult and on how the group in question fits that profile. Second is how the group or leader used specifically identified coercive persuasion techniques to gain undue influence. Third is what we have learned about the particular history of the group or leader and how that demonstrates that further involvement poses a risk and is potentially unsafe, if not dangerous. Finally are the serious concerns that made family and old friends increasingly uncomfortable and ultimately led to the intervention.

At this juncture it isn't necessary for the cult-involved person to make a definitive statement about future involvement with the group or leader. Rather what can be reasonably expected is a commitment to take a break from the group and to think things over more independently. This means thinking things through without any coaching or influence exerted by anyone connected to the group or leader. This process might also include seeking additional input from a professional counselor, lawyer, or consultant who has a particularly relevant and helpful expertise. The impetus behind this commitment should be to prioritize the needed time to further understand the reasons family and friends are so concerned about the group or leader.

There may be agreed-on specific appointments made with a medical doctor, lawyer, or helping professional. Changes may also be made in living arrangements, in regard to group involvement, such as moving out of group housing or out of a living situation with another group member to establish greater independence. Everything should be focused on increasing relative independence and decreasing dependence on the group or leader.

---

[738] M. D. Langone, *Recovery from Cults*, 2nd ed. (New York: W. W. Norton, 1996), 174–175.

[739] P. Tosey and J. Mathison, "Introducing Neuro-Linguistic Programming," Centre for Management Learning & Development, School of Management, University of Surrey, 2006, http://www.som.surrey.ac.uk/NLP/Resources/IntroducingNLP.pdf (accessed May 28, 2014).

[740] J. P. Green et al., "Forging Ahead: The 2003 APA Division 30 Definition of Hypnosis," *International Journal of Clinical and Experimental Hypnosis* 53 (2005): 259–264.

[741] Robert Jay Lifton, "Cult Formation," *Harvard Mental Health Letter*, February 1981.

[742] Ibid.

[743] Margaret Singer, *Cults in Our Midst* (San Francisco, CA: Jossey-Bass, 1996).

[744] Richard Ofshe, "Coercive Persuasion and Attitude Change," *Encyclopedia of Sociology*, vol. 1 (New York: McMillan, 1992), 212–224.

[745] Robert B. Cialdini, *Influence: Science and Practice* (Needham Heights, MA: Allyn & Bacon, 2001).

[746] Robert Jay Lifton, *Thought Reform and the Psychology of Totalism* (Chapel Hill: University of North Carolina Press, 2012), 419–437.

[747] Singer, *Cults in Our Midst*, 58–59.

[748] Edgar H. Schein, *Coercive Persuasion: A Socio-psychological Analysis of the "Brainwashing" of American Civilian Prisoners by the Chinese Communists* (New York: W. W. Norton, 1971).

[749] "Captive Minds: Hypnosis and Beyond." Documentary. Directed by Pierre Lasry. Montreal: National Film Board of Canada, 1983. http://www.youtube.com/watch?v=mQC0nFfp2nc&index=1&list=PL2D64B3CB3D593ACF (accessed May 22, 2014).

[750] Cialdini, *Influence: Science and Practice.*

[751] Ibid.,. 29.

[752] Ibid., 66.

[753] Ibid., 117.

[754] Singer, *Cults in Our Midst*, 170.

[755] Cialdini, *Influence: Science and Practice*, 163.

[756] Ibid., 210.

[757] Ibid., 248.

[758] Betty Fletcher, "Rev. Moon to Serve Jail Time," *Pantagraph* (Bloomington, IL), May 14, 1984.

[759] Victor Dricks, "Immortality Group Fights On," *Phoenix Gazette*, January 27, 1994.

[760] Laurie Goodstein, "Murder and Suicide Reviving Claims of Child Abuse in Cult," *New York Times*, January 15, 2005.

[761] Paul Vallely and Clifford Coonan, "China's Enemy Within: The Story of Falun Gong," *The Independent* (London), April 22, 2006.

CHAPTER 11

BIBLE-BASED GROUP INTERVENTION

A young professional and married mother with small children became involved with an online religious group essentially based on the World Wide Web. For the purpose of this chapter, the group will be identified simply as the Call of God. This small, web-based group included only about twenty to thirty active members, who were recruited and communicated almost entirely through the Internet.

The leader of the group claims he receives revelation directly from God. These revelations are then relayed to the world in the form of "letters from God," which are then archived and downloaded through a group website. Group members maintain cohesiveness through daily communication, but they stay in touch with each other by using online resources, such as Internet conferencing services, frequent e-mails, and text messages. Personal physical contact most often hasn't occurred between the leader and most of his followers.

Those in the core of the Call of God—its most significant and sustaining supporters—are primarily located in North America and Australia. The leader lives in the United States. Contributions to the group are made online through the group website. People generally learn about the Call of God through the same site, and that is also the means of initial contact.

Web-Based "Cult" Groups

Groups called "cults" that use the World Wide Web for the recruitment and retention of members have become increasingly common. Two examples of other groups called "cults" that are essentially web based are Divine Truth, led by Alan John "A.J." Miller in Australia; and the Fellowship of the Martyrs (FOTM), founded by Doug Perry in the United States.

Miller claims to be Jesus reincarnated and says his partner, a young woman named Mary Luck, is actually the reincarnation of the biblical Mary Magdalene, who witnessed the crucifixion of Jesus. Miller has developed a residential complex of properties near Kingaroy, west of Queensland's Sunshine Coast in Australia, where reportedly thirty to forty of his devotees relocated by 2011.[762]

Doug Perry leads FOTM from Liberty, Missouri, near Kansas City. About seventy members of FOTM live in shared apartments in the same neighborhood.[763] Perry also seems to believe that God speaks through him to the world.

Both FOTM and Divine Truth heavily rely on the World Wide Web to recruit new members and raise money. Miller has downloads, and Perry has audiobooks. Both men also use YouTube.com to broadcast their teachings. Perry has accumulated a collection of more than nine hundred videos available online. Miller and Perry often make disparaging remarks about other organized religious groups, apparently implying that they alone possess the complete and uncorrupted truth.

The young mother I worked with had been a member of Call of God for two years before her husband and family contacted me. They became concerned when she announced she would no longer communicate with her parents or sibling due to the undue influence of her group. Her marriage was becoming increasingly strained, though she still lived at home with her husband. He wasn't a member of the group and had repeatedly refused to become involved. The young woman's parents retained me to do an intervention, a choice the woman's husband strongly supported.

I received quite a bit of information from the family through an intake questionnaire and file they had prepared about the group. The father did considerable investigation through public records about the leader's business concerns and assets. I also assembled a file largely based on the Call of God website, which included printouts of various material of interest archived there; I highlighted and noted much of this.

Preparation Meeting

When we met for the preparation meeting before the intervention, we compared our respective files and discussed family concerns in more detail. The preparation meeting included the young woman's parents, her sibling, her sibling's spouse, and her husband. As in all such preparation meetings, we discussed the parameters of our respective roles and what we could reasonably expect.

I emphasized how important it would be to stay focused on the group, its leader, and related behavior, rather than to be drawn into any sort of religious debate. It is important in interventions to stay focused, not allowing the discussion to drift into extraneous concerns that are not immediately relevant. The dialogue must remain tightly focused on the behavior of the group and leader and why there was concern. When people discuss a religious cult, certain beliefs or teachings may come up, but they should be discussed only as they specifically relate to the group's behavior and its pattern of manipulation to gain undue influence.

During the preparation meeting we also talked about how important it would be to temporarily interrupt the group's influence by shutting down all means of communication with them during the intervention. We would accomplish this by turning off and storing all cell phones and terminating all Internet connections. We rehearsed how this step would be taken and agreed that it must be accomplished by the end of the first day.

The young woman would be asked to promise that she wouldn't communicate with the cultic group or anyone associated with the group until the intervention was over. This commitment would encompass the few days when the intervention would take place. I also asked the parents whether it would be possible for her to stay at their home during the intervention so there would be no distractions and so there would be confidence that all means of communication she might use remained shut down. Her husband agreed that this would be best.

Before the intervention began, I suggested that once we had the young woman's agreement about outside communication, the mother would politely ask for her cell phone. It would then be locked up, assuring everyone that she couldn't use it during the intervention to contact the cult group. These precautions would be taken to rule out any coaching or interference from the leader or group members, who might otherwise seek to sabotage the intervention effort.

The Beginning of the Intervention

On the following day the young woman arrived at her parents' home for a special, planned visit. Her parents had pleaded with her that a meeting was necessary so they could better understand the reasoning behind her recently announced decision to cut them off. She expected to share her beliefs and explain to them more about the Call of God. During our preparation for the intervention, we had discussed how such a meeting would provide the necessary and important initial access for them to begin the intervention.

My presence at the meeting was a complete surprise. The young woman also didn't expect her sibling and her sibling's spouse to be there. But everyone had gathered together with her husband's full knowledge and cooperation. The couple's small children had been placed with a caregiver. As agreed, pending her arrival, all phones and Internet access in the family's home were disconnected. She was polite but confused about the purpose of my presence and why others she hadn't expected to see were also present.

Her parents quickly introduced me as a professional consultant they had invited to attend the meeting. They explained that much of what had happened regarding the Call of God was confusing to them, so they had sought outside assistance from an expert consultant. I apologized for the surprise meeting but explained that I had advised the family not to tell her about my inclusion or about others attending the meeting to ensure there would be no interference or coaching by anyone associated with the group. She accepted this apology.

After the initial introduction our conversation first focused on concerns the family expressed. Each member of the family shared his or her specific concerns regarding the group and how it had affected the young woman's behavior. Her parents expressed profound sorrow concerning her recent decision to stop communicating with them. They explained that regardless of what she believed, they would always love her; therefore, they couldn't understand why she had decided to cut them off. Her sibling talked about the many months that had gone by without any word from her and about how much she had been missed. In conclusion her husband explained that the young woman's commitment to the group had seemed to supersede any practical consideration, including their marriage and the care of their small children.

The young woman's parents explained that since she had become involved with the Call of God, she had drifted farther and farther away from family and old friends. Her sibling said the same thing. The husband expressed fears of a marital breakdown and child neglect. He said that due to his disinterest in the group, his wife was increasingly treating him like an unwanted stranger rather than like a loving spouse. He explained that she was so busy with the group that she was increasingly overlooking their small children's needs. The husband said that from his perspective, the situation was progressively becoming worse and that at times his wife seemed hostile and angry when he mentioned his concerns.

After several hours of conversation about family concerns, the young woman became visibly agitated and protested that this was somehow an "attack" on her faith. I assured her that no one present wished to criticize her faith but rather the behavior of the group and the influence of its leader. At this point her mother emphasized that she respected her daughter's faith and could see no conflict regarding religion within the framework of the expressed concerns. The young woman calmed down. I then reiterated that the focus of my work as a consultant was group behavior, not religious beliefs.

We discussed some basic elemental issues concerning Jesus and the New Testament. For example, Jesus once said, "Many shall come in my name, saying, I am Christ; and shall deceive many."[764] We agreed that, according to this scripture, the claim that someone speaks for God may be false. According to the New Testament, Jesus also warned, "Beware of false prophets, which come to you in sheep's clothing, but inwardly they are ravening wolves."[765] He then further explained, "By their fruits ye shall know them."[766] We discussed this process of discernment based on a careful examination of the person's fruits. How did they affect people? What did they produce? How did they behave? Could they be a wolf in disguise? I asked the young woman to become a fruit inspector based on this biblically mandated process, and she agreed.

At the end of the first day of discussion, which took approximately eight hours, the young woman agreed to sleep over at her family's home, turned off her cell phone, and gave it to her mother. We also asked for her commitment not to communicate with anyone associated with the Call of God. She agreed to these terms at the urging of her family and husband.

Defining a Cult

We spent the following day discussing the nucleus for the definition of a destructive cult by examining historical cults. We focused largely on cults that claimed their behavior was based on a true understanding of the Bible and God. For example, we discussed cult leader David Koresh and his group known as the Waco Davidians. The Davidians firmly believed Koresh received special revelation from God. They also accepted him as virtually the exclusive means of truly understanding the Bible and God. The Waco Davidians remained loyal to David Koresh, even when he called on them to do battle with government law enforcement. They then endured a long standoff with authorities, which ended in tragedy. Eighty Davidians, including many children, decided to die in a fire rather than leave their leader.

We then talked about the notorious cult known as Jonestown, which remains the most horrific cult murder/suicide in modern history, claiming the lives of more than nine hundred people. Cult leader Jim Jones, like David Koresh, had a penchant for quoting and twisting scriptures from the Bible and then connecting them to chosen current events. Jones did so to manipulate and control his followers.

I then emphasized that both Koresh and Jones essentially saw themselves as prophets functioning in a pivotal historical role God had ordained to save humanity. Both leaders emphatically told their followers that the end of the world as they knew it was approaching. This doomsday scenario produced a kind of crisis mentality, binding the groups closely together and engendering greater dependence on the leader for a sense of security and safety. In this context doomsday pre-dictions can be seen simply as a device cult leaders use to manipulate and control their followers.

We also discussed the evident mind-set of the Waco Davidians and people at Jonestown. Was it possible for any of them to disagree with David Koresh or Jim Jones? And if they did openly question the au-thority or revelation of these leaders, wouldn't this have been tanta-mount to questioning God or rejecting the Bible?

Despite the controversy surrounding cult deprogrammer Ted Patrick and involuntary deprogramming, it was Patrick who first developed this questioning approach during the 1970s. He said, "The only thing I do is shoot them challenging questions. I hit them with things that they haven't been programmed to respond to." Patrick further explained, "When the mind gets to a certain point, they can see through all the lies that they've been programmed to believe." He concluded that his process of asking such challenging questions results in effectively stimulating the mind "to start working again."[767]

No one doing cult-intervention work today advocates involuntary deprogramming with adults, such as what Patrick did decades ago. But his basic approach of asking thought-provoking questions in the context of a voluntary intervention as a catalyst for critical thinking remains an effective tool contemporary cult-intervention specialists still use.

I then moved the focus of our conversation to the Call of God, asking if it was possible to question the leader of that group. Had he ever admit-ted to making a mistake? Had anyone ever questioned his authority or revelations? Had members of the Call of God ever expressed doubts or disagreements regarding the contents of any of his letters from God?

The young woman responded generally that of course her leader made mistakes and that everyone in the group was free to question him.

When I asked her to please be specific and cite certain examples to illustrate this fact, however, she demurred and was unable to offer a single example. She couldn't describe a particular instance when the leader had admitted to making a serious substantial mistake or had admitted that it was potentially possible for an error or contradiction to exist in one of his revelations or letters from God.

We then discussed the fact that, despite the leader's reluctance to admit mistakes or faults in his teachings, there had historically been disagreements in the group, and these had led to some people leaving. It appears when any disagreement with the leader persisted, this situation would eventually end in the exit or expulsion of a member. Disagreements with the leader weren't really tolerated.

I asked what the group response was like when someone left. What was the attitude of group members toward the person who left? She said that when people left, the exit was typically seen as something negative; the former member had somehow spiritually failed and disobeyed God.

I asked whether it was possible to disagree with the leader and yet still remain faithful and obedient to God. Was it possible or even conceivable that someone in the group might specifically call into question the pronouncements or behavior of the leader but still be considered godly and not antagonistic toward God? The young woman seemed perplexed and said she couldn't imagine why anyone would question the revelations the leader of the group had received. But I suggested that by setting himself up as the exclusive spokesperson or mediator for God through his ongoing revelation, the leader of the group had achieved a position not only of singular importance but also of absolute power and unquestionable authority.

At this juncture to emphasize my point I asked her whether she could think of any group, church, or organization other than the Call of God where people might receive the same spiritual benefits. Was there any alternative, any another group where people might be equally spiritually fed? Was there another leader of equal authority who spoke the equivalent and uncorrupted truth? What group could she specifically think of by name, and where was it located? Like many cult members, she responded to this question by saying there were other true believers out there who weren't members of the Call of God. But when I pressed her to identify by name a specific group, fellowship, or organized gathering of believers that represented an alternative to her group, the young woman couldn't name one.

At this point I offered a possible conclusion based on our discussion. It was impossible in the Call of God to disagree with the leader and remain faithful. That disagreement with the leader was the equivalent of disagreement with God. This thinking then provided the leader with absolute authority and no meaningful accountability. The only way a member could sustain disagreement would be to leave the group entirely, and there was no legitimate reason to leave. Also, there was nowhere to go if the person left, because there was no equally viable alternative group anyone could identify. Only the Call of God had the truth, and everyone else had somehow fallen short and was in some way wrong. Any member who chose to leave was therefore not only a spiritual failure but also one separated from God and lost, according to the group.

Summarizing what we had discussed during the day, we concluded that the leader of the Call of God claimed to occupy a singular position of authority based on his published teachings; he could therefore be seen as the group's defining element and driving force. We discussed the fact that this type of charismatic leadership is described as the first and foremost of the three criteria forming the nucleus for the definition of a destructive cult, according to psychiatrist and noted author Robert Jay Lifton in his paper titled "Cult Formation."[768]

Thought Reform or Coercive Persuasion

The second day we focused on an examination of the use of thought reform or methods of coercive persuasion, which is the second criteria

Lifton lists.[769] We discussed how thought reform might appear and how a Bible-based cult group might employ it. I proposed that the way such control is expressed in such a cult can be seen as a preconceived and carefully constructed trap. In this way the cult victim is trapped and held in a box. This box is constructed with four walls and a floor or foundation, and it is shut tight with a lid.

Two supernatural images coupled with two corresponding claims represent the four walls of the box. The supernatural images are God and Satan, or the devil, and the two corresponding claims are heaven and hell. Whatever the leader or group dictates is what God wants. Therefore, obedience to the group or leader is seen as obedience to God. Anyone or anything else, most especially whoever or whatever opposes the group or leader, is apt to be labeled as the devil and thus be discredited. Lifton recognized this truth in his description of "loaded language," one of eight criteria he used to define thought reform, which is characterized by "'god terms' representative of ultimate good; or 'devil terms' representative of the ultimate evil."[770]

Correspondingly there is the promise of heaven as the reward for obedience to "God," as expressed by the group, and the threat of extermination or hell as the punishment for disobedience.

Ted Patrick talked about the imagery of doomsday cults. "They give [cult members] the same thing over and over again, day in and day out…saying everything outside that door is Satan, that the world is going to end within seven years, and that if you're not in their [group] you're going to burn in hell." A cult member may feel palpable fear regarding the prospect of life outside the perceived protection the box provides. Patrick concludes, "If he goes outside in that bad, evil, world," he "is terrified of what will happen to him out there." [771]

The floor of the box created by Bible-based cults, what can be seen as its functional and operational foundation, is the group leader's idiosyncratic interpretation of the Bible. Specifically, the Bible, as the group interprets it, becomes absolute biblical truth, and anything else is therefore unbiblical and false. Typically, this preferred interpretation of the Bible the group and its leader uses is self-serving and systematically engenders dependence on the group and reliance on it for a sense of safety and security. The Bible, as some groups use it, becomes a tool for manipulation and control.

Caught between these walls, the cult member becomes confined by the group's interpretation of the Bible within the box. The cult member cannot effectively question authority or reflect or reason independently. In this context any alternate perspective is simply seen as striving against the biblical God or aligning with the devil. As Patrick notes, destructive cults frequently devalue critical thinking itself. He says, "It's very painful, because they've been told that the mind is Satan and thinking is the machinery of the Devil."[772]

The cult member thus becomes walled in and isolated. Confined in this space, he or she might have the will to intellectually try scaling a wall, but the box is tightly shut with a lid. This final sealing of the box is accomplished through the call to surrender. In cultic groups members are routinely encouraged to surrender their egos and critical thinking to a higher power. In Bible-based cults people are coercively persuaded to surrender their wills to "God." In such a group, however, surrender to God is really surrender to the group and its authority, since that authority claims to exclusively represent and speak for God.

Authors Conway and Siegelman explained this type of surrender in their book *Holy Terror: The Fundamentalist War on America's Freedoms in Religion, Politics, and Our Private Lives*. They say that such a suggestion to surrender is "employed by cult leaders to induce ongoing states of suspended judgment in their followers, calls to 'surrender' to 'relinquish the will,' to 'let go' or merely 'let things float.'"[773] The authors note that "the principle of surrender is universal to religion, that all spiritual experience requires a 'leap of faith' and a 'giving up of one to something higher'"[774] But Conway and Siegelman found that when authoritarian-controlling groups use it, the "call to surrender may have a profound effect: to serve as a triggering mechanism in the process of indirect control."[775]

To visually demonstrate these points during the intervention, we watched documentaries about two of the most radical cults in modern history, the Waco Davidians and followers of Jim Jones at Jonestown. The purpose of choosing such extreme examples of destructive cults was to demonstrate, through two agreed-on historically destructive cults, that the basic dynamics and mechanics of manipulation found in destructive cults are essentially the same. Despite the biblical and spiritual claims both the Davidians and the followers of Jim Jones made, they have long been historically categorized as destructive cults.

We observed the testimonies of cult members and former cult members, who explained their experiences and the reasoning behind their commitment to their respective groups and leaders. They explained how they had surrendered to the belief that this was a necessary part of the process required to serve God according to the Bible. Of course, they didn't see this as submission to a cult leader but rather submission to God and his Word. But in practice, as historically recorded, surrender in the Waco Davidians and at Jonestown was actually total submission to the authority of cult leaders.

I asked her whether the basic message of salvation in Christianity depended on faith or on submission and devotion to a specific organized group and the dictates of its leader. Apologizing for being a Jewish observer rather than a Christian insider, I intimated that even I knew that Christians didn't cite membership in organizations such as Call of God as the basis for their salvation. I pointed out that, according to the New Testament, "The grace of God has appeared that offers salvation to all people"[776] and that salvation is for anyone who accepts Jesus as his or her savior per the basic beliefs of Christianity.

This belief is not restricted to one small organized group like the Call of God. But the leader of Call of God had routinely condemned any church or religious organization outside his group as lost and without salvation. Making such distinctions is important, because most, if not all, Bible-based cults that claim to be Christian are intolerant and condemning in regard to other Christians if they insist that salvation is essentially bestowed through them exclusively and achieved only by rigid compliance to the dictates and teachings of their leaders. I then linked this understanding to the documentaries about the Waco Davidians and Jonestown and pointed out that both groups shared such beliefs about the exclusivity of their respective groups and the unique authority of their leaders.

On the third day we specifically discussed in some detail the apparent lack of accountability and financial transparency concerning the leader of the Call of God. How was he accountable? Was there an elected board? Had he been elected? Who had appointed him? Where did the money go? How could that money trail be confirmed? Did anyone other than the leader actually know? We discussed that members of the group were expected to tithe and actively engage in fund-raising activities. Some had quit jobs, surrendered significant assets, and made personal sacrifices to support the group. Where did the money and assets go? Was there a published budget? Was there an annual audit?

At this juncture we reviewed the gathered documentation the young woman's father had assembled. These documents, including real estate and corporate disclosure records, which disclosed in some detail the leader's actual assets and most recently declared income. All his disclosed assets were held personally, and no assets could be found specifically titled to the group or a charitable organization. This information directly contradicted what the leader had been telling the group, which was that he had no interest in business or money; nor was he motivated, he said, by any hope for material gain. This discussion about the discrepancy between what the leader said and what the public records demonstrated, seemed to strike home with the young woman.

Cracking the Program

Ted Patrick once said, "When I hit on that one certain point that strikes home, I push it. I stay with that question whether it's about God, the Devil or that person's having rejected his parents. I keep pushing and pushing. I don't let him get around it with the lies he's been told."[777]

The fact that the leader of the group had accumulated substantial assets while simultaneously misleading others about his finances resonated with the young woman and became a point I began to push harder, reviewing document after document to further crack the group programming. Authors Conway and Siegelman summarized Patrick's earlier approach by saying that once he found such a weakness in the cult program, he "hit it head on, until the entire programmed state of mind gave way."[778]

I hammered home the point that, according to the Bible, Jesus and his disciples were disinterested in material possessions and were essentially poor people. I also contrasted the leader of Call of God with the prophets, such as Moses. According to the Bible, in response to God Moses gave up his status and wealth to become a religious leader. Why was the leader of Call of God so preoccupied with accumulating real estate holdings? And why had he deliberately misled his followers to believe he wasn't interested in money? Did this type of dishonesty reflect the pattern of leadership expressed in the Bible?

At this point the group programming began to unravel. As Patrick once said, "When the person realizes he's been lied to by the cult…it's like turning on the light in a dark room."[779] As the lights came on and the cult programming crumbled during the final two days, the young woman increasingly began to ask critical questions. She saw how her group paralleled the examples I had given of other cults and also identified the pattern of coercive persuasion, which had been used to gain undue influence over her life. We went over each of Lifton's eight criteria used to identify a thought-reform program.[780] She could see these same criteria as the dynamics operating in the Call of God.

For example, we discussed how the isolation the group encouraged and its dominant control of information and communication amounted to what Lifton labeled "Milieu Control" or control of the environment. She now could better understand why the leader had encouraged her to cut off her family; by consuming her time, the Call of God had further isolated her, thus negatively impacting both her marriage and parenting.

We also discussed how the leader's special letters from God could easily be seen as what Lifton calls "Mystical Manipulation" or planned spontaneity. That is, "initiated from above, it seeks to provoke specific patterns of behavior and emotion in such a way that these will appear to have arisen spontaneously" but that "directed as it is by an ostensibly omniscient group, [it] must assume, for the manipulated, a near-mystical quality."[781] The supposed letters from God, rather than spontaneous pronouncements from a higher power, seemed to be calculated communications used to manipulate and control the group. This could be seen not only by the way the letters contributed to the authority and power of the leader but also through the way the letters were sometimes addressed to certain issues or people.

Conclusion

On the third day the young woman began to divulge previously unknown and critical inside information about the group. She talked about others in the Call of God who were struggling in their strained marriages and of other parents who were neglecting their children. The young woman also disclosed that one extremely devoted member had ultimately been forced to declare bankruptcy, which she suspected was due in part to the excessive demands of the leader. These disclosures offered immediate evidence that the group influence and control were fading away and that her own previously innate ability to think independently and critically analyze the facts had returned.

At the end of the intervention the young woman's primary concern was how to warn others not to become involved with the Call of God. We discussed the possibility of sharing information online through the Web in some effective way so she might warn others. The young woman ceased her involvement with the Call of God and moved on with her life. She was grateful that her family had made the effort to help her through the intervention effort.

---

[762] "My Name Is Jesus and I'm Serious: Cult Leader Claims to Be Jesus and His Partner Says She's Mary Magdalene," *Daily Mail* (London), May 18, 2011.

[763] Andrew Horansky, "Houston Father Says He Lost Family to Dangerous Cult," *KHOU 11 News*, (Houston, TX), February 16, 2013.

[764] Matt. 24:5 (King James Version).

[765] Matt. 7:15 (KJV).

[766] Matt. 7:16 (KJV)

[767] Flo Conway and Jim Siegelman, *Snapping: America's Epidemic of Sudden Personality Change*, 2nd ed. (New York: Stillpoint Press, 2005), 62.

[768] Robert Jay Lifton, "Cult Formation," *Harvard Mental Health Letter*, February 1981.

[769] Ibid.

[770] Robert Jay Lifton, *Thought Reform and the Psychology of Totalism* (Chapel Hill: University of North Carolina Press, 2012), 4429.

[771] Conway and Siegelman, *Snapping: America's Epidemic of Sudden Personality Change*, 59.

[772] Ibid., 60.

[773] Flo Conway and Jim Siegelman, *Holy Terror* (New York: Delta, 1984), 252.

[774] Ibid., 253.

[775] Ibid., 252.

[776] Titus 2:11 (New International Version).

[777] Conway and Siegelman, *Snapping: America's Epidemic of Sudden Personality Change*, 62.

[778] Ibid.

[779] Ibid.

[780] Lifton, *Thought Reform and the Psychology of Totalism*, 419–437.

[781] Ibid., 422.

CHAPTER 12

FALUN GONG

Before discussing an intervention involving the controversial movement Falun Gong, also known as Falun Dafa, understanding the history and issues surrounding the organization and its founder, Li Hongzhi, is important. The group has been officially declared an "evil cult" in China, and Li now lives as an exile in the United States. At one time there were reportedly millions of Falun Gong adherents in China, though the number of Chinese devotees seems to have steadily dwindled. Falun Gong reportedly has as many as ten thousand practitioners in the United States and four thousand in Canada.[782]

2001—Self-Immolation in Tiananmen Square

A particularly horrific event focused media attention on Falun Gong in 2001. This single event, perhaps more than any other, defined Falun Gong as an "evil cult" in the minds of the Chinese public. On the eve of the Chinese New Year, January 23, 2001, a small group of seven Falun Gong practitioners traveled within China from the city of Kaifeng to Beijing. Once in Beijing the group went to Tiananmen Square and set themselves on fire. A mother and her twelve-year-old daughter died. One man, Wang Jindong, survived but was hospitalized with severe burns. Two women, Hao Huijun and her daughter, Chen Guo, were both hospitalized with very extreme injuries. The two remaining Falun Gong members, including the man who had organized the self-immolation, weren't seriously injured.

Chen Guo later explained, "We wanted to strengthen the force of Falun Gong. We decided burning ourselves was the best way."[783] Chen Guo, once a promising musician, lost both of her hands. Her mother was also severely disabled and disfigured.[784] As the story of the self-immolations was broadcast around the world, Falun Gong refused to accept any responsibility for the tragedy. Spokespeople for the group insisted it was not their teachings or influence that had led to the tragedy; rather it was somehow a Chinese government conspiracy to discredit the organization.[785]

Li Hongzhi

Li Hongzhi, the founder of Falun Gong, was born in northeastern China. He reportedly graduated from high school, worked on a farm, and played the trumpet. During the 1980s he was a clerk at a cereal company. But by 1992 Li decided to join the growing ranks of self-proclaimed "qigong masters" and began giving lectures. In 1995, after Falun Gong was declared an "evil cult," Li Hongzhi moved to the United States. He is now apparently a wealthy man. In 1998 he reportedly bought a house in New York for $293,500. Later the following year he purchased a second home for $580,000 in New Jersey.[786]

Li's followers see him as a "living Buddha."[787] Falun Gong practitioners believe he has "deep insight into the mysteries of the cosmos," and he claims to know "the top secret of the universe." Li tells his followers that "no religion can save people" but only the "almighty Fa,"[788] which he supposedly and exclusively represents.[789] According to his official biography *Zhuan Falun*, Li claims he first recognized his special powers at the age of eight. These powers purportedly include "floating through walls," becoming "invisible," and also having the ability to "rise into the heavens."[790] Li also claims he "can move himself anywhere by thought alone" and that his alleged supernatural powers "averted a global comet catastrophe and the Third World War."[791]

What Is Falun Gong?

Nancy Chen, an anthropologist at the University of California in Santa Cruz, describes what Li Hongzhi teaches as an "amalgam" or "combination of different traditions, a kind of New Age variety."[792] But Guy S. Alitto, professor of history and East Asian languages and civilizations at the University of Chicago, notes, "Falun Gong's demand for doctrinal purity, organizational exclusivity, and its fixed inflexible organizational structure would have been utterly incongruous in traditional Chinese society." Alitto concludes, "Therefore it represents more of a rupture than continuity with Chinese religious traditions."[793] He adds, "Falun Gong gatherings…are devoted completely to the study and discussion of the writings of Li Hongzhi…Falun Gong teachers through the ranks are relegated only to preaching proscribed doctrine."[794] In this sense Falun Gong, like other groups called "cults," appears to be a personality-driven organization largely defined by its leader, Li Hongzhi.

Much of Falun Gong's supposed healing power is based on the belief that Li Hongzhi can telekinetically insert into his disciples the spinning "falun," or mystical "wheel of law." Once this is done, the "living Buddha" can allegedly transfer energy to the believer. Li has said, "The only way to find yourself comfortably free of illnesses is through cultivation practice!"[795] Udo Schuklenk, a professor of philosophy at Queen's University who currently holds the Ontario research chair in bioethics, observes, "Falun Gong adherents believe fervently that practicing Falun Gong can cure ailments ranging from brain cancer to arthritis and many other diseases."[796] Schuklenk warns, "The delusions of the Falun Gong adherents matter, because they might not go themselves to receive life-preserving medical care when they could benefit from it, or worse in another form of child abuse they might not take their children to see a doctor when they could and should have."[797] Chinese officials have reported that nineteen hundred Falun Gong practitioners have died in China due to medical neglect.[798] This was one of the reasons China officially banned Falun Gong in 1999, declaring it an "evil cult."

Li's teachings also include telling his disciples they will appear younger and that elderly devotees "will have less wrinkles and eventually they [the wrinkles] will almost be gone." He also claims that elderly women "will again have their menstrual cycle." Li says that this will be accomplished because "all cells in the bodies of practitioners will be replaced by high energy matter."[799] In response to criticism of this bizarre claim, a practitioner wrote me, "Can you prove that elderly women who practice Falun Gong don't regain their menstrual periods? Have you ever considered the possibility that Li's teachings in this regard are true? I know for a fact that they are true. I suggest you do more research on the subject before mocking these teachings."[800]

Psychologist Margaret Singer noted the apparent lack of reasoning and critical thinking that is common in cult groups and which Falun Gong practitioners often display. In describing her experience with Falun Gong devotees, Singer explained that a practitioner will "actually say 'Don't Think. Just recite the Master's teaching.'" She concluded, "If you want a good description of a cult, all you have to do is read what [Falun Dafa followers] say they are."[801] Singer said, "Imagine an inverted T. The leader is alone at the top and the followers are all at the bottom."[802] A destructive cult is not only totalitarian, but, according to Singer, it employs "the overriding philosophy...that the ends justify the means, a view that allows [such groups] to establish their own brand of morality, outside normal society bounds."[803]

Cult and communication experts Flo Conway and Jim Siegelman describe cultic practices that lead to a diminished ability to process information and employ critical thinking. They said, "Almost every major cult and cult-like group we came upon teaches some form of not thinking…as part of its regular program of activity. The process may take the form of repetitive prayer, chanting or speaking-in-tongues, self-hypnosis or diverse methods of meditation….Such techniques, when practiced in moderation, may yield real physical and mental health benefits….Prolonged stilling of the mind, however, may wear on the brain physically until it readjusts, suddenly and sharply, to its new condition of not thinking. When that happens, we have found, the brain's information-processing capacities may be disrupted or enter a state of complete suspension…disorientation, detachment…hallucinations, delusions and, in extreme instances, total withdrawal."[804]

Racism

Li Hongzhi has also garnered attention because of his racist remarks. He claims that mixed-race people are part of a plot hatched by evil extraterrestrials. In 1998 Li told a gathering in Switzerland, "By mixing the races of humans, the aliens make humans cast off gods." He claims that "mixed races" are supposedly excluded from the "truth" and "have lost their roots, as if nobody in the paradise will take care of them. They belong to nowhere, and no places would accept them… The higher levels do not recognize such a human race."[805] According to Li Hongzhi the offspring of mixed race unions are therefore "intellectually incomplete" or "with an incomplete body." In such cases only he, Master Li, can "take care of it" by resolving that "incomplete" state. This can supposedly be done only if "such a person wants to practice cultivation" according to the precepts of Falun Gong.[806]

Members responding to an article I once wrote about such racist teachings didn't deny that Li Hongzhi made the statements quoted but instead insisted that they must be understood in context. A Falun Gong practitioner defending Li said, "My understanding is that when gods created man, we were created to god's image, different races was created by gods of different races and when a child is born from a marriage of two people from different races it will be hard for the gods to trace the child's origin and therefore hard to save."[807] The strain this must cause affected relationships is not considered, nor is the potential for emotional damage concerning the children of such couples.

Homophobia

Statements by Li Hongzhi also seem to encourage the hatred of homosexuals. Li said, "The disgusting homosexuality shows the dirty abnormal psychology of the gay who has lost his ability of reasoning at the present time," Li Hongzhi wrote this in volume two of *Zhuan Falun* or "Turning the Law Wheel," which was translated into English in 1996. In a talk in Switzerland, Li also stated that "the gods" would eliminate gay people. While visiting Frankfurt, Germany, Li was asked in 1998 whether gays might practice Falun Gong. He answered, "You can cultivate, but you must give up the bad conduct."[808]

During 2006 in the gay-friendly city of San Francisco, city supervisors voted on a resolution of support for Falun Gong; this caused controversy and angered many residents. "What a disappointing vote. I have compassion for the practitioners but I think the supervisors have been duped by the master's party line," Thomas Brown told the press. "I challenge any gay person in this city to get any Falun Gong practitioner to state they do not agree with their master's belief. I have never heard them refute what he has said. There is deception here." He added, "I think it is a vote that will come back to haunt some of the supervisors."[809]

Brown's roommate, Samuel Luo, called the resolution "a huge disappointment" and warned that the group will use it "to recruit members. It makes it hard for people like me to get family members out of the cult." Luo's concern included his parents' involvement with Falun Gong and how the group has affected their lives and family relationships. Thom Lynch, executive director of the LGBT Community Center, told the press, "I think it is great that the leadership in the

Chinese community recognizes the homophobia of this group and I would support their efforts not to let them march [in a Chinese New Year parade]."[810] In response to such statements, one Falun Gong practitioner wrote me, "Actually all orthodox (upright) religions view this matter in the same way, Christianity included, it is very hard to reach heaven when practicing homosexuality."[811]

Falun Gong Media

In 2006 a woman named Wang Wenyi briefly drew attention through what seemed to be a purposely planned publicity stunt. Attending a White House event to honor Chinese president Hu Jintao with an official press pass, Wang unfurled a banner for Falun Gong and screamed at presidents Bush and Hu. Wang had gained entrance to the highly secured area with an official press pass issued through a newspaper called the *Epoch Times*.[812]

Falun Gong appears to have followed in the lead of the Unification Church, which effectively controls the *Washington Times*. Followers of Li Hongzhi control the *Epoch Times*. John Nania, editor in chief of the *Epoch Times* US editions; its Boston editor, Martin Fox; and the newspaper's opinion editor, Stephen Gregory, were reported to be Falun Gong practitioners.[813] A cable television network named New Tang Dynasty Television, which is a New York City nonprofit satellite broadcaster, is also operated by a staff that includes members of Falun Gong.[814] These media interests seem to essentially function as public relations arms for Li Hongzhi and Falun Gong. As one news report about the *Epoch Times* noted, the publication "tends to be remarkably sympathetic to the controversial sect and generally provides a platform to preach Falun Gong's beliefs."[815]

When Wang Wenyi interrupted the White House function, she shouted, "President Bush, stop him from persecuting the Falun Gong! Falun Dafa is good."[816] That wasn't exactly a question from the press or behavior expected from a legitimate journalist. But it does reflect the public relations agenda of Falun Gong. Wang's outburst was described as a "banshee shriek."[817] The *Epoch Times* tried to distance itself from any potential embarrassment due to her inappropriate conduct. An official spokesperson for the newspaper acknowledged, "Dr. Wang attended this event on *Epoch Times* press credentials" but then added the caveat, "However, her actions…were her own. In protesting in this manner, she didn't act on behalf of the *Epoch Times.*"[818] It seems that whenever Falun Gong practitioners engage in unflattering fanatical behavior, the movement attempts to deny any connective culpability and accepts no responsibility.

We can see Wang's protest at the White House as little more than a carefully staged and scripted climax, capping a series she wrote that was run in the *Epoch Times* regarding alleged "organ harvesting in China's labor camps." Chinese officials have repeatedly characterized such sensational claims as "sheer lies."[819] Harry Wu, an outspoken critic of the Chinese government who now lives in exile, expressed skepticism concerning the extreme claims made in the *Epoch Times*. Wu told the press that he doubted the anecdotal accounts Falun Gong recounted about organ harvesting. He characterized the alleged witness statements offered as "unreliable" and concluded that such stories "may be intentionally fabricated."[820] Sixteen Falun Gong practitioners were arrested in China during 2013 for attempting to fake torture photos. One of the suspects reportedly admitted that the group used a concoction of cola and tomato paste to simulate blood.[821]

The Shen Yun dance troop, which is primarily composed of Falun Gong practitioners, is seemingly also intended to be used as a promotional media tool. Once again, Falun Gong seems to be embracing a tradition set by Rev. Moon. Moon funded the so-called Kirov Academy of Ballet as one of his "cultural enterprises."[822] Falun Gong seems to be funding Shen Yun.

The dance company has appeared at the Fox Theater in New York and other large venues in the United States, the United Kingdom, and

Europe. Performances of Shen Yun, however, have not always been well received. One London review said, "What I really object to is that such a politically motivated performance is being smuggled on to stages around Europe in the name of family entertainment." The reviewer further noted, "I am reluctant to welcome the teachings of a man who believes that aliens live among us and that homosexuality and mixed-raced marriages are degenerate."[823] A New York review stated that the audience had been "duped…into paying outrageous sums of money to watch a half-baked advertisement for Falun Gong," which was labeled as an "unconscionable piece of religious propaganda."[824]

Freedom of Speech

Falun Gong supporters have characterized criticism of their conduct at Chinese New Year parades and the refusal of community leaders to allow them to participate in future events as discrimination.[825] The group has repeatedly been criticized for using such high-profile public parades as a vehicle to hand out their literature, including anti-China tracts. This sort of behavior has both angered and alienated many Chinese Americans. San Francisco Chinese Chamber of Commerce president Wayne Hu said, "Falun Dafa brought more than 60 marchers and handed out leaflets along the parade route in violation of our instructions."[826] Ling-Chi Wang, a professor of ethnic studies at UC Berkeley, said Falun Gong "is a religious organization with a political agenda."[827]

In response to such behavior, Falun Gong was not invited to participate in future parades. Falun Gong practitioners then filed a legal action to block the use of a $77,000 public arts grant to support the parade, which left local leaders fuming and gave the public perception that they were spoilers.[828] The San Francisco parade in Chinatown is the largest such celebration in North America, and the Chinese community there is the second largest in the United States following New York. Falun Gong has stirred similar negative sentiments in the New York Chinese-American community. Falun Gong practitioners parading through Chinatown in New York were met with jeers and pelted with water bottles.[829]

Falun Gong's stance concerning freedom of expression appears to be inconsistent when it comes to critics of the movement. In a letter published by a San Francisco newspaper, Samuel Luo noted this apparent contradiction. "Last year when the International Cultic Studies Association organized a program on the Falun Gong in which I was one of the presenters, the Falun Gong threatened the organization with a lawsuit and successfully suppressed our freedom of speech," Luo wrote.[830]

It seems that Li Hongzhi and Falun Gong may have decided to follow the path of the litigious Church of Scientology—that is, threatening or filing lawsuits in what can be seen as an ongoing effort to suppress criticism. The litigiousness of the organization has also included suing an Australian official for restricting the use of loudspeakers and banners outside a Chinese embassy.[831] Falun Gong certainly wants its free-speech rights to be recognized but conversely wants critics like Luo silenced.

Falun Gong Victims

In 2011 I attended an international symposium in Shenzhen, China, concerning cultic studies, sponsored by the Institute of Religious Studies of the Shanghai Academy of Social Sciences. Academics and experts from around the world attended the event and presented papers. The papers examined everything from the evolution of destructive cults to the characteristics of cult members, cult social interaction, and various cultic methodologies.

At the conclusion of the symposium, I had the opportunity to visit with former cult members in China. The two women I spoke with were survivors of the self-immolation tragedy that took place in

Tiananmen Square. After requesting to meet with them, I was told a meeting would be possible after the conference.

The two former Falun Gong practitioners, Hao Huijun and her daughter, Chen Guo, live in Kaifeng. Kaifeng, which is near the Henan provincial capital of Zhengzhou. Historically Kaifeng was the capital of China during the Song Dynasty and once the largest city in the world. Today its population is about eight hundred thousand.

Hao Huijun and her daughter, Chen Guo, live modestly in a government welfare housing project. Their simple one-bedroom apartment includes a private bathroom and large common area with a kitchen. There is a bed placed near the kitchen for an attendant. The fire left both women without hands and disabled. Extensive skin grafts, the result of multiple surgeries, obscured their faces. They have no ears, noses, or lips. Chen Guo has the use of only one eye. But both women have the ability to speak and walk, and they seem to be in stable physical condition. There are no mirrors in their apartment.

After our introductions I asked Hao Huijun about her perspective today and what she feels now, looking back on the time she spent in Falun Gong. Was there something she could share about her experience with others who were concerned about the movement? "I'll take this chance to tell the Falun Gong practitioners in Canada and the US to stop practicing," she stated bluntly. "I suggest they stop practicing Falun Gong and get rid of it," instructed the former schoolteacher of twenty-eight years, who remained quite well spoken and articulate.

Influenced by her mother's commitment, Chen Guo followed the path of Falun Gong, which ultimately led her to that terrible day at Tiananmen Square. She was a twenty-year-old woman who had been recognized as an outstanding student at the time of the tragedy. Early in our discussion Chen Guo left the room, explaining that she didn't feel well. Recalling the time she'd spent in Falun Gong was too distressing. She cried outside the window of the apartment as a friend comforted her. But in her 2002 hospital interview, Chen Guo made the same observation as her mother. She told the press, "I hope those who still believe in this cult can be awakened and throw it away. I don't want to see another victim like me."[832]

Chen Guo's mother explained the context of the horrible event that irrevocably changed their lives forever. "In July 1999 the Chinese Government and the Chinese laws banned Falun Gong. As a citizen, we should have abided by the laws and given up practicing Falun Gong from then on. But we were obsessed at that time. And the suicidal burning occurred later on. We really feel regretful. We all suffered a great deal, brought about by the obsession. So tell [the North American Falun Gong practitioners] to never be obsessed…Please pass my words to Falun Gong practitioners: They should use reason in action…If you look at things in a rational way, you will know what you should do," she said. "Reason is important. In one's life, one should never go to extremes whatever you do. One should use reason to learn how to do things, and have a good understanding."

Over the years Hao Huijun has managed to sort through her experience in Falun Gong. She hopes others might do the same. "Falun Gong caused so many problems," she said. "Why did these problems happen? [Falun Gong practitioners] should think about it with reason, with their own senses, and in a dialectical way. When we look at things from a normal sense, without bias, and with reason, we will know what we should do," Hao Huijun explained.

When told about the conspiracy theories propagated by Falun Gong in regard to the self-immolation tragedy at Tiananmen Square, Hao Huijun responded thoughtfully, placing it again in the context of her own experience in the group. "I thought in a similar way," she said. "But it's time for those who are practicing Falun Gong to calm down and think reasonably…Why were we burning ourselves? It was not that the government forced us into suicide, although the rumors went so. This is not the truth." She concluded, "Before we fully understood, we used the same arguments and same logic in regard to incidents caused by Falun Gong."

I told Hao Huijun that I have received complaints from families in the United States that Falun Gong practitioners often refuse medical care or discontinue medications based on their beliefs. "They should consult a doctor and take medication," she responded. "Tell them to see a doctor when their children fall ill. Don't impose what you regard right on your children," she said. "You can see the disastrous effect this caused my daughter. I really regret that now."

The profound regret Hao Huijun feels is evident. China has mandated a one-child-per-family policy, which means Chen Guo is her only child. Hao Huijun lives every day with her daughter as a constant reminder of what she did while under the influence of Falun Gong. Despite reclaiming her reason, there is nothing she can do to change the physical consequences of her past devotion. This is the burden Hao Huijun must somehow manage to carry for the rest of her life. But she continues to be a teacher and hopes to help others gain the understanding she so painfully acquired.

In China, Falun Gong is labeled an "evil cult," the most literal translation of the Chinese terminology used to describe what English-speaking people might call a "destructive cult." Falun Gong, like other groups called "cults," has denounced that description as "persecution." And Li Hongzhi's followers allege that horrific human rights violations have been committed against them.

This is not unlike the historic response of Scientology to its many critics, who have been labeled "religious bigots." Rather than address the criticism, the strategy seems to be attack or dismiss the critics. Falun Gong has repeatedly tried to shift the focus from its behavior to the behavior of the Chinese government. Li and his followers seem to hope that historic distrust or perhaps anxiety about China's growing power can be used to neutralize any criticism leveled against them. But looking at the facts rather than the fiction confirms what psychologist Margaret Singer observed. "If you want a good description of a cult, all you have to do is read what they say they are."833 And if you want to see the true face of Falun Gong, all you have to do is look into the eyes of Hao Huijun and her daughter, Chen Guo.

---

782 Bob Mims. "Falun Dafa Practitioners Join Millions," *Salt Lake Tribune*, June 12, 1999.

783 Jeremy Page, "Survivors Say China Falun Gong Immolations Real," *Reuters*, April 4, 2002.

784 Ibid.

785 Ibid.

786 Paul Vallely and Clifford Coonan, "China's Enemy Within: The Story of Falun Gong," *The Independent* (London), April 22, 2006.

787 Vallely and Coonan, "China's Enemy Within: The Story of Falun Gong."

788 Peter Carlson, "For Whom the Gong Tolls," *Washington Post*, February 27, 2000.

789 Ibid.

790 Ibid.

791 Vallely and Coonan, "China's Enemy Within: The Story of Falun Gong."

792 Joel P. Engardio, "Spiritual Cultivation," *Los Angeles New Times*, March 23–29, 2000.

793 Guy S. Alitto, "Falun Gong: What Is Old and What is New?" (lecture, International Symposium of Cultic Studies at Assumption University, Thailand, December 15–16, 2011), 54–55.

794 Ibid., 57.

795 Carlson, "For Whom the Gong Tolls."

796 Udo Schuklenk, "Ethical Issues in Societal Interactions with Destructive Cults—Falun Gong and Church of Scientology" (lecture, International Symposium of Cultic Studies at Assumption University, Thailand, December 15–16, 2011), 159.

797 Ibid.

798 Jeremy Paige, "China Nabs Falun Gong Members for State TV Protest," Reuters, April 2, 2002.

[799] Alexander L. Dvorkin, "Falun Gong as a Healing Cult" (lecture, International Symposium of Cultic Studies at Assumption University, Thailand, December 15–16, 2011).

[800] Rick A. Ross, "Li Hongzhi and His PR Machine," *CultNews*, January 29, 2006, http://www.cultnews.com/2006/01/li-hongzhi-and-his-pr-machine/ (accessed May 28, 2014).

[801] Don Lattin, "Falun Gong Derided as Authoritarian Sect by Anti-Cult Experts in Seattle," *San Francisco Chronicle*, April 29, 2000.

[802] Margaret Singer, *Cults in Our Midst* (San Francisco, CA: Jossey-Bass, 1996), 8.

[803] Ibid., 9.

[804] Flo Conway and Jim Siegelman, *Snapping: America's Epidemic of Sudden Personality Change*, 2nd ed. (New York: Stillpoint Press, 2005), 153–154.

[805] Sarah Lubman, "A Chinese Battle on U.S. Soil," *San Jose Mercury News*, December 23, 2001.

[806] Ibid.

[807] Ross, "Li Hongzhi and His PR Machine."

[808] Lubman, "A Chinese Battle on U.S. Soil."

[809] Matthew S. Bajko, "Supes Support 'Homophobic Cult,'" *Bay Area Reporter*, (San Francisco), February 2, 2006.

[810] Ibid.

[811] Ross, "Li Hongzhi and His PR Machine."

[812] Vallely and Coonan, "China's Enemy Within: The Story of Falun Gong."

[813] Mark Jurkowitz, "Times of Change," *Boston Globe*, May 31, 2005.

[814] Dianne Hartman, "Ties to Falun Gong Add Controversy to Chinese New Year Spectacular," *Los Angeles Times*, January 7, 2008.

[815] Vallely and Coonan, "China's Enemy Within: The Story of Falun Gong."

[816] Ibid.

[817] Ibid.

[818] "Statement by the *Epoch Times* on the Events at the White House," April 20, 2006, http://www.theepochtimes.com/news/6-4-20/40651.html (accessed May 28, 2014.

[819] Le Tian, "China's Organ Supply Questioned as Transplants Soar," *China Daily*, (Beijing), April 13, 2006.

[820] Glen McGregor, "Former MP Pushes for Beijing Games Boycott," *Ottawa Citizen*, August 9, 2007.

[821] "Cult Members Arrested over Torture Pics," *Xinhua News Agency*, (China), June 4, 2013.

[822] Emma Brown, "Sun Myung Moon Dies at 92; Washington Times Owner Led the Unification Church," *Washington Post*, September 2, 2012.

[823] Sarah Crompton, "Shen Yun: Propaganda as Entertainment," *The Telegraph* (Kent), February 25, 2008.

[824] Colin Dabkowski, "Played for Fools, by 'Shen Yun' Spectacle Is Nothing More Than Hype and Propaganda," *Buffalo (NY) News*, May 28, 2010.

[825] "Falun Gong, Chamber Square Off over Chinese Parade," *KGO-TV News*, (San Francisco), January 31, 2006.

[826] Justin Jouvenal, "Falun Gong Debate Hits Chinese New Year Parade," *San Francisco Examiner*, January 6, 2006.

[827] Vanessa Hua, "Falun Gong Dispute Hangs over S.F. Chinese Parade," *San Francisco Chronicle*, January 30, 2006.

[828] Ibid.

[829] Colin Moynihan and Cara Buckley, "Falun Gong Marchers Are Jeered in Chinatown," *New York Times*, May 26, 2008.

[830] Samuel Luo, "Falun Gong: Homophobic Mind Control Cult," *San Francisco Sentinel*, January 27, 2006.

[831] "Falun Gong Sues over Protest Restriction," *Sydney Morning Herald*, January 30, 2006.

[832] Page, "Survivors Say China Falun Gong Immolations Real."

[833] Don Lattin, "Falun Gong Derided as Authoritarian Sect by Anti-Cult Experts in Seattle," *San Francisco Chronicle*, April 29, 2000.

CHAPTER 13

FALUN GONG INTERVENTION

In the United States a married mother with young children, all under the age of ten, became involved with Falun Gong through a friend. Initially, she saw the group as an opportunity to simply exercise and become more physically fit. Step-by-step, however, her newfound friends in Falun Gong manipulated the young mother to become more deeply involved. They then progressively broke her down, creating doubts about her personal religious choices and commitments to her chosen Orthodox Jewish life.

The young mother had a Jewish background but had specifically chosen as an adult to become a member of an ultra-Orthodox Jewish sect called the Chabad Lubavitch. She later influenced her parents and other members of her family to follow her into what is often called "ultra-Orthodox" Jewish life. They likewise joined the Lubavitcher sect. The young woman later married another Lubavitcher with a similar history.

The Lubavitchers are a sect within Hasidic Judaism. A charismatic preacher born in the Ukraine named Yisroel (Israel) ben Eliezer

(1700–1760) founded the Hasidic religious movement.[834] Ben Eliezer's brand of Judaism is known for its emotionalism, mysticism, and opposition to the rationalism of more mainstream rabbinic Judaism.[835] [836] After ben Eliezer's death, his disciples eventually splintered as leaders of various groups and spread across Eastern Europe and Russia. Each sect has its own rabbinic leader who wields great authority. Typically when a Hasidic leader dies, there is a succession, and the new leader assumes power. Many Hasidic sects have family dynasties, which sanction power being passed from father to son one generation after another.

The Chabad Lubavitch sect moved from Russia to New York in 1940, led by Rabbi Yosef Yitzhok Schneersohn,[837] who was succeeded by his son-in-law, Rabbi Menachem Mendel Schneerson, Many Lubavitchers came to believe Schneerson was the messiah Jewish prophecies foretold. True believers called him King Moshiach. [838] He died in 1994 at the age of ninety-two.[839] The young woman's entire family was devoutly committed to the Chabad Lubavitch as well as the memory of Schneerson. However, Schneerson died childless, and no one has been chosen to replace him, despite historical precedent.

Hasidic Jews like the Lubavitchers observe very strict dietary rules and stringent guidelines concerning modest dress and contact between men and women. Ultra-Orthodox Jews specifically refrain from any use of modern conveniences, such as cars and electronic devices during the Sabbath, which begins Friday at sunset and ends at the next sunset on Saturday. This period is set aside for the strict observance of the Sabbath.

The young woman's husband and family were shocked when they discovered her growing commitment to Falun Gong, which they viewed as a confusing contradiction of the family's chosen faith and lifestyle. It was an extreme contradiction of that life to engage in a contradictory and alien belief system, which now seemed to dominate her thinking and potentially might influence her children. How could the ultra-Orthodox family remain united in such a conflicted situation and continue their circumscribed life filled with traditional observances and religious restrictions? Why had she become involved with Falun Gong? Didn't she recognize the inherent conflicts posed by her involvement?

Ultra-Orthodox Hasidic Judaism has survived for hundreds of years, largely unchanged within an encapsulated subculture, first largely in Europe and now primarily in the United States and Israel. Most Hasidic Jews largely refrain from interaction with mainstream society outside of business and perhaps political concerns and prefer to live in insular, tightly knit communities. We can see this in the neighborhoods and/or villages they inhabit in New York and Israel. The Chabad Lubavitch is more open and accessible than other Hasidic sects, but Schneerson only recently implemented this change as an outreach effort. Modern Chabad outreach includes fund-raising and proselytizing. These activities, along with messianic claims made about Schneerson, have drawn criticism and generated some controversy.

The family members who retained me for this intervention are the only ultra-Orthodox clients I have had to date. Despite being Jewish myself, my background is with Reform Judaism, which is often considered the most liberal branch of Jewish faith, and Orthodox Jews do not see it as being sufficiently observant. Though I have received many complaints and inquiries from ultra-Orthodox Jews, whom destructive cults have adversely affected, they have been reluctant to retain someone they see as an outsider to help them with such concerns. But after many discussions and considerable deliberation, it seems this family concluded that the risk of not retaining a cult-intervention specialist was unacceptable to them. They felt that Falun Gong was tearing apart the very fabric of their family.

I arrived at the preparation meeting on a Thursday morning. Our meeting took place at the country home where the extended family planned to gather for the beginning of the Sabbath on Friday. The young woman's parents and her husband attended the preparation meeting. The intervention was planned to take place in this somewhat isolated country house. Everyone present was deeply concerned that if the woman's involvement with Falun Gong continued, a divorce and child custody battle would be inevitable.

First, I told those gathered that likely the young woman had initially no idea that Falun Gong contradicted Judaism or that it is was actually a belief system based on faith claims. I explained that a destructive cult is deceptive and that genuine full disclosure isn't part of the recruitment process. That is why they must not blame or shame the young mother. Her Falun Gong friends had tricked her and not allowed her to make truly independent decisions regarding her evolving participation based on fully informed consent.

We agreed that the best time for staging the intervention would be at the country house during the Sabbath, because of the stringent rules observed. This included the Sabbath prohibition concerning work and the use of any electronic device or transportation such as a car. These Sabbath rules would effectively prevent communication with members of Falun Gong. The same rules would create a barrier between the young woman and Falun Gong, which its leaders couldn't easily penetrate to contact or coach her. This would keep them from potentially sabotaging our intervention effort.

An intervention discussion isn't considered work in violation of the Sabbath; rather it is an effort to help someone. The Sabbath or Jewish law can generally be violated to save a life. For example, saving your own life, serving the sick, and rescuing a person in danger are all situations that would supersede the rules of the Sabbath.[840]

Despite the young woman's involvement with Falun Gong, she continued to observe the Sabbath along with the rules and rituals of Orthodox Jewish life. This was yet another indication that Falun Gong had deliberately misled her. Under the group's undue influence, she had come to accept that holding two conflicting belief systems simultaneously was possible or that somehow there was no such conflict between Falun Gong and her Jewish beliefs.

During the preparation meeting we carefully defined the boundaries and purpose of the intervention. I explained that my purpose wasn't to promote any particular religious beliefs or agenda. That is, such decisions must be made individually, and this was not part of my professional work as an intervention specialist. We discussed the need to avoid personal and needless religious arguments and to stay focused on concerns about Falun Gong and how it had affected the young woman's life.

On Friday, after arriving at the country home just before sunset, the family introduced me as an outside expert and consultant. We all sat down in a comfortable room and began our discussion. At this time I further detailed my background and the specific purpose for our meeting.

The young woman plaintively asked her family why this meeting was necessary, considering that Falun Gong was a "harmless" and "benign" group? Each family member individually explained his or her concerns.

Her parents said the family had chosen Orthodox Judaism, which was the basis for their everyday life and that they didn't understand why the young woman had so suddenly rejected that commitment and seemingly abdicated her role as an Orthodox Jewish mother. One family member expressed similar dismay concerning her choices, explaining that she had been the inspiration for the family to choose an Orthodox Jewish life in the first place.

The young woman's husband posed perhaps the most serious questions and concerns. He emphatically asked how she could go against the mutual commitments they had made to each other, their respective families, and their community. He pointed out that never during their courtship had she ever raised any questions concerning that commitment and had instead strongly affirmed that this was her sincere choice. The husband concluded that by embracing Falun Gong, his wife had broken her promises and violated her commitments.

These weren't religious arguments but rather a review of the historical facts. The family wanted to understand how she could so radically change the focus and commitment of her life. Was this her choice? How had that choice been made? They wanted to better understand what the process had been to bring about this sudden and abrupt change and inconsistent behavior.

Repeatedly the young woman assured everyone present that Falun Gong was not a religious choice but rather a physical exercise practice, which didn't contradict her religious beliefs or family values. She also claimed that there had always been problems in her marriage and then broke down in tears.

The family contradicted her claim, however, that the marriage had been historically troubled. Though no marriage was perfect, they said, her marriage appeared to have been reasonably happy until her deepening involvement with Falun Gong became an issue of concern, causing arguments and problems.

At the conclusion of the first evening, we agreed to meet the following day. There was little need to solicit a commitment to cease communication with the group due to the Sabbath rules regulating phones and any electronic communication. Every form of electronic communication in the house had been turned off or shut down. This is exactly what we expected and had planned.

The following morning we began by discussing the nucleus for the definition of a destructive cult as psychiatrist Robert Jay Lifton had provided in his paper "Cult Formation."[841] Lifton's first and foremost criterion is the existence of a "charismatic leader." This is the single most salient feature of a destructive cult, which is the personality-driven nature of the group. The charismatic leader becomes the key defining element, locus of power, and focus of the group members.

Lifton's three primary defining characteristics are as follows:

1. a charismatic leader who increasingly becomes an object of worship as the general principles that may have originally sustained the group lose their power;
2. a process I call coercive persuasion or thought reform;
3. economic, sexual, and other exploitation of group members by the leader and the ruling coterie.[842]

After initially identifying family concerns, defining a destructive cult is often my preferred starting point for most intervention discussions. This is done to establish a foundation or framework for the dialogue, which is based on an objective understanding of the pyramid hierarchy that typically represents the structure of the cultic group. How does this pyramid structure relate to the dynamics and behavior of the group? That is, by definition a destructive cult leader or a very small, tightly knit authoritarian cadre of leaders at the top of the pyramid is the organizational glue that holds the cult together. The leadership can be seen as the hub of the wheel, without which the group typically loses its cohesiveness and would most likely and ultimately collapse.

We discussed the importance and pivotal role of "Master Li," who is regarded as a "living Buddha,"[843] and how this belief might fit into Lifton's first criterion. For example, Li alone defines Falun Gong through his singular role as the most highly regarded and powerful representative of the "almighty Fa," which is the only way to "save people."[844] I explained that this criterion could also be seen through Li's various claims concerning his supposed supernatural powers, which further demonstrate the importance of his personal charisma. Li's powers allegedly include "floating through walls," becoming "invisible,"[845] having the ability to "move…anywhere by thought alone," and being able to "rise into the heavens." I asked if there was anyone else she could think of alive today whom Falun Gong members extolled in the same way with equal significance.

We also discussed an important core teaching of Falun Gong, which is that supposedly Li alone can telekinetically install the spinning "falun," or mystical "wheel of law,"[846] into Falun Gong devotees. The wheel subsequently makes it possible to transfer energy to the believer. I asked if this claim imbued Li with special importance and made him essentially indispensable to the group. And wasn't such a claim about Li's supernatural abilities a pivotal belief, which largely defined Falun Gong? I asked the young woman whether she could see the repeated pattern of such claims and beliefs. That is, didn't they specifically emphasize the singular importance and special significance of Li Hongzhi? Didn't these claims place Li well within Lifton's definition as the focus of Falun Gong? And therefore wouldn't Falun Gong fit in the category of a personality-driven group?

Her response was typical of many cult members. When confronted with uncomfortable facts about the group or leader, the follower will try to change the subject or refocus the discussion on something else. Instead of directly responding to questions about Li Hongzhi, she tried to shift the focus to the Chabad Lubavitch. The young woman replied, "Wouldn't the 'Rebbe' [Rabbi Schneerson] be a cult leader then by that definition?" She elaborated, "There are supernatural claims made about him, and he is revered as the messiah or 'King Moshiach.'"

At this point her family seemed shocked. But before the conversation went completely off track, I agreed with her, tacitly admitting that the Chabad Lubavitch sect could be seen as a personality-driven cult per Lifton's criterion regarding the centrality of a charismatic leader. But I added that the level and seriousness of complaints I had received about Falun Gong far exceeded whatever complaints existed concerning Chabad. Also to my knowledge Schneerson's teachings weren't linked to deaths due to medical neglect, which have been alleged concerning Falun Gong.[847] Certainly there were no Lubavitchers who had engaged in self-immolation as a means of protest; several Falun Gong followers had done so in 2001, resulting in deaths and severe injuries.[848]

I explained that the purpose of my visit, the focus of this discussion, was Falun Gong, not the Chabad Lubavitch. I wasn't there to evaluate messianic claims about Schneerson but rather to address the concerns expressed about how the practice of Falun Gong had affected her life. We then agreed to refocus on the topic of Falun Gong.

We now discussed the meditation practices of Falun Gong and the process of trance induction. Did Falun Gong encourage suggestible, altered states of consciousness? Could some of the group's exercises be seen as self-hypnosis? How could such an altered state of consciousness and increased suggestibility be used to manipulate the thinking or feelings of Falun Gong practitioners? Couldn't this manipulation explain the subjective results achieved through the practice of Falun Gong, which is based on feelings rather than on anything that can be objectively proved or scientifically measured? Other than anecdotal stories, was there really any scientific evidence that Falun Gong had accomplished anything in the realm of healing?

As we discussed this issue, I linked it to Lifton's second criterion, which describes "a process [that is in use] call[ed] coercive persuasion or thought reform."[849] One of the eight criteria Lifton cited[850] to recognize the existence of a thought-reform program is called "Mystical Manipulation." According to Lifton such manipulation "seeks to provoke specific patterns of behavior and emotion in such a way that these will appear to have arisen spontaneously, directed as it is by an ostensibly omniscient group, must assume, for the manipulated, a near-mystical quality."[851]

I asked the young woman whether the type of meditation Falun Gong participants practiced might be seen as a form of Mystical Manipulation. Were the subjective results achieved through such practices really spontaneous, or could they be seen as a planned result? After all, what objective evidence could Li Hongzhi produce to substantiate any of his supernatural claims? I then cited some of the fantastic claims Falun Gong practitioners had made, such as that Falun Gong devotees would appear younger and that elderly devotees "will have less wrinkles and eventually they [the wrinkles] will almost be gone." I pointed out that Li has claimed specifically that elderly women "will again have their menstrual cycle." Li says this will be accomplished because "all cells in the bodies of practitioners will be replaced by high energy matter."[852]

These points were discussed throughout the day and well into the afternoon. The young woman was often resistant and defensive, and she expressed some resentment. She reacted negatively to the suggestion that something was wrong with Falun Gong, which she had somehow failed to recognize. The young mother repeatedly tried to minimize, if not negate, the central role of Master Li and whatever controversy existed regarding his teachings. But she remained respectful of her parents. The young woman endured the stressful discussion to demonstrate that respect, even though she continually refused to recognize the substance and significance of her family's concerns.

As sundown approached the young woman again tried to change the subject and focus of conversation. She pointed out that the supernatural claims made in the context of Judaism could likewise not be proved.

She asked pointed questions. "Did the miracles mentioned in the Bible really occur?" "Did Moses part the Red Sea?" "What about Noah's Ark?" "What accounts in the Bible were actually proved to be historical?" The young woman's questions were an attempt to create an alternate argument that would engage everyone, especially her family.

I then asked her if she meant to imply that the supernatural claims Falun Gong made were the equivalent of the stories found in the Bible—that they should then be understood as religious claims based on faith. She didn't readily respond to this query. But I pursued the point and asked specifically if she meant to say that Li Hongzhi's claims were religious claims. And if so, had that been her understanding when she first made contact with the group? Had Falun Gong been presented to her as a religion, and not just a set of exercises? Had she been recruited or proselytized by a religious group? She didn't answer directly, but these questions seemed to intrigue her.

I then made two points in quick succession. First, if Falun Gong was a religion based on faith claims, she should have been told this fact from the very beginning. It was deceptive if she had been led to believe that Falun Gong was merely a type of physical exercise. Anything less than full disclosure during the initial recruitment phase had been deceptive. Second, if Falun Gong was, in fact, a religion, how could she be expected to practice two religions simultaneously?

The young woman seemed puzzled by this question, but I moved on, realizing there was limited time before sunset and the end of Sabbath restrictions.

We then discussed the racist statements Li Hongzhi had made. Li has stated, "By mixing the races of humans, the aliens make humans cast off gods." He also claims that "mixed races" are supposedly excluded from the "truth" and "have lost their roots." He says that "they belong to nowhere, and no places would accept them…The higher levels do not recognize such a human race."[853] According to Li the offspring of mixed-race unions are somehow "intellectually incomplete" or "with an incomplete body." According to Li only he can "take care of it" by resolving that "incomplete" state. This is supposedly done when "such a person wants to practice cultivation" according to the precepts of Falun Gong.[854]

I pointed out that Adolf Hitler and the Nazis had often expressed such concerns about racial purity. And that such concerns led to ethnic cleansing and the extermination of six million Jews. I asked how she, a Jew, could accept such racial edicts and intolerance.

Her response was to routinely recite Master Li's teachings. She explained that his racist remarks must be understood in the context of a cosmology that included many gods with particular links to specific races. According to Li, he is simply making these distinctions based on this cosmological understanding. His teachings are therefore not racist but an earnest attempt to avoid heavenly confusion with dire earthly consequences.

At this juncture I pointed out an inherent problem for her with Li's teachings. As a Jew she observed the Ten Commandments. For example, we were currently observing the fourth commandment, which states, "Remember the Sabbath, to keep it holy."[855] I asked her what the first and foremost commandment is. She hesitated but finally answered, "You shall have no other gods beside me."[856] At this point I asked her how it was possible for her to hold to two different belief systems simultaneously, especially when they were in such conflict and directly contradicted each other. That is, on one hand Judaism is monotheistic and has only one God, but Falun Gong practitioners preach there is a plurality of many gods.

I also asked her if Falun Gong practitioners had explained all this to her when she initially made contact with the group. And if this wasn't the case, wasn't this evidence of deliberate deception during what could be seen as their recruitment process? That is, the Falun Gong practitioners knowingly withheld or obscured information about the specific religious nature of their group, which forms the foundation for their practice. Hadn't she deserved to know about all this before becoming more involved?

As the sun set she seemed to have reached an impasse. The young woman insisted that somehow her involvement with Falun Gong was possible without any conflict. She then promised her husband and family that her children would be raised in a "Jewish home." But I reiterated that monotheism was the single most important and consistent feature of Judaism and therefore the basis for a Jewish home. If she expected to honor her stated commitment to raise her children as Jews, how could she do so honestly while simultaneously embracing the teachings of Master Li? Wasn't this a contradiction? How was it possible? How could she reconcile Falun Gong within the traditional framework of her very structured and regulated Jewish life? A life she had repeatedly said she would honor and which she expected her children to follow and understand? How would this work?

At this juncture there was a kind of meltdown. The young woman tearfully refused to talk further and said our discussion must be concluded. It was near sundown, and soon the Sabbath restrictions concerning travel and communication would be over. The intervention had consumed about a day and half, which wasn't enough time to cover everything, but it had been sufficient to share substantial information, raise some serious questions, and touch on key concerns and relevant issues.

Ultimately everyone agreed to honor the young woman's wishes and end the intervention—but with the understanding that the couple would participate in professional marriage counseling with someone they would both mutually agree on. The young woman also implicitly agreed to completely terminate her involvement with Falun Gong or anyone associated with the group. I had serious concerns regarding the sincerity of her commitments, but I subsequently received no complaints from her family that she had broken any of her promises.

---

[834] Christian D. Von Dehsen and Scott L. Harris, *Lives and Legacies: Philosophers and Religious Leaders* (Westport, CT: Greenwood, 1999), 95.

[835] Ibid.

[836] M. Avrum Ehrlich, *The Messiah of Brooklyn: Understanding Labavitch Hasidism Past and Present* (Jersey City NJ: KTAV Publishing House, 2004), 78.

[837] Rachel Altein, *Out of the Inferno: The Efforts That Led to the Rescue of Rabbi Yosef Yitzchak Schneersohn of Lubavitch from War-Torn Europe in 1939–40* (Brooklyn, NY: Merkos L'Inyonei Chinuch, 2002), 270.

[838] Liz Leyden, "5 Years after Death, Messiah Question Divides Lubavitch," *Washington Post*, June 20, 1999.

[839] Ibid.

[840] George Robinson, *Essential Judaism: A Complete Guide to Beliefs, Customs and Rituals* (New York: Atria Books, 2001), 200.

[841] Robert Jay Lifton, "Cult Formation," *Harvard Mental Health Letter*, February 1981.

[842] Ibid.

[843] "China's Enemy Within: The Story of Falun Gong," *The Independent* (London), April 22, 2006.

[844] Peter Carlson, "For Whom the Gong Tolls," *Washington Post*, February 27, 2000.

[845] Ibid.

[846] Ibid.

[847] Jeremy Page, "China Nabs Falun Gong Members for State TV Protest," *Reuters*, April 2, 2002.

[848] Jeremy Page, "Survivors Say China Falun Gong Immolations Real," *Reuters*, April 4, 2002.

[849] Lifton, "Cult Formation."

[850] Robert Jay Lifton, *Thought Reform and the Psychology of Totalism* (Chapel Hill: University of North Carolina Press, 2012), 419–437.

[851] Ibid., 422.

[852] Alexander L. Dvorkin, "Falun Gong as a Healing Cult" (lecture, International Symposium of Cultic Studies at Assumption University, Thailand, December 15–16, 2011).

[853] Sarah Lubman, "A Chinese Battle on U.S. Soil," *San Jose Mercury News*, December 23, 2001.

[854] Ibid.

[855] Exod. 20:8–11 (Hebrew Scriptures or Holy Bible).

[856] Exod. 20:3–6 (Hebrew Scriptures or Holy Bible).

CHAPTER 14

SCIENTOLOGY

Before detailing an intervention concerning a Scientologist, having a basic understanding of about the organization and its history is important. Some of the most notable and historically significant events in the history of groups called "cults" are tied to Scientology. Scientology can be seen as perhaps the most notorious cult in the United States. It certainly seems to be the most reported about and the enduring focus of public fascination. This is largely due to the many celebrities who are Scientologists, such as Tom Cruise, John Travolta, and Kirstie Alley.

Scientology has a relatively long history, beginning in the 1950s. There are certain key events during its more than five decades of history that provide some perspective and context so we can better understand Scientology, its development, and its current position.

1977—FBI Raids on Scientology

In 1977 FBI raids on Scientology churches led to the indictment of eleven people, including the third wife, Mary Sue Hubbard, of L. Ron Hubbard, the founder of Scientology. The defendants received sentences of one to five years in prison. But L. Ron Hubbard remained an "unindicted co-conspirator."[857]

Scientology's covert criminal operation called "Snow White" during the 1970s remains astounding in its scope and success in penetrating the US government. Scientologists reportedly undertook this operation "to spy on and burglarize multiple federal offices, including the IRS and Justice Department, with the aim of stealing and destroying government documents about Scientology."[858] The operation also included spreading stories about Scientology's perceived enemies.

Historically L. Ron Hubbard is a controversial figure. In the introduction to his book about Hubbard and Scientology titled *Bare-Faced Messiah*, author Russell Miller writes, "Scientology has vigorously promoted an image of its founder, L. Ron Hubbard, as a romantic adventurer and philosopher whose early life fortuitously prepared him, in the manner of Jesus Christ, for his declared mission to save the world. The glorification of 'Ron,' superman and savior, required a cavalier disregard for facts: Thus it is that every biography of Hubbard published by the church is interwoven with lies, half-truths and ludicrous embellishments."[859] L. Ron Hubbard claimed to be a nuclear physicist and said he had traveled into outer space without his body. California superior court judge Paul Brekenridge described Hubbard as "a pathological liar."[860]

Lafayette Ronald Hubbard was born in Tilden, Nebraska, on March 13, 1911. After "flunking out" of George Washington University in 1932, he became a "pulp fiction writer."[861] In 1950 Hubbard published *Dianetics: The Modern Science of Mental Health*, proclaiming it was "a milestone for man comparable to his discovery of fire and superior to his inventions of the wheel and arch."[862] The book became a best seller and spawned "Dianetics groups" across the United States.[863] Eventually, what had started out as a self-improvement program became a religion. Hubbard's son said his father "told [him] and a lot of other people that the way to make a million was to start a religion."[864] In 1954 Hubbard launched the Church of Scientology.

L. Ron Hubbard taught that the human spirit is immortal and lives on through many lifetimes. He wrote that Scientology is "the means to attain true spiritual freedom and immortality."[865] Purportedly this goal is accomplished through Scientology courses, training, and what is called "auditing" or "spiritual counseling."[866] One of Hubbard's pivotal points to explain the need for such auditing is the continuing influence of ancient spirits.

Hubbard wrote that Xenu (pronounced Zee-new), "the head of the galactic federation" seventy-five million years ago, to resolve an over-population problem, killed millions of people by blowing them up volcanically on earth. Xenu then packaged their disembodied spirits in "clusters" so that many spirits could live on in one body. Hubbard labeled these spirits "body thetans" or BTs.[867] The story about Xenu and details concerning BTs are disclosed to Scientologists when they reach a certain level of training known as OT-3 (Operating Thetan Level 3).[868] At that point Scientologists learn how Hubbard's teachings can free them from the influence of these ancient, shackled spirits.

Along this prescribed path, or what is called the "Bridge to Total Freedom," a Scientologist eventually reaches what is called the state of "clear" and then begins to move on through the various Operating Thetan (OT) levels, which are graded from OT-1 through OT-8. The story of Xenu is strictly withheld until a Scientologist reaches OT-3; only then can it be shared, despite its substantial importance within Scientology's belief system.

David Touretzky, avid researcher of Scientology and a professor at Carnegie Mellon University, told the *New Yorker* that to pay for the course work and auditing necessary to reach the "upper levels," it could potentially cost hundreds of thousands of dollars.[869] When asked about Scientology, Cynthia Kisser, the executive director of an organization devoted to exposing cults, told *Time* magazine, "No cult extracts more money from its members."[870]

When L. Ron Hubbard died at the age of seventy-four in 1986, he reportedly "left behind a $640 million dollar fortune."[871] According to the coroner's report, Hubbard apparently took an antianxiety drug hydroxyzine (Vistaril); his assistants reportedly said that this was "only one of many psychiatric and pain medications Hubbard ingested over the years."[872] This is an interesting detail considering that Scientology, as ordained by its founder, is generally an outspoken critic of psychiatry, psychiatrists, psychiatric medications, and mental health professionals.

1995—The Death of Lisa McPherson

On December 5, 1995, Lisa McPherson, a longtime member of Scientology, died under strange circumstances. McPherson had been staying at Scientology's Fort Harrison Hotel in Clearwater, Florida, for seventeen days immediately preceding her death. When Scientologists brought McPherson to a hospital ER in Port Richey, she had already stopped breathing and had no heartbeat. The young woman was also described as gaunt, and her body was bruised.[873] According to Scientology, McPherson had checked into the hotel for "rest and relaxation" and "suddenly fell ill."[874] The coroner initially concluded that there was no way McPherson "suddenly fell ill."[875]

Lisa McPherson had been a devoted Scientologist since the age of eighteen. She'd moved from Texas to Florida in 1994 to be closer to Scientology's headquarters in Clearwater. She worked for a Scientology-linked company and was committed to the church's training. In 1995 McPherson reached the state of "clear," but only a month later, after a minor traffic accident, it appears that she had a mental breakdown. After getting out of her car, McPherson took off her clothes in the street. She told a paramedic, "I need help. I need to talk to someone." The young woman was then taken to a nearby hospital and received a psychiatric evaluation, which is the equivalent of a sacrilege to Scientologists. McPherson subsequently signed out of the hospital against the doctor's advice.[876]

It is from this point that the situation seemed to devolve under the control of Scientology. McPherson was brought to the Fort Harrison Hotel and put under the constant watch of Scientologists there. This included feeding her, doling out "valerian root capsules," administering "herbal sleeping preparations," and giving McPherson various dietary supplements consistent with Scientology's beliefs.

Copious notes concerning McPherson's condition and treatment were taken each day.[877] According to those log entries, she was "blabbering" and "shaking." And at times she spoke "incoherently for hour after hour." McPherson "refused to eat" and was at times "violent," "combative," and/or "confused." And she experienced "difficulties even to swallow a bit of water."[878] A Scientologist "cut her nails" to "reduce the risk of scratches," but the Scientologists involved with her care didn't take McPherson back to the hospital for more than two weeks. The two crucial last days of log entries were destroyed. But days before McPherson died, it was noted that she was "not strong enough" to stand.[879]

Almost three years after Lisa McPherson's death, after a police investigation and lengthy review by a state prosecutor, Scientology was charged with two felonies: "practicing medicine without a license and abuse of a disabled adult."[880] In its defense Scientology commissioned studies concerning the cause of McPherson's death, challenging the coroner's conclusions. Dr. Joan Wood, the coroner, received thousands of pages of documents and numerous subpoenas. "It became very difficult," said Jacqueline Martino, a former chief investigator who worked with Wood for sixteen years. "I think she almost tried to stand alone against this behemoth, Scientology."[881] Ultimately under considerable pressure, Wood amended the death certificate from cause of death "undetermined" to "accident." The coroner had first said the death was due to a blood clot brought on by "severe dehydration."[882] Because of the change Wood made concerning the cause of death, criminal charges against Scientology were dropped.[883]

Lisa McPherson's family filed a wrongful death lawsuit in February 1997 against Scientology, and it was settled out of court in May 2004. The terms of that settlement remain confidential.[884]

In September 2003 certain Scientology release forms were made public through the Internet. These releases and/or agreements contain the statement that the signer opposes psychiatric treatment and that if the signer should become mentally ill, Scientology is authorized to "extricate" him or her from treatment or care by mental health professionals. Rather than receiving such care or treatment, he or she agrees to submit to the so-called Introspection Rundown, a Scientology practice L. Ron Hubbard had devised.

It appears that Lisa McPherson was subjected to this Scientology procedure.

The release form reads, "I understand that the Introspection Rundown… includes being isolated from all sources of potential spiritual upset, including, but not limited to family members, friends or others with whom I might normally interact. As part of the Introspection Rundown, I specifically consent to Church members being with me 24 hours a day at the direction of my Case Supervisor." Moreover, "the Case Supervisor will determine the time period in which I will remain isolated" and that "such duration will be completely at the discretion of the Case Supervisor." The release form or legal contract concludes, "I further understand that by signing below, I am forever giving up my right to sue the Church…for any injury or damage suffered in any way connected with Scientology religious services or spiritual assistance."[885]

Dr. Joan Wood, who served as a medical examiner for eighteen years and performed more than fifty-six hundred autopsies, never recovered from the one she did on Lisa McPherson. That event in Wood's life reportedly so "scarred" the coroner that she went into a "reclusive retirement."[886] "Sadly, the Scientology episode took its toll on Joan Wood, [and] that was her demise," lawyer Denis de Vlaming said. When Wood died in 2011 at the age of sixty-seven, no one she knew professionally through her long career found out until it appeared in a newspaper.

2012—Alleged Abuses of David Miscavige

2012 would prove to be a very bad year for Scientology, both in court and generally through negative media exposure. Seemingly endless bad press would engulf the purported cult, first through former members claiming the church had abused them and also through the breakdown of its most famous member's marriage, that of movie star Tom Cruise.

In January 2012 Debbie Cook, formerly one of the most high-ranking staff members of Scientology, sent out an e-mail raising questions about the organization's fund-raising tactics. It seems that Cook hoped to reform the church from within and urged thousands of Scientologists who received her e-mail to take on what she called the "responsibility that every Scientologist has" regarding the legacy of L. Ron Hubbard.[887] Cook claimed that despite seemingly endless appeals for needed money, Scientology actually held more than $1 billion in cash reserves.

Fifty-year-old Cook had served Scientology faithfully since she was a teenager. She'd risen in its ranks and assumed command of the church's important hub in Clearwater, Florida, reportedly "the most revered Scientology spiritual center anywhere." Cook ran Clearwater for seventeen years before leaving in 2007.[888] In a prepared statement she said after her January e-mail, "I am not trying to pick a fight with the Church, nor am I bitter, or blasting or any of the other things concocted by other media outlets. I am simply asking my friends to do their part, the part that Mr. Hubbard asked of all Scientologists, which is to make sure that they only follow the workable technology laid out in policy and bulletins written by Hubbard exactly as he wrote them. This is the responsibility every Scientologist has—to keep it unadulterated."[889]

Cook and other former Scientology staff seem to feel that David Miscavige, Hubbard's successor and the current head of Scientology, has somehow adulterated Hubbard's teachings. Like Cook, David Miscavige started with Scientology when he was very young. His father, Ron Miscavige Sr., brought him into the organization as a small and sickly boy, suffering from asthma and severe allergies. But by the time he was twelve, David Miscavige was reportedly already providing Scientology's version of religious counseling, called "auditing."[890] Dropping out of high school at sixteen, Miscavige embraced Scientology full time. "I wanted to dedicate my life to this…The thought of hanging around two more years in that existence so that I could match up with the status quo meant nothing to me because I knew that in two years I would go and work with the church anyway," he explained in an interview.[891]

Miscavige became a staff member of Scientology in what is known as the Sea Organization (Sea Org), working within the "Commodore's Messenger Organization." "Commodore" was the title Hubbard gave himself when he created a personal navy within Scientology. Miscavige's job as a messenger was to help in the implementation and management of Hubbard's policies. He was housed, like many other Sea Org members, within Scientology facilities at Clearwater and encapsulated within its subculture. At the age of nineteen in 1979, he rose to the rank of "action chief." And in the wake of the "Snow White" program, Miscavige played an increasingly important and pivotal political role within the organization. He is credited with obtaining the resignation of Mary Sue Hubbard in 1981. "I knew if it was going to be a physical takeover we're going to lose because they had a couple thousand staff and we [the 'messengers'] had about 50." Nevertheless his takeover succeeded. He later commented, "Nobody gives you power. I'll tell you what power is. Power in my estimation is if people will listen to you. That's it."[892]

Two years after Mary Sue Hubbard was deposed, it seems David Miscavige had largely consolidated and sealed his position of power in Scientology. When questions were raised about L. Ron Hubbard's status and competency by his son, a sworn statement emerged in 1983, signed by the reclusive Scientology founder. Hubbard's statement included fingerprints for the purpose of identification and reportedly used a "special ink" to date his signature. In this document, which a judge later ruled authentic, Hubbard called Miscavige his "trusted associate" and "good friend" who reportedly kept his "affairs in good order." When L. Ron Hubbard died in 1986, it appears that Miscavige was firmly in control and had effectively become the new "Commodore."[893]

In 1991 *Time* magazine featured Scientology on its cover as the "Cult of Greed,"[894] But two years later David Miscavige won a great victory. After seemingly endless litigation and conflict with the US Internal Revenue Service (IRS), Scientology was finally awarded the tax-exempt status it had sought for forty years.

Jazz musician Chick Corea, a longtime Scientologist, later told the *St. Petersburg Times*, "The one incredible thing that we all needed was what David did...[He] came and took all the dropped balls and caught them all and kind of saved the organization from splintering apart, and put it back together again for all our sakes."[895] But Vaughn Young, a former Scientology insider who'd spent twenty years in the organization, saw things somewhat differently. In a 1989 interview Young said many Scientologists looked on Miscavige with "a combination of admiration and fear." Young warned, "He's got a serious vicious streak in him that you don't want to trigger."[896]

It was this alleged "vicious streak" that became the focus of press attention in 2012. After Debbie Cook sent her e-mail expressing concerns about fund-raising and Miscavige, she was sued. Scientology claimed Cook had been paid $50,000 severance and had signed a strict confidentiality agreement, which prohibited her from discussing anything about Scientology. After receiving the money, Cook moved to San Antonio, Texas, with her husband. When she appeared in a Texas court, her testimony was shocking.

Under oath Cook testified in March 2012 that in 2007 she had been held under guard in "the hole," a pair of double-wide trailers within Scientology's "Gold Base" compound located in the desert near Los Angeles. Cook said dozens of former Scientology executives were held there. She testified that in the hole they were fed "slop" and reportedly "forced to sleep on an ant-infested floor."[897] Cook testified that she spent seven weeks in the hole, where she was screamed at in a volatile and often violent environment. At times the electricity was turned off, even though temperatures exceeded one hundred degrees. Cook testified that she had been made to stand in a trash can while fellow executives poured water over her and screamed that she was a lesbian. Cook stated that at one point she witnessed David Miscavige punching one executive in the face. Another executive was told to lick the bathroom floor, which he did for thirty minutes. Cook said David Miscavige ordered an employee to break one of her fingers. The Scientology employee then bent back one of her fingers but didn't fracture it.[898]

Cook explained under oath that at the end of her ordeal, she signed the confidentiality agreement. "I would have signed that I stabbed babies over and over again and loved it. I would have done anything basically at that point," she said.[899] Debbie Cook stated that she was "basically imprisoned" during the last months she spent in Clearwater. Her attorney concluded that the agreement his client signed was "unenforceable" because she had been put under duress.[900]

Scientology denied everything.

But Cook said her testimony represented only "the tip of the iceberg."[901]

Weeks after Debbie Cook's testimony in San Antonio, Scientology decided to settle the lawsuit. Neither Cook nor Scientology's spokesperson would offer further comment. The document disclosed stated that neither party would pay the other anything. Cook's website and Facebook page were then shut down.[902] Debbie Cook and her husband, Wayne Baumgarten, sold their car, furniture, and household possessions. Then they moved to Guadeloupe, an island in the Caribbean. Jon Donley, who had once worked at the couple's marketing company in Texas, asked them if their move was a condition of the settlement. "They looked me right in the eyes and said, 'We can't talk about that,'" Donley said.[903]

Other former Scientology staffers have spoken out about alleged abuse by David Miscavige. According to former insiders, Miscavige had smashed Scientology executive Mike Rinder's head into a wall. Rinder claimed that Miscavige had attacked him repeatedly. "That happened more than once." he told the press. In 2009 four former Scientology staffers claimed David Miscavige had assaulted them.[904]

Scientology has described the allegations of such former members as "total lies." [905]

When Oscar-winning screenwriter Paul Haggis resigned from Scientology after thirty-five years, the event drew considerable press attention. In 2011 an article published in the *New Yorker* magazine explicitly outlined the reasons for Haggis's action. The screenwriter discussed in some detail Scientology's policy of "disconnection," which encourages members to cut off family, friends, and associates who have been declared suppressive persons or SPs. An SP is often someone who in some way has expressed criticism of the organization.

In a CNN interview an official spokesperson for Scientology, Tommy Davis, was asked about the disconnection policy. He answered, "There's no such thing as disconnection as you're characterizing it." However, Haggis publicly took issue with Davis. "We all know this policy exists. I didn't have to search for verification—I didn't have to look any further than my own home." Haggis was referring to his wife who was told to disconnect from her parents when they left the church. He then concluded, "To see [Tommy Davis] lie so easily, I am afraid I had to ask myself: what else [is Tommy Davis] lying about?" Haggis later lamented, "What kind of organization are we involved in where people just disappear?"[906] Lawrence Wright, the reporter who wrote the article in the *New Yorker* about Haggis, later expanded the story into a sensational book about Scientology.[907]

Jenna Miscavige Hill, the niece of David Miscavige, wrote a book about her own odyssey in Scientology.[908] She told the press, "My experience in growing up in Scientology is that it is both mentally and at times physically abusive." Ms. Hill claimed, "We got a lousy education from unqualified teachers, forced labor, long hours, forced confessions, being held in rooms not to mention the mental anguish of trying to figure out all of the conflicting information they force upon you as a young child."[909] Like other defectors, Hill says she has been branded an SP.[910]

2012—Katie Holmes and Tom Cruise Divorce

In 2012 when actress Katie Holmes filed for divorce against movie star Tom Cruise, all the historically troubling issues surrounding Scientology seemed to congeal and become fodder for the press. And the issue of disconnection in particular—and its potential for parental alienation—was discussed in some depth. It appears the famous couple was preparing for a contentious court battle over the custody of their six-year-old daughter, Suri Cruise. Holmes reportedly was unhappy about Scientology and didn't want her child to be indoctrinated.

The divorce became a magnet drawing increasingly bad press for Scientology. Former Scientologists were interviewed, and details about their allegations of abuse in the organization were reported about and broadcast globally. Media magnate Rupert Murdoch even weighed in, calling Scientology "a very weird cult" and Scientologists "creepy, maybe even evil."

Josh Forman, a matrimonial attorney and partner at Chemtob Moss Forman & Talbert in New York, opined, "I don't think it would be very good for Tom's career if he is seen as having a huge, dragged-out custody battle with Katie. I think they should really settle, and I see this as settling."[911] Less than two weeks after the divorce filing, that is exactly what happened. Cruise quickly settled the divorce.[912] In that settlement Katie Holmes was reportedly granted "sole custody of Suri," while Cruise received "'meaningful' visitation rights."[913] Further details reportedly revealed that the settlement contained a prohibition concerning attendance at any "residential school" of any kind, which seems to preclude the possibility of potential Scientology indoctrination. Tom Cruise is also required to pay for his daughter's education, health care, and dental costs, though apparently Katie Holmes will be the parent who specifically decides what type of care and education Suri Cruise will receive in the future.[914]

Narconon

Narconon is a drug rehabilitation program closely associated with Scientology. Narconon CEO Gary Smith said, "It's not accurate to say it is Scientology-based, because Scientology is a religion. We're not a religion." However, Smith admitted that Narconon is based on the teachings of Scientology's founder, L. Ron Hubbard, and that it receives funding from Scientology.[915]

Board-certified forensic psychiatrist Dr. Ryan Estevez said, "Anybody can see if you look into [Narconon], the philosophy that is brought into the rehabilitation program is the same philosophy that is brought into their religion of Scientology."[916]

The rehabilitation program Narconon provides includes what is called the "purification rundown," which is a Scientology ritual L. Ron Hubbard prescribed. This is about a month-long regimen of vitamins that includes taking large doses of niacin, ingesting cooking oil, running on a treadmill, and sweating in a sauna at temperatures reportedly set from 140 to 180 degrees Fahrenheit.[917] Dr. Estevez warned, "From a physician perspective, they are also doing something that could be very dangerous."[918]

A similar Scientology-linked detoxification program run in New York City called Downtown Medical sought to involve city rescue worker who responded to the World Trade Center attack and were exposed to toxic materials. Participants were reportedly asked to cease taking prescribed medications as part of the program. Dr. David Prezant, deputy chief medical officer of the New York Fire Department (FDNY), said, "It's risky for anybody to stop any type of medication without guidance and a plan from their own treating physician." The FDNY refused to endorse the program.[919]

Narconon also ran an antidrug educational program, which was banned from San Francisco public schools in 2004.[920] In 2005 the California Medical Association unanimously supported dropping Narconon as a source for drug education for students due to its "factually inaccurate approaches." Medical experts specifically called attention to erroneous teachings such as "Drugs accumulate indefinitely in body fat, where they cause recurring drug cravings and flashbacks for years, even after the user quits" and that "the vitamin niacin pulls drugs from fat, and saunas sweat them from the body."[921]

Narconon Arrowhead in Oklahoma became the focus of a multiagency investigation by the Oklahoma State Bureau of Investigation, the Pittsburg County sheriff's office, and the Department of Mental

Health. The investigation began with the death of Stacy Dawn Murphy, twenty, at Arrowhead in 2012 but would eventually include the additional Narconon Arrowhead-related deaths of Hillary Holten, twenty-one; Gabriel Graves, thirty-two; and the 2009 death of Kaysie Dianne Werninck, twenty-eight. During 2013 a number of lawsuits were filed across the United States against Narconon. Five lawsuits filed against the Arrowhead facility in Oklahoma alleged fraud, deceit, breach of contract, and civil conspiracy.[922]

Lucas Catton, once the president of the Arrowhead facility in Oklahoma, left in 2004. In an interview Canton said, "It's all based on deception. Everything from the success rate to their counseling certifications, to their general requirements of what it takes to be a staff member to their connection to the Church of Scientology—every single one of those things is deceptively portrayed to the general public versus what really goes on behind the closed doors."[923]

Search warrants were executed at a Narconon-related rehabilitation clinic during April 2013. Narconon in Georgia is under investigation for insurance fraud. One patient's insurer was reportedly billed $166,275 for doctor's visits that never took place. At the time the warrants were executed, Danny Porter, the Gwinnett County district attorney, said, "We are actively and vigorously pursuing an investigation."[924] Concerned families claimed that Narconon financially exploited them. "No one ever said, 'We're going to open up two credit cards in your name,'" said Scott Maxey, a Chicago man who received new credit cards in the mail that were already charged to their limits to pay Narconon.[925]

Scientology Shrinking

Despite its prodigious efforts in recent years, which includes buying and renovating impressive buildings Scientology calls its "Ideal Orgs," or operational urban hubs, census figures seem to demonstrate that Scientology is in decline with a shrinking membership. For example, according to a 2011 census there are only 2,163 Australians who call themselves Scientologists. This reflects a 13.7 percent drop in Australian membership alone over the past five years.[926] The US Census Bureau and American Religious Identification Survey (ARIS) estimates appear to reflect the same. ARIS estimated that there were fifty-five thousand Scientologists in the United States in 2001, but by 2008 that number reportedly dwindled to about twenty-five thousand.[927]

[857] Colin Rigley, "L. Ron Hubbard's Last Refuge," *New Times* (San Luis Obispo, CA), May 28, 2009.

[858] Ibid.

[859] Ruth Eglash, "Who Was L. Ron Hubbard?" *The Jerusalem Post*, December 7, 2006.

[860] Joseph Mallia, "Judge Found Hubbard Lied about Achievements," *Boston Herald*, March 1, 1998.

[861] Michael Crowley, "L. Ron Hubbard," *Slate*, July 15, 2005.

[862] Ibid.

[863] Ibid.

[864] "Interview with L. Ron Hubbard Jr.," *Penthouse*, June 1983.

[865] Ibid.

[866] Ibid.

[867] L. Ron Hubbard, Operation Thetan (OT) Level III. (L. Ron Hubbard's handwritten version is available through the Web) http://www.american-buddha.com/scientologyNEW0T3.pdf (accessed May 28, 2014).

[868] Lawrence Wright, "The Apostate: Paul Haggis vs. the Church of Scientology," *New Yorker*, February 14, 2011.

[869] Ibid.

[870] Rich Behar, "Scientology: The Cult of Greed," *Time*, May 6, 1991.

[871] Mallia, "Judge Found Hubbard Lied about Achievements."

[872] Janet Reitman, "Inside Scientology," *Rolling Stone*, February 23, 2006.

[873] "Lisa McPherson Case: Events Leading to the Death of Scientologist Lisa McPherson," *St. Petersburg Times*, May 21, 2009.

[874] Ibid.

[875] Ibid.

[876] Ibid.

[877] Ibid.

[878] Ibid.

[879] Ibid.

[880] Ibid.

[881] "Lisa McPherson Scientology Case Drove Joan Wood from Medical Examiner to Recluse," *St. Petersburg Times*, July 30 2011.

[882] Ibid.

[883] "Lisa McPherson Case: Events Leading to the Death of Scientologist Lisa McPherson."

[884] Ibid.

[885] David Touretzsky and Peter Alexander, "A Church's Lethal Contract," *Razor Magazine*, December 2003.

[886] "Lisa McPherson Case: Events Leading to the Death of Scientologist Lisa McPherson."

[887] Joe Childs and Thomas C. Tobin, "In Letter, Former Scientology Leader Debbie Cook Renews Concerns about Church Fund-Raising," *Tampa Bay Times*, January 7, 2012.

[888] Ibid.

[889] Ibid.

[890] Thomas C. Tobin, "The Man behind Scientology," *St. Petersburg Times*, October 25, 1998.

[891] Ibid.

[892] Ibid.

[893] Ibid.

[894] Rich Behar, "The Thriving Cult of Greed and Power," *Time*, May 6, 1991.

[895] Tobin, "The Man behind Scientology."

[896] Ibid.

[897] Joe Childs and Thomas C. Tobin, "Ex-Scientology Leader Debbie Cook Tells of Fear and Pursuit by Church Officers," *Tampa Bay Times*, March 7, 2012.

[898] Joe Childs and Thomas C. Tobin, "Ex-Clearwater Scientology Officer Says She Was Put in 'the Hole,' Abused for Weeks," *Tampa Bay Times*, February 10, 2012.

[899] Ibid.

[900] Childs and Tobin, "Ex-Scientology Leader Debbie Cook Tells of Fear and Pursuit by Church Officers."

[901] Joe Childs and Thomas C. Tobin, "Former Clearwater Scientology Leader Settles Lawsuit with Church," *Tampa Bay Times*, April 24, 2012.

[902] Ibid.

[903] Joe Childs and Thomas C. Tobin, "Ex-Scientology Leader Debbie Cook Moving to Caribbean Island," *Tampa Bay Times*, June 20, 2012.

[904] Joe Childs and Thomas C. Tobin, "Strength in Their Numbers," *St. Petersburg Times*, August 1, 2009.

[905] Joe Childs and Thomas C. Tobin, "Scientology Response to Church Defectors: 'Total Lies,'" *St. Petersburg Times*, June 20, 2009.

[906] Wright, "The Apostate: Paul Haggis vs. the Church of Scientology."

[907] Lawrence Wright, *Going Clear: Scientology, Hollywood, and the Prison of Belief* (New York: Random House Audio, unabridged edition, January 17, 2013).

[908] Jenna Miscavige Hill and Lisa Pulitzer, *Beyond Belief: My Secret Life inside Scientology and My Harrowing Escape* (New York: William Morrow, 2013).

[909] Matt Blake, "Scientology Leader's Niece to Reveal 'Strange and Disturbing' Details about Life inside Church in Tell-All Memoir," *Daily Mail* (London), September 25, 2012.

[910] Ibid.

[911] Piya Sinha-Roy, "Holmes Faces Cruise, Scientology in Fight for Suri," Reuters, July 2, 2012.

[912] Sheila Marikar, "Katie Holmes, Tom Cruise Settle Divorce," *Good Morning America*, ABC, July 9, 2012.

[913] "Tom Cruise's Cheap Divorce: Katie Holmes Receives Just $400,000 a Year in Child Support from Multi-millionaire Ex-husband," *Daily Mail* (London), August 24, 2012.

[914] Tom Hicks, "Tom Cruise and Katie Holmes Divorce Settlement Leaks," *Contra Costa Times*, August 24, 2012.

[915] "Is the Narconon Drug Treatment Program a Scientology Front?" *WTSP-TV 10 News*, February 8, 2013.

[916] Ibid.

[917] John DeSio, "The Rundown on Scientology's Purification Rundown," *New York Press*, May 30, 2007.

[918] "Is the Narconon Drug Treatment Program a Scientology Front?"

[919] Michelle O'Donnell, "Scientologists Treatments Lure Firefighters," *New York Times*, October 4, 2003.

[920] Nanette Asimov, "Narconon Banned from S.F. Schools," *San Francisco Chronicle*, August 25, 2004.

[921] Nanette Asimov, "Doctors Back Schools Dropping Flawed Antidrug Program," *San Francisco Chronicle*, March 27, 2005.

[922] Jeanne LeFlore, "Narconon Arrowhead: Five Lawsuits Filed Allege Fraud and Deceit and Other Charges," *McAlester News-Capital*, March 28, 2013.

[923] Ann Schecter, "Scientology-Linked Rehab Narconon under Fire from Two Former Executives," *Rock Center NBC News*, April 4, 2013.

[924] Christian Boone, "Search Warrants Executed at Narconon Rehab Clinic," *Atlanta Journal-Constitution*, April 26, 2013.

[925] Jodie Fleischer, "Families Say Rehabilitation Clinic Opened Credit Cards without Permission," *WSBTV-News*, May 6, 2013.

[926] Steve Cannane, "Scientology Membership in Drastic Decline," *Australian Broadcast Corporation*, June 29, 2012.

[927] Tony Ortega, "Scientologists: How Many of Them Are There Anyway?" *Village Voice*, July 4, 2011.

CHAPTER 15

SCIENTOLOGY INTERVENTION

A middle-aged Scientologist confronted his wife and served her with divorce papers. He was determined to leave his family in an effort to become a full-time member of the Sea Organization, commonly called Sea Org. First established by L. Ron Hubbard, Scientology's founder, Sea Org is now composed of the full-time staff serving at Scientology centers or what are called "Orgs" around the world.

Most people who join Scientology begin as "publics," people who pay for Scientology courses and services but are not on staff.[928] Celebrity Scientologists like actors Tom Cruise and John Travolta are essentially publics, but they are catered to and receive special treatment, such as special handling at Scientology's so-called celebrity centers.[929] Scientology courses and services can be quite expensive and therefore potentially represent a substantial financial burden to the average income earner and at times even for the wealthy.[930] Some publics have joined Sea Org in the hope that further training and services would be available, essentially in exchange for work. Sea Org members have signed "billion year contracts" tying themselves to Scientology seemingly forever, based on a belief in past and future lives.[931]

After nearly thirty years as a public Scientologist, the husband wanted to do more to "clear the planet." "Clearing the planet" is Scientology jargon that essentially means recruiting people into Scientology so they can supposedly become cleared of negativity through Scientology courses and training. The husband felt that at this point in his life he could best accomplish this task by serving Scientology as a staff person. Now that his two children were adults and not living at home, only his marriage remained as an obstacle. He must leave his wife, who had never fully embraced Scientology, and move on.

After more than twenty years of marriage, the husband had never been able to convince his wife to do more than take a few Scientology courses. The couple owned a home and had raised their two children together, but now the husband was restless. He must fulfill his destiny through Scientology. And since his wife wouldn't support this full-time mission, he must leave her and go it alone.

After receiving divorce papers, the wife called her children, and a kind of family intervention took place. The wife and children cried and pleaded. They begged the husband and father not to separate from the family by going into relative seclusion in the Sea Organization. They knew that Sea Org members may cut off their families and have little, if any, meaningful communication. And if family members questioned such behavior or offered any criticism of Scientology, they might be labeled "suppressive persons," or SPs, and then summarily be dismissed through what Scientologists calls the "disconnection" process.

After the emotional catharsis of the family intervention, the husband agreed to pause and reconsider the situation. His family's pleas affected him deeply, but he was confused and torn between his dual loyalties of Scientology and family.

At this juncture the wife called her sister-in-law. The husband's family had long been concerned about his involvement in Scientology, but much like his wife, they had kept their criticism private for fear of losing him. Now with the evidence mounting that he might submerge completely in Scientology, they decided to take immediate action and retained me to facilitate an intervention.

Before beginning the intervention, we held a preparation meeting, which included the husband's sister, his wife, and his children at my hotel room. We spoke at length for hours about the complexities of the intervention process and about how each person must fulfill his or her role. This talk included the usual warnings about boundaries and undue criticism at inappropriate moments. The intervention would require their full support, cooperation, and assistance for me to fulfill my role and facilitate this effort.

We decided during the preparation process that the best approach for the intervention would be a friendly visit from the sister at the family home. This was planned in advance, and the children would be there. We would begin on a weekend. The sister and I would come to the house, and she would introduce me.

We arrived in the morning. The wife greeted us at the door and let us in. It wasn't long before the husband and I were engaged in a friendly conversation about his home improvement projects, art collection, and hobbies. We chatted about his interest in art history and architecture for some time before he finally asked, "Why are you here?" My answer was candid and to the point, explaining that his family had serious concerns about his plans for the future. It seems that he had decided to postpone those plans, though there was still some palpable fear among his family members. We agreed to have a deeper conversation about their fears. Were all these apprehensions misplaced, or were there legitimate reasons for concern?

Our conversation soon moved to the subject of Scientology. The husband explained that he had been a member of the organization for almost three decades. He added that his wife and children had neither opposed nor fully embraced Scientology and that historically there had been no real arguments or serious disagreements about his commitment to the controversial organization. Instead, at times his wife and children had agreed to take Scientology courses and had been passive or generally agreeable to his ongoing involvement.

At this point his wife entered the conversation, explaining that her relative passivity in the past regarding Scientology didn't mean she had no concerns about it. The husband's sister explained that after learning about the proposed divorce and his plans to abruptly change his living arrangements, she became seriously concerned. Both of the adult children likewise expressed fears about Scientology's influence in the current situation. They wanted to know why their father had decided to leave their mother and move in to Scientology group housing.

His explanation was that after years of taking courses and moving through Scientology training as a public member, he wanted to make Scientology his total focus and mission in life. The husband felt that the only way he could do this effectively was to become a full-time staff member of Scientology. Since his children were both adults now, they no longer needed a full-time father. And his wife had enough property and assets to ensure her security. When I asked whether Scientology or Scientologists had played any role in his decision-making process, the husband's response was stony silence.

During the first day we discussed the nucleus for a definition of a destructive cult, as described by Robert Jay Lifton.[932] Might Scientology potentially fit within that basic framework? Did the founder of Scientology, L. Ron Hubbard, parallel the first characteristic Lifton had described, fulfilling the role of a defining charismatic and authoritarian leader? Wasn't it Hubbard's legacy of writings that formed the foundation of Scientology and completely defined the group? In this sense couldn't Scientology be seen as a personality-driven organization? These thought-provoking questions stimulated our discussion and moved the conversation forward. The husband acknowledged the singular and pivotal importance of Hubbard and his writings. He said that without L. Ron Hubbard, Scientology had no basis for existence or meaningful substance.

After Hubbard's death in 1986, Sea Org member David Miscavige ultimately became chairman of the board of the Religious Technology Center tasked with the responsibility to "preserve, maintain and protect the Scientology religion."[933] Today he "holds the ultimate ecclesiastical authority regarding the standard and pure application of L. Ron Hubbard's religious technologies."[934]

In our discussion about Hubbard, we touched on the mythology that seemed to surround the man. This included Hubbard's personal biography, as promoted by Scientology, which reportedly is often misleading, generally inflated, and grossly exaggerated.[935] Who was L. Ron Hubbard? We examined some of the relevant research about Hubbard's education, military career, and time as a science fiction writer. But it was his role as the creator of Scientology that ultimately became Hubbard's most lasting and important historical legacy.

What was Scientology without L. Ron Hubbard? After a day of discussion, we agreed that the personalities of Hubbard and Scientology were so intertwined, synonymous, and inseparable that neither had any historical significance without the other. Scientology would simply be unable to function without Hubbard's legacy. Therefore the most salient single feature of a destructive cult was evident in Scientology—that is, a charismatic leader comes to define the group and is its driving force. Our first day was consumed with establishing this fact. We examined the life of Hubbard through whatever objective historical documentation or existing news reports could be verified rather than through the mythology Scientology had developed about the man.

At the end of the first day, there was no difficulty in obtaining the husband's agreement that he would continue the dialogue the following day and not contact anyone associated with Scientology. He stayed with his wife and two children at the family home, and his sister and I returned to our respective hotel rooms, not far away, for the night. Per our previous preparation, the family understood that during the intervening evening they wouldn't discuss Scientology or any related topics we had touched on through our conversation that day. Instead, they would use that time to unwind, relax, and engage in casual conversation not connected to the intervention.

On day two we discussed the second characteristic Lifton identified in his core definition of a destructive cult—that is, evidence that the group or leader uses a thought-reform program. Lifton lists eight criteria that, taken together, constitute proof that a thought-reform program is in place and ongoing.[936] Lifton explains that such a program can be run effectively using a minimum of six of these criteria. We discussed which of the criteria might be applicable to Scientology.

The first and foremost of Lifton's eight criteria of thought reform is control of the environment or what he calls "Milieu Control."[937] This aspect of thought reform provides the foundation or platform for the following seven operating characteristics. I asked the husband to explain what extent his social network of friends extended to beyond Scientology. He explained that virtually all his present friends were Scientologists. Other than members of his immediate family and extended family, he really didn't have any deep or meaningful relationships with anyone outside of Scientology. After decades of involvement in Scientology, whatever old friends he'd once had outside the organization had long since fallen away.

To better understand how this aspect of relationships might relate to cultic control, we went over a chart psychologist Margaret Singer composed that correlated the research of MIT professor Edgar

Schein regarding coercive persuasion with the findings of Lifton and her own interpretation of how this information applied to cults.[938] Singer noted how "control [of] the person's time and, if possible, physical environment" correlated with Milieu Control.[939] We talked about how such social isolation is also one of the "key factors" sociologist Richard Ofshe cited in his explanation of coercive persuasion.[940] In other words, that's "the use of an organized peer group" to "promote conformity."[941] Singer also noted the work of Arizona State University professor Robert Cialdini,[942] who included "liking" as a principle of influence used to gain compliance. Singer correlated this dimension to cults: "We obey people we like."[943] I asked the husband whether his relatively tight-knit group of Scientology friends had effectively served as an element of control in his decision-making process. Did he obey Scientology largely because he liked them? Cialdini also points out the influence of what he calls "social proof"; one way to "determine what is correct is to find out what others believe is correct."[944]

We also discussed the husband's many years of taking courses, going through auditing, and doing other Scientology-related activities. Certainly during that time Scientology or Scientologists had exercised ongoing control over the environment. Specifically we focused on how the organization can potentially encapsulate an individual. I then pointed out that Sea Organization members represented the most extreme example of Scientology's control of an environment. Sea Org members lived in Scientology housing, were full-time staffers who were barely socializing in any meaningful way with the outside world, and became effectively cocooned in Scientology. We discussed how control of the environment and the flow of information laid the groundwork for control of the mind. As Cialdini observed, "People often view a behavior as more correct in a given situation—to the degree that we see others performing it."[945] To the extent that an organization or leader can control environment, everything a person sees, experiences, and does in social interaction, that group or leader can substantially control the mind. Ofshe summarized this control as "the

manipulation of the totality of the person's social environment to stabilize behavior once modified."[946]

On the second day we also touched on other aspects of Lifton's
thought-reform criteria such as "Mystical Manipulation" and the
"Cult of Confession."[947] How might those characteristics be expressed
in Scientology? Scientologists are put through a process called "auditing," which is a form of counseling based on questioning conducted
by an auditor while the subject is physically connected to what is essentially a galvanic response-measuring device. Scientologists call
this apparatus an "e-meter."[948] A Scientologist is told that the e-meter
measures the "negative reactive mind," but in fact it is little more than
a means of measuring nervous tension during what can be seen as an
interrogation process. The US Food and Drug Administration (FDA)
categorized the e-meter as a "religious artifact" without any meaningful medical application.[949]

Perhaps auditing might be seen as somewhat like a Roman Catholic
confessional process with a priest but without confidentiality and the
added element of technology. The so-called e-meter is one aspect of
what is often called a "lie detector" machine or polygraph. How potent
and penetrating does that make Scientology's form of confession? An
auditor or confessor is aided by a form of technology, which helps him
or her identify and delve deeper into the subject's secrets and vulner-
abilities. We talked about the fact that auditors take copious notes for
each auditing session, which then become part of a file compiled about
that individual. We discussed how the auditing process could be used
to manipulate the subject, who is in a highly suggestible state.

According to Lifton, Mystical Manipulation "uses every possible
device at the milieu's command, no matter how bizarre or painful.
Initiated from above, it seeks to provoke specific patterns of behavior and emotion in such a way that these will appear to have arisen
spontaneously, directed as it is by an ostensibly omniscient group, and

must assume, for the manipulated, a near-mystical quality."[950] This comment also parallels Ofshe's observation concerning the primary aspects of coercive persuasion, which includes the "intense interpersonal and psychological attack to destabilize an individual's sense of self to promote compliance."[951] We also reviewed Singer's research, which identified the net result of such personal manipulation as "powerlessness, covert fear and dependency."[952]

As we continued to move forward through the second day, the husband remained engaged and seemed very interested. But he did repeatedly offer counterpoints defending both Scientology and its practices. He said, "Other religions are the same." But as the husband offered a new apology, it was also an opportunity to raise additional questions about the integrity and transparency of Scientology.

For example, other religious groups are typically much more open about their beliefs, faith claims, and doctrines. Why does Scientology deliberately withhold information about important components of its belief system? Do Christians withhold certain information they know about Jesus? Do Jews conceal the story of Abraham?

These questions emphasize the point that Scientology deliberately withholds important information about its basic beliefs. No one who enters Scientology is initially told about Xenu (pronounced Zee-new), "the head of the galactic federation" who ruled seventy-five million years ago and killed millions of people by blowing them up volcanically on earth. Only when a Scientologist reaches OT III (Operating Thetan Level 3)[953] does he or she learn about how Xenu packaged disembodied spirits in "clusters" or body thetans (BTs), which would live on as one body. Only when a Scientologist reaches OT III does he or she learn the relevance of this history, which is linked to the process of cleansing oneself of negativity. This process includes addressing the negative influence of BTs, which can effectively be accomplished only through Scientology.

I asked the husband whether he thought Scientology might be seen as deceptive or at least less than forthcoming by not openly sharing the story of Xenu and BTs with people from the beginning. Would Christians neglect to explain the importance of the virgin birth or resurrection as an important part of Christianity? Would Jews fail to disclose the epoch of Exodus and its relevance to the Ten Commandments?

Despite the importance of Xenu to Scientology, his existence is not disclosed until a Scientologist reaches a predetermined point, which may take years to accomplish. Only then is this information shared. We talked about Singer's delineation of the differences between indoctrination and thought reform—for example, that religious indoctrination is typically not deceptive but that thought reform "is deceptive."[954]

There are eight OT levels in Scientology. As we discussed this aspect, everyone agreed that progressing through these various levels could be quite costly.[955]

But how could someone make an informed decision about such an investment of time and money if he or she doesn't have the necessary information to fully understand Scientology? If Scientology expects someone to pay for courses and training, why isn't there more meaningful disclosure about the beliefs that form the basis for much of that course work?

The husband struggled with these questions and could neither easily address them nor offer solid answers. His family members reiterated their concerns—that if he was going to dedicate the rest of his life to Scientology as a full-time staffer, such issues must be addressed. Again we agreed to meet the following day, ending our second day with serious questions we would follow through on the next morning.

On the third day the husband seemed almost anxious to begin. He wanted answers to the perplexing questions surrounding Scientology.

We discussed yet another aspect of Lifton's criteria concerning thought reform. Is Scientology what Lifton calls a "Sacred Science"? Lifton writes that in a group using thought reform, there is "an aura of sacredness around its basic dogma, holding it out as an ultimate moral vision for the ordering of human existence." He adds, "This sacredness is evident in the prohibition (whether or not explicit) against the questioning of basic assumptions, and in the reverence which is demanded for the originators of the Word, the present bearers of the Word, and the Word itself, while thus transcending ordinary concerns of logic."[956] Singer describes this as a "closed system of logic" that will "allow no real input or criticism" as opposed to education, where a "two-way pupil-teacher exchange is encouraged."[957] Singer also says a legitimate educational effort "is not deceptive."[958]

Could Scientology be considered such a "Sacred Science" and "closed system of logic"? Scientologists have said they hope to "clear the planet" through their technology. Cannot such a plan be seen as tantamount to proposing "an ultimate moral vision for the ordering of human existence"? Is there a meaningful two-way exchange during Scientology training? Certainly there is reverence of L Ron Hubbard as the "originator of the Word" as well as considerable deference demonstrated to both the current leader, Miscavige, and the organization as "the current bearers of the Word." And there is absolute acceptance of the word itself. We also discussed how Cialdini's principles of influence might be applied in this context. That is, the use of authority, according to Singer, uses "a deep-seated sense of duty to authority figures" to solicit obedience and compliance.[959]

We watched A&E cable network's investigative report about Scientology.[960] This two-hour presentation, broadcast during December 1998, was the last media interview of David Miscavige. A&E apparently had the full cooperation of Scientology. The producers seemed to make sure that ample time was afforded for Scientologists to rebut any criticism and present the organization's views and official positions. Miscavige noted, "All of our source materials, original teachings will be taught and practiced the same way fifty years from now, hundred years from now, thousand years from now."[961] Miscavige ultimately concluded, "Scientology, we believe, is a point where science and religion have truly met."[962]

Entertainer Isaac Hayes, who was also interviewed for the A&E program, emphasized the absolute nature of Scientology teachings as written by Hubbard. Hayes said, "We will not allow it to become aberrated [subject to an aberration], [and] we will not change it."[963] This sentiment Hayes expressed seems to reflect Lifton's description concerning "the prohibition against the questioning of basic assumptions" of the group.

But then how could Scientology be the point where "science and religion have truly met" if it is such a closed system that is not subject to change? We discussed this issue during the intervention; that is, science is certainly subject to change based on new discoveries and research. Scientologists like Hayes, however, appeared to see any change as an unwanted aberration. For example, Hubbard posited the theory that toxins are indefinitely held in the fatty tissues of the body. I pointed out that science has proved Hubbard wrong.[964] Yet Scientologists who support the Scientology-linked drug rehabilitation and education program, known as Narconon, refuse to accept this scientific fact. They will not accept that L Ron Hubbard was wrong.

We discussed this issue during the third day. After all, Hubbard wasn't a doctor or a scientist but rather a science fiction writer without a college degree. Isn't it possible that such a man, writing decades ago, got some things wrong? For example, there is now new research regarding the brain and its chemistry. In the 1950s Hubbard wasn't aware of this—that is, scientific research hadn't yet been done. How could Scientology be scientific if it isn't subject to new discoveries and research? How could it "meet science" without critical questioning or change?

As we watched the A&E investigative report, other issues came up. A Scientologist tried to explain the cost of courses and training. He said, "Donations are requested." I asked the husband whether this statement was disingenuous; that is, Scientology has specific pricing for its courses and services, and they are not simply paid by "donations." He agreed and was aware of the prices set for services; he saw that the word *donation* was misleading.

At another point during the A&E program, the practice of "disconnection" was discussed. Disconnection is the process in Scientology that provides for the official shunning of declared or designated people outside the organization. Scientologists are expected to cease association and communication with people who have been declared "suppressive persons" (SPs). During the A&E program Mike Rinder, then an official spokesperson for Scientology, claimed that those people declared for disconnection were "antagonistic." Ironically Rinder himself would years later leave Scientology, be declared an SP, and be subject to disconnection.

I asked the husband whether in his experience everyone who went through disconnection had demonstrated that he or she was somehow antagonistic. He responded that not everyone declared that he knew had been antagonistic regarding Scientology or Scientologists. Many had simply opted to leave or discontinue their involvement with Scientology, and subsequently they had been declared SPs. We concurred on this point, then reviewed news reports about former Scientologists and affected families, who claimed Scientology had cut them off.[965] Many complained about the lack of meaningful communication from loved ones in the Sea Organization.

We continued to watch the A&E report, which served to frame other issues. At one point Isaac Hayes said, "The more you know, the less likely you are to be victimized." Hayes meant that people should learn more about Scientology. But couldn't this concept be applicable to almost anything? I asked the husband whether this principle might be applied to our current discussion about Scientology. He agreed. Another day was ending. After we finished watching the A&E report, our third day was done.

At the beginning of the fourth day, we continued our dialogue about Lifton. At this point we delved into what Lifton called "loaded language." He wrote, "The language of the totalist environment is characterized by the thought-terminating cliché. The most far-reaching and complex of human problems are compressed into brief, highly reductive, definitive-sounding phrases, easily memorized and easily expressed. These become the start and finish of any ideological analysis."[966] We talked about how the label SP might fit the category of a thought-terminating cliché. We discussed how labeling people as SPs not only makes them social pariahs but also effectively ends any consideration of their ideas or personal accounts of abuse in the organization. In this sense the loaded language linked to disconnection could not only terminate thinking but also dispense with the very existence of those so declared.

"The Dispensing of Existence" is yet another of Lifton's criteria used to identify the existence of a thought-reform program or what some might call "brainwashing." This characteristic is an expression of how "the totalist environment draws a sharp line between those whose right to existence can be recognized, and those who possess no such right."[967] At this point we discussed how this quotation might be linked to Scientology's disconnection policy. How people passed in and out of existence depending on their status or designation, according to Scientology. A person's existence could be dispensed with if he or she left the organization, because there was no legitimate reason to leave. Therefore, whenever someone left, he or she was wrong and was potentially an SP; he or she could be declared an SP and then be subject to disconnection. Wasn't Scientology's disconnection policy an expression of what Singer described as a "closed system" that was intolerant of criticism and resisted logic?

Was it simply coincidental that so many aspects of Scientology paralleled Robert Jay Lifton's nucleus for a definition of a destructive cult? Was it happenstance that so many of Lifton's criteria concerning thought reform and coercive persuasion techniques, as researchers such as Schein, Singer, and Ofshe explained, seemed to be evident in Scientology?

The husband didn't experience an epiphany or sudden moment of clarity. Instead, through the days as we worked together, his realization of Scientology gradually unfolded. Bit by bit and piece by piece, the program instilled in his mind over a period of decades gradually unraveled and fell apart. He increasingly asked critical questions, and on the fifth day he said he would no longer be involved in Scientology. Needless to say, his family was greatly relieved. But most importantly, he came to this conclusion through his own thought processes, analysis, and critical thinking—which the intervention had only facilitated and encouraged.

On the fifth day he began to disclose previously unknown information to his family about Scientology and its inner workings. He admitted that Scientologists had encouraged him to divorce his wife and leave his family. It seems those who had advised him saw the husband as more useful in Sea Org as a full-time staffer than just continuing to take courses and receive auditing and training.

In the months that followed, I received several phone calls from the husband, his sister, and his wife. Sometimes there were concerns regarding the difficulties he was experiencing in his social transition away from Scientology. He was sometimes lonely and missed his Scientology friends. It appears that he wasn't officially declared, but his Scientology friends began to drop him, and he needed to move on with his life. This meant finding new friends and interests.

The husband received some professional counseling, but largely found solace from the input, support and advice of family.

[928] Tony Ortega, "Scientology Cruise Ship as Hellhole: The Ramona Dienes-Browning Story," *Village Voice*, December 4, 2011.

[929] Douglas Frantz, "Celebrity Faithful Strive to Put Halo atop Organization," *San Diego Union-Tribune*, February 15, 1998.

[930] Joseph Mallia, "Inside the Church of Scientology," *Boston Herald*, March 1, 1998.

[931] Ibid.

[932] Robert Jay Lifton, "Cult Formation," *Harvard Mental Health Letter*, February 1981.

[933] Jamie Doward, "David Miscavige: A Cult Figure in the Fame Game," *The Guardian* (New York), July 7, 2012.

[934] Ibid.

[935] Joseph Mallia, "Judge Found Hubbard Lied about Achievements," *Boston Herald*, March 1, 1998.

[936] Robert Jay Lifton, *Thought Reform and the Psychology of Totalism* (Chapel Hill: University of North Carolina Press, 2012), 419–437.

[937] Ibid., 420–422.

[938] Margaret Singer, *Cults in Our Midst* (San Francisco, CA: Jossey-Bass, 1996), 63.

[939] Ibid.

[940] Richard Ofshe, "Coercive Persuasion and Attitude Change," *Encyclopedia of Sociology*, vol. 1 (New York: McMillan, 1992), 212–224.

[941] Ibid.

[942] Robert B. Cialdini, *Influence: Science and Practice* (Needham Heights, MA: Allyn & Bacon, 2001).

[943] Singer, *Cults in Our Midst*, 169.

[944] Cialdini, *Influence: Science and Practice*, 117.

[945] Ibid.

[946] Ofshe, "Coercive Persuasion and Attitude Change," 212–224.

[947] Lifton, *Thought Reform and the Psychology of Totalism*, 420–423.

[948] Mark Pilkington, "Clear Thinking," *The Guardian* (New York), February 17, 2005.

[949] Ibid.

[950] Lifton, *Thought Reform and the Psychology of Totalism*, 422.

[951] Ofshe, "Coercive Persuasion and Attitude Change," 212–224.

[952] Singer, *Cults in Our Midst*, 63.

[953] Lawrence Wright, "The Apostate: Paul Haggis vs. the Church of Scientology," *New Yorker*, February 14, 2011.

[954] Singer, *Cults in Our Midst*, 63.

[955] Ibid.

[956] Lifton, *Thought Reform and the Psychology of Totalism*, 427–428.

[957] Singer, *Cults in Our Midst*, 58.

[958] Ibid., 59.

[959] Ibid., 169.

[960] Heidi Ewing, "Inside Scientology," *Investigative Reports*, A&E, December 9, 1998.

[961] Ibid.

[962] Ibid.

[963] Ibid.

[964] Nanette Asimov, "Doctors Back Schools Dropping Flawed Antidrug Program," *San Francisco Chronicle*, March 27, 2005.

[965] Lawrence Wright, *Going Clear: Scientology, Hollywood, and the Prison of Belief* (New York: Random House Audio, unabridged edition, January 17, 2013).

[966] Lifton, *Thought Reform and the Psychology of Totalism*, 429.

[967] Ibid., 433.

CHAPTER 16

LARGE GROUP AWARENESS TRAINING (LGAT)

Before detailing an intervention regarding large group awareness training (LGAT), discussing the historical concerns surrounding some controversial LGATs is helpful. Today there are many for-profit, privately owned companies and organizations around the world that sell this type of training through extended weekends or longer retreats and seminars.

An LGAT organization or company is typically based on selling the philosophy of its founder. The purpose of the training, other than making money as a product of the business, is to essentially persuade participants to accept and embrace that philosophy. This is done over a period of days in the context of an intensely emotional and frequently confrontational group encounter format. The philosophy LGAT proponents propose and promote is typically seen as the means for addressing virtually any human problem and often as an all-encompassing framework for curing the ills of humanity. A primary leader usually facilitates the LGAT, and that facilitator is most often carefully scripted. The underlying assumption is that adoption of the LGAT belief system will lead to a better and more productive life.

LGAT participants are expected to undergo days of confrontation and scrutiny through a facilitated group encounter designed to promote a catharsis of change, culminating in an expected epiphany or sudden illumination. Despite discomfort, many new initiates do not leave due to peer pressure and the constraints of group influence. In their new state of engineered enlightenment, they have effectively embraced the LGAT's philosophy. This is the requisite realization and planned outcome of a LGAT experience. In this sense LGATs demand a rather rigid conformity and adherence to a group mind-set. That is why some past participants and others have alleged that LGATs are engaged in a kind of "brainwashing." Whatever trait an individual possesses that fails to conform to the LGAT paradigm is likely to be seen as negative and therefore should be purged from the participant or be destroyed.

Psychologist Margaret Singer observed, "LGAT programs tend to last at least four days and usually five."[968] She explained, "Such programs seem designed more to get participants emotionally pumped up, suspending their judgment and following orders of the 'trainers,' than to impart anything connected with job performance."[969] Once the initial training is completed, it is often followed up and reinforced by continuing group involvement and a commitment to ongoing coaching through the LGAT organization.

Subsequent to their enlightenment through the LGAT process, participants may become enmeshed in a kind of subculture revolving around the LGAT. This may include volunteer work for the LGAT despite the fact that most LGATs are for-profit, privately owned enterprises, not charities. LGAT graduates may also be encouraged to recruit and enroll others, essentially serving as a volunteer sales force for the LGAT company or organization. Such recruitment efforts not only provide the company with more paying customers but also serve to solidify the loyalty of its true believers.

Frequently in an LGAT environment, emotions or feelings can become a subjective substitute for cognitive processes and objective reality. Reality in this sense can be turned on its head, denigrated, and even dismissed as if nonexistent. Psychologist Margaret Singer said, "The draw of these groups was the idea that each person is able to create his or her own reality."[970]

The stripping away of individual defenses, coupled with the seemingly arbitrary labeling of thoughts and emotions as either "good" or "bad" according to the LGAT philosophy, has at times produced very negative results. In his book *The Politics of Transformation: Recruitment-Indoctrination Processes in a Mass Marathon Psychology Organization*,[971] author Philip Cushman warned about what he called "mass marathon training," also known as LGATs. Cushman found that four potentially dangerous characteristics concerning encounter groups could also often be seen in mass marathon training. For this purpose he specifically cited the research of Irvin D. Yalom, MD, an authority concerning group dynamics, and his fellow researcher, Morton A. Lieberman, PhD.[972] The four warning signs Yalom and Lieberman identified—and which Cushman referenced—are the following:

1. "Leaders had rigid, unbending beliefs about what participants should experience and believe, how they should behave in the group and when they should change."
2. "Leaders had no sense of differential diagnosis and assessment skills, valued cathartic emotional breakthroughs as the ultimate therapeutic experience, and sadistically pressed to create or force a breakthrough in every participant."
3. "Leaders had an evangelical system of belief that was the one single pathway to salvation."
4. "Leaders were true believers and sealed their doctrine off from discomforting data or disquieting results and tended to discount a poor result by, 'blaming the victim.'"

The following examples of controversial LGAT programs provide a better understanding of why some LGATs have often been called deceptive and potentially unsafe.

2004—Executive Success Programs (ESP) Suicide

In February 2004, thirty-five-year-old Kristin Marie Snyder killed herself. According to authorities, she paddled a kayak into a glacier-fed bay in Alaska and capsized it. Her body was never found, but she was officially declared dead. Left behind was a suicide note. The environmental consultant with a master's degree in plant ecology had written, "I attended a course called Executive Success Programs [ESP] based out of Anchorage, Alaska and Albany, New York. I was brainwashed and my emotional center of the brain was killed/turned off. I still have feeling in my external skin, but my internal organs are rotting. Please contact my parents…if you find me or this note. I am sorry life; I didn't know I was already dead. May we persist into the future."[973]

At the time Snyder had been attending a sixteen-day "intensive" offered by a for-profit privately owned company run by a former multilevel marketing guru named Keith Raniere. On the second day of that program, Snyder reportedly seemed "delusional."[974] Her domestic partner, Heidi Clifford, said she had stopped sleeping and was threatening suicide.

Kristin Snyder had been involved with ESP, now known as NXIVM (pronounced nexium).[975] Her parents said they had become concerned when their daughter came home for a visit after her first sixteen-day ESP intensive. In conversation they questioned the cost of ESP, specifically the $7,000 she paid for an intensive. She then cut them off and called her "coach."[976] Snyder reportedly spent more than $16,000 in four months before she was done with ESP.[977]

"I do, indeed, feel that her involvement in ESP was a first-cause factor in her death," Kristin Snyder's father told the press. "As it was, her personality disintegrated right before their eyes, and no one knew how to pick up the pieces. I do not believe that Kris wanted to kill herself. She cried out for help for almost a week, but was totally ignored," her father said.[978]

Carlos Rueda, chairman of the Department of Psychiatry at Our Lady of Mercy Hospital in New York City, stated that he treated three ESP/NXIVM students for psychological disorders he believed were related to its training. One case included a "psychotic episode" and required hospital care in January 2003. Rueda told the press, "I think that the stress and the way the courses are structured may make people who have a tendency to have a psychotic disorder have an acute episode."[979] The press contacted the woman who had experienced the breakdown, and she claimed that ESP/NXIVM told her, "We have to break you to reconstruct you." She then concluded, "But they rebuild you how they want to rebuild you." A spokesperson for ESP stated that "no civil action has ever been alleged against ESP in that regard."[980]

Other controversial LGAT programs include EST (Erhard Seminar Training), now known as Landmark Education, Lifespring, and the Mankind Project. These LGATs have also garnered press attention, complaints, and in some instances personal injury lawsuits.

Psychologist Margaret Singer was specifically critical of EST and its program the Forum, which was sold in 1991 and then became known as Landmark Education[981] in her book *Cults in Our Midst*,[982] Singer later said, "I do not endorse them—never have."[983] Landmark sued Singer, and as a part of an agreed settlement after years of protracted litigation, she stated that the group was not a cult or sect.[984]

There is little to suggest that training through companies like Landmark actually produce anything other than subjective results. A group of researchers, led by Jeffrey D. Fisher, Purdue professor of psychology, studied the effects of Landmark training.[985] They concluded, "In fact, with the exception of the short-term multivariate results for perceived control, there was no appreciable effect on any dimension which could reflect positive change." However, even this perception of control among the Landmark participants studied dissipated after eighteen months.[986] Author Stephen J. Kraus later referred to the Fisher study and said, "People who attend EST or the Landmark Forum generally report positive benefits from the experience, but a study that compared attendees with a control group of non-attendees suggests that the seminar produces only a short-term boost in locus of control, and no measurable long-term effects."[987] The British Psychological Society later cited the Fisher study,[988] and an article in *Nova Religio*, published by University of California Press, cited it as well.[989]

Concerns about Erhard's training are well documented. In 1977 it was reported that seven individuals suffered serious psychiatric disturbances after participating in EST.[990] Concerned psychiatrists alerted their colleagues through an article published by the *American Journal of Psychiatry* of the possibility that some people might develop devastating effects regarding EST training.[991] One of the authors Dr. Leonard L. Glass said, "We don't know if more people become psychotic after EST than after riding on the F train." But he opined, "There's enough possibility of a real connection between EST and psychotic breaks to cause us to want to alert psychiatrists and psychologists."[992]

Apparently reflecting continuing concerns about the potential for such problems, Mark Kamin, a Landmark Education spokesperson, stated in a 2002 interview that the company had implemented a screening process devised by a board of psychiatrists. Kamin said, "We have a requirement that people must be emotionally stable at that time to participate in our programs."[993] A wrongful death lawsuit filed against Landmark in 2004 claimed that Landmark training had contributed to the mental state of a man who murdered a postal carrier.[994] A court found the killer legally insane. He allegedly had been removed from a Landmark seminar for behaving strangely and extremely erratically.

The lawsuit filed by the postal carrier's surviving family was later dismissed.[995]

Landmark Education, now called Landmark Worldwide, has become a global concern with offices around the world located in Hong Kong, Singapore, Bangkok, Nagoya, Seoul, Tokyo, Osaka, New Delhi, Mumbai, Bangalore, Melbourne, Sydney, Perth, Auckland, London, Nairobi, Bogata, Cape Town, Tel Aviv, Toronto, Vancouver, Montreal, and Mexico City.[996] The company continues to maintain many offices across the United States including New York, Los Angeles, Chicago, Philadelphia, Houston, Phoenix, Dallas, Washington, DC, Seattle, San Diego, San Francisco, San Jose, Orange County, Atlanta, Denver, Detroit, Boston, and Ft. Lauderdale.[997]

John Hanley Sr. founded Lifespring in 1974. Perhaps the most notable Lifespring graduate is Virginia Thomas, wife of US Supreme Court justice Clarence Thomas. She became involved with the group in the early 1980s but later left and sought counseling. Thomas told the *Washington Post* in 1987, "I had intellectually and emotionally gotten myself so wrapped up with this group that I was moving away from my family and friends and the people I work with. My best friend came to visit me and I was preaching at her using that rough attitude they teach you." Virginia Thomas eventually sought help from private consultant and cult-intervention specialist Kevin Garvey.[998]

At least thirty lawsuits were filed against the LGAT company Lifespring.[999] In 1984 a jury in Virginia awarded $800,000 to a past participant who'd suffered a breakdown and was subsequently hospitalized. A Washington, DC, attorney who received Lifespring training received a $300,000 judgment for similar injuries. Lifespring reportedly settled many claims out of court. The company settled a wrongful death claim in 1982 regarding a suicide linked to its training. And in 1993 Lifespring agreed to a $750,000 settlement for a trainee who was institutionalized for two years after receiving training from Lifespring.[1000] The company eventually dissolved, but many of its former trainers and associates went on to start their own LGAT companies. LGAT companies that use techniques inspired by Lifespring continue to thrive and expand. One example is AsiaWorks, which Chris Gentry founded in 1993.[1001] Thousands have participated in AsiaWorks training.[1002] The company now has offices in Beijing, Singapore, Jakarta, and Bangkok.[1003]

Kevin Garvey, who studied LGATs for decades, said many use the same influence techniques through what he identified as their "conceptual core." He noted "patterns of information control, language control, disorientation through altering food and sleep patterns [and] the manipulation of the environment through praise and discouragement."[1004] Garvey claimed that such techniques are "designed and orchestrated to undercut any comprehensible discussion, all behind the facade of being this profound self-exploration." He warned, "The outcome for some people is very extreme."[1005] Psychologist Margaret Singer echoed Garvey's sentiments. Singer said that, and she included LGATs in her book *Cults in Our Midst* "because they represent forms of coordinated programs of intense persuasion and group pressure."[1006]

The Mankind Project (MKP) is an LGAT that offers a program called the "New Warriors Training Adventure" (NWTA). In 2005, just fifteen days after completing the NWTA program near Houston, a young man committed suicide. Michael Scinto became distraught during the training, and it appears he never recovered.

He wrote a letter to the Madison County sheriff's office before his death, detailing his experience. Scinto said, "They provoked the men into a rage," He wrote that when he asked to leave, a group leader said that "if I left, I would be causing harm to the other participants." The young man further stated, "I was convinced that if I ran, they would catch me," and "at this point I feared for my life." Scinto was found in his apartment with a self-inflicted gunshot wound to his head.[1007] His family sued the Mankind Project in 2007, and the wrongful death lawsuit was settled in 2008.[1008]

As part of that settlement, MKP of Houston was required to make certain changes. This included the requirement that a mental health professional screen potential participants. Allegedly the settlement specifically cited three changes to be made by MKP:

1. "Members will be released from their confidentiality agreements and will be encouraged to tell anyone who inquires about the initiation and other MKP programs."
2. "The organization will revise its website and provide a detailed description of the initiation as well as publish new, detailed brochures."
3. "MKP will modify its confidentiality agreements and training program to reflect this new found transparency."

Many LGAT creators appear to have drawn on the same themes and/or origins. Werner Erhard and John Hanley Sr. were both once involved in Mind Dynamics.[1009] Erhard studied Scientology[1010] and reportedly blended its themes along with other idiosyncratically gathered concepts, such as Dale Carnegie, Zen, Gestalt, Encounter groups,[1011] and the teachings of the German philosopher Martin Heidegger[1012] to create his composite LGAT philosophy.[1013] The particular paradigm put forth through the ESP/NXIVM intensive is called "rational inquiry." This philosophy espoused by Keith Raniere is reportedly a blend of Objectivism (based on the writings of Ayn Rand)[1014] and Scientology jargon[1015] presented through EST-like seminars by an organization structured much like a multilevel marketing scheme.[1016]

Raniere is known as "Vanguard" to his devoted "Espians," which gather for an annual week-long celebration of his birthday called "Vanguard Week."[1017] Raniere was an only child of a ballroom dance instructor. His mother largely raised him alone and died from heart disease when he was in college.[1018] Keith Raniere earned bachelor's degrees in biology, physics, and math at Rensselaer Polytechnic Institute in Troy, New York.[1019] Like Werner Erhard, who in a previous incarnation was a used-car salesman,[1020] [1021]Raniere once worked as an

406 | CULTS INSIDE OUT

Amway salesman and later launched his own multilevel marketing company called Consumer Buyline. But that company was shut down amid lawsuits and an investigation the attorney general of New York launched.[1022] It was after this business failure that Raniere embarked on creating an LGAT.[1023]

Keith Raniere was featured on the cover of *Forbes Magazine* in its October 13, 2003, issue. The article was titled "Cult of Personality" and described Raniere as "the world's strangest executive coach." One unhappy customer was apparently billionaire Edgar Bronfman Sr., who once took a course and endorsed ESP. He later told *Forbes*, however, "I think it's a cult."[1024] But despite Bronfman's less-than-glowing words, NXIVM reportedly "swallowed as much as $150 million" of the inherited wealth of his two daughters, Sara and Clare Bronfman. The two Seagram's fortune heiresses became deeply involved with Raniere and NXIVM.[1025]

2011—James Arthur Ray and "Sweat Lodge" Deaths

On November 18, 2011, fifty-three-year-old self-help motivational entrepreneur James Arthur Ray, once a featured guest on *The Oprah Winfrey Show*,[1026] was sentenced to two years in an Arizona state prison for negligent homicide. Kirby Brown, thirty-eight; James Shore, forty; and Liz Neuman, forty-nine, died while attending Ray's five-day LGAT called "Spiritual Warrior" due to heat stroke. The deaths were directly related to a so-called sweat lodge ceremony. Following a four-month-long trial, the jury deliberated ten hours before returning a guilty verdict. [1027] Juror Phillip Lepacek said, "It was a no-brainer there was heat. These people were baked."[1028]

James Ray, a "preacher's son,"[1029] ended his formal education when he dropped out of Tulsa Junior College in 1978. After various jobs, Ray worked in the sales department of AT&T, where he would eventually manage some training for the company, according to June Maul, a retired AT&T district manager. While at AT&T Ray became somewhat familiar with Stephen Covey, author of *Seven Habits of Highly Effective People*. Ray later claimed that he worked for Covey. However, Debbie Lund, a Franklin/Covey spokeswoman, said, "None of us remember him ever working for the company, nor ever being a contract employee."[1030]

It seems Ray was given to embellishing his biography. Moreover, ethical questions reportedly arose concerning his unauthorized use of training techniques borrowed from other sources and the inappropriate use of shamanic rituals and seemingly contrived claims concerning his association with mystical teachers.[1031] "You are not, nor have you ever been, certified to conduct holotropic breathwork," an attorney wrote Ray in 2011 on behalf of psychiatrist Stanislav Grof, the creator of that training.

Likewise, Lance Giroux, the managing director of yet another training and consulting firm, resented Ray's unauthorized use of his trademarked Samurai Game. Dr. Matthew James, president of Kona University, warned Ray to stop using shamanic rituals associated with the Hawaiian Huna tradition.[1032] Ray had attended some workshops regarding the rituals and then started holding his own Huna ceremonies. "I had someone from my office call [Ray] up and say 'what you're doing is improper, you weren't given permission, you need to stop right away,'" James said. Ray also claimed that he had studied the Q'ero traditions for three years with a shaman in Peru named Don Jose Luis. However, Denise Kinch, the author of a book about Q'ero traditions, told the press that Jose Luis is not a Q'ero or medicine man but rather a guide who runs weekends in Peru about Q'ero rites.[1033]

James Ray seemingly shifted his emphasis from a spiritual quest to the material pursuit of money. "I happen to think money is pretty cool, and I can help you attract a lot of it," Ray said. In 2007 he announced his intention to become the first "spiritual teaching billionaire."[1034] And it would be billionaire Oprah Winfrey who provided the platform for Ray to begin realizing those financial dreams. Ray was a speaker tapped to talk for *The Secret* a popular DVD, which Winfrey heavily promoted. Ray was a guest twice on Oprah Winfrey's daytime talk show during February 2007. The cache of Oprah greatly enhanced Ray's career and substantially increased his income. In 2005 Ray's revenue from his training seminars was $1.5 million, but in 2008 after appearing with Oprah Winfrey, his income reached $9.4 million.[1035]

Like Keith Raniere's Executive Success Programs, Ray's pricey retreats would supposedly somehow enlighten people. Participants paid between $9,000 and $10,000 to attend one of his programs. When he rented the Angel Valley Retreat Center for an event near Sedona, Arizona, quite a few people signed up. About fifty Ray enthusiasts were packed into the makeshift sweat lodge. Two hours after it began, the group ceremony abruptly ended with an emergency call. Two participants died that day, while another, Liz Neuman, passed away later in a medical center. Almost half (twenty-two) of the attendees were hospitalized.[1036]

Days of Ray's retreats were consumed with lectures, and participants watched film clips from the movie *The Last Samurai* starring Tom Cruise. They were then taken to the desert to undergo what was called Vision Quest. This consisted of being individually isolated in a ten foot circle with no food or drink for thirty-six hours. After that crucible came the final day and the so-called sweat lodge ceremony.[1037]

Explaining what the retreat was like, Beverley Bunn, the roommate of deceased Kirby Brown, testified in court, "You learn through the course of the week that you don't question Mr. Ray on anything." She added, "As you go through the week you learn that there's consequences or reprimand for you to be called out…if you question Mr. Ray or don't play full on."[1038] A recording of James Ray, played at his trial, detailed what "full on" meant. "You will have to get to a point where you surrender to death…When you are going into the lodge symbolically you are going back into the womb of Mother Earth…It is such a great metaphor…My body dies but I never die,"[1039] Ray said. He further explained, "There's no lodge like my lodge...By the second or third round, I'm thinking why the hell am I me? Why couldn't I just do a weenie-ass lodge like everyone else? And the reason is, when you emerge you will be a different person. When you face your own death, life's never the same. It's just not."[1040]

Wambli Sina Win, a former Oglala Sioux tribal judge and authority concerning authentic sweat-lodge practices, told the press, "Whatever he led was not a sweat-lodge ceremony as I understand it...He evidently learned bits and pieces and created a Frankenstein." Linda Andresano, a nurse who had attended traditional sweat lodges but passed out and had to be carried out of Ray's version, testified, "It was much hotter than any one I'd been in before." She explained that in a traditional sweat lodge, leaders "would ask how everybody was doing, and pass water around."[1041]

In one segment of his training, called the Samurai Game, Ray literally commanded participants to feign death. Connie Joy, a frequent participant of Ray retreats, said, "You have to picture him in the Samurai Game dressed in a white robe, pointing at people. When they say he said to die, I mean in a booming voice, pointing at you and saying, 'Die!' And if you didn't drop instantly, he really started screaming at you to die." Typically, the command to die followed an infraction of Ray's rules or some form of noncompliance. Joy, who became disenchanted with Ray after problems at one of his retreats held in Peru, told the press, "He enjoyed playing God."[1042]

"This could have happened to any of us. If you're with a group of people for a week, and everyone walks into a situation, you're going to go, too. And if your leader tells you it's OK, you're going to believe him. As you spend time together, a group mentality develops," explained Christine B. Whelan, PhD, a visiting assistant professor of sociology at the University of Pittsburgh who has studied the self-help industry.[1043] Sweat-lodge participant Dennis Mehraver described how reliant he had become on James Ray's leadership. "With all my experiences before with Mr. Ray I believed he knew how far I could go better than myself," Mehraver stated in court.[1044] "He was strong with the people. They were too intimidated, they were too committed to him," Jennifer Haley observed. Haley was a volunteer member of what Ray called his Dream Team.[1045] Ray also used various techniques including Holotropic Breathing, an accelerated breathing technique to reach an "altered state of consciousness."[1046]

James Ray reached a financial settlement with the families of those who had died in his sweat lodge. They were each paid $3 million. This money came from James Ray's insurers.[1047] After his criminal conviction and subsequent sentencing, Ray sold his home in the Beverly Hills area of California for $3.015 million.[1048] In 2012 James Ray claimed he was broke and $11 million in debt. He requested that the court declare him "indigent" for the purpose of costs associated with his appeal.

Prosecutor Sheila Polk said shortly before sentencing that Ray "led the life of a pretender, and there are predictable consequences when one leads a life of pretense."[1049] Polk later received the 2012 Arizona State Bar Criminal Justice Award for her outstanding work as a prosecutor.[1050] Beverly Bunn, an orthodontist from Texas who endured Ray's sweat lodge, offered this impression of her former self-help guru. "James Ray preaches that thoughts, feelings and actions are all connected. That was true in his own life."[1051]

LGATs suggest that their philosophy can potentially solve almost any life problem, from personal issues to professional performance. However, it is doubtful that this "one size fits all" prescription is in fact a meaningful solution. Instead of succumbing to the lure of LGATs, there are far safer and more focused ways to address professional and personal concerns. Professionals can seek career enhancement through continuing education at accredited institutions. Those struggling with personal problems can seek counseling from a licensed professional or advice from a trusted friend. There are also support groups that may specifically address a perceived problem recommended by local community services. This approach to self-improvement is more proved and pragmatic and largely avoids the accountability and safety issues that seem inherent in many LGATs.

Psychologist Margaret Singer summarized her impressions. "Having observed a number of LGATs and having interviewed many persons who attended variants of these programs as part of their work assignments, I am astonished at the gross childishness and unkindness of humiliating anyone under the guise of education, experiential learning, or the claim that participation in such travesties enhances work performance."[1052] She labeled such LGATs as "high-confrontation, psychologically intense programs"[1053] and said, "They are a modern-day, corporate version of social and psychological influence techniques that make people deployable without their knowledge or consent—precisely my objection to cults."[1054]

---

[968] Margaret Singer, *Cults in Our Midst* (San Francisco, CA: Jossey-Bass, 1996), 42.

[969] Ibid., 190.

[970] Ibid., 42.

[971] Philip Cushman, *The Politics of Transformation: Recruitment—Indoctrination Processes in a Mass Marathon Psychology Organization* (New York: St. Martin's Press, 1993), http://www.culteducation.com/brainwashing9.html (accessed May 28, 2014).

[972] Irvin D. Yalom and Morton A. Lieberman, *A Study of Encounter Group Causalities* (New York: Guilford Press, 1992), 16-30..

[973] Dennis Yusko, "An Espian's Brief Life," *Albany Times-Union*, February 1, 2004.

[974] Ibid.

[975] Ibid.

[976] Ibid.

[977] Ibid.

[978] Ibid.

[979] Dennis Yusko, "New Vision for Mind in Eye of Beholder," *Albany Times-Union*, September 28, 2003.

[980] Ibid.

[981] "Self-Help Guru Werner Erhard Selling Empire," *San Francisco Chronicle*, February 17, 1991.

[982] Singer, *Cults in Our Midst*, 42, 192–196, 202, 205.

[983] Amanda Scioscia, "Drive-Thru Deliverance," *Phoenix New Times*, October 19, 2000.

[984] Margaret Singer, "Statement per Settlement Agreement with Landmark Education," May 7, 1997.

[985] Jeffrey D. Fisher et al., *Evaluating Large Group Awareness Training: A Longitudinal Study of Psychosocial Effect* (New York: Springer-Verlag, 1990).

[986] John Gastil, *The Group in Society* (Los Angeles: Sage Publications, 2009), 228–229.

[987] Stephen J. Kraus, *Psychological Foundations of Success* (San Francisco: Next Level Science, 2003), 235.

[988] Gidi Rubinstein, "Characteristics of Participants in the Forum, Psychotherapy Clients, and Control Participants: A Comparative Study," *Psychology and Psychotherapy: Theory, Research and Practice*, Leicester: British Psychological Society 78, no. 4 (2003): 481–492, http://www.researchgate.net/publication/7416493_Characteristics_of_participants_in_the_Forum_psychotherapy_clients_and_control_participants_a_comparative_study (accessed May 28, 2014).

[989] Sefi Melchior and Stephen Sharot, "Landmark in Israel: Recruitment and Maintenance of Clients in a Human Potential Organization," *Nova Religion* 13, no. 14 (May 2010): 61–83.

[990] Jane Brody, "Reports of Psychosis after Erhard Course," *New York Times*, April 24, 1977.

[991] Michael A. Kirsch and Leonard L. Glass, "Psychiatric Disturbances Associated with Erhard Seminar Training: II. Additional Cases and Theoretical Considerations," *American Journal of Psychiatry* 134, no. 11 (November 1977): 1254–1258.

[992] Brody, "Reports of Psychosis after Erhard Course."

[993] Marisa Agha and Mara H. Gottfried, "Not the Woman We Knew," *Pioneer Press* (St. Paul, MN), March 1, 2002.

[994] Weed v. Landmark Education Corp, in the District Court of Tulsa County State of Oklahoma Case No. CJ-2003-02541 (May 2004).

[995] Weed v. Landmark Education Corp, in the District Court of Tulsa County State of Oklahoma Case No. CJ-2003-02541 Final Judgment (May 3, 2007).

[996] "Contact Your Local Office," Landmark Education official website 2013, http://www.landmarkworldwide.com/when-and-where/office-location-finder (accessed May 28, 2014).

[997] Ibid.

[998] Laura Blumenfeld, "The Nominee's Soul Mate," *Washington Post*, September 10, 1991.

[999] Anne McAndrews, "I Lost My Husband to a Cult," *Redbook Magazine*, May 1994.

[1000] Ibid.

[1001] Ruth Mathewson, "Yuppies Happy to Pay for Vision of New Life," *South China Morning Post*, September 24, 1994.

[1002] Jason Tedjasuakmana, "Looking for a New Path," *Time*, August 21, 2000.

[1003] "Contact AsiaWorks Training," AsiaWorks website, http://www.asiaworks.com/contact-us/ (accessed May 28, 2014.

[1004] Enzo Di Matteo, "In the Grip of the Therapy Tough-Guys," *Toronto Now Magazine*, April 20–26, 2000.

[1005] Ibid.

[1006] Singer, *Cults in Our Midst*, 196.

[1007] Chris Vogel, "Naked Men: The Mankind Project and Michael Scinto," *Houston Press*, October 4, 2007.

[1008] Chris Vogel, "Mankind Project Decides to get Transparent," *Houston Press*, August 31, 2009.

[1009] J. Gordon Melton and James R. Lewis, *Perspectives on the New Age* (Albany, NY: SUNY Press, 1992), 129–132.

[1010] Jesse Kornbluth, "The Fuhrer over EST," *New Times* (New York), March 19, 1976.

[1011] Megan Rosenfeld, "Encountering Werner Erhard," *Washington Post*, April 14, 1979.

[1012] Anthony Gottlieb, "Heidegger for Fun and Profit," *New York Times*, January 7, 1990.

[1013] Paul Boyer, "Book World: Erhard from EST to Worst," *Washington Post*, December 9, 1993.

[1014] Suzanna Andrews, "The Heiresses and the Cult," *Vanity Fair*, November 2010.

[1015] James M. Odato and Jennifer Gish, "The Secrets of NXIVM," *Albany Times-Union*, February 12, 2012.

[1016] Ibid.

[1017] Odato and Gish, "The Secrets of NXIVM."

[1018] Ibid.

[1019] Ibid.

[1020] Boyer, "Book World: Erhard from EST to Worst."

[1021] Rich Behar and Ralph King Jr., "The Winds of Werner," *Forbes*, November 18, 1985.

[1022] David Orenstein, "Consumer Buyline of Clifton Park Was Forced to Close after 25 Separate Investigations," *Albany Times-Union*, August 24, 1997.

[1023] Odato and Gish, "The Secrets of NXIVM."

[1024] Michael Freedman, "Cult of Personality," *Forbes*, October 13, 2003.

[1025] Andrews, "The Heiresses and the Cult."

[1026] Lloyd Grove, "Oprah and the Sweat Lodge Guru," *Daily Beast*, October 29, 2009.

[1027] Felicia Fonesca, "US Self-Help Guru Convicted in Ceremony Deaths," *Associated Press*, June 23, 2011.

[1028] "Weak Defense in Guru Case, Juror Says," *Associated Press*, July 3, 2011.

[1029] Ann O'Neill, "Inside the Sweat Lodge: Witnesses Describe a Ritual Gone Wrong," *CNN*, March 14, 2011.

[1030] Bob Ortega, "Sweat-Lodge Trial: James Arthur Ray Often Misused Teachings, Critics Say," *Arizona Republic*, April 10, 2011.

[1031] Ibid.

[1032] Ibid.

[1033] Ibid.

[1034] Ibid.

[1035] Craig Harris and Dennis Wagner, "Story Unfolds of James Ray, Who Hosted Fatal 'Sweat Lodge,'" *USA Today*, October 27, 2009.

[1036] Felicia Fonesca, "3rd Person Dies in Arizona Sweat Lodge Ceremony Case," *Associated Press*, October 18, 2009.

[1037] Christopher Goodwin, "At the Temple of James Arthur Ray," *The Guardian* (New York), July 8, 2011.

[1038] "Emotional Witness Describes Horror outside Sweat Lodge," *CNN*, March 12, 2011.

[1039] Ibid.

[1040] O'Neill, "Inside the Sweat Lodge: Witnesses Describe a Ritual Gone Wrong."

[1041] Ortega, "Sweat-Lodge Trial: James Arthur Ray Often Misused Teachings, Critics Say."

[1042] "Former Follower Speaks Out about Enlightenment Tactics," *ABC TV-News 15*, (Phoenix, AZ), March 2, 2011.

[1043] Roxanne Patel Shepelavey, "When the Quest for Self-Improvement Kills," *MSNBC News*, September 14, 2010.

[1044] Mark Duncan, "Sweat Lodge Survivors Say Ray Did Little or Nothing to Aid Victims," *Prescott Daily Courier*, March 10, 2011.

[1045] O'Neill, "Inside the Sweat Lodge: Witnesses Describe a Ritual Gone Wrong."

[1046] Ortega, "Sweat-Lodge Trial: James Arthur Ray Often Misused Teachings, Critics Say."

[1047] "Sweat Lodge Lawsuits Settled for $3M," *Associated Press*, December 3, 2011.

[1048] Lauren Beale, "Self-Help Guru James Arthur Ray Sells His Beverly Hills-Area Home for $3.015 Million," *Los Angeles Times*, December 2, 2011.

[1049] Bob Ortega, "James Arthur Ray Gets Prison Time in Sweat Lodge Deaths," *Arizona Republic*, (Phoenix, AZ) November 19, 2011.

[1050] "Polk Wins State Criminal Justice Award," *Daily Courier* (Prescott, AZ), June 18, 2012.

[1051] Goodwin, "At the Temple of James Arthur Ray."

[1052] Singer, *Cults in Our Midst*, 190.

[1053] Ibid.

[1054] Ibid., 196.

CHAPTER 17

LGAT INTERVENTION

At the urging of his adult son, a medical doctor agreed to attend the Forum, which is large group awareness training (LGAT) run by Landmark Education, a privately owned for-profit company. The son persuaded his father to participate with him when he repeated the initial weekend of training called the Forum. The doctor thought the weekend offered an opportunity to spend quality time with his son. The son believed the training would improve their relationship and bring them closer together. The son also thought the LGAT had helped him with many personal problems.

The Forum weekend can be a deeply cathartic and stressful experience. This LGAT format serves as the vehicle through which participants are introduced to the world view and philosophy of the LGAT creator and its "Source," Werner Erhard, formerly known as Jack Rosenberg.[1055]

Erhard reportedly created "a consciousness-raising cult," which combined a mix of "Scientology, Zen and Gestalt."[1056] His idiosyncratic philosophy is funneled through an LGAT format to paying participants.

Landmark staff members, with frequent assistance from volunteers, facilitate this process. The Forum can be confrontational and emotionally draining. Many Landmark graduates subjectively believe the training is a virtual panacea and means of addressing almost any problem or issue in life.

The father dutifully endured the rigors of the LGAT, but neither his wife nor some of his professional colleagues appreciated the changes the training had wrought. According to his spouse, he changed from a self-effacing humble man, who was more concerned about others than about himself, to an arrogant, often-condescending, and increasingly self-centered person.

The doctor also became involved in a kind of subculture composed of Landmark graduates. It seemed to his wife and some of his coworkers that almost every conversation with the doctor somehow now included Landmark jargon or allusions to its philosophy. This had become a source of friction since others didn't appreciate Landmark's philosophy and had no interest in participating in the training, which the doctor now promoted to anyone who would listen.

It's important to note that some people emerge from LGATs and move on with little, if any, further connection to the training, the company that provides the training, or other graduates. But some graduates of such training appear to become something like "LGAT junkies," enthusiastically enrolling in more training and at times even repeating the same courses. Such avid enthusiasts also often seem to be absorbed in a kind of subculture, which the LGAT has spawned and sustained. This may include ongoing volunteer work and an evolving and expanding group of friends who are also deeply devoted to the same LGAT and its philosophy.

The changes in personal behavior and lifestyle, which an LGAT can bring about, can be disturbing and at times alarming to family and friends. In some situations family and old friends may also become involved and support the LGAT. But when such support doesn't develop, concern may increase regarding someone who has become deeply involved and enmeshed within such a group. In the doctor's situation, his wife was decidedly unimpressed with Landmark and distressed about its growing influence over her husband. After wrestling with this perceived problem for some time, the wife decided an intervention was necessary.

The wife and I met for a preliminary preparation session the day before the intervention. According to our planning, the effort to disentangle the doctor from the LGAT would include only the three of us and no one else. The wife assured me that her husband, though a doctor, was a very humble and approachable person. We discussed the boundaries and our respective roles during the intervention. The wife repeatedly assured me that her husband would be reasonable and that she would be able to persuade him to stay and participate.

The following morning the wife ushered me into the kitchen of her home, where the doctor was quietly reading while sipping his morning coffee. I was introduced as a private consultant whom she had asked to sit in and assist in a discussion about her personal concerns about Landmark Education. The doctor seemed indifferent at first and said he couldn't understand why there were any concerns. The wife explained that she was unhappy and very concerned about what she regarded as radical recent changes in his behavior since he became involved with Landmark.

The doctor immediately responded that the LGAT had been a very positive experience and that he failed to see why his wife saw his continuing involvement or enthusiasm about the training as a problem that required discussion with a consultant.

At this point the doctor's wife explained that his behavior had substantially changed and that she saw those changes as negative, not positive. Specifically she cited that he was constantly talking about Landmark to their friends and his colleagues at work. She said people outside Landmark didn't appreciate this, especially at the workplace, where it was most often not only unwanted but inappropriate. She concluded that, in her opinion, the LGAT and its philosophy engendered an intensely self-centered and frequently offensive demeanor and that her husband's apparent obsessiveness with it had become increasingly difficult to deal with and endure.

Again the doctor reacted by stating there was nothing wrong with the LGAT and that it was instead an inspiration, it was enlightening, and it addressed many human problems.

At this juncture I asked the doctor if he had studied the history of Landmark Education. Based on his comments, it was evident that he hadn't. I opened my bag and brought out a prepared file filled with research, including news reports and other relevant material regarding Landmark, formerly known as Erhard Seminar Training or EST. I explained that the privately owned company had a deeply troubled history of complaints, lawsuits, labor violations, and bad press. We looked over news articles from the United States and the United Kingdom. These reflected the continuing controversy that has historically surrounded the company and its founder, Werner Erhard, for decades.

Recounting Werner Erhard's personal history, I asked the doctor how it could be that the originator of Landmark's training hadn't evidently benefited directly from the philosophy in his personal life. Erhard has been married and divorced twice, and he has reportedly had deeply troubled relationships with his children.[1057] But this personal turmoil occurred largely after his supposed epiphany of self-realization. Why hadn't his philosophy been more effective in helping him with his own personal relationships? And if the EST/Landmark philosophy had largely failed its founder, how could it be expected to help others in their marital and family situations?

The doctor disregarded Erhard's personal history and simply said that the training had worked for him. Once again, however, his wife immediately disagreed and pointed out the strain she felt and said the LGAT seemed to be causing a rift in their relationship.

I pointed out similar complaints regarding the strain EST and Landmark training had caused in families and marriages, specifically the estrangement it might potentially create if a spouse or family member disagreed or objected to the LGAT or its philosophy. The husband responded with the apology that Landmark perhaps wasn't right for everyone. He said any company or product had its detractors. My response was to point out that LGATs had a particularly bad track record of complaints linked to their training. I pointed out that LGATs appear to have inherent structural problems concerning their dynamics and corresponding behavior, which has hurt people.

We now focused on an article about "mass marathon training."[1058] Historically this is another label used to describe LGATs. Written by a mental health professional who attended an LGAT, the article cites certain aspects of such groups that parallel encounter groups researchers have deemed "dangerous."[1059] The first characteristic cited is that the "leaders had rigid, unbending beliefs about what participants should experience and believe, how they should behave in the group and when they should change."[1060] I asked the doctor whether this characteristic was evident during his experience in the Forum. We then discussed how rigid and intensely confrontational the process could be and that "getting it," according to Landmark's jargon, essentially means accepting Erhard's world view and philosophy, which is the expected net result of the training. The doctor didn't disagree with this assessment.

I asked the doctor whether he felt the Forum leader had expressed any meaningful flexibility about Landmark's beliefs or the basic assumptions of its philosophy. He couldn't recall a specific example of significant flexibility expressed during the training. We then discussed that the purpose of the training appeared to be to change people through a carefully scripted and relatively rigid process. Such change was expected to occur by the conclusion of the training. The husband didn't dispute this assessment.

We moved on to the second criteria in the article, that an LGAT leader has "no sense of differential diagnosis and assessment skills."[1061] The doctor acknowledged that the Forum leader was certainly not a mental health professional and was therefore not specifically trained or licensed concerning such skills. I asked the doctor whether during his Forum experience the leader seemed to value "cathartic emotional breakthroughs as the ultimate therapeutic experience" or had "pressed to create or force a breakthrough in every participant." Again, researchers cited these additional aspects as potentially dangerous.[1062]

The doctor was silent. At this point I noted and referred to reported complaints about Landmark in news reports that directly corresponded with these characteristics.[1063] [1064] [1065] That is, Landmark often emphasized such "breakthroughs," and Forum leaders have often been described as bullies who intimidate people, pushing participants to experience such predetermined breakthroughs.

We now explored the third listed characteristic, that leaders expressed "an evangelical system of belief" and that their philosophy was seen as the "one single pathway to salvation."[1066] This characteristic appears to be evident in the application of Erhard's world view, or "getting it" as the ultimate, most effective, and reliable means of resolving personal issues and problems.

I asked the husband whether he felt Landmark Education regarded its philosophy as the only meaningful and truly effective framework for resolving life's issues or problems. And if this wasn't the case, what alternative approach did the Forum leader specifically cite or mention that might be seriously considered as equal to the LGAT? The doctor demurred; he couldn't recall any such alternative the Forum leader specifically discussed during his training.

Finally, we discussed the fourth criterion or warning sign cited in the article. Did the Forum leader and Landmark volunteers appear to be "true believers"? Was the attitude they expressed one that researchers said essentially "sealed their doctrine off from discomforting data or disquieting results and tended to discount a poor result by 'blaming the victim'"?[1067] He admitted that someone said information posted through the Internet that was critical of Landmark should be disregarded and that a Forum participant who didn't "get it" or was somehow resistant to the training might be labeled as "uncoachable."

We then reviewed the three basic building blocks of coercive persuasion, which Edgar Schein historically described.[1068] Could these stages of coercive persuasion generally correlate with the process of training Landmark provided? Weren't Forum participants essentially subjected to a similar three-stage process, which included what Schein described as "unfreezing," "changing," and "refreezing"?[1069]

For example, didn't Landmark training first go through a kind of confrontational and confessional breaking or thawing phase, as Schein described? Wasn't this then followed by a period of intense pressure focused on changing participants' perspectives and perceptions? Did the Forum process end by locking in Erhard's ideas through group pressure and agreement? Was it probable that this locking down or freezing at times was also further accomplished through a kind of embedding socialization within a kind of Landmark subculture?

This simple, fundamental three-stage structure of classic coercive persuasion, as Schein outlined, correlates to both the eight criteria psychiatrist Robert Jay Lifton used to establish the existence of a thought-reform program and the six conditions psychologist Margaret Singer used to describe "the tactics of a thought-reform program."[1070]

We examined both the three stages and the detailed correlations Lifton and Singer offered to see how they might potentially parallel Landmark. Singer stated that during the unfreezing phase there is an effort to "destabilize a person's sense of self" and that the subject is kept largely "unaware of what is going on."[1071] I asked the doctor whether he had precisely and in detail understood before he began the training what would be presented during the Landmark Education weekend seminar, known as the Forum. The doctor responded that he had actually known very little about Landmark before beginning the training other than what his son had said, which included a rather vague general description of the program.

We talked about how a Forum leader typically solicited and facilitated frequently painful confessionals from participants; during this process the leader might be quite demanding, harsh, and judgmental. Singer stated that the purpose of such tactics is to coerce the subject to "drastically reinterpret his or her life's history and radically alter his or her worldview and accept a new version of reality and causality."[1072] Singer describes that the net result of this process can be "dependence on the organization" and that a person may then largely become "a deployable agent of the organization."[1073] I asked the doctor whether he had met Landmark enthusiasts who repeated their training and did ongoing volunteer work for the company. Might that behavior be seen as somewhat dependent? Was Landmark using those people? He admitted that someone could perhaps perceive the situation that way but that he didn't.

We also discussed how the Forum might be compared in some ways to group therapy. Unlike group therapy led by a licensed mental health professional, however, a landmark leader has no specific licensing requirements and corresponding accountability to a licensing board or body. Moreover, a Forum leader, unlike a licensed counseling professional, has no requirement to disclose the exact nature and structure of his or her counseling approach before beginning.

We also talked about some of the liabilities researchers had cited about certain types of potentially problematic encounter groups. For example: "They sometimes ignore stated goals, misrepresent their actual techniques, and obfuscate their real agenda."[1074] I pointed out again that he hadn't been told in advance that Forum training was designed as a vehicle to impart or download Werner Erhard's philosophy. Had he understood in detail that this was, in fact, the intent of the training? Had he made a fully informed choice to accept the ultimate goal of the LGAT?

We then discussed another important liability that can be readily recognized in many LGATs such as Landmark. That is, they "lack adequate participant-selection criteria."[1075] We talked about how almost anyone might attend the Forum and potentially be impacted by its training, which again can be stressful, cathartic, and at times quite confrontational. We talked about how some people may be able to cope with such pressure, but for other participants, it might be too difficult, and they could begin to unravel and eventually experience a kind of breakdown. In fact, I pointed out that Landmark has admitted that this is an apparent issue and ongoing liability concern for the company. A Landmark spokesperson claimed that this concern has been effectively addressed by implementing a "screening process."[1076] I told the doctor this was necessary because Landmark Education, formerly known as EST, had a history of breakdowns tied to its training.[1077] I shared an article two medical doctors had coauthored about psychiatric disturbances associated with EST.[1078]

At this juncture we talked about other cited liabilities associated with encounter groups, which might potentially lead to harm done to participants. For example, if they lacked "reliable norms, supervision, and adequate training for leaders,"[1079] how could Landmark take into consideration and "adequately consider the 'psychonoxious' or deleterious effects of group participation"?[1080] That is, without proper educational background and licensed supervision, how could a Forum leader or Landmark volunteer recognize when a participant was psychologically or emotionally unraveling or experiencing a breakdown during the training?

The doctor struggled with these citied liabilities. He understood the value of education and proper supervision. He tried to apologize for Landmark by talking about his "breakthroughs." This included his subjective feeling of clarity and the final epiphany he had experienced, which he believed somehow made better or exonerated any of the negative aspects of the Forum and excused Landmark. The doctor's only direct response to the specifically cited problems posed by such high-demand training was that maybe Landmark wasn't for everyone. But he then reiterated that for him it had ultimately been a positive experience. I responded by pointing out yet another one of the cited liabilities of some encounter groups; they "devalue critical thinking in favor of 'experiencing' without self-analysis or reflection."[1081]

At this point the doctor's wife once again interjected that for her the net result of her husband's Landmark training hadn't been positive. Instead it had been disruptive and at times personally painful for her. She said that in her opinion the training had turned out to be a negative influence, not a positive one. She repeated emphatically how obsessive her husband had become regarding Landmark and how this obsessiveness had adversely impacted both his personal and professional lives. Most importantly, the wife explained that Landmark's undue influence had hurt their relationship. She also stated that her husband's professional colleagues had begun to question his judgment due to the doctor's apparent fixation on Landmark and the related jargon he repeated at work. At home she said her husband had become increasingly self-centered, distant, and dismissive regarding her feelings. She also complained that his social life was becoming more centered on Landmark and Landmark graduates than on their mutual old friends.

The doctor continued to dismiss all the accumulating critical information, negative news reports, and accompanying research. He waved his hand and explained that what had been presented wasn't his experience and was therefore invalid. After running into this persistent, rhetorical roadblock more than once, I tried to reframe the importance of the presented material. Weren't historical information, research, and relevant studies important parts of a deliberate process of exploration when reviewing options or addressing a particular problem?

At this point the doctor exploded, raising his voice. He exclaimed, "I'm a doctor, dammit!" My response was to point out that there had been a medical doctor present at Jonestown when the cyanide was dispensed. There is no special protection afforded to doctors, I said, that somehow immunizes them to coercive persuasion. We are all equally susceptible to such schemes, especially during a particularly painful or vulnerable time, or when someone we trust introduces us to a new group or leader.

Despite the doctor's indignant and angry response, I asked him what the basis was for due diligence in the field of medicine. Would a medication or procedure be suggested without proper investigation and meaningful inquiry to establish through facts and research the efficacy and safety of the treatment or procedure under consideration?

Rather than respond to this question, the doctor turned to his wife and asked what was required to end the intervention discussion. At this point the doctor's wife began crying. He couldn't understand why she was behaving so emotionally, and he asked her what was wrong. The wife answered that she had no idea how brainwashed he had become.

The doctor asked what he could do to satisfy his wife and end the intervention. She responded that he must completely stop his involvement with Landmark and cease associating with anyone associated with the company other than his son. She added that if he didn't take these steps, they might be headed for a divorce. The doctor nodded and agreed to her terms. He then looked at me and said we were done. This response concluded our first and final day.

When the doctor's wife drove me back to the hotel, she explained that her husband must be deeply embarrassed but believed he finally and fully understood her concerns and would end his involvement with Landmark. She assured me that usually the doctor was a cheerful and courteous man, not abrupt or rude. It was his cheerful disposition, sense of humor, spontaneity, and casual and unpretentious manner that had first attracted her to him. It was when these personality traits seemed to suddenly shift and change that she began to suspect something was wrong with Landmark.

Through follow-up calls I subsequently learned that the doctor maintained his commitment and completely ended his involvement with Landmark.

[1055] "Werner Erhard," *60 Minutes*, CBS, March, 1991.

[1056] Richard Behar and Ralph King Jr., "Winds of Werner," *Forbes*, November 18, 1985.

[1057] "Werner Erhard," *60 Minutes*.

[1058] Philip Cushman, *The Politics of Transformation: Recruitment—Indoctrination Processes in a Mass Marathon Psychology Organization* (New York: St. Martin's Press, 1993), http://www.culteducation.com/brainwashing9.html (accessed May 28, 2014).

[1059] Irvin D. Yalom and Morton A. Lieberman, *A Study of Encounter Group Causalities* (New York: Guilford Press, 1992), 16-30.

[1060] Ibid.

[1061] Ibid.

[1062] Ibid.

[1063] Elise Lucet, Alain Roth and Jean-Marie Abgrall, "Voyage to the Land of the New Gurus," Video, directed by Karima Tabti, *France 3*, May 24, 2004.

[1064] James O'Brien, "Defending Your Life," *GQ*, May 2005.

[1065] Roland Howard, "Mindbreakers," *Daily Mail* (London), July 23, 2001.

[1066] Yalom and Lieberman, *A Study of Encounter Group Causalities*.

[1067] Ibid.

[1068] Edgar H. Schein, *Coercive Persuasion: A Socio-psychological Analysis of the 'Brainwashing' of American Civilian Prisoners by the Chinese Communists* (New York: W. W. Norton, 1971).

[1069] Ibid.

[1070] Margaret Singer, *Cults in Our Midst* (San Francisco, CA: Jossey-Bass, 1996), 63.

[1071] Ibid.

[1072] Ibid.

[1073] Ibid.

[1074] Louis A. Gottschalk, E. Mansell Pattison, and Donald W. Schafer, "Training Groups, Encounter Groups, Sensitivity Groups and Group Psychotherapy," *California Medicine: The Western Journal of Medicine* 115, no. 2 (August 1971): 87–93.

[1075] Ibid.

[1076] Marisa Agha and Mara H. Gottfried, "Not the Woman We Knew," *Pioneer Press* (St. Paul, MN), March 1, 2002.

[1077] Jane Brody, "Reports of Psychosis after Erhard Course," *New York Times*, April 24, 1977.

[1078] Michael A. Kirsch and Leonard L. Glass, "Psychiatric Disturbances Associated with Erhard Seminar Training: II. Additional Cases and Theoretical Considerations," *American Journal of Psychiatry* 134, no. 11 (November 1977): 1254–1258.

[1079] Gottschalk, Pattison, and Schafer, "Training Groups, Encounter Groups, Sensitivity Groups and Group Psychotherapy," 87–93.

[1080] Ibid.

[1081] Ibid.

CHAPTER 18

ABUSIVE, CONTROLLING RELATIONSHIPS

Before detailing an intervention about abusive or controlling relationships, it's beneficial to have a better understanding of such relationships—how to define them, what behavior might be evident—and recount some historical examples.

As noted in a previous chapter, destructive cults can be quite small. All a cult actually requires to exist is a leader and at least one follower. In the book *Captive Hearts, Captive Minds,* a "cultic relationship" or "one-on-one cult"[1082] is described as follows:

> The one-on-one cult is a deliberately manipulative and exploitative intimate relationship between two persons, often involving physical abuse of the subordinate partner. In the one-on-one cult, which we call a cultic relationship, there is a significant power imbalance between the two participants.

The stronger uses his (or her) influence to control, manipulate, abuse, and exploit the other. In essence the cultic relationship is a one-on-one version of the larger group. It may even be more intense than participation in a group cult since all the attention and abuse is focused on one person, often with more damaging consequences.[1083]

Like the leaders of destructive cults, the majority of abusive, controlling partners, according to some observers, are apparently men.[1084] Some of the warning signs to watch for include pushing the relationship too fast, demanding undivided attention, determining to "be in charge," and insisting on always winning. There are repeated broken promises. He cannot handle criticism and won't accept responsibility for his behavior or actions. He also often blames others to avoid taking responsibility. He is extremely jealous and unpredictable, and he has anger issues. He appears to lack respect for the opinions of others. You feel you can never be good enough. His love seems to be highly conditional, and the relationship makes you feel increasingly uneasy.[1085]

Anecdotal evidence seems to suggest that many abusive and controlling partners are grossly insensitive, extremely ego-driven personalities given to self-indulgent behavior and obsessed with their own importance. Such abusive partners also appear to have little, if any, meaningful empathy or sympathy for the feelings of others.

These characteristics could potentially place some abusive or controlling partners in the narcissistic personality disorder (NPD) general profile that typically defines a narcissistic personality. "Prevalence of lifetime NPD was 6.2%, with rates greater for men (7.7%) than for women (4.8%)."[1086]

The following characteristics are common among those diagnosed with NPD:[1087]

1. He or she has a grandiose sense of self-importance. For example, the person exaggerates achievements and talents and expects to be recognized as superior without commensurate achievements.
2. He or she is preoccupied with fantasies of unlimited success, power, brilliance, beauty, or ideal love.
3. He or she believes he or she is "special" and unique and can be understood only by associating with other special or high-status people (or institutions).
4. He or she requires excessive admiration.
5. He or she has a sense of entitlement; in other words, he or she has unreasonable expectations of especially favorable treatment or automatic compliance with his or her expectations.
6. He or she is interpersonally exploitative; in other words, he or she takes advantage of others to achieve his or her own ends.
7. He or she lacks empathy and is unwilling to recognize or identify with the feelings and needs of others.
8. He or she is often envious of others or believes others are envious of him or her.
9. He or she shows arrogant, haughty behaviors or attitudes.

A pervasive pattern of grandiosity, coupled with an insistent need for admiration and a lack of empathy, along with five or more of the warning signs above, is a strong indication of NPD.[1088] This can be a daunting realization for someone suffering in an abusive, controlling relationship. This is because someone with a narcissistic personality is unlikely to recognize he or she has a problem and therefore sees any reason to change.

The abused partner in an abusive, controlling relationship can often seem "brainwashed." As noted in a previous chapter about brainwashing, Candace Waldron, executive director of Help for Abused Women and Their Children in Ipswich, Massachusetts, remarked that such a relationship "becomes almost like a brainwashing environment" because victims most often are isolated and "don't have a lifeline to the outside."[1089] Research has shown that a "lack of institutional and informal social support, and greater avoidant coping styles were related to lowered self-esteem and more severe depressive symptoms."[1090]

Dr. Lenore Walker, a psychologist and professor at the Center for Psychological Studies at Nova Southwestern University, wrote *The Battered Woman*.[1091] In her book Walker puts forth the theory that some women develop a kind of "learned helplessness" (LH), which explains why they don't leave an abusive, controlling relationship. Walker summarizes LH as "the understanding that random and negative behavior towards a person can produce the belief that the person's natural way of fighting such abuse will not succeed in stopping it. Thus, the person stops trying to put an end to the abuse and rather develops coping strategies to live safely with the possibility he or she will continue to be abused."[1092] Walker coined the term "battered woman" and subsequently the "battered women's syndrome." She is the foremost authority in this area of research and its application, which initially began in the 1970s.

In many cases the net result of LH seems to be a kind of paralysis, which renders the victim psychologically and emotionally unable to leave the situation, coupled with depression and decreasing self-esteem.

1987—Hedda Nussbaum and Joel Steinberg

On November 2, 1987, New York City police responded to an emergency call made by a frantic mother, who said her six-year-old daughter, Lisa, was hurt and not breathing. When police arrived at the Greenwich Village apartment of Hedda Nussbaum and her partner, attorney Joel Steinberg, they found the couple's adopted daughter bruised and comatose. She never regained consciousness and died.[1093]

Steinberg was arrested and charged with second-degree murder and first-degree manslaughter. The following year he was convicted of manslaughter and sentenced to twenty-five years in prison.

As the story unfolded in press accounts and through the televised trial, the reported abuse shocked the public. Steinberg had not only beaten his daughter to death but also subjected Nussbaum to a decade of horrific abuse. When police took Nussbaum into custody, she had a ruptured spleen, a broken knee, fractured ribs, broken teeth, a cauliflower ear, and scars covering her body.[1094] Her nose had been broken five times and ultimately required plastic surgery to repair.[1095]

Hedda Nussbaum was a former associate editor of children's books at Random House in Manhattan. Though she was well educated and from a good family, Steinberg had reportedly "brainwashed" her.[1096] Nussbaum later said, "It's incredible how low I had sunk without realizing it. I became a walking zombie."

The process Steinberg used to break Nussbaum down and turn her into a "zombie" was at first subtle and slow, unlike the rapid and radical transformation of Patty Hearst by the SLA. It is somewhat reminiscent, though, of "the game" played at Synanon. He began by confronting Nussbaum with criticism, such as offering an ongoing critique of her social skills. Steinberg in effect became Nussbaum's "therapist" and boyfriend. He also isolated her, explaining that her family was "evil." Steinberg convinced Nussbaum that she had done "horrible sexual things" but that he would be her "savior." Three years passed before the physical abuse began.[1097]

Hedda Nussbaum tried to run away five times, but she never told anyone the truth about her relationship with Steinberg.[1098] It wasn't until after her daughter's death that she finally regained her independence, largely due to separation the authorities imposed on the couple. That separation broke Steinberg's control over Nussbaum and allowed the battered woman to think independently.

Years later Hedda Nussbaum became a speaker on the subject of domestic violence. In an interview connected to a college lecture, she said, "I'm sorry. I'm sorry I didn't see. I'm sorry it's too late to see. But we can help others."

Joel Steinberg was released from prison in 2004 after serving two-thirds of his sentence. Despite his conviction the disbarred lawyer never took responsibility for his daughter's death. In an interview shortly after leaving prison, Steinberg called himself a "good father."[1099]

When asked for her reaction to Steinberg's release, Hedda Nussbaum said, "I'm not his puppet any longer and I'm taking precautions against him finding me."[1100]

2002—Lee Boyd Malvo, John Muhammad, and the "D.C. Sniper" Murders

For three weeks during October 2002, a reign of terror took place in the area known as the Washington, DC, Beltway. The so-called D.C. sniper created panic in the city and its surrounding suburbs. During this period ten people were shot and killed, and three were injured. A police investigation would eventually lead to the arrest of John Allen Williams, a forty-two-year-old Gulf War veteran with ten years of military service. Williams had taken the name John Muhammad after joining the Nation of Islam.[1101] Also arrested was his accomplice, a seventeen-year-old named Lee Boyd Malvo.[1102]

The image that emerged through their criminal trials was that of a deeply close overlapping relationship between the middle-aged Muhammad and teenage Malvo. A psychiatrist testified that Malvo "displayed a pathological loyalty" and that the teenager had effectively "merged with Muhammad." Defense lawyers argued that Malvo had been "brainwashed"[1103] and that the process of molding the boy's mindset had taken place over a period of years. Muhammad taught Malvo that emotions were his enemy and that right and wrong were merely artificial constructs.[1104]

Lee Boyd Malvo grew up in poverty in Kingston, Jamaica. His parents separated when he was five, and his mother raised him. In 2000, after moving to Antigua, he met John Muhammad and quickly became enthralled with the charismatic man, who would ultimately become his surrogate father.

Muhammad had fled to the Caribbean with his three children after a bitter custody dispute.[1105] Eventually the children were returned to their mother, and Malvo became Muhammad's "pseudo son."[1106]

In late 2000 Malvo's mother temporarily gave her son to Muhammad as collateral for fake travel papers to the United States.[1107] The boy and his mother later traveled to Florida in 2000, but after only a few months, the teenager ran away to be with Muhammad. He seemed to crave the stability the older man appeared to represent. Psychologist and cult expert Paul Martin later testified, "Instability is a factor in indoctrination. People seek relief from that instability, that sense of insecurity in their life."[1108]

Once Malvo reunited with Muhammad, the older man's influence and control became complete. Malvo even adopted an American accent and called Muhammad "Dad." His new father filled the boy's head with hate. He gave Malvo audiotapes of racist diatribes, which the boy listened to until he fell asleep. Mohammad's grandiose plan was to start a revolution through random murders and then ransom the government he now despised for the funds to build a "Utopian Society."[1109] The teenager, once reportedly "sweet and obedient," was transformed under Mohammad's influence into a cold-blooded killer.

At trial Malvo's lawyer compared his client to "the acolyte of a cult."[1110] Mohammad refused to testify as a witness at the Malvo trial[1111] despite the fact that he had already been convicted of murder at his trial and sentenced to death.[1112] He chose instead to abandon his pretended "son."

Despite use of an "insanity defense,"[1113] Malvo was found guilty of terrorism and capital murder.[1114] The presiding judge, Marum Roush, said the insanity defense required proof that Malvo was incapable of making the distinction between right and wrong. "I imagine someone is going to have to say at some point that the indoctrination in this case was so severe that it made Mr. Malvo unable to know right from wrong," she said. "I would be sorely disappointed if there is no such testimony."[1115]

Testimony was provided by psychologist Paul R. Martin, founder of Wellspring Retreat, a licensed mental health facility in Ohio devoted to the rehabilitation of former cult members. There were numerous objections regarding the relevance of Martin's testimony. The prosecutor said, "There is no evidence of a cult in this case." Martin disagreed. "We call the situation a cult of one."[1116]

Paul Martin didn't interview Lee Boyd Malvo, but a social worker, Carmeta Albarus, did for seventy hours. She testified that one could understand the relationship between Malvo and John Muhammad by watching *The Matrix*. Albarus testified, "I saw Neo as Lee" and "Morpheus as Muhammad." The social worker elaborated, "Neo was 'the One,' who was going to contribute significantly to changing the system, Morpheus was to me the authoritative figure and the mentor."[1117]

Ultimately the jury decided against the death penalty for Malvo despite the recommendations of the prosecution. Lee Boyd Malvo was sentenced to six terms of life imprisonment without the possibility of parole.[1118]

John Muhammad would again be tried for murder in the state of Maryland in 2006, and during that trial he acted as his own attorney. Muhammad cross-examined Malvo in the courtroom. When the one-time mentor Muhammad referred to his former protégé as "son," the young man interrupted him. "I would prefer you address me by my name," he said.[1119] The prosecutor asked Malvo how Mohammad had made him feel about white people. "Hate," he responded.

John Muhammad was executed on November 10, 2009. He offered no final words and never demonstrated any remorse for his crimes.[1120]

Later in an interview Lee Boyd Malvo said, "I was a monster. If you look up the definition, that's what a monster is. I was a ghoul. I was a thief. I stole people's lives. I did someone else's bidding just because they said so…There is no rhyme or reason or sense." Explaining the relationship between Muhammad and him, Malvo said, "He picked me because he knew he could mold me…He knew I could be what he needed me to be…He could not have chosen a better child. I was unable to distinguish between Muhammad the father I had wanted and Muhammad the nervous wreck that was just falling to pieces." Explaining Muhammad's influence, Malvo said, "He understood exactly how to motivate me by giving approval or denying approval. It's very subtle. It wasn't violent at all. It's like what a pimp does to a woman."[1121]

Lee Boyd Malvo also later disclosed that Muhammad sexually abused him. "For the entire period when I was almost 15 until I got arrested, I was sexually abused by John Muhammad," he said. "I couldn't say no. I had wanted that level of love and acceptance and consistency for all of my life, and couldn't find it. And even if unconsciously, or even in moments of short reflection, I knew that it was wrong, I did not have the willpower to say no."[1122]

Much like the victims of destructive cults, individuals dominated through abusive, controlling relationships became dependent on an absolute leader to determine their value judgments. As can be seen from the historical examples, as this type of relationship continues and deepens, the passive person largely loses the ability to think independently and function autonomously. The growing dependence such a relationship engenders often depends on increasing isolation and control of environment and information. All these qualities parallel the similar control features destructive cults use, leading to the description of "cultic relationships" to describe some abusive or controlling situations.

[1082] Madeleine Landau Tobias and Janja Lalich, *Captive Hears, Captive Minds* (Alameda, CA: Hunter House, 1994), 17.

[1083] Ibid., 17.

[1084] Kelly Glasscock, "Speaker Discusses Personal Experiences in Abusive Marriage," *Kansas State Collegian* (Manhattan, KS), March 15, 2000.

[1085] Ibid.

[1086] Stinson FS, Dawson DA, Goldstein RB, Chou SP, Huang B, Smith SM, Ruan WJ, Pulay AJ, Saha TD, Pickering RP, Grant BF, "Prevalence, correlates, disability, and comorbidity of DSM-IV narcissistic personality disorder: results from the wave 2 national epidemiologic survey on alcohol and related conditions.," *Journal of Clinical Psychiatry*, 2008 Jul;69(7):1033-45 http://www.ncbi.nlm.nih.gov/pubmed?term=Stinson%20FS[Author]&cauthor=true&cauthor_uid=18557663 (accessed May 29, 2014).

[1087] "Narcissistic Personality Disorder," Diagnostic and Statistical Manual of Mental Disorders Fourth Edition Text Revision (DSM-IV-TR) *American Psychiatric Association* (2000), http://www.psi.uba.ar/academica/carrerasdegrado/psicologia/sitios catedras/practicas_profesionales/820_clinica_tr_personalidad_psicosis/material/dsm.pdf (accessed May 29, 2014).

[1088] Ibid.

[1089] Stacie N. Galang, "Reason Why Abuse Victims Return Often Complex, Experts Say," *Salem (MA) News*, April 10, 2008.

[1090] Roger E. Mitchell and Christine A. Hodson, "Coping with Domestic Violence: Social Support and Psychological Health among Battered Women," *American Journal of Community Psychology* 11 (6) (1983), 629-54.

[1091] Lenore E. Walker, *The Battered Woman* (New York: William Morrow, 1980).

[1092] Lenore E. Walker, *The Battered Woman Syndrome*, 3rd ed. (New York: Springer, 2009), 84.

[1093] Hedda Nussbaum, interview by Larry King, *Larry King Live*, CNN, June 16, 2003.

[1094] Ibid.

[1095] Marianne Garvey, "Hedda: I'll Flee Once Evil Joel Gets Sprung," *New York Post*, May 23, 2004.

[1096] Kelly Glasscock, "Speaker Discusses Personal Experiences in Abusive Marriage," *Kansas State Collegian* (Manhattan, KS), March 15, 2000.

[1097] Ibid.

[1098] Ibid.

[1099] "Steinberg Calls Himself 'a Good Father,'" *New York Times*, August 7, 2004.

[1100] Garvey, "Hedda: I'll Flee Once Evil Joel Gets Sprung."

[1101] Hal Bernton and David Heath, "Nation of Islam Farrakhan Says Muhammad Is a Member," *Seattle Times*, October 22, 2002.

[1102] Kevin Johnson, "D.C. Sniper Executed in Virginia," *USA Today*, November 11, 2009.

[1103] Ibid.

[1104] "Brainwashed Malvo a Puppet," *Associated Press*, November 12, 2003.

[1105] Alex Tizon, "Sniper Suspect John Allen Muhammad's Meltdown," *Seattle Times*, November 10, 2002.

[1106] Rosie Dimanno, "Convicted Murderer Vows to Stay Silent," *Toronto Star*, December 2, 2003.

[1107] Andrea F. Siegel, "Defense Pushes Theory of Malvo Brainwashing," *Baltimore Sun*, December 2, 2003.

[1108] "Cult Expert Says Malvo May Have Been Vulnerable to Brainwashing," *Associated Press*, December 6, 2003.

[1109] Paul Bradley and Kiran Krishnamurthy, "Critical Malvo Witness Grilled," *Richmond Times-Dispatch*, December 9, 2003.

[1110] Adam Liptak, "Defense Portrays Sniper Suspect as Indoctrinated," *New York Times*, November 21, 2003.

[1111] Dimanno, "Convicted Murderer Vows to Stay Silent."

[1112] Kiran Krishnamurthy and Bill Geroux, "Jury Chooses Death for Mohammad," *Richmond Times Dispatch*, November 24, 2003.

[1113] Adam Liptak, "Younger Sniper Suspect's Lawyers Press Insanity Defense," *New York Times*, December 5, 2003.

[1114] "Malvo Convicted of Sniper Murder," *CNN*, December 18, 2003.

[1115] Liptak, "Younger Sniper Suspect's lawyers Press Insanity Defense."

[1116] Ibid.

[1117] Ibid.

[1118] "Young Sniper Is Sentenced to 6 Life Terms," *Associated Press*, November 8, 2006.

[1119] "Muhammad Questions Malvo about His Sanity," *Associated Press*, May 24, 2006.

[1120] "D.C. Sniper's Execution Met with Grief, Bitterness," *CNN*, November 11, 2009, http://www.cnn.com/2009/CRIME/11/11/virginia.sniper.execution/ (accessed May 29, 2014).

[1121] Josh White, "Lee Boy Malvo, 10 Years after D.C. Area Sniper Shootings: 'I Was a Monster,'" *Washington Post*, September 29, 2012.

[1122] Ian Sager and Scott Stump, "D.C. Sniper Lee Boyd Malvo: 'I Was Sexually Abused by My Accomplice,'" *NBC Today News*, October 24, 2012.

CHAPTER 19

ABUSIVE, CONTROLLING RELATIONSHIP INTERVENTION

Parents contacted me about their teenage daughter, who had become deeply enmeshed in an abusive and controlling relationship and was subsequently estranged from her family.

This situation initially developed during a family summer vacation when the daughter met a young man, who was several years older. He was staying at the same resort with his mother. Before the family's relatively brief vacation had ended, the two young people seemed inseparable.

At the beginning the girl's parents reserved judgment, even though the relationship had developed so rapidly. But after the family returned home, the daughter spent hours every day, locked in her bedroom and talking with the boyfriend through the Internet. Day after day these conversations continued and soon became the focus of the teenage girl's life. The daughter appeared to be obsessed with the relationship and left little time for anything else in her life. She became increasingly isolated from her family and old friends.

The fall came, and it was time for the daughter to begin her first year of college. The school she attended was away from home and offered dormitory rooms for its students. The parents hoped their daughter would find some meaningful balance between school and the boyfriend. In a few weeks, however, the girl dropped out of college and moved into an apartment with the boyfriend in another state. All these changes rapidly occurred within the space of only two months.

Alarmed by the abrupt changes in their daughter's life, the father and mother became profoundly concerned about the relationship. When they discussed their concerns with their daughter, communication with her subsequently became less frequent and far more difficult. It seemed like the girl was being coached before and sometimes during her conversations. After some consideration the mother and father concluded that their daughter was under undue influence.

The parents contacted me for a consultation. I was careful to explain that my intervention approach is purely educational and doesn't include any form of counseling or therapy. I advised the parents that if they wanted counseling, therapy, a psychological evaluation, or assessment for their daughter, I wasn't qualified to provide it.

After a meeting at my office and further consideration, they determined that an intervention was necessary. Together we began to carefully plan how and when this intervention would take place.

The mother's birthday was coming up, and after a considerable conciliatory effort, the family was able to persuade the daughter to come home and celebrate the event with her family. The intervention was scheduled to take place during her visit. The daughter agreed to come alone without the boyfriend. At first the boyfriend was reluctant about the trip, but when the parents intimated that they might be willing to help their daughter out financially, he changed his mind.

The parents and I met for our preparation at my hotel the day before the intervention was set to begin. We agreed that no one else would attend the intervention, with the possible exception of a former babysitter, who was very close to their daughter. We decided that the babysitter wouldn't attend the first day of the intervention but might participate later with their daughter's consent. Our concern was not to overwhelm the daughter by having too many people present at the beginning.

We also discussed the importance of temporarily blocking communication between the boyfriend and the daughter during the intervention. That is, the parents agreed to shut down any potential means of contact. This specifically meant shutting down all Internet access and putting away in safekeeping any devices in the house.

We discussed the necessity of asking the daughter to agree to a temporary suspension of communication with the boyfriend. This agreement would be in effect until our discussion was concluded, which might be a period of three days. I emphasized that by the end of the first day, she must agree to surrender her cell phone or any device she might potentially use to contact her boyfriend. I repeatedly focused on the importance of parental supervision to maintain this commitment during our preparation meeting. The parents couldn't physically enforce such an agreement, but they could remind their daughter and persuade her to keep her promise.

We also discussed the possibility that their daughter might suddenly panic and leave the house, perhaps in the middle of the night, and then contact the boyfriend. I advised them that throughout the intervention, particularly between each of our daily sessions during the evening, they must be vigilant. That is, they must maintain constant awareness of where their daughter was and what she was doing at any given time until we were done. If she insisted on leaving the house for some reason, they must accompany her to make sure she didn't use that time as an opportunity to contact her boyfriend.

The first day after their daughter arrived, there was a birthday celebration. She also took some time to visit with old friends. The following morning I arrived at the family home. The daughter had no idea that my visit had been planned, and it was a complete surprise. Her parents began the discussion with the simple explanation that they felt overwhelmed by recent events and were so deeply concerned that they had decided to consult a professional. The mother and father then introduced me as the professional they had consulted, and I quickly entered the conversation and began facilitating further discussion.

At first the daughter was visibly upset and somewhat angry. She didn't appreciate being surprised by such a sudden meeting. But despite that initial negative reaction, the discussion moved forward and continued, with everyone in the room actively engaged in dialogue.

I introduced myself and said I wasn't there to provide any form of counseling or therapy; I was there only to deliver educational information based on my expertise. The daughter asked what my area of expertise included, and I replied that my work centered on controversial groups called "cults" and the coercive persuasion techniques they use to gain undue influence.

The daughter was surprised, but her parents quickly explained that they had some concerns they wished to address about recent events in her life that appeared to reflect undue influence.

I then began to recount specific stories of abusive, controlling relationships. I used as examples the personal accounts of women such as Hedda Nussbaum,[1123] Nicole Brown Simpson,[1124] and Tina Turner, described in the iconic singer's book.[1125] I explained that highly educated, sophisticated, and often seemingly strong women had been victimized through the use of coercive persuasion in such relationships.

We then discussed some basic "warning signs" Hedda Nussbaum had once cited at a college lecture about abusive and controlling relationships.[1126]

One warning sign might be that the controlling partner pushes the rapid development of the relationship. This may often seem too fast, and long-term plans are being made quickly. We discussed how this warning sign aligned with the daughter's experience. Her recent relationship had begun as a casual meeting at a resort while on vacation, but it quickly developed and led to dropping out of school, leaving her hometown, and moving in with the boyfriend in another state. All this had occurred in less than sixty days. I asked the daughter if she would agree that her life had changed very rapidly. The daughter nodded but resisted the idea that this might actually be a warning sign of an abusive, controlling relationship.

Another point Nussbaum cited was that typically controlling male partners often seem to have a strained relationship with their mothers. This was evident regarding the young man in question. The daughter knew this was true, even though the boyfriend had apparently agreed to spend some time with his mother on vacation.

The young man also exhibited another telling characteristic, which was his fervent striving for the daughter's undivided attention. He also wanted to "be in charge" at all times. These were both warning signs Nussbaum had cited in her lecture.

The boyfriend further fit the profile through his highly competitive nature coupled with a constant need to win. The daughter recalled how aggressively the young man played team sports, often bullying young children in games at the resort where they first met. She also admitted that he wouldn't tolerate criticism and always justified his actions. The boyfriend always blamed someone or something else rather than accept responsibility for his mistakes or failings.

Another characteristic that fit the profile we discussed was the boyfriend's unreasonable jealousy regarding the girl's friends and family. He demanded her total devotion and complete attention, and when anyone else wanted time with her, he seemed to feel threatened and was likely to become envious or even angry. The girl had also seen evidence of his "nasty temper." It seemed that the boyfriend had little, if any, respect for the opinions of others unless they agreed with him.

During the previous two months, the daughter had experienced situations when the boyfriend seemed to threaten to withdraw his love and approval based on her compliance. He often pushed her to do things that made her uneasy, such as dropping out of school and moving away to another state, where she knew no one. Again, this history matched the same pattern of behavior Nussbaum had described in her lecture.

The young man could be quite demanding, and at times the daughter felt that she could never do enough to satisfy him. We discussed how the feeling of never being good enough engendered dependency and how that dependency might provide the basis for further dominance and control.

The repeated parallels between the cited warning signs associated with abusive, controlling partners and the history of her own relationship and current situation seemed to take the daughter aback.

As we moved forward through the first day of the intervention, we examined the definition of what has been called a "cultic relationship."[1127] In such a relationship one individual is "deliberately manipulative and exploitative," and "there is a significant power imbalance between the two participants. The stronger uses his (or her) influence to control, manipulate, abuse, and exploit the other." But unlike a cult, which is typically a group dominated by an authoritarian, charismatic leader, the cultic relationship instead includes only two people. In such a situation "all the attention and abuse is focused only on one person, often with more damaging consequences."[1128]

As our day together drew to an end, I asked the daughter whether she would agree to resume our discussion the following day. She nodded in agreement and also made an explicit commitment not to contact her boyfriend in any way, shape, or form. Per our previous preparation, her parents had shut down any and all means of communication within their home. The girl gave her cell phone to her mother.

The following morning the daughter seemed more interested in conversation and less angry about the initial surprise nature of our meeting. We now discussed another profile that frequently appeared to fit some abusive and controlling partners. That is, many abusive partners seem to match much of the behavior attributed to narcissistic personalities or what has been labeled NPD (narcissistic personality disorder).[1129]

Some of the characteristics we subsequently discussed, which are linked to NPD, included a person who seemed to have a grandiose sense of self-importance, someone given to exaggeration regarding his or her achievements, and a person who often expressed a desire to be recognized as superior. Such a man or woman might frequently be preoccupied with fantasies about future success, power, and/or ideal love. I asked the daughter whether these traits might be attributed to her boyfriend. She was quiet at this point.

I discussed in further detail how such a person might have a belief that he or she is "special" and warrants excessive admiration. When dealing with such an individual, he or she seems to express a sense of entitlement or unreasonable expectation for special treatment. The individual may also lack empathy or the ability to easily recognize the needs and feelings of others. Often such individuals may seem arrogant, aloof, and egotistical.

The daughter looked down at the floor. These characteristics seemed to resonate regarding the boyfriend's behavior. I explained that people who fit such a profile rarely make significant or major changes regarding their personality and behavior. If someone fits such a profile, it is more likely that he or she will remain the same and continue to express the same pattern of behavior.

As we moved into the latter part of the second day, the daughter agreed to invite the babysitter and longtime family friend to sit in on our discussion. This young woman, who was well known and whom everyone in the family respected, had once been involved in an abusive, controlling relationship.

After the babysitter arrived, she explained in some detail the history of her past relationship. The young woman thought that telling her story might potentially help the daughter in sorting through her own recent experience. The daughter trusted the babysitter and highly regarded her honesty and integrity.

The babysitter related the history of her troubled relationship, which lasted years and caused her tremendous pain. She said that at first everything seemed to be wonderful, but then the relationship rapidly changed and became abusive and controlling. The babysitter's boyfriend fit the same profile we had discussed over the past two days. The young woman described him as intensely possessive, jealous, dominating, and narcissistic.

The babysitter said that as a direct result of her boyfriend's influence and his demands, she became increasingly isolated from old friends and family. Her boyfriend became an overwhelming and dominant force in her life and monopolized all her time. Eventually the babysitter had little time for anything or anyone else. She said it felt like being slowly but methodically suffocated.

The babysitter explained that she tried to fix the relationship but that her boyfriend never accepted any responsibility for whatever needed to be fixed. Near the end of the relationship, after one breakup, the babysitter's boyfriend threatened suicide. She went back to him, believing that to do so was necessary to save his life. At that point the babysitter also believed that whatever was wrong with the relationship must be her fault. And her boyfriend convinced her that she would never find another person who would love her as much as he did.

The babysitter eventually came to the painful realization, however, that her boyfriend's frequent professions of total commitment were being used like tools to manipulate her. Looking back over years of emotional and sometimes physical abuse, the young woman wished she had come to her realization earlier. Concluding her contribution to our discussion, the babysitter expressed admiration for the mother and father who had risked the daughter's wrath rather than ignore the situation. The babysitter said she wished her family had been brave enough to do the same.

We were now almost at the end of the second day, and the daughter broke down and wept. Crying, the girl said she had reached her own point of realization about the boyfriend and the controlling nature of their relationship. The daughter said she could see how her situation in many ways paralleled the babysitter's story and the warning signs we had discussed. The girl also admitted that many of the attributes describing a narcissistic personality were directly applicable to the boyfriend.

It was at about this juncture that the doorbell rang. When the mother opened the door, she faced two local police officers. One policeman explained that the boyfriend had contacted them; because the daughter hadn't contacted him for almost two days, he suspected that the girl was being held as a prisoner in her parents' house. After talking with the daughter privately, the officers were satisfied that the girl wasn't a prisoner; she was unharmed and safe.

One of them asked, "Is this like a cult deprogramming?" I responded that it was more like a family intervention. After a few more questions, the policeman assured the parents that no one would bother them again and that they would warn the boyfriend about making false reports to the police.

The next morning, when we resumed our discussion, I cited the incident with the police to make a point. The boyfriend was so controlling that he couldn't allow the daughter to spend two uninterrupted days with her family, even though the occasion was to celebrate her mother's birthday. Instead, he expected the daughter to check in with him constantly by texting him, calling in, or e-mailing him at multiple intervals throughout each day.

I asked the daughter whether his apparent expectation regarding constant ongoing contact seemed normal. Was this a reasonable routine or excessively controlling and manipulative? Was it a normal reaction to call the police after less than two days? Why had he sent the police to the family home? Did he really think her parents would hurt her?

We then moved on to discuss what has been called "brainwashing" but more specifically what can be seen as a synthesis of thought reform[1130] or coercive persuasion techniques[1131] a predatory group or person uses to gain undue influence.

We discussed the three most basic stages of coercive persuasion, according to MIT professor Edgar Schein. These include "unfreezing," "changing," and then "refreezing" a person after the desired mind-set has been achieved.[1132]

How had the daughter's boyfriend unfrozen her?

Psychologist Margaret Singer calls the unfreezing phase of coercive persuasion "the destabilizing of a person's sense of self."[1133] How had the boyfriend destabilized the daughter? We discussed the laser-like intensity of their relationship—the seemingly endless talks they had and how much time the boyfriend had demanded. This aspect had been evident first at the vacation resort, later through their ongoing Internet calls, and ultimately through his demands that she drop out of school and move in with him.

I asked the daughter whether the boyfriend had used their prolonged talks as a means to change her life goals and alter her family values. She agreed that this constant conversation and communication were the impetus and catalyst for the changes that had taken place in her personal and academic life. Through these discourses the boyfriend had managed to alter the daughter's direction in life, including her goals and individual values.

We then discussed in more detail how the boyfriend had persuaded her to drop out of school and move in with him in less than sixty days. Wasn't that a sudden change? Had she previously considered making such dramatic changes in her life before meeting the boyfriend?

The girl's parents said they became concerned not only because these changes were happening so fast but also because their daughter had given up her personal goals, friends, and family. It appeared that she had sacrificed everything in her life to satisfy the needs of the boyfriend.

I then pointed out how such rapid and singularly motivated change fit within the framework of coercive persuasion, as Singer suggested. Had the boyfriend manipulated the daughter to reinterpret her life? As Singer summarized, had she ultimately accepted "a new version of reality"?[1134] How had the boyfriend impacted the historical relationships in her life? Did this explain why she had so suddenly changed her goals and family values?

How had the daughter changed from a loving family member, concerned about friends, to someone who barely communicated with anyone other than the boyfriend?

The daughter acknowledged that the rapid and radical changes in recent months had occurred as a direct result of the boyfriend's persuasive power and growing influence.

At this juncture in the intervention, we began to examine the basic characteristics of thought reform, as psychiatrist Robert Jay Lifton outlined.[1135] The single most basic and important element of thought reform, as Lifton defined, is "Milieu Control"—that is, control of the environment.

We now began to discuss how isolated the daughter had recently become. The parents commented about the apparent control of communication between them and their daughter in recent weeks. They said it had seemed like the boyfriend was now filtering everything. Was this pattern of control similar to Lifton's Milieu Control? Could control over communication and growing isolation be the means to achieve such Milieu Control? I pointed out the research of sociologist Richard Ofshe, who stated that "the control of communication" can express milieu control.[1136]

At this point the parents offered specific examples of how increasingly impaired the communication with their daughter had been. At times they could hear the boyfriend coaching their daughter during a phone call. They said this was an abrupt change in their daughter's behavior and caused them concern. The parents said that in the past the daughter had always been easy to talk to despite her many friends and busy schedule.

As we continued to discuss the eight criteria Lifton had cited to establish the existence of a thought-reform program, the daughter repeatedly saw parallels to the dynamics of her relationship and the behavior of the boyfriend. She also connected these features to the babysitter's account of her experience from the day before.

By the end of the third day, the daughter announced that she had decided to end the relationship.

The local police who had previously visited the family home helped the daughter recover her personal belongings from her boyfriend's apartment.

I later learned that the daughter had reenrolled at college and resumed her normal life again. Interestingly, she also became a knowledgeable resource for other young women on campus affected by, or struggling with, abusive and controlling relationships.

[1123] Hedda Nussbaum, interviewed by Larry King, *Larry King Live, CNN*, June 16, 2003.

[1124] William Claiborne, "Testimony Opens in Simpson Trial with account of Physical Abuse," *Washington Post*, February 1, 1995.

[1125] Tina Turner and Kurt Loder, *I, Tina: My Life Story* (New York: It Books, 2010).

[1126] Kelly Glasscock, "Speaker Discusses Personal Experiences in Abusive Marriage," *Kansas State Collegian* (Manhattan, KS), March 15, 2000.

[1127] Madeleine Landau Tobias and Janja Lalich, *Captive Hears, Captive Minds* (Alameda, CA: Hunter House, 1994), 17.

[1128] Ibid.

[1129] "Narcissistic Personality Disorder," Diagnostic and Statistical Manual of Mental Disorders Fourth Edition Text Revision (DSM-IV-TR) *American Psychiatric Association* (2000), http://www.psi.uba.ar/academica/carrerasdegrado/psicologia/sitios_catedras/practicas_profesionales/820_clinica_tr_personalidad_psicosis/material/dsm.pdf (accessed May 29, 2014).

[1130] Robert Jay Lifton, *Thought Reform and the Psychology of Totalism* (Chapel Hill: University of North Carolina Press, 2012).

[1131] Richard Ofshe, "Coercive Persuasion and Attitude Change," *Encyclopedia of Sociology*, vol. 1 (New York: McMillan, 1992), 212–224.

[1132] Edgar H. Schein, *Coercive Persuasion: A Socio-psychological Analysis of the "Brainwashing" of American Civilian Prisoners by the Chinese Communists* (New York: W. W. Norton, 1971).

[1133] Margaret Singer, *Cults in Our Midst* (San Francisco, CA: Jossey-Bass, 1996), 62.

[1134] Ibid.

[1135] Lifton, *Thought Reform and the Psychology of Totalism*, 419–437.

[1136] Ofshe, "Coercive Persuasion and Attitude Change," 212–224.

CHAPTER 20

GURU GROUP INTERVENTION

A husband concerned about his wife's involvement in a yoga and meditation group retained me for an intervention. The couple had been married for more than ten years and had two small children. The wife had been involved in the group for approximately two years. A well-educated former executive, she had stopped working to raise the children as a stay-at-home parent.

The wife's history serves as yet another example of the manipulative and often misleading recruitment practices of destructive cults. This account should likewise disabuse people regarding the myth that somehow only unintelligent or unsophisticated people are susceptible to cults.

Encouraged by a friend, the wife attended yoga classes at a local studio. Her motivation was simply physical fitness through what has become a popular form of regular exercise. She didn't initially understand that this particular yoga studio was run by a guru and that most, if not all, of the yoga students were his devoted followers. Yoga is historically linked to Hindu ritual and sacramental hymns.[1137] However, the overwhelming majority of those involved in yoga, as practiced in the United States, aren't tied to either religious groups or destructive cults.

As the young mother began to practice yoga at the studio, she became increasingly aware of the guru's philosophy and spiritual agenda. Members of this relatively small and close-knit group of devotees demonstrated extreme deference to the guru and seemed willing to do almost anything to serve or please him. The guru also maintained a retreat in Southeast Asia in addition to his facility in the United States.

As the wife's involvement deepened and her level of commitment escalated, this devotion caused conflict and led to a marital rift. The wife increasingly neglected her children as she struggled to meet the demands the guru imposed on her through a heavy schedule of group activities. After several heated arguments about the conflict between family commitments and the yoga group, the couple separated. The wife moved out of the family home and rented an apartment in a building largely occupied by other group members.

After being retained, I began to coach the husband in coping strategies. Subsequently he stopped arguing with his wife about her involvement with the group and apologized for any angry outbursts that had previously occurred. He also began to carefully filter his ongoing communication, avoiding negative comments and criticism about his wife's behavior, the yoga group, and its guru. As a direct result of using this strategy, after a few weeks the friction diminished, as did much of the tension; though still separated, the couple became increasingly friendly. Their level of communication greatly improved. Eventually the wife later even agreed to go on a family vacation.

After returning from the vacation, the husband requested that I facilitate an intervention as soon as possible. His wife had advised him during the trip that she would soon be moving from her apartment into group housing. The husband felt the timing was crucial to begin the intervention before his wife became embedded in the more controlled group environment. We also agreed that an intervention would be far more difficult after such a move due to increased group influence, control of communication, and the probability of more limited access.

I soon flew in to begin my preparation work. Upon my arrival I met with the husband and his wife's family members, who were to be included in the intervention effort. This included both of the wife's parents and her brother. I coached the family about what to say and what not to say regarding the boundaries of their participation. I encouraged the family to offer their firsthand observations about the group and the guru's influence and to explain how this had caused them concern. But they were cautioned not to become needlessly argumentative, accusatory, or excessively confrontational.

We also discussed who had the most emotional pull, which could be used as leverage to keep the wife from ending the intervention and leaving. We discussed this in some detail and rehearsed how to handle such a situation. The woman's parents agreed that they would both follow her out if she attempted to leave in an effort to convince her to return. The brother also understood that part of his role was to emphasize to his sister the importance of staying, listening, and participating in the discussion.

We reviewed the four main blocks of the intervention. Family members asked general questions about our schedule, breaks, food arrangements, and what to do throughout the intervening time in the evenings between each day of the intervention. The family understood that they must not discuss the group or any related topic while I was gone and should instead wait until my return the following day. This would be done to avoid any argument or conflict that could potentially end the intervention. Our preparation process took several hours on the day before the intervention began.

The plan we agreed on and set in place involved the husband's requesting that his wife come to their home to watch the children while he attended a business meeting. But when she arrived at the house, her parents, brother, and I would all be waiting, and relatives at another location would actually be taking care of the children.

Upon her arrival the wife immediately recognized that she had walked into some type of family intervention. She reacted angrily and initially refused to participate, running back to the garage and waiting there to be driven back to her apartment. Her parents quickly followed her and, as I had coached them the day before, pleaded with her to return and talk things out. After about thirty minutes of heated discussion, she complied and returned.

At this point the husband introduced me as a professional he had hired to facilitate a meeting and provide expert consultation. The wife asked me numerous questions about my background, work experience, and the ultimate goal of our meeting. I answered each question directly and explained that the purpose of the intervention was to share meaningful information from various perspectives based on research. I also said that the reason this particular meeting had been planned as a surprise was to avoid any interference from her yoga group or guru. I added that the family had some serious concerns and that it would be reasonable to set aside adequate time to address those concerns and review the research material.

Everyone present assured the wife that the final decision to separate, divorce, or continue with the yoga group was hers to make. We expressed hope that part of her decision-making process about these issues might include consideration of relevant research and the information to be shared through our discussion.

In response to her questions about my background, I talked about my many years of experience dealing with controversial groups and movements, some that were quite similar to her guru-led yoga group.

I also pointed out that I had reviewed materials the guru had produced about his history and the organization he headed, which pertained to the structure, practices, and purpose of the group. I concluded by telling the wife that an organization with nothing to hide has no reason to fear examination or discussion about its practices and behavior. At this point the wife agreed to stay and participate.

During the first day of the intervention, we discussed an array of topics linked in some way to the four blocks of the intervention process. I previously outlined. This included talking about what can be seen as the nucleus for a definition of a destructive cult as psychiatrist Robert Jay Lifton outlined in his paper "Cult Formation,"[1138] which proposes the primary characteristics, general structure, and dynamics of a thought-reform program as expressed by destructive cults.

We also touched on some of the concerns her spouse and family had expressed regarding dramatic recent changes in her life that seemed related to group influence. Our first day of discussion laid the foundation for further dialogue, tested what areas of discussion were most important to her, and maintained her interest. The first day easily consumed eight hours.

At the conclusion of the first day, I asked the wife whether she would agree to meet again the following day. I also asked her to refrain from having contact in any way, shape, or form with anyone associated with the yoga group or guru. This prohibition specifically included e-mail, text messaging, phone calls, and communication of any kind. I explained that the many hours she had previously spent with the group and guru had been uninterrupted. Therefore, in fairness our discussion on balance must also not be interrupted. The family also expressed concern that her responses to the information presented must be genuine and spontaneous. Whatever she said would be her thoughts and not something coached or somehow based on instructions from the group or guru.

These conditions prompted another emotional outburst. The wife expressed considerable anger toward her parents and especially her husband, accusing them of interfering in her life and trying to control her. At this point her brother stood up and offered his emotional response to the situation. He stated that, in his opinion, the situation was so serious that he'd given up time with his wife and children, driving several hours to attend the intervention. The wife noted her brother's concern and responded positively to the importance of continuing our dialogue. We agreed to meet the following morning, and she also specifically agreed that there would be no communication with the group. The wife also decided not to return to her apartment and instead stayed overnight with her family at the house.

As the husband drove me to my hotel, we went over the instructions I've given them during the previous day of preparation. I warned him to avoid an argument that might explode without me there to moderate the situation.

The following morning we resumed our discussion. During this second day we focused specifically on the primary characteristics of a destructive cult in considerable detail. This discussion included specific examples of cultlike behavior, dynamics, and structure; we covered how these might parallel the yoga group and its guru. For example, what is the role of the guru in this particular yoga group? Is he a charismatic leader? Is he the defining element and driving force of the group? Can this yoga group be seen as personality driven and totalitarian? Working from this foundation, we reviewed the yoga group's published literature, website information, and some e-mail communication between members of the group and the guru, which the husband had copied.

We also watched a documentary, *You Can Go Home Again*,[1139] which contains some historical footage about an assortment of groups called "cults." The documentary also puts considerable emphasis on interviews with former cult members. We discussed the repeated pattern and similarity of their statements. Even though the former cult members came from completely different groups, they seemed to share a common experience. That is, they had all been involved in groups that a charismatic and authoritarian leader had dominated and defined. The former members interviewed for the documentary also said they had been deceived, subjected to various levels of environmental control, and manipulated, resulting in their personal exploitation. This documentary concluded our second day.

At this juncture the wife seemed to be curious. She repeatedly asked questions to further understand the points made in our discussion and was neither angry nor argumentative. She readily agreed to meet again a third day without any difficulty.

On the third day we discussed in some depth the thought-reform process various cults use and the specific techniques of coercive persuasion they employ. This conversation included discussion about the published works of psychiatrist Robert Jay Lifton,[1140] psychologist Margaret Singer,[1141] Professor Edgar Schein,[1142] sociologist Richard Ofshe,[1143] and the study of influence as defined researcher and Professor Robert Cialdini in his book *Influence*.[1144]

Core excerpts of the assembled material were printed out and reviewed. These studies and research formed the basis for much of our discussion on the second day. Once again, frequent comparisons were made between the internal dynamics and behavior of the guru-led yoga group and what Lifton described as "thought reform." For example, we discussed how the group had increasingly dominated her time and social interaction, and how this influence could be seen as effectively controlling her environment and frame of reference. We also discussed the three fundamental stages of coercive persuasion as Schein defined them—"unfreezing," "changing," and then "refreezing."

Had the group encouraged her to abandon her "ego" and former identity? What changes had group members encouraged? How had they used peer pressure to enforce this process? How did the group reinforce changes once they were accomplished? We connected these questions and issues with the experiences of ex-cult members we'd seen in the documentary and which we had discussed the day before.

Toward the end of the third day, we watched another documentary on DVD, *Captive Minds: Hypnosis and Beyond*,[1145] which very specifically focuses on psychological and emotional manipulation. The documentary included a detailed review of the trance-induction process through hypnosis, meditation, and other techniques. For example, the documentary demonstrated how easily people could be manipulated by a stage hypnotist but also showed how a trance state could be achieved by other means, such as the overload of the senses or through rhythmic drumming and chanting.

The documentary also included some discussion about the use of indirect directives, which can be seen as a covert means of obtaining compliance. This can be done through such things as the tone of voice, body language, or a repeated emphasis on certain words. The documentary demonstrated the seemingly benign use of indirect directives in a counseling session with a psychiatrist.

We then discussed how suggestible people are once they are in an altered state of consciousness. We then correlated this state of suggestibility to the yoga group and certain meditation practices the guru encouraged. How suggestible and vulnerable were the people in the yoga group during such an experience? Did the guru sometimes subtly employ indirect directives to gain compliance?

At the conclusion of the third day, the wife appeared to be intensely interested in, though deeply disturbed by, the information we had covered. She also seemed to be much more at ease with her family and particularly comfortable with her husband. There was no hesitation regarding an agreement to meet for a fourth day.

On the fourth day we discussed the history of the small yoga group and its guru. We reviewed certain corporate documents, disclosure statements, real estate records, and finally personal e-mail communications between the guru and some of his followers, which the husband had copied and printed out for me. A pattern emerged regarding the guru's evident financial gain and accumulated assets through the group. Also clear was how he had repeatedly exploited and profited from the free labor his followers had provided.

The yoga group as an organizational entity purportedly had a charitable purpose, which supposedly was based on human improvement. However, the guru apparently lived a life of ease and luxury at the expense of his followers. We could see this fact in the documentation, in living arrangements at the group retreat in Southeast Asia, and through the persistent personal demands the guru made through his e-mails. Did this evidence reflect the personality of an "egoless" or "enlightened" being? Or was it rather the behavior of a selfish opportunist?

We reviewed news reports about controversial gurus that encouraged some practice to achieve an altered state of consciousness for the purported purpose of self-improvement and fulfillment. For example, the notorious Bhagwan Shree Rajneesh,[1146] the Japanese cult Aum "Supreme Truth,"[1147] both found guilty of terrorism, and the so-called Hare Krishna movement, which declared bankruptcy when faced with child abuse claims.[1148]

The family repeatedly interjected their personal observations about the yoga group and its influence on the wife's life, including how group activities had overwhelmed her daily schedule and how she had become increasingly isolated. As her group involvement increased, family members said, they saw her less, and communication began to wither away. This isolation became even more pronounced when she moved into an apartment building other group members also occupied.

Near the conclusion of the fourth day, the wife was very quiet, and finally she began to cry. She asked her family for their forgiveness. She said, "How could I be so stupid?" At this point I interjected that it had been impossible for her to realistically evaluate the group given the deceptive way in which she had been recruited and gradually manipulated. I said that her harsh self-judgment seemed misplaced. How could she have made an informed decision about group involvement without having the necessary information? What about the group and its leader? Didn't the guru, and perhaps some of his prominent devotees, have the responsibility to disclose their agenda from the beginning? Weren't they responsible for the negative consequences of their influence? Why didn't they deserve some, if not all, of the blame?

The conclusion of this intervention was quite emotional, but it was a happy one. The husband and wife reconciled, and she had no further contact with the group or the guru. Not long after the intervention, the wife contacted me about her concerns that the group might harass or bother her in some way. I assured her that if she ignored them by refusing to respond to their e-mails, text messages, and calls, they would eventually give up and move on. It seems they did just that.

[1137] Georg Feuerstein, *The Yoga Tradition: Its History, Literature, Philosophy and Practice*, 3rd ed. (Chino Valley, AZ: Hohm Press, 2001), 538.

[1138] Robert Jay Lifton, "Cult Formation," *Harvard Mental Health Letter*, February 1981.

[1139] Maurice Davis, "You Can Go Home Again."DVD. Directed by Elliot Bernstein, New York: Union for Reform Judaism, 1982.

[1140] Robert Jay Lifton, *Thought Reform and the Psychology of Totalism* (Chapel Hill: University of North Carolina Press, 2012).

[1141] Margaret Singer, *Cults in Our Midst* (San Francisco, CA: Jossey-Bass, 1996).

[1142] Edgar H. Schein, *Coercive Persuasion: A Socio-psychological Analysis of the "Brainwashing" of American Civilian Prisoners by the Chinese Communists* (New York: W. W. Norton, 1971).

[1143] Richard Ofshe, "Coercive Persuasion and Attitude Change," *Encyclopedia of Sociology*, vol. 1 (New York: McMillan, 1992), 212–224.

[1144] Robert B. Cialdini, *Influence*, rev. ed. (New York: HarperCollins, July 15, 1993).

[1145] "Captive Minds: Hypnosis and Beyond." Documentary. Directed by Pierre Lasry. Montreal: National Film Board of Canada, 1983. http://www.youtube.com/watch?v=mQC0nFfp2nc&index=1&list=PL2D64B3CB3D593ACF (accessed May 22, 2014).

[1146] "Escaping the Bhagwan," *The Age* (Sydney), April 11, 2009.

[1147] Murray Sayle, "Nerve Gas and the Four Noble Truths," *New Yorker*, April 1, 1996.

[1148] "Hare Krishna Plan OK'd by U.S. Court," Associated Press, May 24, 2005.

CHAPTER 21

AMWAY INTERVENTION

A college student became involved in a multilevel marketing scheme known as Amway or Quixtar, Inc. Over a period of months, the young man became so obsessed with Amway that he neglected his studies. As his grades slipped and the possibility arose that he might have to leave college, his parents became concerned. His father, a certified public accountant (CPA), tried to explain the flaws and pitfalls linked to multilevel marketing schemes like Amway. But despite the father's effort, his son refused to be dissuaded from his commitment to the company.

As the prospects for the young man's successful completion of college continued to dim, his father contacted me. We soon arranged for an intervention schedule based on a long weekend visit that had already been planned. I would be the family's surprise guest during that weekend to facilitate the intervention effort.

On the day before the intervention began, we met to discuss details. The father explained that he couldn't understand how his son, who was bright and studying business in college, could have been so easily fooled by what he considered to be a blatantly opportunistic scheme. As a trained professional accountant, he had explicitly explained to his son why Amway's business plan often failed to generate any significant income for those involved. But no matter how many times the father went over the numbers and identified the flaws he saw in Amway's business plan, his son seemed to be beyond reason and somehow unable or unwilling to acknowledge the facts.

The father asked me whether it was possible that Amway had "brainwashed" his son. When we went over the basic structure of the intervention, I noted that one of the primary topics we would focus on during our discussion was coercive persuasion, which is commonly called "brainwashing."

The father seemed convinced that if an outside consultant presented more negative information, such as a more in-depth, critical analysis of the Amway business plan, this would be the key to unlock his son's ability to independently and critically think again. It is impossible to predict which specific area or category of discussion is most likely to connect and solicit a thoughtful and meaningful response during an intervention. It could be the negative history of a particular group or leader or perhaps the emotional pull of family concerns. Or it could be the unmasking of a process of manipulation a group employed to shut down critical thinking. I urged the parents not to press any specific point or category during the intervention but rather to let the dialogue unfold in a way that allowed their son to focus on whatever interested him the most.

During the preparation process I also explained to the parents that though there would be four basic blocks of the intervention, there was no specific order in which these blocks would be covered. I again emphasized the need to stay focused on whatever topic drew their son's interest to keep him engaged and interested in the conversation. The ultimate purpose of any intervention is to stimulate independent thinking by engaging in an educational process that includes critical analysis. The person who is the focus of the intervention must be personally engaged and interested, or no meaningful exchange of ideas will occur, and the effort will fail.

On the morning when the intervention began, the young man was courteous and deferential to his mother and father. He repeatedly said he wanted to satisfy whatever concerns they had about his involvement in Amway and agreed not to contact anyone associated with the company during our time together. His father's persistence in pursuing the subject of Amway somewhat annoyed him, but ultimately he welcomed the opportunity to explain the positive aspects of the Amway business plan once again.

Initially, our conversation centered on Amway's troubled history, which included a pattern of complaints about its practices, negative press reports, and litigation.

We discussed some of the fundamental flaws in many multilevel marketing schemes. These often included the issue of market saturation—that is, "a situation in which no more of a product or service can be sold because there are no more possible customers."[1149] For example, similar businesses so saturate a given area that the prospects of other similar businesses in the same area become limited. This is why many businesses do studies regarding the issue of market saturation to determine whether an area is oversaturated.

As an example I offered a study done in Wisconsin concerning the casino market to determine whether more casinos would benefit the state and were therefore feasible. The study determined that the market was already saturated and that adding more casinos was therefore not advisable.[1150] I asked the young man what limits Amway had set regarding how many distributors were selling its products in a given area to avoid market saturation. What specific policies or rules reflected Amway's ongoing effort to avoid having too many distributors in the same place? Did Amway set limits concerning distributors by area?

The young man couldn't think of any limitations Amway had ever set regarding the number of distributors in an area. In fact, distributors were encouraged to recruit more distributors in their area regardless of how many there might already be in the neighborhood, city, state, or region.

Another focus of discussion was how Amway or Quixtar people make money. That is, what is the primary focus of Amway? Is it the sale of its products or the promotion of its multilevel business plan in an effort to recruit more distributors? I pointed out that historically lawsuits filed against Amway have asserted that distributors are pressured to buy products and "motivational materials" and that it is a relatively small group of "kingpins" presiding over thousands of down-line distributors who make significant amounts of money. Reportedly, I said, Amway's elite make most of their money selling materials, known within Amway or Quixtar as the "tool and function" end of the business. The ratio of tools income as opposed to regular Amway business is reportedly "nine-to-one or more."[1151]

The son readily admitted that he had paid for such motivational materials and that based on his experience, the focus in Amway was often on recruiting more distributors rather than on simply selling company products. He also acknowledged that he and other distributors were pressured to purchase Amway products.

I pointed out that reportedly "Amway distributors earn an average of just $115 a month." And that "just a quarter of 1% (0.26%) make more than $40,000 a year."[1152] I asked the young man whether it was really possible for him to make enough money through Amway to support himself, considering the expense of buying Amway products and tools. This analysis seemed to disturb the young man. He said that all businesses included some risk but admitted that it wasn't rational to be in a business without the reasonable hope of future success and profitability. He, like other Amway distributors, hoped to somehow be not an average distributor but rather an exceptional one. But was it reasonable to expect this outcome given the numbers?

The question now was why anyone would engage or remain in a business without a reasonable hope for meaningful success. Didn't Amway/Quixtar people understand that the odds were stacked against success, as the numbers reflected? Why would people make a business commitment if it wasn't in their own best interest? After all, isn't business about making money? At this juncture I pointed out that Amway had settled a class action lawsuit for $56 million. The lawsuit alleged that the company had engaged in predatory practices including "racketeering, among other charges."[1153]

Why would people knowingly allow themselves to be preyed on? We touched on what some Amway critics have called the "cultlike" nature of the organization, a kind of rigid mind-set expressed by Amway enthusiasts who echo the same jargon and seem totally enthralled with the company. Does Amway have a preferred way of thinking that denigrates objective and critical analysis? Do Amway and Quixtar devotees behave like people in cultlike groups? Do Amway distributors recognize that multilevel marketing often ignores basic business principles like market saturation? Or do they obscure such reasonable guidelines with the company's slogans and jargon?

Later on during the first day, we touched on what might be seen as "Loading the Language" in Amway. That is what psychiatrist Robert Jay Lifton describes as "highly reductive, definitive-sounding phrases, easily memorized and easily expressed" that become "the start and finish of any ideological analysis."[1154] Loaded language is one of the characteristic components of what Lifton calls "thought reform" or what is more commonly labeled "brainwashing."

We talked about how Amway appears to use such verbiage through phrases such as "building the business," which essentially means recruiting more "downlines"[1155] or distributors by showing "the plan."[1156]

The plan means the multilevel marketing scheme Amway and Quixtar uses. The lure for many potential participants is referred to as "chasing the dream"[1157] of wealth and success. Someone who criticizes Amway/Quixtar is apt to be labeled a "dream stealer,"[1158] a derogatory label denoting that someone somehow represents opposition or is an impediment to the dream fulfillment attributed to Amway. People or things that distract someone from following the plan are "negative"[1159] and therefore avoided. This might include a regular job, television, or in some situations family and old friends.

The young man was familiar with all these expressions. He had often heard them through his involvement with Amway/Quixtar. His "sponsor" or "upline," who mentored him, sometimes spoke of them.

Reviewing this particular form of insider language and how it paralleled Lifton's definition of loaded language drew the young man's interest. He listened intently to the explanation of how such language could restrict critical thinking and ultimately constrict the mind itself. I commented how this might partly explain why people stayed in Amway, even when it didn't produce meaningful income. They were following "the plan" and caught between "chasing the dream" and being "negative."

We also discussed the environmental control exerted through Amway's subculture composed of "downlines" and "uplines." How much time did he actually spend with people outside those tied into the multi-level marketing company? Were his preexisting friendships outside of Amway being nurtured and meaningfully maintained, or were they withering and falling away? To what extent had Amway come to dominate his daily life and environment? How much significant feedback did he really receive from people outside the Amway subculture that now surrounded him?

These questions solicited answers from the young man that provided further evidence of the pervasiveness of Amway's influence in his life. He admitted that his time was increasingly taken up with Amway and that the people he now socialized with were largely other Amway distributors. We also discussed his attendance at Amway conferences, seminars, and meetings and looked at how the company and its supporters controlled these activities and environments.

Didn't all these factors contribute to the creation of a kind of encapsulated Amway world or subculture, in which only positive affirmations about the company were encouraged, recognized, and allowed? How could anyone within such a subculture meaningfully consider alternate ideas? Was it really possible for alternate ideas to penetrate this environment? Could any criticism of Amway and its business practices be seriously considered and thought through within this environment? These questions ended our first day.

At the beginning of the second day, we discussed in more detail how Amway, through its subculture and domination of time and associations, could be seen as what psychiatrist Robert Jay Lifton calls "Milieu Control."[1160] I asked whether it was possible that his new Amway life had effectively come to control much of his communication and had effectively shut out, dismissed, or eliminated anything negative that might contradict or criticize Amway's basic assumptions or its business plan. At this point the young man became uneasy and asked whether this meant that Amway was somehow engaged in what could be called "brainwashing."

Building on the thought-reform model, I cited another criterion Lifton described called "Sacred Science." That is, the group or organization encourages "an aura of sacredness around its basic dogma," and "this sacredness is evident in the prohibition (whether or not explicit) against the questioning of basic assumptions, and in the reverence which is demanded for the originators of the Word, the present bearers of the Word, and the Word itself."[1161]

I asked the young man whether seriously questioning the Amway business plan was possible. Would criticism of the plan be tolerated?

He answered that any distributor who criticized the business plan was likely to be pressured to cease such criticism. If the distributor persisted in criticism, he or she would probably be labeled as negative and made to feel so uncomfortable that he or she would leave Amway.

I asked whether the plan was possibly wrong in some aspect. Could Amway's business plan be improved based on constructive criticism— for example, addressing the issue of market saturation? The young man responded that he couldn't recall an instance when any mistakes or imperfection was acknowledged in regard to the Amway business plan. He added that if a distributor didn't get positive results through the plan, the failure was somehow due to that distributor's personal failure to execute the plan properly. There was never any criticism of the plan itself.

I asked him whether a perfect business plan actually existed. Didn't businesses frequently benefit by encouraging constructive criticism from within? Wouldn't acknowledging mistakes in a business plan lead to improvement, positive change, and a better business plan? Wouldn't an improved plan provide more profits? Wasn't that the goal of positive, evolving change? Isn't that often a goal of good business? The young man appeared perplexed but admitted that these were basic business principles that made sense; he'd studied them in college. His father interjected emphatically that all businesses were subject to changing conditions and that no business plan was perfect.

I then asked the young man another question. Did he feel there was noticeable reverence expressed toward the leaders in Amway who achieved elevated positions in the organizational multilevel marketing scheme, such as distributors who had reached the rank of "emerald" or "diamond"? He admitted that such people were greatly admired, if not revered, and put forth as examples or role models to be imitated. I mentioned that this reverence for the "bearers of the Word" or plan could be seen as another expression of "Sacred Science" in Amway. The young man appeared to be more interested in the process of coercive persuasion used to gain undue influence than in criticism of the business practices of Amway.

On the third day we delved into the subject of social influence. We discussed six basic principles of influence, which professor of psychology Robert Cialdini outlined.[1162] How might these principles be used to manipulate people in Amway? For example: "The principle of social proof…states that one means we use to determine what is correct is to find out what other people think is correct; the principle applies especially to the way we decide what constitutes correct behavior. We view a behavior as more correct in a given situation to the degree that we see others performing it."[1163] Cialdini elaborates, "Usually, when a lot of people are doing something, it is the right thing to do. This feature of the principle of social proof is simultaneously its major strength and its major weakness."[1164]

I asked whether it was possible that Amway had created a false social proof by using the company's relative control of the environment through its monopolization of the young man's time and social interactions. That is, if everyone around him was enthusiastically echoing and providing confirmation of Amway's business plan and saying it was wonderful through successive meetings, conferences, and social gatherings, did that influence his thinking? He agreed that social proof was a factor that initially encouraged and later intensified his participation in Amway.

We also explored how the interlocking principles of "liking" and "authority" might influence thinking in a multilevel marketing scheme. Specifically, it is true that "we most prefer to say yes to the requests of someone we know and like."[1165] For example, as Cialdini points out, "how much more difficult it is for us to turn down a charity request when it comes from a friend or a neighbor." The young man admitted that his relationships in Amway with people he liked had greatly contributed to his growing commitment and often served as a kind of organizational glue. He also acknowledged the powerful influence authority figures, such as emeralds and diamonds, exerted in Amway. We examined the "deep-seated sense of duty to authority within us all."[1166] Cialdini notes, "We are trained from birth that obedience to proper authority is right and disobedience is wrong."[1167] How had the powerful authority figures in Amway used the aura of authority to influence the thinking of distributors?

At this point during the third day, the young man broke down and began crying. He said that before our discussion began he'd had no idea how the organization manipulated him. But now that he had examined the process of coercive persuasion and the techniques commonly used to gain undue influence, he felt that he had been brainwashed and that this realization was deeply disturbing. I explained that the process people often call brainwashing is really quite subtle and comes on gradually in increments that are deceptive. I added that typically those the process exploits are therefore actually unaware of what is going on, and in this sense they never knowingly give their fully informed consent to go through such a process.

As the third day continued, we expanded our discussion of why people stay in multilevel marketing schemes such as Amway, even when they lose money or earn a minimal income that is inconsistent with the time they invest. Cialdini describes "our nearly obsessive desire to be (and to appear) consistent with what we have already done."[1168] This is accomplished through "personal and interpersonal pressures to behave consistently with that commitment. Those pressures will cause us to respond in ways that justify our earlier decision."[1169] This is the basis for the principles of "commitment and consistency," which Cialdini says can become the "hobgoblins of the mind."[1170]

We now discussed how the young man's hobgoblins of commitment had effectively anchored him to Amway so that he felt locked in by his commitment despite the financial setbacks and lack of meaningful income. The young man also explained that he had experienced pressure to remain—personally through his own sense of commitment and externally through other Amway distributors and "uplines." This, in part, explained his seeming determination to remain loyal to Amway despite whatever hardships occurred and the serious questions his concerned family and friends raised about the business.

As the day ended we discussed what sociologist Benjamin Zablocki calls the "exit costs" cult members consider as "disincentives for leaving." Zablocki lists "costs ranging from financial penalties, to relational commitments."[1171] I added that this might also include a sense of personal equity after much time, effort, and money have been invested and hardships endured.

At this point the young man looked at his parents and me and said he was done with Amway. Despite whatever exit costs existed, he had decided to stop being an Amway distributor. He explained that it was better to cut his losses now and move on than to suffer the probable greater costs of leaving later.

[1149] *Cambridge Dictionaries Online*, "market saturation," accessed May 29, 2014 http://dictionary.cambridge.org/us/dictionary/business-english/market-saturation.

[1150] Cary Spivak, "Study Concludes Wisconsin Casino Market Is Saturated," *Milwaukee Journal Sentinel*, September 27, 2012.

[1151] Dan Margolies, "Lawsuit Contends Amway's Profits Come Mostly out of Distributors' Pockets," *Kansas City Star*, August 12, 2003.

[1152] Jayne O'Donnell, "Motivational Marketing or Pyramid? Sales People Find it Hard to Earn Much," *USA Today*, February 10, 2011, http://usatoday30.usatoday.com/money/industries/retail/2011-02-07-multilevelmarketing03_CV_N.htm.

[1153] Chris Knape, "Amway Agrees to Pay $56 Million, Settles Case Alleging It Operated a 'Pyramid Scheme,'" *Michigan Live*, November 3, 2010.

[1154] Robert Jay Lifton, *Thought Reform and the Psychology of Totalism* (Chapel Hill: University of North Carolina Press, 2012), 429.

[1155] Dan Hansen, "Chasing The Dream: Amway Culture Has Own Vocabulary Glossary Offers Gateway Into Corporate Language," *Spokesman-Review* (Spokane, WA), October 13, 1996.

[1156] Ibid.

[1157] Ibid.

[1158] Ibid.

[1159] Ibid.

[1160] Lifton, *Thought Reform and the Psychology of Totalism*, 420–422.

[1161] Ibid., 427–429.

[1162] Robert B. Cialdini, *Influence: Science and Practice* (Needham Heights, MA: Allyn & Bacon, 2001).

[1163] Ibid., 117.

[1164] Ibid.

[1165] Ibid., 163.

[1166] Ibid., 208.

[1167] Ibid., 210.

[1168] Ibid., 66.

[1169] Ibid.

[1170] Ibid.

[1171] Benjamin D. Zablocki, "Exit Cost Analysis: A New Approach to the Scientific Study of Brainwashing," *Nova Religion* 2, no. 1 (1998): 219.

CHAPTER 22

FAILED INTERVENTIONS

It is important to understand the basis on which a successful intervention is determined. That is, what defines "success" and "failure" in my work as a professional consultant or cult-intervention specialist?

Success

Historically about 75 percent of the people who have retained me to help them due to concern about someone in a cultlike group or cultic situation have experienced a successful outcome. That is, by the end of our working relationship, the person who was the focus of concern ended his or her group involvement or cultic relationship.

It must be understood that my success rate includes all the people who have retained me. That means anyone who has paid me professional fees for assessment, consultation, or intervention work. This includes every billed client regardless of the level of work provided or amount of time spent in that working relationship.

Clients who retain me typically expect my work to culminate in an intervention effort. This usually means that there is a set date for the intervention, which is most often agreed on before I'm retained. The intervention typically takes three to four days.

Failure

A failure occurs when the person who is the focus of concern decides to stay with the cultlike group or leader despite the work I performed through the consultation or intervention effort.

The determination of whether my work has been a success or failure is therefore based on a simple question. Has the cult-involved person ended his or her involvement with the group or cultic situation as the direct result of my professional effort?

I have participated in approximately five hundred interventions (1982–2013). I don't typically follow up with clients unless they subsequently decide to contact me. This is my policy based on professional boundaries regarding respect for privacy. But some clients have decided to follow up with me, particularly if there is a problem.

I can recall only two or three occasions when former clients contacted me to say that a person who had decided to leave a group or cultic situation by the end of an intervention effort later changed his or her mind and returned to the same group or situation. Based on this feedback from former clients, the rate of relapse after an initially successful interventions would seem to be less than 1 percent. That is, less than 1 percent of the successful intervention outcomes were later reversed when a cult member changed his or her mind and returned to his or her former situation.

Some families have later contacted me to report that though they initially experienced failure through an intervention effort, which I facilitated, the person who was the focus of the intervention later decided to leave the group. This change of mind was largely due to the information they received and the dialogue that occurred during the intervention. Such outcomes have occurred numerous times. Based on this feedback from my former clients, it appears that the rate of such delayed departures substantially exceeds 1 percent.

Statistics

In recent years I have substantially changed the mix of my work. I no longer devote all my time to interventions. My work now includes court expert testimony, media consulting, and lectures. I focus much of my time on the Web presence of the Cult Education Institute, an on-line database and research library devoted to the study of controversial groups and movements, some of whom have been called "cults."

Between 2005 and 2013 seventy-seven clients retained me due to concerns about an individual involved in a cultic situation.

Based on the previously stated definitions for success and failure, my success rate within this historical group of clients (2005–2013) was 72.3 percent. That is, fifty-five clients experienced success when the individuals who had caused concern due to a cultic situation left that situation as the direct result of my work.

Among this same historical group, twenty-one clients experienced failure. That is, regardless of the professional services I provided, the person involved in the cultic situation didn't leave it. Two of these failures later resulted in people leaving a cultic situation, but this reversal didn't occur immediately at the conclusion of my work.

Communication and Access Are Crucial

The single most pivotal issue that provides the foundation for any cult intervention or consultation effort is meaningful access to the cult-involved individual. Many families who have contacted me over the years have said they have little to no contact with a loved one who is in a cultic group or under undue influence in some type of cultic situation. Readers must understand that without substantial communication and meaningful access, effectively planning for any sort of intervention is virtually impossible.

When such unfortunate and difficult circumstances exist, I recommend that those who are concerned develop coping and communication strategies that may ultimately lead to improved contact and regular access. Essentially such strategies include scrupulously avoiding confrontation, arguments, and the expression of negative sentiments. Instead they should focus on more positive things, such as continuing affirmation of family support and affection. Using such strategies (see the chapter on "Coping Strategies") can potentially produce a viable basis for an intervention, which can then be considered as a possible option.

My Shortest Intervention

Perhaps the briefest intervention of my career involved an American engineer who worked around the world. He retained me for an intervention effort focused on his former fiancée. The engineer had fallen in love while working in Europe. After becoming engaged, he brought his fiancée to the United States for an extended visit to meet his family. The engineer had previously met his fiancée's parents, sister, and friends while working in Italy. The young woman and her sister belonged to what seemed to be a very tight-knit social group. When the couple was in the United States, however, it became apparent to the engineer that a single leader actually dominated and controlled this close-knit group of friends.

During the couple's stay in the United States, the engineer began to question the constant phone calls between his fiancée and the group's leader. It seemed to him that there were no boundaries in this relationship and that the leader's advice was always adhered to without question; in fact, it governed every aspect of his fiancée's life. The engineer began to openly question the propriety of such profound influence, and after a somewhat heated discussion about this with his fiancée, she abruptly left the United States and returned to Europe. The engineer was devastated. He repeatedly tried to communicate with his estranged girlfriend, but she didn't respond.

The engineer then contacted me, hoping to arrange for an intervention. I explained that an intervention was impossible without meaningful communication and access. He said he would somehow devise a strategy to provide a point of access to his former girlfriend. The engineer insisted that he must at least try to approach her, and he came up with a precarious plan based on the return of his former fiancée's abandoned belongings, which she had left behind in the United States.

The engineer's plan revolved around shipping the baggage back to Italy and arranging for it to be returned to the young woman through an intermediary. He retained a private investigator in Italy. The private investigator called the young woman and advised her that he had received her luggage and boxed belongings sent from the United States, which she could pick up at his office at a scheduled time. The engineer said this would be the only opportunity for us to at least meet with her briefly. We would surprise her when she came to the office, and he hoped she would stay long enough for us to convince her to set aside more time for discussion in the following days.

I remained deeply skeptical that this approach had any hope of success, and I told the engineer his plan would most likely fail. He admitted that it was a desperate attempt but said this was the only way he could reliably contact her. The engineer believed, or wanted to believe, that somehow his plan would work, because his former fiancée still loved him.

I traveled to Italy, where I met the engineer and the private investigator. The private investigator provided us with additional detailed information. Though the group and its leader were relatively obscure, it had drawn some attention in this region of Italy, and people called it a "cult." The leader often recruited people through personal and family relationships. It seems likely that the leader may have believed he could recruit the engineer through his love interest.

The investigator had also interviewed the parents of the engineer's former fiancée. He told us that her older sister, an early devotee of the leader, had recruited her. We later met with her parents, who explained that both of their daughters had completely cut them off after they raised critical concerns about the group. It had been years since the mother or father communicated with either of their children. They were quite surprised but happy when their daughter briefly visited them accompanied by the engineer to announce her engagement. They didn't fully understand the situation, but hoped the marriage might end the leader's control over their daughter. Though sympathetic, the parents now felt that the situation was hopeless and wouldn't assist in any intervention effort.

We waited at the private investigator's office one morning to meet the young woman. As planned, she appeared promptly at the scheduled time to pick up her belongings. But when she saw us, she immediately became furious. The meeting ended quickly, in less than fifteen minutes, and was a complete failure. The only aspect of this effort that might be considered meaningful was that the engineer experienced a kind of closure. But he left Italy disappointed and heartbroken.

This failed intervention illustrates a very important point. Without ongoing communication and meaningful access, there is no basis for likely success through an intervention effort.

In my opinion, though a desperate approach like the one the engineer devised may at times be the only alternative, such an approach will most likely end in failure. If at all possible, waiting for a more viable alternative is almost always better. This may take considerable time and planning, and it may also involve some investigation to locate the cult-involved person and learn more about his or her daily life. For example, does he or she live independently or with members of a particular group? Is there any level of communication that currently exists and can be developed? Is there a possibility that the cult-involved person might visit family members or old friends outside the group? Does the cult-involved person communicate with anyone on a regular basis outside the group? Is he or she independently accessible in some other way through a workplace situation or somewhere else outside the group?

If the answers to such questions repeatedly lead to the conclusion that there is no way to communicate with, or have any meaningful access to, the cult-involved person, then there is no reason to retain a cult-intervention specialist or consultant. Before retaining a professional to further assess, prepare for, or plan for an intervention, there must be a basis for contact firmly established and created through improved communication and resulting in reliable and regular access. There's no need to hire a professional before this goal has been effectively reached.

Time Doesn't Always Equal Success

One failed intervention involved a married couple with children in the United States. The husband was the member of a secretive group for more than a decade. The group was so secretive that his wife didn't fully understand its existence or appreciate her husband's level of commitment. After some years of marriage, the husband finally introduced his wife to the group and its leader through private gatherings. After attending some of these meetings and a retreat, the wife determined that the group seemed to fit the definition of a destructive cult. That is, a living leader who was dictatorial and engaged in coercive persuasion for the explicit purpose of exploiting his or her followers dominated and defined the group.[1172] The wife contacted me to begin planning and preparing for an intervention.

Eventually with the husband's full knowledge and cooperation, the intervention took place. We agreed that we would spend five full days discussing destructive cults in general, the coercive persuasion techniques such groups use, the group the husband was involved in, and why his wife was concerned about it.

The husband was a very successful businessman and a generous supporter of the group and its leader. His financial support, along with the substantial contributions of other wealthy group members, afforded the leader a rather lavish lifestyle. Because of this and his many years of devotion, the husband held a position of special recognition and privilege in the group. Other group members treated him very respectfully, even deferentially, and the leader particularly honored him.

Each day during the intervention we spent about eight hours, going over detailed research regarding destructive cults, the dynamics of such groups, and how the husband's group specifically fit in this context. He didn't disagree that his group could be seen as a cult according to the cited common characteristics, but he repeatedly said he hadn't been personally harmed and was comfortable within it.

Former members of the group attended some of our meetings to discuss their perceptions of the leader. They offered a distinctly different perspective than the husband. Former members reported abuses in the group, which included excessive demands for payments that strained their finances. They also complained about the leader's micromanagement of their personal lives, which had caused harm to relationships. The husband's response was to simply say again and again that this hadn't been his experience; therefore, though some former members may have experienced some problems, they didn't concern him.

After days of discussion the intervention ended. The husband was unmoved and made it clear that he would continue as an active member of the group. Even when his wife threatened divorce, the husband remained adamant about his group commitment. The intervention was a failure. The couple soon separated and later divorced.

Looking back at this intervention effort, I see there was more than enough time to share the necessary information and discuss relevant concerns in considerable depth. But in my opinion this effort failed largely because the husband felt deeply invested in the group and enjoyed the personal attention he received. The leader made him feel very special. And his group involvement conferred on him a sense of esoteric status and empowerment. Through the group the husband felt that he had reached an elite level of awareness and was recognized as a philosopher. He seemed to think that without the group he would lose this special status.

After years of personal and financial investment, the husband also appeared to have a sense of equity in the group. In my opinion it was his perception of what has been called "exit costs"[1173] that basically blocked any serious consideration of leaving the group. Sociologist Benjamin Zablocki sees such exit costs as an important facet in the calculations of cult members. That is, such exit costs, as cult member perceive them, are "disincentives for leaving."[1174]

In most cases the more time during an intervention is allotted to discuss concerns, examine research, and compare the parallels between a particular group and other groups called "cults," the more likely it is that the intervention will end in success. But there are situations, despite the time spent, that may still end in failure. Each individual involved in a cult or cultic situation must ultimately face his or her personal exit costs based on his or her emotional needs and history.

Runaway

Another intervention centered on a nineteen-year-old girl. Her parents had been long-time members of a well-known cult when they decided to leave it. But they had raised their children in the group for many years. The couple's minor children willingly left the group with little problem, but their older sister refused to leave and was legally considered an adult.

The parents' cult departure caused a rift. Their eldest child left their home and moved in with another member of the group. Communication became strained, but the daughter continued to regularly call and visit with her family.

The parents retained me to undertake an intervention. The intervention took place in the context of a family visit with relatives in a neighboring city. Participants included the mother, father, an aunt, and an uncle. We all met in a hotel room where the family was staying. The uncle and aunt lived in town and also attended the initial meeting.

The intervention was difficult, and bursts of anger largely consumed the first day. Frequently the daughter angrily walked out of the hotel room and came back only after her uncle pursued her and persuaded her to return. Such interruptions occurred several times throughout the day.

A former member of the group participated in the intervention. Sharing her personal story of group involvement at a relatively high level of responsibility seemed to impress the daughter and stimulate her critical thinking. During the first day we were also able to review a substantial amount of research material specifically gathered about this particular group and its leadership. This historical documentation was difficult for the daughter to dispute but took time to digest.

At the end of our first day, the parents expected their daughter to stay overnight with them at the hotel. But she refused, insisting instead on staying at her uncle's nearby home. She agreed to return the following day to continue our discussion and promised not to communicate with the group or anyone associated with the group in any way, shape, or form until we had concluded our discussions.

Through the previous preparation process, the family knew the importance of closely monitoring the evenings between each intervention day. That is, every evening posed the potential for problems. We had discussed the need to closely watch their daughter throughout the intervention and pay particular attention to her communication. Everyone understood that this meant turning off cell phones and blocking Internet access through any device until the intervention effort was over. My concern, as always, was focused on contact with the group. If there was such contact, the group would certainly use it to obstruct or sabotage our effort. Cultic groups inherently know that the more time there is for discussion and sharing information about them through an intervention, the more likely it is that they will lose a follower.

Before the daughter left to stay with her uncle overnight, I briefed him again about the importance of blocking all contact and communication with the group and said he must watch over his niece until they returned the next day. The uncle assured me that he would closely monitor her and make sure there was no opportunity for her to make contact with members of the group. He would then bring her back to the hotel the following morning to resume the discussion.

But the nineteen-year-old never returned for a second day. The following morning her uncle left her alone in his house when he dropped his children off for school. When the uncle returned, his niece was gone. She had run away, and days passed before her parents knew where she had gone. The intervention had ended in failure.

The daughter probably intended to fulfill her commitments, but during an intervention cult members often feel conflicted between their loyalty to the group and whatever loyalty continues to remain intact regarding their families. An intervention can be stressful, and in that context a troubled cult member may reach out for guidance from the group, which has deliberately encouraged dependency on them for answers. For this reason I strongly suggest that families involved in an intervention closely monitor the situation and specifically any and all communication during the intervention process.

In my opinion this intervention might have been successful if the daughter hadn't been left alone. This opportunity allowed her to contact the group during a critical period. After the failed intervention the cultic group carefully controlled the daughter's communication with her family for many months, and she seemed to be somewhat scripted. There would be no opportunity for another intervention.

Internet Interference

Another of my failed interventions involved a husband who was concerned about his wife's involvement with a local group. The group, which its charismatic leader dominated and defined, was a small faction that had broken away from a much larger organization, which was frequently called a "cult."

The husband became concerned, because the group increasingly dominated his wife's time and thinking. The couple had a small child, and the teachings of the group, which largely focused on the evils of the world and an imminent apocalyptic end of the world, seemed terrifying. The group leader told his followers that they must prepare for doomsday. The husband's work required extensive travel. When he was away, his wife often took their child to group meetings.

Our intervention included the husband and his parents. He said his mother and stepfather were quite close to his wife and that she respected their judgment. We hoped their presence during the intervention would be helpful. I met with everyone the day before the intervention to explain the boundaries and components of our collective effort. I emphasized how important the role of the family would be in keeping the wife grounded, engaged, and interested.

We were in a somewhat isolated rural area, and neither the cultic group nor any of its members were nearby. The group building was located some distance from the house, so it would be rather difficult for the leader or group members to interfere. Nevertheless, I warned the family about phone and Internet access, and they agreed to have everything shut down.

The first day of the intervention went fairly well, though I was deeply disappointed by the mother and stepfather's level of participation. They didn't seem to have anything to say despite earlier conversation about their concerns during our preparation process. The wife was cooperative and courteous, though she scrupulously avoided any direct indication of her true feelings. She instead tried to alleviate any concerns by minimizing her level of involvement with the group.

By the end of the first day, we had covered quite a bit of ground, including research about cults in general and particularly about the larger organization, to which her group was historically linked. We also discussed in some depth the doomsday teachings of the leader of her group and noted that they were similar to groups called "doomsday cults." There were several contradictions in the group leader's teachings that didn't seem to make any sense. By the end of our day of discussion, the wife tacitly acknowledged that these contradictions existed and expressed some concern about them. We agreed to meet the following morning to begin our discussion again.

The second day, when the husband picked me up at my hotel, he said his parents would not be participating any further. He explained that they felt awkward and uncomfortable and had decided to leave. This was a disappointment that certainly compromised the effectiveness of the continuing intervention effort. And this is why it's so important to make sure anyone agreeing to participate in an intervention is completely supportive and will see it through to the conclusion. Unfortunately the husband's parents decided to do otherwise.

When we arrived at the house, his wife seemed greatly changed. She was curt and argumentative rather than the courteous, open person I had met the previous day. We picked up the discussion about the leader's teachings and how at times they seemed confusing and contradictory. The wife's response now appeared almost rehearsed. When I pressed the wife about what source of information she relied on to form her opinions, she admitted that she had studied the group's website overnight. The husband had failed to disconnect the Internet access, as we had agreed.

When I tried to unwind the group's explanation of seemingly contradictory teachings for the purpose of closer examination, the wife became angry. Rather than engage in an analysis of the material posted at the group website, the wife insisted that we end our conversation and soon left the room. Now only the husband was there to persuade his wife to resume the dialogue. He couldn't convince her to continue. The intervention ended in failure.

In my opinion this intervention effort primarily failed for two reasons. First, the family couldn't pull together consistently and support the effort all the way through. Having the right people involved when undertaking an intervention is vitally important. If someone is ambivalent about the effort, he or she shouldn't become involved. Instead, hopefully others can be found who can be more supportive and consistently provide a better basis for success.

In addition, despite my warnings, the husband decided not to disconnect Internet access at the house. He later explained this was because he was afraid his wife would be angry if she later found out he had done this. The husband's failure to follow through on this important point, however, allowed his wife to download scripted answers from the group rather than to engage in independent critical thinking. The wife had promised not to contact the group during the intervention but rationalized that visiting the group website was somehow not the equivalent of directly contacting group members.

Breakdown

A family contacted me regarding concerns about their son, who had recently returned home after prolonged involvement with a certain highly demanding group. His behavior was now erratic, and the parents were concerned that their son had been brainwashed.

Substantial historical documentation was available about this particular group through news reports and court records. The organization had often been called a "cult." I assembled a file and flew in to prepare the family for the intervention. When I met with them the day before the intervention, we discussed what could potentially go wrong and what our respective roles would be during the process.

On the day of the intervention, when I met the son for the first time, talking with him was difficult. Hours passed, but we were unable to maintain an ongoing exchange of ideas. He would talk—often, it seemed, to himself—then drift away into an apparent alternate world of his own, disconnected from his surroundings.

After almost a day of the parents and me trying to engage the young man, without success, I asked his mother and father to meet with me privately in another room. I explained that it was impossible for me to share information without a meaningful level of communication. I advised the parents to seek help from a doctor in their local area. The situation was outside my expertise, and I couldn't help them.

Later doctors established that the young man had experienced a kind of mental breakdown, and he was hospitalized. His cultic involvement may have caused this in part, or there may have been an underlying condition his group involvement somehow exacerbated. In any event the problem wasn't something an intervention could address; it instead required the immediate attention of a doctor.

Hopefully, these examples of failed interventions can help those who are concerned better understand the possible problems that may develop during an effort.

It has been said that whenever information is shared during an intervention, the effort can be seen as successful. When families retain a cult-intervention consultant, however, they usually expect much more defined results. That is why I have very specifically defined the net result of a successful intervention. That is, the person who is the focus of the intervention decides to leave the group or cultic situation by the conclusion of that effort.

It's important to reiterate again that meaningful communication and access are the foundations for any intervention. Until those crucial elements or ingredients are developed or are evident, there is no need to retain a specialist or consultant for an assessment or to prepare for an intervention.

[1172] Robert Jay Lifton, "Cult Formation," *Harvard Mental Health Letter*, February 1981.

[1173] Benjamin D. Zablocki, "Exit Cost Analysis: A New Approach to the Scientific Study of Brainwashing," *Nova Religion* 2, no. 1 (1998).

[1174] Ibid., 219.

CHAPTER 23

MOVING ON

Generally most cult members eventually move on and leave the group. Sadly, this separation may take place after they have experienced years of deception, exploitation, and destructive consequences in their personal lives. Cult members frequently experience psychological, emotional, and at times physical or sexual abuse. The experience of each former cult member will vary according to his or her individual involvement in the group and its level of destructive behavior.

Members in many destructive cults are encouraged to become increasingly dependent through the use of coercive persuasion techniques. The net result of such cultic manipulation culminates in a form of undue influence. In this state of mind, the cult member is induced to accept erroneous perspectives, such as that individual autonomy or independent thinking is somehow an expression of arrogance, inflated ego, pride, or even "sinful." The cult member is coerced to accept that others must make decisions and value judgments for him or her.

Even though most cult members live at home, work at a regular job, and don't reside in a compound, they can nevertheless become isolated through their immersion in the group, which dominates most, if not all, of their otherwise free time. Due to this immersion, cult members become increasingly dependent on the group or leader. This is often because they have been largely cut off from the outside world.

In this state of relative isolation, they may develop unreasonable fears about leaving the group, seemingly irrational concerns about outsiders, and an apparent disconnection from reality. This may include the fear that the cult or leader might retaliate in some way if they left. This fear of retaliation by former cult members is most often exaggerated or misplaced, but it may take time for it to dissipate. It's important to recognize that such unreasonable fears former cult members express are not unusual and are actually quite common.

Psychologist Margaret Singer said this cultic mind-set was the cumulative result of what she called "the five Ds," which includes deception, debilitation, dependency, dread, and desensitization.[1175]

In their book *Snapping: America's Epidemic of Sudden Personality Change*, authors Flo Conway and Jim Siegelman recounted information they had gathered after disseminating one thousand questionnaires to former cult members throughout the United States and Canada. They received four hundred responses from people who had spent time in forty-eight different groups called "cults."[1176]

A substantial percentage of former cult members reported back to Conway and Siegelman that they experienced "ongoing problems of confusion, disorientation and dissociation."[1177] The authors found that two-thirds of the respondents experienced substantial residual emotional difficulties. "One in six reported hallucinations or delusions for up to twelve years after leaving their groups."[1178] One former cultist said, "It hurts to think, it physically aches."[1179] According to their survey results, the substantial recovery from a cultic experience took "on an average sixteen months."[1180] Conway and Siegelman specifically noted that "the psychological trauma the new sects and therapies may inflict on their members is directly proportional to the amount of time people spend in mind-altering rituals and self-help practices."[1181]

Conway and Siegelman also reported that "one in five of [their] survey respondents experienced some physical health problem."[1182] Dr. Cathleen Mann, a PhD in psychology, has been a licensed counselor for over eighteen years and has helped many former cult members. According to Mann the first priority for every exiting cult member is a medical checkup. She says, "Since most cults use a drastic change in diet, sleep deprivation, over activity, assaults to the body in other ways, it is highly likely that the former member has potential physical consequences."[1183]

Other studies of former cult members seem to confirm a similar pattern of results regarding the negative effects cultic involvement produces. One such study included sixty-six former members of Rev. Moon's Unification Church and was published in the *American Journal of Psychiatry*. It found that 36 percent of the former members experienced emotional problems after leaving and that 61 percent said church leaders had "negatively impacted" their lives.[1184][1185]

A study of the American Family Foundation (AFF), now known as the International Cultic Studies Association (ICSA), yielded a similar pattern of results. The AFF/ICSA study included 308 former members of 101 groups called "cults."[1186] About 67 percent experienced emotional disorders including depression, 76 percent were angry with their former leaders, and 83 percent had lower self-confidence. These results are quite comparable to those previously reported through the surveys Conway and Siegelman took.[1187]

Mann notes that "the scant research we have is anecdotal and consists of former members' self-report." She warns about unfounded assumptions. "I think the most troubling problem is twofold: (1) assuming everyone from a particular group is always traumatized at all or in the same way; and (2) presenting specialized counseling as the only solution." Mann concludes, "This is problematic because it strikes at a person's ability to make informed choices about counseling and because counseling does not work for everyone."[1188] It is important to keep in mind that destructive cults and leaders often present themselves as the single solution.

Those hoping to help former cult members must not impose their assumptions or solutions on them as the cult once did. Instead, information must be transparently shared about various alternatives and choices regarding recovery.

Singer said, "Most persons leaving cults are not severely mentally ill, but those occasional ones who are should, of course, be referred to a psychiatrist or psychologist knowledgeable about cults."[1189] A persistent myth concerning cult involvement is that it can be explained by some preexistent and underlying mental illness or condition. In fact, the overwhelming majority of cults reject those who are mentally or physically ill and are interested only in recruiting high-functioning, healthy, and therefore potentially useful people.

Singer observed, "Most cult veterans are neither grossly incompetent nor blatantly disturbed. But they report and their families confirmed cognitive inefficiencies and crucial changes that take time to pass. Excultists often have trouble putting into precise words these inefficiencies, which they want to explain." Singer characterizes this temporary cognitive disability as a combination of both the "blurring of mental acuity" along with "uncritical passivity." [1190]

When someone leaves a cultic situation, confronting him or her with criticism, a judgmental attitude, or blame is unwise. It is also incorrect to assault him or her with negative attacks concerning his or her former group or leader. Instead, be a good listener. Remember that a destructive cult cannot be all bad and that there may have been some positive aspects or associations linked to cultic involvement. Time in the group or under the undue influence of a leader may have produced some positive changes, developments, or realizations. It's important for those who are concerned not to make sweeping generalizations and needlessly negative comments. Destructive cults prey on and exploit human frailties and emotions to fulfill their needs. Those hoping to help former cult members must recognize their fragility and be sensitive to their situation.

Don't be critical of spirituality, idealism, or some form of awareness. The stated goals and ideals of the group may have been laudable despite the bad behavior. No one willingly joins a "cult" or volunteers to be abused and exploited. People are essentially tricked into cultic involvement.

Don't try to convince or convert a former cult member regarding a certain set of beliefs. Respect individual expression and the personal process of discovery. Each former cult member must begin to make his or her own choices, free of coercive persuasion and undue influence.

As the surveys indicate, many cult members may take some time redeveloping their critical-thinking skills and beginning to think independently again. Likewise, their ability to tolerate ambiguity may slowly return. No one can reasonably expect an instant, overnight transformation after departing from a cultic situation.

Placing pressure on former cult members to speed up the process is also unwise. As Conway and Siegelman noted, the longer a person has been in a destructive cult, the longer it may take him or her to sort things out and regain his or her past cognitive abilities. This may also depend on the severity of the group or leader. Some groups called "cults" are more destructive than others. Conway and Siegelman found that this was true depending upon the degree of personal involvement and the level of destructive behavior and control within a particular group.

Because there are so few support groups devoted to the issue of cult involvement, simply reading books on the subject of cults and thought reform may be easier. It is also possible to gather historical informa- tion about cults and their coercive persuasion techniques through the World Wide Web. Understanding the common elements of deception, coercive persuasion, and undue influence inherently present in de- structive cults may help to sort through postcult issues and serve to assuage unreasonable fears, ease stress, and reduce anxiety.

The family and friends of a former cult member may also require help understanding cultic influence to better cope with someone who has re- cently ended such a situation. Again, this can be accomplished through a similarly focused educational process, which includes reading helpful books about cults and relevant research. Much like a former cult member who is coming to terms with the broader context of his or her involvement by learning about how cults affect others, family and friends can also ben- efit by broadening their knowledge base in regard to this subject.

Not placing blame on the family is also important. Mann states, "We do know that there is no connection in the research between family dysfunction, prior mental illness, or 'looking for answers' and cult involvement." She points out, "Blaming historical and familial pro- cesses takes the onus of responsibility from the deception of cult re- cruiters, and places it on the cult member."[1191]

Some people who leave cults become activists, hoping to help others. They may do so by sharing their cult experience with others in the hope that such knowledge will help others avoid destructive cults. Or former cult members may try to help those left behind in the group to leave as they have done. This may produce positive results and per- haps provide a sense of empowerment or closure in regard to their own past cult involvement.

But it is practical and important to take care of personal priorities first. Former cult members are not obligated to become activists, and most do not. Most simply move on. If someone has left behind family members in a particular group, it may be more important to preserve whatever goodwill and communication is possible rather than to engage in activism against the group.

Australian Jan Groenveld, a former member of controversial religious groups, began her cult education work in 1979. She said, "After 15 years wandering through the world of the cults, including time in both Mormonism and Jehovah's Witnesses, I finally realized that I was being controlled rather than controlling my own life. I found myself alone with no access to information that would help me recover."[1192]

In an effort to "make it easier for others," Groenveld launched a website in 1990 to share information through the Internet. Her website, Cult Awareness and Information Centre (CAIC), explains, "The Internet is the only medium where both cult members and nonmembers are on a level playing field."[1193]

Groenveld, like many others who have left cultic situations, suffered through what was sometimes a painful transition back to mainstream life. She explained some of the pitfalls of this process in an article widely posted on the World Wide Web titled "It Hurts."[1194]

Jonestown survivor Deborah Layton explains, "It's an abusive relationship. Often by the time you figure that out it's too late, because you can't see how to extricate yourself without hurting yourself or your family. You are like a caged animal."[1195] Groenveld laments the loss. "Leaving a cult is like experiencing the death of a close relative or a broken relationship…like having been betrayed by someone with whom you were in love. You feel you were simply used." Groenveld describes her subsequent "grieving process." She explains, "Most people understand that a person must grieve after a death, [but] they find it difficult to understand the same applies in this situation." This grieving process includes the recognition of painful feelings, which are the direct result of the deception and harm done by a cultic experience.

Nori Muster, a longtime devotee of the International Society of Krishna Consciousness (ISKCON) who later left the movement, noted deception in the recruitment process. "I don't know that they actually join ISKCON, They come to the temple, but that's something different."[1196] Muster was once ISKCON's public relations secretary and editor of its newspaper. After she left, Muster wrote a book about the abuses in ISKCON titled *Betrayal of The Spirit*.[1197] These abuses caused many members to leave.[1198] Groenveld said that the sense of betrayal many former cult members feel cuts deep. "It hurts to discover you were deceived [by]...people you trusted implicitly, whom you were taught not to question." And it hurts "when you learn that those you were taught were your 'enemies' were telling the truth after all."

Jayanti Tamm was born into a group called a "cult" led by Guru Sri Chinmoy. She writes, "Cults are designed to keep a clear separation between those inside and outside. The more faithful a follower, the more reliant the person is on the group. It becomes everything—family, friends, church, home, work, dwelling, community. Extracting oneself from that after decades is difficult, and sometimes impossible. It is both terrifying and isolating."[1199] Like Muster, Tam later wrote a book about her experience titled *Cartwheels in Sari*.[1200] Groenveld relates how difficult it can be to "start all over again" and that there may be profound sadness if substantial time has been lost. "Your self-confidence and self-worth are almost non-existent," she said.[1201]

Tamm describes the mind-set many cult members have when considering another life in the outside world. "It's hard to leave and finally admit that what you put your whole life into is something that isn't really true," she said.[1202] Groenveld says that shame may follow such a realization about "what you were" and a terrible feeling that "you are all alone." This is coupled with a painful realization that the "love and acceptance" once experienced within the group "was conditional" and dependent on "remaining a member of good standing." Groenveld even wondered if she might be "better off" back in the group. She also experienced a longing "for the security…in the organization" despite the knowledge that she could never "go back."

Conway and Siegelman found that deprogramming was beneficial to cult members. About 73 percent of the former cult members they surveyed had been deprogrammed, half on a voluntary basis and the other half on an involuntary basis through an intervention. "As a group, they reported a third less, and in many cases only half as many, post-cult effects than those who weren't deprogrammed," the authors said.[1203] There was also a significant difference in recovery time for those who had been deprogrammed. "Average rehabilitation time was one-third longer—more than a year and half—for those who weren't deprogrammed compared to just over a year for those who were. Overall, deprogrammees reported a third fewer months of depression, forty percent less disorientation [and] half as many sleepless nights."[1204]

When commenting about former cult members who hadn't gone through a formal intervention, Singer said, "It has become apparent that participation in an exit-counseling session is far better than ordinary psychiatric or psychological treatment…for helping those who have already left but are having trouble understanding and handling what went on during their cult days and the types of problems they are experiencing in the aftermath of their cult involvement."[1205]

Singer cites two reasons why the educational process of a cult intervention is preferable to psychiatric or psychological treatment. "First, former cult members need information and explanations about what produced changes in them while they were in the cult," she said. Singer's second reason cited is that "ordinary psychiatric and psychological counseling focuses almost exclusively on early life experiences and childhood history and the impact of these early years." Singer calls this "a blind spot." Instead the psychologist states that the focus must be "on adult experiences of intense social influence and group situations."[1206]

The cult "deprogramming," process has often helped cult members sort through their experience and formed the foundation for their recovery. Singer notes, "I have noticed that those who have deprogrammed or counseled out make the easiest, best, and quickest returns to normal life."[1207]

Mann also sees the second necessary step for former cult members after addressing possible health concerns is "an educational process in critical thinking." She explains, "Critical thinking is not mere recitation of criticism of the group, but is a process by which former members learn the basis of rational thought, skepticism, deductive and inductive reasoning, and recognizing logical fallacies to premises of indoctrination practices." Mann clarifies, "This needs to be education, not therapy," and it "is an important preliminary step that should occur before any counseling is considered."[1208]

Wellspring Retreat is a licensed mental health facility in Ohio. Founded in 1986, the short-term residential retreat features a program focused on the recovery of former cult members. Founder and psychologist Dr. Paul Martin explains, "The program is intensive, but also specialized. Much of the early segment of the treatment program is geared to increasing ex-members' understanding about the dynamics of thought reform and helping them explore how their group practiced thought reform and how the thought reform program affected their personality and their relationship to the world outside the cult."[1209] Martin adds, "Wellspring's approach to treating the dissociation begins therapy by reconstructing the client's experiences in terms of a systems model of thought reform. Typically, clients' awareness of what happened to them is restricted because they lack a conceptual framework that can adequately attach meaning to their experiences."[1210]

Some cult members leave one group only to join another similar group. Many former cult members never effectively sort through what went wrong, what caused them to leave, and why. Many blame themselves or others outside the group rather than analyze the destructive internal dynamics of their former group or criticize a leader. Singer says some cult members can "debrief themselves of the cult experience through reading, contact with other ex-members, and in some cases therapy dealing with cult-related issues before they come to understand the impact that the cult experience has and on their emotional and daily life."[1211]

Mann notes, "Many former cult members recover by themselves over time." She adds, "We do know that counseling is not an answer for everything." It also must be noted that the effectiveness and scientific basis for some forms of counseling has been called into question by the critical analysis provided in books like *Science and Psuedoscience in Clinical Psychology*.[1212] Mann says that there are "varying degrees of harm from any one cult to any one individual." She warns that failing to recognize such variations and distinctions is a "common mistake."[1213]

Singer categorizes the difficulties that emerge for many former cultists during their postcult adjustment period. Much like Groenveld, Singer focuses on what hurts most when cult members decide to move on. There is guilt, shame, self-blaming, unreasonable fear, and excessive doubt. In some very extreme situations, there is even the possibility of panic attacks. There can be a sense of loneliness after leaving such a tightly knit social environment.[1214] Singer says, "Each former member wrestles with a number of the problems…Some need more time than others to resolve all the issues they face, and a few never get their lives going again."[1215]

Groenveld once described her temporary deficiencies and said she found it "difficult to make decisions" and at times thought she had "lost touch with reality."[1216] To move on effectively, Singer says that former cult members must build "a new social network." In some situations "former cult members often feel like immigrants or refugees entering a foreign culture," the psychologist says. But Singer adds, "In most cases, however, they are actually reentering their own former culture...Unlike the immigrant confronting novel situations, the person coming out of a cult is confronting the society she or he once rejected."[1217]

Singer warned about what she called "the 'fishbowl' effect,"[1218] which is the feeling that family and friends are closely watching a former cult member and fearing that almost anything might cause him or her to go back. To avoid that effect, family and friends can be sympathetic and supportive but not hovering and controlling.

Other issues former cult members may be challenged by include "aversions and hypercritical attitudes" the cult inculcated and nurtured. Also, as a direct result of the pain and sense of betrayal felt over their past commitment, former cult member may develop a "fear of commitment."[1219] But Singer says they must overcome such disillusionment and learn how to trust again.[1220] This can be done based on their new knowledge, increased awareness, and ongoing interaction with the world around them.

According to the AFF/ICSA study, "As ex-cultists come to understand the mechanisms operating in the cultic environment, they become more capable of effectively grieving the loss of friends, time, career pursuits, idealism, and other aspirations that were lost as a result of spending time in and leaving the cult."[1221]

Despite the difficulties and pain Jan Groenveld went through, she said, "Yes it hurts, but the hurts will heal with time, patience and understanding. There is life after the cult."[1222] After twenty-five years of cult life, Jayanti Tamm moved on and made a life of her own. She married, had a daughter, and eventually became an English professor.[1223]

Singer concludes, "A free mind is a wonderful thing. Free minds have discovered the advances of medicine, science, and technology; have created great works of art, literature, and music; and have our rules of ethics and the laws of civilized lands."

The end of a cult experience can be the beginning of an educational process of discovery about how cultic, coercive persuasion and undue influence take place. This can potentially be both a life-affirming and personally enriching journey. Many former cult members develop deep insights and a keen appreciation of what it means to critically think and function independently. Perhaps more than most people, they have come to fully understand the value of a free mind.

A sure sign that a former cult member has resolved to move on in his or her recovery process is criticism of his or her former group and a willingness to understand the deceptive and manipulative techniques that led to his or her recruitment and continued cult involvement. Finding critical balance and integration regarding the cultic experience, based on an individual's personal situation and needs, is the ideal goal for a successful recovery.

[1175] Margaret Singer, *Cults in Our Midst* (San Francisco, CA: Jossey-Bass, 1996), 270.

[1176] Ibid., 188.

[1177] Flo Conway and Jim Siegelman, *Snapping: America's Epidemic of Sudden Personality Change*, 2nd ed. (New York: Stillpoint Press, 2005), 187.

[1178] Ibid., 191.

[1179] Ibid., 192.

[1180] Ibid., 193.

[1181] Ibid.

[1182] Ibid., 191.

[1183] Cathleen Mann, e-mail message to author, May 21, 2013.

[1184] M. Galanter, "Unification Church 9 'Moonie' Dropouts: Psychological Readjustment after Leaving a Charismatic Religious Group," *American Journal of Psychiatry* 140 (1983): 984–989.

[1185] Conway and Siegelman, *Snapping: America's Epidemic of Sudden Personality Change*, 199.

[1186] Paul R. Martin, "Post-Cult Symptoms as Measured by the MCMI before and after Residential Treatments," *Cultic Studies Journal* 9, no. 2 (1992): 219–250.

[1187] Conway and Siegelman, *Snapping: America's Epidemic of Sudden Personality Change*, 199.

[1188] Mann, e-mail message to author.

[1189] Singer, *Cults in Our Midst*, 295.

[1190] Margaret Singer, "Coming Out of Cults," *Psychology Today*, January 1979.

[1191] Mann, e-mail message to author.

[1192] "About Jan Groenveld," Cult Awareness and Information Centre (CAIC), http://www.culthelp.info/index.php?option=com_content&task=view&id=2&Itemid=3 (accessed May 28, 2014).

[1193] "What Is CAIC," Cult Awareness and Information Centre (CAIC), http://www.culthelp.info/index.php?option=com_content&task=view&id=3&Itemid=4 (accessed May 28, 2014).

[1194] Jan Groenveld, "It Hurts," Cult Awareness and Information Centre (CAIC), http://www.culteducation.com/group/17915-it-hurts.html (accessed May 28, 2014).

[1195] Andrew Gumbel, "'A Cult Is like Abusive Relationship...You Are Trapped, like a Caged Animal,'" *The Independent* (London), March 20, 2000.

[1196] Dorie Clark, "Where Have All the Krishnas Gone?" *Boston Phoenix*, February 2, 2001.

[1197] Nori Muster, *Betrayal of the Spirit: My Life behind the Headlines of the Hare Krishna Movement* (Champaigne, IL: University of Illinois Press, 2001).

[1198] Sujor Dhar, "Sex, Drugs, Embezzlement Chant Today's Hare Krishna," *Asian Times Online*, July 25, 2001, http://atimes.com/ind-pak/CG25Df05.html (accessed May 29, 2014).

[1199] Jayanti Tamm, "Leaving a Cult," *Washington Post*, April 2, 2009.

[1200] Jayanti Tamm, *Cartwheels in a Sari: A Memoir of Growing Up Cult* (New York: Harmony, 2009).

[1201] Groenveld, "It Hurts."

[1202] Colin Gustafson, "Greenwich Native Calls Chinmoy's Ministry a 'Cult,'" *Greenwich Time* (Greenwich, CT), June 12, 2009.

[1203] Conway and Siegelman, *Snapping: America's Epidemic of Sudden Personality Change*, 197.

[1204] Ibid.

[1205] Ibid.

[1206] Singer, *Cults in Our Midst*, 296.

[1207] Ibid., 297.

[1208] Mann, e-mail message to author.

[1209] Martin, "Post-Cult Symptoms as Measured by the MCMI before and after Residential Treatments," 219–250.

[1210] Ibid.

[1211] Singer, *Cults in Our Midst*, 296.

[1212] Scott O. Lilienfeld, Steven Jay Lynn, and Jeffrey M. Lohr, *Science and Pseudoscience in Clinical Psychology* (New York: Wiley, 2004).

[1213] Mann, e-mail message to author.

[1214] Ibid., 300–301.

[1215] Ibid., 304.

[1216] Groenveld, "It Hurts."

[1217] Ibid., 319.

[1218] Ibid., 323.

[1219] Ibid., 324.

[1220] Ibid., 332.

[1221] Martin, "Post-Cult Symptoms as Measured by the MCMI before and after Residetial Treatments."

[1222] Groenveld, "It Hurts."

[1223] Nanette Morges, "Growing Up Cult in Connecticut," *The Hour* (Norwalk, CT), July 14, 2009.

POSTSCRIPT

It has been decades since the cult phenomenon first impacted public consciousness through the fund-raising and recruitment tactics of the Unification Church ("Moonies") and International Society of Krishna Consciousness ("Hare Krishnas"). In 1978 Jonestown, the utopian dream turned nightmare, claimed the lives of more than nine hundred people, including hundreds of children. Much has changed since then, and much has remained the same. Incredible changes in technology have provided previously unimaginable access to information about cults, quite literally at the fingertips of people around the world. But the problems destructive cults pose have remained the same.

The primary issue that continues to concern the public is the harm destructive cults do. Leaders may preach and teach people whatever they wish, but concerns arise when harm is done in the name of those beliefs and teachings. This harm has included such serious consequences as deaths due to medical neglect, orchestrated suicides, murders, subway gassing, suicide bombers and self-immolation.

In recent years the ubiquitous nature of cults has become evident and more commonplace. The larger organized groups called "cults," such as Scientology, the International Society of Krishna Consciousness, and the Unification Church, have continued and become more established, while small groups called "cults" have proliferated across the modern landscape. These smaller groups, often with fewer than one hundred members, operate largely unnoticed until a tragedy occurs and attracts media attention.

Small cults may operate from a house in a residential neighborhood or from a retreat in a rural area. There are evidently thousands of such groups in the United States alone, and the proliferation of such small cults continues to be a growing global phenomenon. Some governments have taken steps to reign in the excesses of such groups through law enforcement, while others have, to some extent, ignored them. In the United States some religious cults have historically used the First Amendment of the Constitution, which guarantees freedom of religion, as a shield to protect them from legal consequences regarding their bad behavior.

The new interconnectivity and ubiquitous access to information, which the Internet has wrought and the relatively new social media has furthered and allowed us to watch such behavior in virtual real time. This same technology has also allowed law enforcement, child welfare, and health and protection services the ability to monitor the harm cults do much more closely than ever before.

Destructive cults have also effectively used the World Wide Web and expanding social media and have employed new technologies to their advantage. This has included the use of websites and online videos as promotional, fund-raising, and recruitment tools. This new technology has also facilitated networking between disparate groups—for example, the networking of hate groups in certain countries and increasingly on a global scale.

Despite the advantages new information technologies provide, the advent of the so-called Information Age has proven to be more of a bane than a blessing for destructive cults. Today people can do a simple search using the Internet and quickly access information about a controversial group, movement, or leader from their home, office, or almost anywhere using a handheld device. This easy access to information afforded through ever-improving technology has made it more difficult for destructive cults to deceive the public or obscure their history. Almost instantly anyone can find historical information about cults through online archived news reports, public records, or complaints about a group or leader by former members or other concerned parties.

One of the most pivotal features of any destructive cult's process of coercive persuasion and its ability to maintain undue influences is the control of information. But it has become increasingly difficult for cults to block access to such critical information due to the Internet. As a direct result many organizations called "cults," such as Scientology, have found it virtually impossible to contain their secrets or deny their recorded history.

In an effort at damage control, some groups have prohibited members from using the Internet, while others have encouraged the use of limiting software or modified devices. Inevitably information released or made available through the Internet spreads across the World Wide Web and cannot ever be reliably contained again. New information technology has forever changed the ability of cults to effectively conceal or withhold information, and many people have ultimately left cults as a direct result of this reality.

Nevertheless an unsettling aspect of our modern information age and the advent of social media is the potential for cultlike cocooning, which can take place whenever groups or individuals either intentionally or unintentionally filter their world.

This cocooning can effectively occur when we choose to access news only through preferred sources that represent a certain point of view. Such cocooning can also be accomplished by selectively communicating with our chosen friends on Facebook and following our favorites on Twitter, who likewise reflect a similar point of view. This effect can be augmented by repeatedly watching narrowly focused YouTube channels, listening to a chosen list of talk radio personalities, and relying on the opinions of bloggers who express the same world view. This can create a kind of bubble or what has been called an "echo chamber" or "alternate universe."

This virtual bubble of relative isolation, which only "true believers" inhabit while reinforcing groups and people, can become relatively resistant and rather watertight to any outside frame of reference, alternate ideas, or perspectives, regardless of the facts. This cocooning can promote what can be seen as a kind of cultlike mind-set, which includes an inherent "we vs. them" mentality. This cocooning phenomenon may explain the growing societal polarization that now appears to be intensifying in the United States.

But cultlike bubbles of isolation using the tools modern information technology and communication has provided is not just an American phenomenon; it can potentially occur anywhere in the world as people increasingly go online and become connected.

Virtual communities or subcultures can gather and easily flock together through the Internet. In this sense our easy access to information can be used either positively for education and increased awareness or negatively as a means to isolate people and cut them off from reality.

In an effort to use the Internet for the purpose of education about destructive cults and coercive persuasion, I launched a website archive in 1996. The site was first known as simply RickRoss.com, but as it grew exponentially, it eventually became the Ross Institute of New Jersey, which was granted tax-exempt, educational nonprofit status. The Ross Institute website continues to evolve as an online database research resource and is now known as the Cult Education Institute, an institutional member of both the American and New Jersey library associations

It is my hope that more online libraries devoted to the research and study of destructive cults will be made available free to the general public. By having information about cults immediately accessible to anyone through the Internet, deceptive cult-recruitment tactics are directly impacted. People who are able to access this information before cult groups approach them are better informed and prepared to resist their recruitment tactics. Online historical information about specific groups can also provide balance when someone is considering association with a certain group.

In this sense Internet archives provide the basis for an inoculation against the harm destructive cults do by serving as a public educational resource. This includes both information about cultic coercive persuasion techniques and what might otherwise be the hidden histories of particular groups. Such online educational resources can also serve former cult members by helping them to more easily sort through and understand what happened to them as a result of involvement with a destructive cult.

Law enforcement and other regulatory authorities around the world have increasingly taken a firmer stance regarding the criminal activities of destructive cults and fanatical fringe groups. Once there seemed to be a certain level of expediency that existed concerning the activities of such groups. But more commonly today, cults that hurt people are being held accountable—for example, the many arrests and prosecutions of parents in faith healing groups in the United States. Previously when children died in such groups due to medical neglect, the authorities often failed to take any meaningful action. The trend today in America is that parents who neglect their children to death will be arrested, prosecuted, and sentenced to prison time. Adults within some faith healing groups may believe the rejection of modern medicine is a religious right, but the US courts have ruled that they have no right to impose that belief on children and prevent proper medical care.

The well-being and proper care of minor children in cults have become a growing focal point of interest and public concern. In the

United States adults have the right to be affiliated with any group, including hate groups, extremists, and destructive cults. But that right of association doesn't include subjecting minor children to abuse. One of the most disturbing realities about destructive cults is that minor children in them are never allowed an alternative choice. Law enforcement, child welfare agencies, and public health and labor authorities must respond quickly to any allegations of abuse to protect the most vulnerable members of destructive cults, the children.

As the world seems to grow smaller every day through ever-expanding communication and the global sharing of information, we have come to collectively realize that the problems posed by destructive cults aren't restricted to any one country or continent. Cult tragedies have occurred on every region of the globe and caused many governments concern. History has proved that the cult phenomenon isn't somehow restricted to a particular country, continent, race, or ethnic group. Instead it is a reality that can potentially affect anyone around the world. For this reason sharing what we now know about this problem is an important tool in beginning to solve it or at least to lessen the damage destructive cults do.

As the world faces the continuing problems of fanaticism and terrorism, we often see the same mind-set. That is, extremists in groups can be manipulated and motivated through a process of recruitment and retention not unlike cult brainwashing. Many of the common characteristics found in destructive cults parallel the structure and dynamics of terrorist groups such as al-Qaeda or ISIS. The same state-of-mind that prompted the tragedy at Jonestown is essentially the same mind-set that brought down the World Trade Center towers, ending thousands of lives and now threatens whatever hope there is for stability and peace in the Middle East. Understanding this mind-set and potentially learning how to deprogram it is a meaningful tool in combatting some of the radicalization that produces global terrorism.

International conferences sponsored by organizations in Europe, Asia, and the United States have historically allowed for the exchange and sharing of meaningful information about destructive cults. These exchanges can stimulate and facilitate further research and study. Law enforcement personnel around the world can also potentially use the knowledge coalesced from this networking about destructive cults, enhancing their ability to monitor the criminal activities of cults.

Some in academia and the media generally defend cults and often seem to apologize for their bad behavior. These apologists have often characterized any critical examination of such groups as "persecution" or a "human rights" violation. It is not persecution or a human rights issue, however, to hold cults and their leaders accountable to the same laws and ordinances as everyone else. And of course if groups called "cults" behaved better and ceased doing harm, such critical analysis wouldn't be necessary.

The key means of responding to destructive cults has always been education. This is the basis for effective intervention work, and it is the basis for protecting the general public from destructive cults. People who are aware of destructive cults and how they work are much better prepared to avoid their recruitment tactics and exploitation. This is why some groups called "cults" have ranted against the Internet, the media, and former members who disclose their secrets—they don't want the public educated about their behavior and history. We can persuade cults to change and hold them accountable not only through law enforcement but also through public education by sharing the information about them to increase cult awareness.

Over the decades some cults have frequently targeted me for harassment. They have hired people to go through my garbage, illegally review my private bank and phone records, post diatribes about me online, and threaten my life. Knowing that the impact of my work has warranted such attention from cults is heartening. Otherwise why would they bother to harass me?

What began for me as a personal effort to protect my grandmother from fanatics during the early 1980s evolved into a journey spanning decades—first as an anticult activist and community organizer and now as a cult-intervention specialist, court expert witness, and lecturer.

Hopefully this book will make a difference and stimulate more critical analysis, research, and education about destructive cults. Others may also find this work compelling and begin a journey of their own. That is the purpose of this book—to build on the information we have and share it in such a way that others may continue the ongoing educational process. Educating and thus helping people to be free of cults can be both a personally fulfilling experience and a purposeful, professional life.

ACKNOWLEDGMENTS

I'm deeply grateful for the many people who have made my journey of exploration concerning the world of cults and this book possible.

Rabbi Albert Plotkin, the first community leader who responded to my questions about cults, was a tireless, ecumenical organizer. He inspired my earliest efforts as an anticult activist and community organizer.

Annette Daum was the director of the department of interreligious affairs for the Union for Reform Judaism. She brought me to New York, and her pioneering work in the field of cult education further informed my understanding of the cult phenomenon.

Lois Tuchler, executive director of Jewish Family & Children's Service of Greater Phoenix, provided me the opportunity to professionally coordinate community programs. She impressed on me that success is measured not just by direct results but also by contributions to change.

Priscilla Coates, executive director of the Cult Awareness Network, was an icon of information about cults. Her focus on the importance of recalling and archiving historical facts about destructive cults was a key inspiration in my work. Priscilla's piercing insights provided the basis for a better understanding of cult tragedies.

Aaron Scholar, executive director of the Bureau of Jewish Education of Greater Phoenix, urged me to create and teach classes about cults to better prepare young people. He understood that education is the best hope of protecting young people from cults that frequently recruit on college campuses across the United States.

Margaret Singer, eminent cult expert and psychologist, was required reading and a friend. Her dry wit and sage advice were indispensable. She was there at the very beginning of the modern cult era and served as a member of the advisory board of the Cult Education Institute, formerly known as the Ross Institute of New Jersey. Margaret understood the educational potential and importance of the Internet. She foresaw that it would become a key component of cultic studies.

Flo Conway and Jim Siegelman, authors of *Snapping: America's Epidemic of Sudden Personality Change* and *Holy Terror: The Fundamentalist War on America's Freedoms in Religion, Politics, and Our Private Lives*, first inspired me through their books and public appearances and later as good friends. I'm deeply grateful for their help regarding this book. Flo and Jim were a pivotal influence in sorting through and organizing the structure of the book. They also helpfully reviewed the chapters concerning the definition of a destructive cult and cult brainwashing. Their feedback made this a better book. Thanks so much, Flo and Jim, for always being there.

Psychologist Paul Martin, his wife, Barbara Martin, and the staff at Wellspring Retreat, a licensed mental health facility devoted to assisting cult victims, helped me to better understand the shared problems of former cult members and their recovery process.

I could never have survived professionally without the pro bono help numerous lawyers and law firms provided over the years. They protected not only me personally but also the online archives of the Cult Education Institute.

In Arizona, law firms like Lewis and Roca and Brown and Bain of Phoenix helped me through litigation when I lived in Phoenix. I want to specifically thank Arizona attorneys William Wolf, Bret Maidman, Paul Eckstein, and Daniel Barr for their successful work.

Since my move to New Jersey, the law firm Lowenstein Sandler has generously provided me with much needed legal help. Peter Skolnik, a partner at Lowenstein Sandler, diligently persevered through two harassment lawsuits—first, defending me in a lawsuit filed by Landmark Education and later defending me against a particularly vexatious litigant NXIVM in a lawsuit that dragged on for more than a decade.

I also want to thank attorneys Robert Rivas of Florida, Douglas Brooks of Massachusetts, Michael Norwick and Thomas Dolan of New Jersey, and Thomas Gleason of New York for their tireless work and dedication to protecting the principle of free speech.

The organizations Public Citizen and the Berkman Center for Internet and Society at Harvard University were also quite helpful regarding ongoing litigation concerns.

I want to thank Drs. Guy S. Alitto, Paul Morris, and Udo Schuklenk for their feedback and comments at an international symposium on cultic studies in Thailand during 2011. One night after a day of presentations, I had a friendly and private debate with Drs. Morris and Shuklenk about the core definition of a destructive cult. That discussion became much of the impetus for forming an understanding of the nucleus for a definition of a destructive cult in this book.

I want to thank Dr. Monica Pignotti and journalist Tony Ortega for reviewing chapters about Scientology and offering their invaluable feedback.

Most of all, I am deeply grateful to Dr. Cathleen Mann, who contributed substantially to the process of writing this book through her ongoing critique of chapters. Dr. Mann was extremely generous and pushed me to write a better book through her always-constructive criticism. Thanks, Cathleen, for being so patient and precise. Your commitment and consistent ethical professionalism exemplify how anyone seriously addressing the issue of destructive cuts and helping cult victims should behave and conduct his or her work.

BIBLIOGRAPHY

Aaronovitch, David. *Voodoo Histories: The Role of the Conspiracy Theory in Shaping Modern History.* New York: Riverhead Books, 2010.

Abrahams, Kyria. *I'm Perfect, You're Doomed: Tales from a Jehovah's Witness.* New York: Touchstone, 2009.

Acocella, Joan Ross. *Creating Hysteria: Women and Multiple Personality Disorder.* San Francisco, CA: Jossey-Bass, 1999.

Albarus, Carmeta, and Jonathan Mack. *The Making of Lee Boyd Malvo: The D.C. Sniper.* New York: Columbia University Press, 2012.

Arnott, Dave. *Corporate Cults: The Insidious Lure of the All-Consuming Organization.* New York: AMACOM, 1999.

Atack, Jon. A *Piece of Blue Sky: Scientology, Dianetics, and L. Ron Hubbard Exposed.* Fort Lee, NJ: Lyle Stuart, 1999.

Ayella, Marybeth F. *Insane Therapy: Portrait of a Psychotherapy Cult.* Philadelphia: Temple University Press, 1998.

Bailey, Brad, and Bob Darden. *Mad Man in Waco: The Complete Story of the Davidian Cult, David Koresh, and the Waco Massacre.* Waco, TX: Wrs Pub, 1993.

Barkun, Michael. *Religion and the Racist Right: The Origins of the Christian Identity Movement.* Chapel Hill: University of North Carolina Press, 1996.

Bergen, Peter. *Holy War Inc.: Inside the Secret World of Osama bin Laden.* New York: Free Press, 2001.

Bernstein, Albert J. *Emotional Vampires: Dealing with People Who Drain You Dry.* New York: McGraw-Hill, 2000.

Berry, Jason. *Lead Us Not into Temptation: Catholic Priests and the Sexual Abuse of Children.* Urbana: University of Illinois Press, 2000.

Bjorklund, David F. *False-Memory Creation in Children and Adults: Theory, Research, and Implications.* London: Psychology Press, 2000.

Blee, Kathleen M. *Inside Organized Racism: Women in the Hate Movement.* Oakland, CA: University of California Press, 2002.

Brackett, D. W. *Holy Terror: Armageddon in Tokyo.* Trumble, Connecticut: Weatherhill, 1996.

Brainerd, Charles J., and Valerie J. Reyna. *The Science of False Memory.* Oxford, UK: Oxford University Press, 2005.

Brandis, Gabriel. *Servant of the Lotus Feet: A Hare Krishna Odyssey.* Bloomington, IN: iUniverse, 2004.

Breault, Marc, and Martin King. *Inside the Cult: A Member's Chilling, Exclusive Account of Madness and Depravity in David Koresh's Compound.* New York: Signet, 1995.

Brown, Sandra L., and Liane J. Leedom. *Women Who Love Psychopaths.* San Francisco: Health and Well-Being, 2008.

Bruni, Frank, and Elinor Burkett. *A Gospel of Shame: Children, Sexual Abuse and the Catholic Church.* New York: Harper Perennial, 2002.

Bryan, Gerald B. *Psychic Dictatorship in America.* Livingston, MT: Paolini International, 2000.

Bugliosi, Vincent, and Curt Gentry. *Helter Skelter: The True Story of the Manson Murders.* New York: Bantam, 1995.

Burks, Ron, and Vicki Burks. *Damaged Disciples: Casualties of Authoritarian Churches and the Shepherding Movement.* Grand Rapids, MI: Zondervan, 1992.

Butterfield, Stephen. *Amway: The Cult of Free Enterprise.* Brooklyn, NY: South End Press, 1999.

Camp, Gregory S. *Selling Fear: Conspiracy Theories and End Times Paranoia.* Grand Rapids, MI: Baker Books, 1997.

Cantril, Hadley. *Invasion from Mars: A Study in the Psychology of Panic.* Piscataway, NJ: Transaction Publishers, 2005.

"Captive Minds: Hypnosis and Beyond." Documentary. Directed by Pierre Lasry. Montreal: National Film Board of Canada, 1983. http://www.youtube.com/watch?v=mQC0nFfp2nc&index=1&list=PL2D64B3CB3D593ACF (accessed May 22, 2014).

Caroll, Todd. *The Skeptic's Dictionary: A Collection of Strange Beliefs, Amusing Deceptions, and Dangerous Delusions.* Hoboken, NJ: John Wiley & Sons, 2003.

Carlone, Judith L. *Nineteen Years in a Manhattan Cult: The Cult Next Door.* Closter, NJ: Ace Academics, 2005.

Carter, Ruth. *Amway Motivational Organizations: Behind the Smoke and Mirrors.* Winter Park, FL: Backstreet, 1999.

Chalmers, David M. *Hooded Americanism: The History of the Ku Klux Klan.* Durham, NC: Duke University Press Books, 1987.

Cialdini, Robert B. *Influence.* Rev. ed. New York: Collins, 1993.

Compton, Vicki, and Ellen Zelda Kessner. *Saving Beauty from the Beast: How to Protect Your Daughter from an Unhealthy Relationship.* New York: Little, Brown, 2003.

Conway, Flo, and Jim Siegelman. *Snapping: America's Epidemic of Sudden Personality Change.* 2nd ed. New York: New York: Stillpoint Press, 2005.

Conway, Flo, and Jim Siegelman. *Holy Terror: The Fundamentalist War on America's Freedoms in Religion, Politics, and Our Private Lives.* New York: Delta, 1984.

Corydon, Bent. *L. Ron Hubbard: Messiah or Madman?* Rev. ed. Fort Lee, NJ: Barricade Books, 1987.

Dan, Lou Michael, and Dan Harbeck. *American Terrorist: Timothy McVeigh and the Oklahoma City Bombing.* New York: Harper, 2001.

Daniel, William R. *Shootout at Miracle Valley.* Tucson, AZ: Wheatmark, 2008.

Davis, Maurice. "You Can Go Home Again." DVD. Directed by Elliot Bernstein, New York: Union for Reform Judaism, 1982.

Davison, Bruce, Lori Lethin and John Putch. "The Wave." DVD. Directed by Alexander Grasshoff. Thousand Oaks, CA: BN Publishing, 1980.

Dees, Morris, with James Corcoran. *Gathering Storm: America's Militia Threat.* New York: Harper Perennial, 1997.

Deikman, Arthur J. *The Wrong Way Home: Uncovering the Patterns of Cult Behavior in American Society.* Boston, MA: Beacon Press, 1994.

Deikman, Arthur J., and Doris Lessing. *Them and Us: Cult Thinking and the Terrorist Threat.* Pt. Richmond, CA: Bay Tree, 2006.

De Rivera, Joseph, and Theodore R. Sarbin. *Believed-In Imaginings: The Narrative Construction of Reality.* Washington, DC: American Psychological Association (APA), 1998.

Dobratz, Betty A. *The White Separatist Movement in the United States: White Power, White Pride.* Baltimore, MD: Johns Hopkins University Press, 2000.

Drain, Lauren, with Lisa Pulitzer. *Banished: Surviving My Years in the Westboro Baptist Church.* New York: Grand Central, 2013.

Duignan, John, and Nicola Tallant. *The Complex: An Insider Exposes the Covert World of the Church of Scientology.* Dublin, Ireland: Merlin, 2008.

Duncan, Wendy J. *I Can't Hear God Any More: Life in a Dallas Cult.* Dallas, TX: VM Life Resources, 2006.

Emmett, Andrea Moore. *God's Brothel: The Extortion of Sex for Salvation in Contemporary Mormon and Christian Fundamentalist Polygamy and the Stories of 18 Women That Escaped.* San Francisco, CA: Pince-Nez Press, 2004.

Emmons, Nuel. *Manson in His Own Words.* New York: Grove Press, 1988.

Engel, Beverly. *The Emotionally Abused Woman: Overcoming Destructive Patterns and Reclaiming Yourself.* New York: Fawcett Columbine, 1992.

Enroth, Ronald. *The Jesus People: Old-Time Religion in the Age of Aquarius.* Grand Rapids, MI: Wm. B. Eerdmans, 1972.

Enroth, Ronald. *Churches That Abuse.* Grand Rapids, MI: Zondervan, 1992.

Evans, Patricia. *The Verbally Abusive Relationship: How to Recognize It and How to Respond.* 2nd ed. New York: Adams Media, 2003.

Ezekiel, Raphael S. *The Racist Mind: Portraits of American Neo-Nazis and Klansmen.* New York: Penguin Books, 1996.

Faith, Karlene. *The Long Prison Journey of Leslie Van Houten: Life beyond the Cult.* Lebanon, NH: Northeastern University Press, 2001.

Fenster, Mark. *Conspiracy Theories: Secrecy and Power in American Culture.* Minneapolis, MN: University of Minnesota Press, 2001.

Festinger, Leon, Henry W. Riecken, and Stanley Schachter. *When Prophecy Fails.* Redford, VA: Wilder, 2011.

Fikes, Jay Courtney. *Carlos Castaneda, Academic Opportunism and the Psychedelic Sixties.* Victoria, BC: Millennia Press, 1993.

Finch, Robert. *Without the Guru: How I Took My Life Back after Thirty Years.* Charleston, NC: BookSurge, 2009.

Fitzpatrick, Robert, and Joyce K. Reynolds. *False Profits: Financial and Spiritual Deliverance in Multi-Level Marketing and Pyramid Schemes.* Harrisonburg, VA: Herald Press, 1997.

Forward, Susan. *Emotional Blackmail: When the People in Your Life Use Fear, Obligation and Guilt to Manipulate You.* Reprint, New York: William Morrow Paperbacks, 1998.

Franz, Raymond. *Crisis of Conscience.* 3rd ed. Winston, GA: Commentary Press, 1992.

Garden, Mary. *The Serpent Rising: A Journey of Spiritual Seduction.* 2nd ed. Victoria, Australia: Sid Harta, 2003.

Gardner, Martin. *The New Age: Notes of a Fringe-Watcher.* Amherst, NY: Prometheus Books, 1991.

Gardner, Martin. *Weird Water and Fuzzy Logic*. Amherst, NY: Prometheus Books, 1996.

Gilpin, Geoff. *The Maharishi Effect: A Personal Journey through the Movement That Transformed American Spirituality*. New York: Tarcher, 2006.

Goldberg, Robert Alan. *Enemies Within: The Culture of Conspiracy in Modern America*. New Haven, CT: Yale University Press, 2001.

Goldhammer, John D. *Under the Influence: The Destructive Effects of Group Dynamics*. Amherst, NY: Prometheus Books, 1996.

Gordon, James S. *Golden Guru: The Strange Journey of Bhagwan Shree Rajneesh. New York:* Penguin Books, 1988.

Gorenfeld, John. *Bad Moon Rising: How Rev. Moon Created the Washington Times, Seduced the Religious Right, and Built an American Kingdom*. San Francisco, CA: PoliPointPress, 2008.

Gortner, Marjoe. "Marjoe." DVD. Directed by Sarah Kernochan and Howard Smith. New York: New Video Group, 2006.

Guerra, Jim. *From Dean's List to Dumpsters: Why I Left Harvard to Join a Cult*. Pittsburgh, PA: Dorrance, 2000.

Guest, Tim. *My Life in Orange: Growing Up with the Guru*. New York: Mariner Books, 2005.

Hare, Robert. *Without Conscience: The Disturbing World of the Psychopaths among Us*. New York: Guilford Press, 1999.

Harmon-Jones, Eddie, and Judson Mills. *Cognitive Dissonance: Progress on a Pivotal Theory in Social Psychology*. Washington, DC: American Psychological Association (APA), 1999.

Harrison, Barbara G. *Visions of Glory: A History and a Memory of Jehovah's Witnesses.* New York: Touchstone, 1980.

Hawkins, Kay. *The House of Yahweh: My Side of the Story.* Bloomington, IN: Author House, 2012.

Headley, Marc. *Blown for Good: Behind the Iron Curtain of Scientology.* Los Angeles, CA: BFG, 2009.

Hearst, Patricia Campbell, with Alvin Moscow. *Every Secret Thing.* New York: Pinnacle Books, 1982.

Herman, Judith. *Trauma and Recovery.* Reprint, New York: Basic Books, 1997.

Hill, Jenna Miscavige, and Lisa Pulitzer. *Beyond Belief: My Secret Life inside Scientology and My Harrowing Escape.* New York: William Morrow, 2013.

Hoffer, Eric. *The True Believer.* New York: HarperCollins, 1989.

Hoffman, Bill, and Cathy Burke. *Heaven's Gate: Cult Suicide in San Diego.* New York: HarperCollins, 1997.

Hoffman, Bruce. *Inside Terrorism.* New York: New York: Columbia University Press, 1999.

Holenbach, Margaret, David Farber, and Beth Bailey. *Lost and Found: My Life in a Group Marriage Commune.* Albuquerque, NM: University of New Mexico Press, 2004.

Hong, Nansook. *In the Shadow of the Moons: My Life in the Reverend Sun Myung Moon's Family.* New York: Little, Brown, 1998.

Hotchkiss, Sandy. *Why Is It Always About You?: Saving Yourself from the Narcissists in Your Life.* New York: Free Press, 2002.

Hubner, John, and Lindsey Gruson. *Monkey on a Stick*. New York: Onyx Books, 1990.

Jackson, Forrest, and Rodney Perkins. *Cosmic Suicide: The Tragedy and Transcendence of Heaven's Gate*. Dallas, Texas: Pentaradial Press, 1997.

Jeffs, Brent W. *Lost Boy*. New York: Broadway Books, 2009.

Jessop, Carolyn, and Laura Palmer. *Escape*. New York: Broadway Books, 2007.

Juergensmeyer, Mark. *Terror in the Mind of God: The Global Rise of Religious Violence*. Oakland, CA: University of California Press, 2000.

Johnson, David, and Jeff VanVonderen. *The Subtle Power of Spiritual Abuse: Recognizing and Escaping Spiritual Manipulation and False Spiritual Authority within the Church*. Ada, MI: Bethany House, 1991.

Jones, Christina, Celeste Jones, and Juliana Buhring. *Not Without My Sister*. New York: Harper Collins UK, 2007.

Joshi, S.T. *Documents of American Prejudice: An Anthology of Writings on Race from Thomas Jefferson to David Duke*. New York: Basic Books, 1999.

Joy, Connie. *Tragedy in Sedona: My Life in James Arthur Ray's Inner Circle*. Transformation Bloomington, IN: Media Books, 2010.

Kamentsky, Ellen. *Hawking God: A Young Jewish Woman's Ordeal in Jews for Jesus*. Atlanta, GA: Sapphire Press, 1993.

Kaplan, David E., and Andrew Marshall. *The Cult at the End of the World: The Terrifying Story of the Aum Doomsday Cult; From the Subways of Tokyo to Arsenals in Russia*. New York: Crown, 1996.

Keiser, Thomas W., and Jacqueline L. Keiser. *The Anatomy of Illusion: Religious Cults and Destructive Persuasion*. Springfield, IL: Charles C. Thomas, 1987.

Kent, Stephen, and Benjamin Zablocki. *From Slogans to Mantras: Social Protest and Religious Conversion in the Late Vietnam Era*. Syracuse, NY: Syracuse University Press, 2001.

King, Dennis. *Lyndon Larouche and the New American Fascism*. New York: Doubleday, 1989.

Kramer, Joel, and Diana Alstad. *The Guru Papers: Masks of Authoritarian Power*. Berkeley, CA: North Atlantic Books, 1983.

Laake, Deborah. *Secret Ceremonies: A Mormon Woman's Intimate Diary of Marriage and Beyond*. New York: Random House Value, 1995.

Langone, Michael D., ed. *Recovery from Cults*. New York: W. W. Norton, 1995.

Lau, Frederick, Max Riemelt and Jennifer Ulrich. "Die Welle [The Wave]." DVD. Directed by Dennis Gansel. Munich, Germany: Constantin Video, 2008.

Layton, Deborah. *Seductive Poison*. New York: Anchor Books, 1999.

Lee, Brenda. *Out of the Cocoon: A Young Woman's Courageous Flight from the Grip of a Religious Cult*. Brandon, OR: Robert D. Reed, 2010.

Lieberman, David J. *Get Anyone to Do Anything and Never Feel Powerless Again: Psychological Secrets to Predict, Control, and Influence Every Situation*. New York: St. Martin's Press, 2000.

Lifton, Robert Jay. *Thought Reform and the Psychology of Totalism*. Chapel Hill: University of North Carolina Press, 1989.

Lifton, Robert Jay. *The Nazi Doctors: Medical Killing and the Psychology of Genocide*. Da Capo Press ed. New York: Basic Books, 2000.

Lifton, Robert Jay. *Destroying the World to Save It: Aum Shinrikyo, Apocalyptic Violence, and the New Global Terrorism*. New York: Picador, 2000.

Loftus, Elizabeth, and Katherine Ketcham. *The Myth of Repressed Memory: False Memories and Allegations of Sexual Abuse*. New York: St. Martin's Griffin, 1996.

Low, Marsha Goluboff. *The Orange Robe: My Eighteen Years as a Yogic Nun*. Bloomington, IN: iUniverse.com, 2011.

Mabee, Carleton. *Promised Land: Father Divine's Interracial Communities in Ulster County*. St. Fleischmanns, NY: Purple Mountain Press, 2008.

Madigan, Tim. *See No Evil: Blind Devotion and Blood Shed in David Koresh's Holy War*. Fort Worth, TX: Summit, 1997.

Mancusco, Nick, Saul Rubinek and Meg Foster. "Ticket to Heaven." DVD. Directed by Ralph L. Thomas. La Crosse, WI: Echo Bridge Home Entertainment, 2007.

Many, Nancy. *My Billion Year Contract: Memoir of a Former Scientologist*. Los Angeles, CA: CNM, 2009.

Maran, Meredith. *My Lie: A True Story of False Memory*. San Francisco, CA: Jossey-Bass, 2010.

McMurrin, Sterling M., Irwin Altman, and Joseph Ginat. *Polygamous Families in Contemporary Society*. Cambridge, England: Cambridge University Press, 1996.

Meeink, Frank, and Jody M. Roy. *Autobiography of a Recovering Skinhead: The Frank Meeink Story as Told to Jody M. Roy, Ph.D.* Portalnd, OR: Hawthorne Books, 2010.

Mehta, Gita. *Karma Cola: Marketing to Mystic East*. New York: Vintage, 2012.

Melz, Raymund, Deborah Melz and Joaquin Sullivan. "Join Us." DVD. Directed by Ondi Timoner. Pasadena, CA: Interloper Films, 2008.

Milgram, Stanley. *Obedience to Authority: An Experimental View*. New York: Harper Perennial Modern Classics, 2009.

Milkman, Harvey, and Stanley Sunderwith. *Craving Ecstasy.* San Francisco, CA: Jossey-Bass, 1998.

Miller, Russell. *Bare-Faced Messiah: The True Story of L. Ron Hubbard.* New York: Michael Joseph, 1987.

Mitchell, Dave. *The Light on Synanon: How a Country Weekly Exposed a Corporate Cult—And Won the Pulitzer Prize.* New York: Wideview Books, 1982.

Morantz, Paul, and Hal Lancaster. *Escape: My Lifelong War against Cults.* Los Angeles, CA: Figueroa Press, 2012.

Muster, Nori. *Betrayal of the Spirit: My Life behind the Headlines of the Hare Krishna Movement.* Champaign, IL: University of Illinois Press, 2001.

Muster, Nori. *Child of the Cult.* Seattle, WA: Amazon Digital Services, 2012.

Nathan, Debbie. *Sybil Exposed: The Extraordinary Story behind the Famous Multiple Personality Case.* New York: Free Press, 2011.

Neiwert, David A. *In God's Country: The Patriot Movement and the Pacific Northwest.* Pullman, WA: Washington State University Press, 1999.

Neufeld, Gordon K. *Heartbreak and Rage: Ten Years under Sung Myung Moon.* College Station, TX: Virtualbookworm.com, 2002.

Nolen, William R. *Healing: A Doctor in Search of a Miracle.* Greenwich, CT: Fawcett, 1987.

Nussbaum, Hedda. *Surviving Intimate Terrorism.* Baltimore, MD: Publish America, 2005.

Oakes, Len. *Prophetic Charisma: The Psychology of Revolutionary Religious Personalities.* Syracuse, NY: Syracuse University Press, 1997.

Olsen, Elizabeth, Sarah Paulson, John Hawkes. "Martha Marcy May Marlene." DVD. Directed by Sean Durkin. *x*. DVD. Los Angeles, CA: 20th Century Fox, 2012.

Olsson, Peter A. *Pied Pipers of Our Time: A Psychological Study of Destructive Cult Leaders from Rev. Jim Jones to Osama bin Laden.* Baltimore, MD: Publish America, 2005.

Packard, Vance. *The Hidden Persuaders.* Updated, New York: Pocket, 1984.

Paolini, Talita, and Kenneth Paolini. *400 Years of Imaginary Friends; A Journey into the World of Adepts, Masters, Ascended Masters and Their Messengers.* Livingston, MT: Paolini International, 2000.

Patrick, Ted, with Tom Dulack. *Let Our Children Go.* New York: E. P. Dutton, 1976.

Penton, James. *Apocalypse Delayed: The Story of Jehovah's Witnesses.* 2nd ed. Toronto, Canada: University of Toronto Press, 1997.

Perry, Bruce, and Maia Szalavitz. *The Boy Who Was Raised as a Dog: And Other Stories from a Child Psychiatrist's Notebook—What Traumatized Children Can Teach Us about Loss, Love and Healing.* Reprint, New York: Basic Books, 2007.

Pesinger, Michael A., Norman J. Carrey, and Lynn A. Suess. *TM and Cult Mania.* North Quincy, MA: Christopher Pub House, 1980.

Peters, Shawn Francis. *When Prayer Fails: Faith Healing, Children, and the Law.* Oxford, UK: Oxford University Press, 2007.

Peterson, Beth E. *People Who Play God: How Ultra-Authorities Enslave the Hearts, Minds, Souls of Their Victims.* Philadelphia, PA: Xlibris, 2003.

Pinker, Steven. *How the Mind Works.* New York: W. W. Norton, 1999.

Pratkanis, Anthony, and Elliot Aronson. *Age of Propaganda: The Everyday Use and Abuse of Persuasion*. Revised, New York: W. H. Freeman, 2001.

Quebedeaux, Richard. *By What Authority: The Rise of Personality Cults in American Christianity*. New York: Harper Collins, 1981.

Ragas, Matthew W., and Bolivar J. Bueno. *The Power of Cult Branding*. New York: Prima Venture, 2002.

Reich, Walter. *Origins of Terrorism: Psychologies, Ideologies, Theologies, States of Mind*. Woodrow Washington, DC: Wilson Center Press, 1998.

Reiterman, Tim. *Raven: The Untold Story of the Rev. Jim Jones and His People*. New York: Tarcher, 2008.

Reitman, Janet. *Inside Scientology: The Story of America's Most Secretive Religion*. Boston, MA: Boston, MA: Houghton Mifflin Harcourt, 2011.

Rudin, James A. *Prison or Paradise: The New Religious Cults*. Minneapolis, MN: Fortress Press, 1980.

Rudin, Marcia. *Cults on Campus: Continuing Challenge*. Bonita Springs, FL: American Family Foundation, 1991.

Sargent, William. *Battle for the Mind*. Cambridge, MA: Malor Books, 1997.

Sanchez, Steve. *Spiritual Perversion*. Seattle, WA: Amazon Digital Services, Inc., 2010. Kindle edition.

Scheibeler, Eric. *Merchants of Deception: An Insider's Chilling Look at the Worldwide, Multi-Billion Dollar Conspiracy of Lies That Is Amway and Its Motivational Organizations*. Charleston, SC: BookSurge, 2009.

Schacter, Daniel L. *The Cognitive Neuropsychology of False Memories: A Special Issue of Cognitive Neuropsychology*. Milton, Oxfordshire, UK: Psychology Press, 1999.

Scheeres, Julia. *A Thousand Lives: The Untold Story of Hope, Deception, and Survival at Jonestown.* New York: Free Press, 2011.

Schein, Edgar H. *Coercive Persuasion: A Socio-psychological Analysis of the "Brainwashing" of American Civilian Prisoners by the Chinese Communists.* New York: W. W. Norton, 1971.

Schlick, Theodore Jr., and Lewis Vaughn. *How to Think about Weird Things: Critical Thinking for a New Age.* 2nd ed. Mountain View, CA: Mayfield, 1998.

Schultz, Tim. *The Fringes of Reason.* New York: Harmony, 1988.

Scobee, Amy. *Scientology: Abuse at the Top.* Puyallup, Washington: Scobee Publishing, 2010.

Shermer, Michael. *Why People Believe Weird Things: Pseudoscience, Superstition and Other Confusions of Our Time.* Revised, New York: Holt Paperbacks, 2002.

Simi, Pete, and Robert Futrell. *American Swastika: Inside the White Power Movement's Hidden Spaces of Hate.* Lanham, MD: Rowman & Littlefield, 2010.

Simon, George K. Jr. *In Sheep's Clothing: Understanding and Dealing with Manipulative People.* Little Rock, AK: A. J. Christopher, 1996.

Singer, Margaret. *Cults in our Midst.* San Francisco, CA: Jossey-Bass, 1995.

Singer, Margaret, and Janja Lalich. *Crazy Therapies—What Are They? Do They Work?* San Francisco: San Francisco, CA: Jossey-Bass, 1996.

Siskind, Amy B. *The Sullivan Institute/Fourth Wall Community: The Relationship of Radical Individualism and Authoritarianism.* Westport, CT: Praeger, 2003.

Smith, Joe. *Herding the Moo: Exploits of a Martial Arts Cult.* 2nd ed. Bloomington, IN: Trafford, 2006.

Solomon, Dorothy Allred. *Daughter of the Saints: Growing Up in Polygamy*. New York: W. W. Norton, 2004.

Spencer, Irene. *Shattered Dreams: My Life as a Polygamist's Wife*. New York: Center Street, 2007.

Stern, Kenneth S. *A Force upon the Plain: The American Militia Movement and the Politics of Hate*. Norman, OK: University of Oklahoma Press, 1997.

Srasser, Todd. *The Wave*. New York: Ember, 2013.

Storr, Anthony. *Feet of Clay: Saints, Sinners, and Madmen; A Study of Gurus*. Reprint, New York: Free Press, 1997.

Sweeney, John. *The Church of Fear: Inside the Weird World of Scientology*. Worcestershire, UK: Silvertail Books, 2013.

Szalavitz, Maia. *Help at Any Cost: How the Troubled-Teen Industry Cons Parents and Hurts Kids*. New York: Riverhead, 2006.

Tamm, Jayanti. *Cartwheels in a Sari: A Memoir of Growing Up Cult*, New York: Harmony, 2009.

Tarlo, Luna. *The Mother of God*. New York: Plover/Autonomedia, 1997.

Taylor, Kathleen. *Brainwashing: The Science of Thought Control*. Oxford, UK: Oxford University Press, 2006.

Thompson, Damian. *Counterknowledge: How We Surrendered to Conspiracy Theories, Quack Medicine, Bogus Science and Fake History*. London, UK: Atlantic Books, 2008.

Tobias, Madeline Landau, Janja Lalich, and Michael Langone. *Take Back Your Life: Recovering from Cults and Abusive Relationships*. 2nd ed. Berkeley, CA: Bay Tree, 2006.

Tomson, Oliver. *Easily Led: A History of Propaganda.* Stroud, UK: Sutton, 1999.

Tourish, Dennis, and Tim Wohlforth. *On the Edge: Political Cults of the Left and Right.* New York: Sharpe, 2000.

Underwood, Barbara, and Betty Underwood. *Hostage to Heaven: Four Years in the Unification Church.* New York: C. N. Potter, 1988.

Van Der Braak, Andre. *The Enlightenment Blues: My Years with an American Guru.* New York: Monkfish, 2003.

Van Wagoner, Richard S. *Mormon Polygamy: A History.* 2nd ed. Salt Lake City, UT: Signature Books, 1992.

Vrij, Andrew. *Detecting Lies and Deceit: The Psychology of Lying and Implications for Professional Practice.* Hoboken, NJ: John Wiley & Sons, 2000.

Wade, Craig. *The Fiery Cross: The Ku Klux Klan in America.* Reprint, Oxford, UK: Oxford University Press, 1998.

Walker, Lenore E. *The Battered Woman.* Reprint, New York: William Morrow, 1980.

Wassil-Grimm, Claudette. *Diagnosis for Disaster: The Devastating Truth about False Memory Syndrome and Its Impact on Accusers and Families.* New York: Overlook Press, 1996.

Watters, Ethan, and Richard Ofshe. *Therapy's Delusions: The Myth of the Unconscious and the Exploitation of Today's Walking Worried.* New York: Scribner, 1999.

Weiss, Elaine. *Surviving Domestic Violence: Voices of Women Who Broke Free.* 2nd ed. Scottsdale, AZ: Agreka Books, 2000.

Weyermann, Debra. *Answer Them Nothing: Bringing Down the Polygamous Empire of Warren Jeffs.* Chicago, IL: Chicago Review Press, 2011.

Williams, Miriam. *Heaven's Harlots: My Fifteen Years as a Sacred Prostitute in the Children of God.* New York: Harper Perennial, 1999.

Windle, Patricia Baird, and Eleanor J. Bader. *Targets of Hatred: Anti-Abortion Terrorism.* Palgrave New York: Macmillan, 2001.

Winell, Marlene. *Leaving the Fold.* Berkeley, CA: Apocryphile Press, 2006.

Winn, Denise. *The Manipulated Mind: Brainwashing, Conditioning, and Indoctrination.* Cambridge, MA: Malor Books, 2000.

Wooden, Kenneth. *The Children of Jonestown.* New York: McGraw-Hill, 1980.

Woods, Bonnie. *Deceived: One Woman's Stand against the Church of Scientology.* London: Bonnie Woods, 2009.

Wright, Lawrence. *Going Clear: Scientology, Hollywood, and the Prison of Belief.* New York: Random House, 2013.

Yeakley, Flavil R. Jr. *The Discipling Dilemma: A Study of the Discipling Movement among Churches of Christ.* Nashville, TN: Gospel Advocate, 1988,

Yenner, William. *American Guru: A Story of Love, Betrayal and Healing: Former Students of Andrew Cohen Speak Out.* Rhinebeck, NY: Epigraph, 2009.

Zablocki, Benjamin David. *Alienation and Charisma: A Study of Contemporary American Communes.* New York: Free Press, 1980.

Zablocki, Benjamin, and Thomas Robbins. *Misunderstanding Cults: Searching for Objectivity in a Controversial Field.* Toronto, Canada: University of Toronto Press, 2001.

Zeskind, Leonard. *Blood and Politics: The History of the White Nationalist Movement from the Margins to the Mainstream.* New York: Farrar, Straus and Giroux, 2009.

Zimbardo, Philip. *The Psychology of Attitude Change and Social Influence.* New York: McGraw-Hill, 1991.

Zimbardo, Philip. *The Lucifer Effect: Understanding How Good People Turn Evil.* Reprint, New York: Random House, 2008.

INDEX

ABOUT THE AUTHOR

Rick Alan Ross is one of the leading experts on cults in the world to-day. He has consulted with the FBI, the BATF, and various other law enforcement agencies, as well as the governments of Israel and China, on the topic of cults.

Ross is a private consultant, lecturer, and cult-intervention specialist. He began his work as an anticult activist and community organizer in 1982. Ross first became concerned about controversial groups and movements in response to a radical religious group that had covertly targeted his grandmother's nursing home. Since that time he has raised awareness about cults and facilitated more than five hundred interventions to rescue people from cultic situations.

He has been qualified and accepted as an expert court witness in eleven different states, including the US federal court. He has also worked as a professional analyst for CBS News, CBC of Canada, and Nippon and Asahi in Japan.

Ross has appeared in thirteen documentaries and numerous network television interviews and has been interviewed and quoted in media all over the world.

He is the founder of the Cult Education Institute, whose website is one of the largest sources of information regarding cults on the Internet. It was originally founded in 1996, but was recently redeveloped as a more modern database. See www.culteducation.com for more information.

Printed in Dunstable, United Kingdom